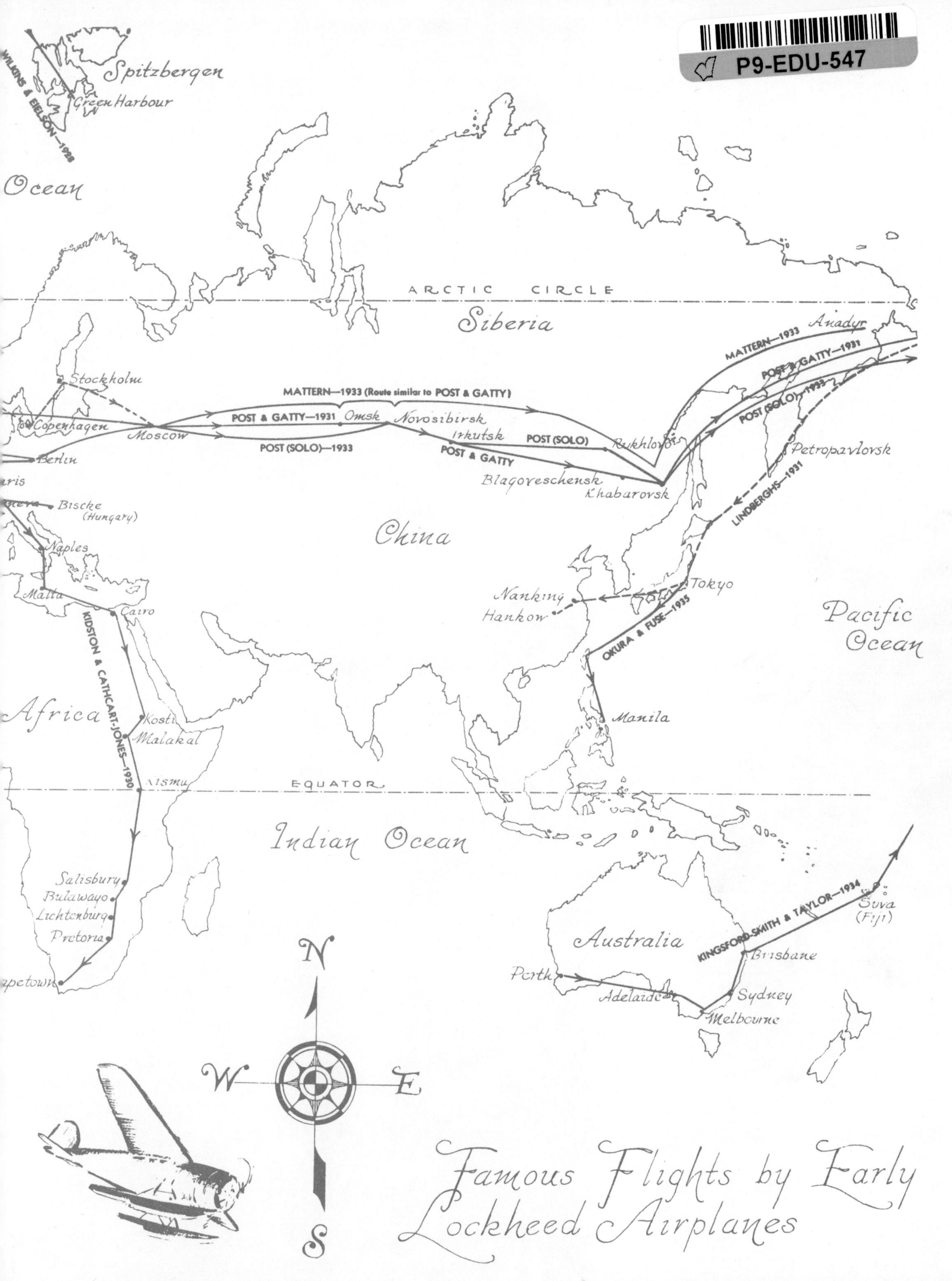

Famous Flights by Early Lockheed Airplanes

LOCKHEED

REVOLUTION IN THE SKY

REVOLUTION IN THE SKY

The Lockheeds of Aviation's Golden Age

RICHARD SANDERS ALLEN

REVISED EDITION

ORION BOOKS / NEW YORK

The author is grateful to the following companies, individuals, and institutions, past and present, whose generosity made illustrations available for inclusion in this book: The Aeroplane, Harold Andrews, Juan Arraez, P. Badre, John C. Barbery, Joseph H. Barry, Jim Barton, Warren M. Bodie Archives, Walter J. Boyne, Peter M. Bowers, Braniff International Airways, J. R. Brinkley III, Richard M. Bueschel Collection, James Carmody, Harvey Christen, Lionel Clark, *Cleveland Plain Dealer,* Continental Airlines, Thor Dahl, Harry Davidson, R.E.G. Davies, John M. Davis, Carlos Dufriche, Felipe Ezquerro, Angelo Emiliani, Herbert G. Fales, Lesley N. Forden, General Electric Company, Robert J. Gleason, B. F. Goodrich Company, Patricia Groves, Daniel P. Hagedorn, H. Allen Herr, Gerald Howson, Stephen J. Hudek Collection, David D. Jameson, Lloyd R. Jarman, Walter Jefferies Collection, Chalmers Johnson Collection, T. R. Judge, William A. Kelly, Leo J. Kohn, Gregory C. Krohn Collection, William T. Larkins, Edward Leiser, Lockheed Aircraft Corporation, Lockheed Air Terminal, Charles G. Mandrake Collection, Justo Miranda, K. M. Molson, Morrison Flying Service, National Air Museum, Northwest Orient Airlines, Pan American Grace Airways, Paramount Productions, Edward Peck, Dr. Daniel A. Poling, Pratt & Whitney Aircraft Corporation, Rev. Boardman C. Reed, Theron K. Rinehart, Matthew E. Rodina, Jr., Franklin Rose, Irving Rosenberg Collection, James A. Ruotsala, San Diego Aerospace Museum, Thomas Sarbaugh, Warren D. Shipp, A. J. Shortt, Cecil O. Shupe, Richard K. Smith, Socony Mobil Oil Company, M. K. Sponholz, Paul L. Stephenson, Bryan B. Sterling, Emil Strasser, Tallmantz Aviation, Inc., Robert Taylor, Don Thomas, Roscoe Turner, John W. Underwood, Adolfo Villasenor Collection, Truman C. Weaver, Walter Walsh, William F. Yeager Collection.

Frontispiece: *1930s International Nickel Company executive Herbert G. Fales's Lockheed Vega over a Florida lagoon.*

Published by Orion Books, a division of Crown Publishers, Inc., 225 Park Avenue South, New York, New York 10003,
ORION and colophon are trademarks of Crown Publishers, Inc.
Manufactured in the United States of America

Library of Congress Cataloging-in-Publication Data

Allen, Richard Sanders
Revolution in the sky/Richard Sanders Allen—Rev. ed.
p. cm.
Bibliography: p.
Includes index.
1. Lockheed airplanes—History. 2. Aeronautics—History.
I. Title.
TL686.L6A37 1988 88-9839
629.133'340423—dc19 CIP

ISBN 0-517-56678-8
10 9 8 7 6 5 4 3 2 1
Revised Edition

To My Son
Robert Bishop Allen

CONTENTS

A LETTER FROM CHARLES LINDBERGH

October 6, 1964

Dear Mr. Allen:

I returned last week from an extended trip abroad, and my wife handed me the copy of *Revolution in the Sky* which you so considerately sent us. Very many thanks.

I have been reading your book with interest and, as you can imagine, with some nostalgia. I am impressed by your detailed research and resulting accuracy. Obviously the manuscript involved a great many dedicated hours.

For your records I will amplify slightly the story of ordering the first Sirius. I wanted to obtain a low-wing, long-range plane for my survey flying. (Low-wing for safety in a forced landing, wider wheel spread, quicker take-off from rough fields, better vision in airport traffic, etc.) Nothing of this kind was being built in the United States. I met Jerry Vultee at the Cleveland National Air Races in 1929. I had flown Lockheed Vegas and liked them. Vultee and I discussed low-wing types—advantages and disadvantages. I offered to buy a low-wing Lockheed at the price of the standard Vega, and the deal was concluded on this basis. I am under the impression that my check to the Lockheed Corp., for $17,825.00, included the engine. (I am not certain about this.) All engineering and tooling costs of the new type were to be borne by Lockheed and written off on hoped-for future orders.

My recollection is to the effect that our flying suits were heated by the engine gear-driven generator (page 36).

I had ordered a retracting landing gear for the Sirius, and a wing with this gear was completed shortly before our 1930 transcontinental, record-breaking, flight. But the gear looked to me so wobbly that I did not want to attempt a heavy-load take-off on it, and left it at Burbank for further development. I intended, at that time, to have the retracting-gear wing installed on our Sirius. Later plans for converting the Sirius to a seaplane resulted in our never operating the plane with a retracting gear. The Army Air Corps asked for the retracting-gear wing, and I authorized the Lockheed Corp. to turn it over to the Army.

On page 94, it is stated that Carranza attempted his fatal New York–Mexico City flight in a replica of the *Spirit of St. Louis.* Actually his plane was basically the regular Ryan model, equipped with additional fuel tanks.

On page 104 it is stated: "Pan American had cached gasoline and supplies at prearranged way stops, and wired money ahead for such purchases in Siberia and Japan." Actually, I arranged and paid for all gasoline and supplies used on our flight to the Orient in 1931. Pan American did furnish the radio equipment we carried in the Sirius, since it was by far the most advanced available. We used Canadian Air Force gasoline caches in northern Canada. The Standard Oil Company arranged to send fuel to our Siberian stops.

On our 1933 Atlantic-survey flights, Pan American organized and financed the ground and water expedition which worked with us in the *Jelling* in the Labrador-Greenland areas of our survey. At a number of landings we used fuel cached or carried by the *Jelling.*

As you state in the book, I was working as consultant to Pan American. In this connection I wanted to become acquainted with northern routes and flying conditions. The results of my surveys and experience were, of course, fully available to Pan American. But I conceived of, and, with the exceptions outlined above, financed, the 1931 Orient and 1933 Atlantic survey flights myself.

The above is simply factual information, a result of the consulting relationship I maintained with Pan American and other organizations. It was my business to keep abreast of airline problems in general. My flights with the Sirius were independent of but closely related to (in most instances) the organizations I was consultant to. This arrangement seemed to work out advantageously from all standpoints, including Pan American's.

On page 105 it is stated that "Instead of the original orange, her [the Sirius's] wings and tail were now red." I am not under the impression that the color was changed. According to my memory, it was always an orange-red (black and orange so it would have the maximum contrast under various ground-color conditions in case of a forced landing and search).

All of the above items are detail, and stated as a matter of interest and record. On the whole I think you have achieved extraordinary accuracy in your book. Regardless of how much research one does, it is impossible to keep minor discrepancies from slipping in. My congratulations on a fine job go to you along with my appreciation.

With best wishes,

Charles A. Lindbergh

CHARLES A. LINDBERGH

To Mr. Richard Sanders Allen

A PERSONAL WORD

This book is concerned with the single-engine Lockheed, a very special kind of airplane, and a glamorous symbol of a turning point in aviation history.

Recent literary emphasis has been on the achievements and design of military aircraft in both World Wars, yet the intervening years of peace had their share of great planes and heroic flyers as well. This period saw the phenomenal growth of aviation, even in the face of an economic depression, and it was accompanied by avid public interest in airplanes and adulation for their pilots.

As a boy, I was part of the great air-minded throng of Americans who ran outdoors to watch the skyborne passage of *any* airplane. Like thousands of others, I kept scrapbooks, built models, hung around flying fields. Clear in my mind is the Saturday that my big brother took me to the airport at Newark, New Jersey. There, parked on the apron, was a shiny red-and-white Lockheed Vega.

The date was October 26, 1929. Though I had my first plane ride the next day from famous Roosevelt Field, it was an anticlimax after seeing the wonderful Vega at Newark. To me that sleek, cowled and panted ship *was* Aviation. Just delivered from the Lockheed factory in California, the plane was like a living thing, just aching to be flown, an object of speed and power and the kind of beauty that a boy can best appreciate.

That spark of youthful enthusiasm lay smoldering through thirty years of work that only occasionally touched on flying and airplanes. It was rekindled in 1958 when my son tucked in my Christmas stocking a model kit of the famous Vega *Winnie Mae*. Nostalgic, I proceeded to dig out from the attic my tattered clipping "file" on aircraft. Putting the model together, along with poring over the frail old newsprint brought it all back: those daydreams of airborne journeys, and the hours spent searching through each week's rotogravure section for such pictures as those showing the Lindberghs in the Orient, Post and Gatty tired but game in Berlin, and all the parade of Lockheeds with their young and smiling pilots.

What, I wondered, ever happened to all those famous Lockheeds and the men and women who flew them through uncharted skies? As a writer on historical and engineering subjects, I began to feel strongly that these planes deserved serious research and investigation. Seeking data, I found the stories behind the planes were available only in bits and pieces. An overall account of this glamour plane of aviation's Golden Age had never been chronicled.

In this book, I have tried to pay tribute to these first Lockheed airplanes, the very sight of which could fire so much admiration, and to their builders, owners, and pilots. What I have put together in the pages beyond is *not* a "company history" of the Lockheed Aircraft Corporation. Rather, it is simply the story of the background and accomplishments of these nearly two hundred single-engine Lockheeds, which were produced between 1927 and 1937.

Assembling this book has been largely a seeking-out of the written, photographed, and remembered fact. My old clippings were a nucleus, and the aviation and general press and magazines of the period provided basic groundwork. Over a period of three decades, I have consulted, either in person or by mail, some five hundred people who were directly involved in the story of the Lockheed Vega and its wooden and metal sister ships. Their cooperation has been overwhelming.

The components of aviation history, though comparatively recent, can be nebulous. The memories of fifty years ago can be excellent, haphazard, or even nonexistent. One man who was on the spot will recall an event as happening "just this way." Another will be positive of an entirely different time, place, even people. To add to the confusion, contemporary newspapers may give still different versions.

In many cases I have arrived at what I believe is a reasonably accurate account only by comparison, deduction, and downright guess. The evidence of photographs is usually conclusive, but once in a while even these were retouched, or faked—and so provide a trap for the researcher.

The historical and factual sketches, tables, and charts in the Appendix have been compiled from basic information in the files of the Federal Aviation Administration and the Lockheed Aircraft Corporation, and from material supplied by serious students of aviation history.

When I began to do research on the early Lockheed

First Lockheed Vega seen by author, factory fresh.

airplanes, I had only my dog-eared file of newspaper and magazine clippings dating from 1928–31. But my fellow aviation historians and many interested individuals are a generous lot. Support for and contributions to the project came, literally, from all over the world. The people listed below are only a small portion of those who can never be sufficiently thanked: John C. Barbery; Joseph H. Barry; Owen Billman; Warren M. Bodie; Peter M. Bowers; Walter J. Boyne; Dustin W. Carter; Harvey Christen; Mark Clevenger; Lesley N. Forden; Janet Greene; Stephen Greene; Stephen J. Hudek; David D. Jameson; Lloyd Jarman; Walter Jeffries; Chalmers A. Johnson; Phil Juergens; Leo J. Kohn; Gregory C. Krohn; William T. Larkins; Harvey H. Lippincott; Charles G. Mandrake; Robert C. Mikesh; Erik Miller; Ken Molson; Don Rampton; Rev. Boardman C. Reed; Lester G. Robinson; Matthew E. Rodina, Jr.; Irving Rosenberg; James Ruotsala; Kenn C. Rust; James J. Sloan; Emil Strasser; Bob Taylor; John W. Underwood; Janz Vanderveer; Adolfo Villasenor; Truman C. Weaver; William F. Yeager.

LOCKHEED

REVOLUTION IN THE SKY

". . . the door blew off, but they continued on to Mines Field with the wind howling and eddying through the cabin. There Yankee Doodle taxied triumphantly up in front of the grandstand—the sole entry to complete the race."

1

THUNDER OUT OF BURBANK

The dusty Midwestern airfield lay basking in the fall sunshine which slanted off the roof of the new tin hangar. The crowd had driven out from town in Model As, plus a Marmon and Packard or two, and by now was strung along the makeshift rope barrier, snacking on pop and Crackerjack. Straw boaters and cloche hats shielded eyes that searched the horizon, eager to spot the approach of the lead planes of the 1929 National Air Tour.

Before long, specks appeared in the distance and grew larger to become airplanes. Their engines filled the sky with an increasing hum as, one by one, they took shape: the metal, wood, fabric, and wire products of America's budding aviation industry, sent out on display.

Steeped in the lore he'd found in the pages of *Model Airplane News,* a youngster in knickers importantly announced the arrivals to a knot of grownups near by.

"Those biplanes now, they're Wacos, and there's two Great Lakes, and that one coming in—yep, it's that lady pilot in an American Eagle."

Quickly the boy pointed out the broad-winged Bellancas, the Fairchild monoplane, and the hulking bimotored Curtiss Condor. The landing of two gleaming all-metal Ford Trimotors caused a minor stir among the spectators.

Finally, swooping out of the sunlight, two new planes made a thundering pass over the field and all eyes swung to watch. Just a glance recognized them as far different from the bulky, square-cut ships that had preceded them.

The freckled kid was fairly hopping with excitement.

Winnie Mae, *greatest Vega of them all, gets set to take off from Harbour Grace, Newfoundland, for Atlantic leg of Post and Gatty's round-the-world flight in 1931.*

"Lockheeds!" he shouted above the din of the snarling engines. "Boy, what a plane!"

The perfectly streamlined shapes banked steeply at the end of the sod field, and circled to land. Descriptions like "winged bullet," "torpedo plane," and "flying cigar" went through the crowd, and the bull voice of the announcer came in snatches from a megaphone: ". . . now landing . . . Lockheed Vega, made in Burbank, California . . . piloted by Mr. Post . . . the red one is flown by Captain Hawks . . . a Lockheed Air Express . . . this plane holds three transcontinental speed records. . . ."

As the sleek planes taxied to a stop down the line, the boy's eyes were shining.

"Lockheeds!" he breathed, almost reverently. "Gee, how I'd like to fly in one of those!"

His desire was echoed many times in the late twenties and early thirties. Thousands of air-minded kids during these years of aviation's Golden Age could spot a Lockheed in seconds. The image of their speeding, bulletlike shape became etched on the mind of anyone who read a newspaper and followed the exploits of men and women like Colonel Lindbergh, Wiley Post, Amelia Earhart, and Sir Charles Kingsford-Smith.

It wasn't just kids. To fly a Lockheed was the ultimate wish of hundreds of top pilots who witnessed the planes' rocketing entry onto the aviation scene, and a surprising number realized their ambitions.

Many of the famous aircraft manufacturers were well established when the first Lockheed Vega made its appearance in 1927. There was Boeing in Seattle, Curtiss-Wright at Garden City, Consolidated in Buffalo, and Douglas in Santa Monica. All these companies considered the Army and Navy their only real and steady customers, and for years they concentrated primarily on biplane development. Their output consisted of two-wingers of varying sizes, their framework skeletons of wood and welded metal tubing covered by taut, highly doped, and painted fabric. After months and years of testing with the armed services, "the big four" developed and marketed an occasional commercial model. But monoplanes from their factories were a long time coming.

Other good firms built fine aircraft, too. There was Fairchild of Farmingdale, Long Island, Bellanca of New Castle, Delaware, and Travel Air of Wichita, Kansas—all pioneers in the building and sale of passenger monoplanes. Their products, with broad braced wings and boxy fuselages, were a common sight at any sizable airport. Another popular job was the Ryan Brougham, the 5-passenger version of Lindbergh's famed *Spirit of St. Louis*.

From Hasbrouck Heights, New Jersey, came the American-built Fokker Universals, with their big unsupported cantilever wings. Only two companies made all-metal planes. The Hamilton company of Milwaukee, better known for its propellers, built a well-designed monoplane clad in aluminum alloy, as did the Ford Motor Company with its famous Ford Trimotor.

Pitted against this array of biplanes and fabric-covered monoplanes, plus the two newfangled metal jobs, the early Lockheeds were a complete innovation in style and performance. Their unique single-shell, wooden monocoque construction put them far ahead when it came to speed and long-range capability, and they immediately proceeded to outclass everything that flew.

These fast wooden monoplanes, built in six distinct models over a period of seven years, brought streamlined good looks to workaday aircraft. Between 1927 and 1934 the consensus of the flying world was that Lockheed built the fastest, finest, and most desirable airplanes on the market.

Even with massive public recognition and flyers' acceptance, only 198 Lockheeds of this early single-engine series were built. But no other group of aircraft, produced in such small numbers, ever made so great a contribution to aviation.

From the little factory in Burbank, California, came many glamorous airplanes, record-breakers and ocean-hoppers almost as famed as the pilots who flew them. Then, after time and distance were conquered, a good share of the first Lockheeds became workhorse commercial airliners, carrying mail, passengers, and cargo over far-flung airways on through the years. Individual pilots flew them simply for pleasure; they were also the nucleus of America's great fleet of executive transports.

Best-known model of the original line of speedy wooden Lockheeds was the high-winged Vega, the most famous of which was Wiley Post's world-circling *Winnie Mae*. A later model, the low-winged Orion, introduced fully retractable landing gear and high-speed schedules to infant airlines in both America and Europe. In between were other versions that regularly took the air from Burbank: the parasol-wing Lockheed Air Express and the specialized long-distance Explorers. The Lockheed Sirius found fame with the trail-blazing survey flights of the Lindberghs. And a final two-seater was the Altair, from which was evolved the U.S. Army's very first low-wing fighter plane.

All these models made aviation history. A list of Lockheed records and "firsts" runs to hundreds of entries, and includes dozens of speed records, unprecedented round-the-world and intercontinental flights, plus pioneer crossings of both the Atlantic and Pacific oceans. Men and women recognized as the finest flyers of the era flew Lockheeds over every continent of the globe.

The Vega and its sister ships brought into useful being the present-day concept of streamlined airplane configuration. Thus barely half a lifetime ago, and in the space of a few short years, they carried out a true revolution in the sky.

With their coming, aviation outgrew the box kite.

2

SEEKERS OF A DREAM PLANE

The story of the fabulous Lockheeds could be said to open in 1913, with the takeoff of a gawky biplane that gave little promise of the streamlined performers that were later to blaze through the sky. Actually, though, it began with the dreams of Allan Haines Loughead, a Californian whose Scots-Irish name, in its phonetic spelling, became the hallmark of some of the world's most famous aircraft.

Red-haired Allan was the son of John and Flora Haines Loughead, and the youngest of his mother's four children. At the time of his birth in 1889 the family lived in Niles, inland from the southeast shore of San Francisco Bay. Allan's parents separated when he was young, and his mother took the family to Alma in the Santa Cruz foothills, where she operated a thirty-five acre fruit ranch. College trained and talented, Mrs. Loughead derived extra income from writing novels and poetry. Some of her feature stories were published in the *San Francisco Chronicle*. Allan, slowed by poor health as a child, never finished grammar school, but his mother supplied an education with her fine tutoring.

Young Loughead and his older brother Malcolm enjoyed ranch life, but much preferred tinkering with machinery. At seventeen Malcolm got a job as a mechanic in San Francisco, working on White steam motorcars. Allan also forsook raising grapes and prunes when he reached seventeen, and went up to the big city himself. His first job was in a hardware store at $10 a week, but he soon took a cut in pay to work, like Malcolm, as an automobile mechanic.

Meanwhile, Victor, the eldest of the three brothers,

Lougheads' second ship: F-1 was world's largest seaplane in 1918, had 74-foot wingspread and a triple tail.

worked as a consulting engineer in Chicago, where he spelled his name Lougheed. He was one of the founder members of the Society of Automotive Engineers, but he was an aerodynamics theorist and writer on the side, and his *Vehicles of the Air* and *Airplane Designing for Amateurs* were widely read, discussed, and used by would-be aeronauts—including his brothers.

Through Victor, Allan Loughead found work in 1910 as an airplane engine mechanic in Chicago and soon had a chance on the side to make his first flight. Sharing the seat of a homemade airplane erected in a Chicago barn, Allan was "copilot": he manipulated the aileron wires while the ship's builder worked rudder and elevators. It was one of the first recorded dual-controlled flights in aviation history.

The thrill lingered with him as he tuned the power plant for the plane of his employer, James E. Plew, a truck distributor who was trying to break into aviation. Plew's Curtiss-type pusher, with a 35-hp engine, was made ready for demonstration flights from a nearby race track. Allan yearned to be more than just the man who adjusted sparkplugs and carburetor as he watched with envy while the regular hired pilots tried to get the ship off the snow-covered ground. When they gave up, Plew listened to the pleas of his erstwhile mechanic—and gave him a try. Cocky young Loughead coaxed the flimsy pusher into the air, gradually orienting himself to the controls and the shoulder harness that worked the ailerons. Jerkily, he circled around and around the track oval and landed triumphantly in one piece. Of his first solo he said:

"It was partly nerve, partly confidence, and partly damn foolishness, but I was now an aviator!"

Allan had barely an hour and a half in the air himself when he began working as a "flying instructor." He also indulged in a brief career as an exhibition flyer, which came to an abrupt end at Hoopeston, Illinois. Piloting a water-soaked and underpowered Curtiss, Loughead left the ground in fine style, but could not gain altitude. His journey into the late-afternoon dusk was suddenly interrupted by contact with some low-hanging telegraph lines. Like a paper glider, the fragile Curtiss came to gentle rest in a tangle of wires, hanging with one wing impaled on the cross-arm of a pole. Allan switched off the engine, which was still popping, and scrambled unhurt from the dangling wreckage.

Experiences on the county-fair circuit taught Loughead what was good—and bad—about the flying machines of 1911. Not trusting his luck too far, and with a wife to support, he returned to San Francisco to work in a garage until such time as he might be able to build an airplane of his own. The design for a 3-place seaplane was already occupying his mind. It should be a tractor type, with the engine ahead, he thought: he was tired of worrying about a heavy motor mounted behind, hanging there in readiness to crush the pilot should the plane come down nose first.

The self-taught birdman often discussed aerodynamic problems with his brother Malcolm, and at length the two mechanics joined forces to build their own plane. A hydroplane was the logical choice because of the unlimited facilities in and around the Bay area, and San Francisco's longtime interest in boating. Cannily the Lougheads termed their brain child the Model G to give the impression that this was their seventh, rather than first, foray into aircraft manufacture.

The brothers kept their jobs and worked every other waking moment on their airplane. To help them, Max Mamlock of the Alco Cab Company invested $4,000 in their enterprise. The Lougheads contributed their time, tools, and design skill, together with a great deal of elbow grease. For a year and a half, a small former garage at the corner of Pacific Avenue and Polk Street was the scene of ever-increasing activity as the new airplane took shape.

Model G, the first Loughead-built airplane, was a sizable ship. A biplane, its upper wingspread was 46 feet and its triangular fuselage was 30 feet long. It was equipped with mid-wing ailerons, and, in the manner of French design, the entire tail swung on a universal joint. The main center float was an affair like a sled, and outrigger pontoons kept the wing tips from dipping into the water. When its Kirkham 6-cylinder engine burst its crankcase after fifteen minutes of operation, the designers

Allan and Malcolm's first design: lanky Model G is airborne June 1913 over San Francisco Bay.

Model G on land to show off features making it one of the earliest successful tractor-type seaplanes. Note rare horseshoe Kirkham radiator to cool 80-hp Curtiss V-8 power plant, open-air passenger seating.

substituted an 80-hp water-cooled Curtiss V-8 power plant, with the Kirkham's horseshoe-shaped radiator retained. The Model G had only one instrument: an old tachometer taken from a motor boat.

On the afternoon of June 15, 1913, Allan and Malcolm eased their creation into the waters of the Golden Gate from the beach at the foot of Laguna Street, just west of the Army's transport dock at Fort Mason. Allan climbed in, started the engine and, swinging into the wind, got the G on step. Soon the slap of the waves below ceased and the plane was airborne. The ship was very sensitive to handle, but a short hop was enough to show that months of work had produced success. Allan, highly pleased, returned to the beach and took Malcolm aboard. This time the "hydro-aeroplane" made a 10-mile flight, cruising around the island of Alcatraz, soaring in grand style some 300 feet above fascinated spectators on Market Street.

The Lougheads' Model G was one of the first successful tractor-type seaplanes ever built. It was highly unusual for this tender age of flight in that it could carry more than one person.

The G was well proved, but a minor landing mishap and general financial conditions put the plane in storage for two years. Allan went back to his old trade of keeping San Francisco's motorcars in running condition. Malcolm, ranging further afield, tried to sell the Chinese a Curtiss pusher, only to have the plane confiscated as contraband by the British at the outbreak of World War I.

Both brothers would occasionally knock off work and go up in the Mother Lode country to prospect for gold, but never returned with more than a nugget or two. The Model G, gathering dust in storage, bothered them. Then came the opening of San Francisco's Panama-Pacific Exposition in 1915 and an opportunity to use the ship. Backed by fresh capital, the Lougheads bought control of their plane and picked up the flying concession at the Pan-Pacific. During fifty flying days at the fair, they safely carried more than 600 passengers and made themselves $4,000. Allan and Malcolm decided to move to Santa Barbara after the exposition closed. Since the gas tank of the Model G held only eight gallons, the boys couldn't attempt to fly the ship the 300-odd miles south, so the plane had to go by flatcar.

Early 1916 found them settled in southern California and launching a new project: the Loughead (pronounced "Lock-heed") Aircraft Manufacturing Company. For the third time, the energy and obvious ability of Allan and Malcolm attracted financial backing. It came in this instance from Burton R. Rodman, a Santa Barbara machine-shop owner. Anthony Stadlman, a friend from Allan's exhibition flying days in Chicago, was made factory superintendent. Operations began with a handful of workers in the rear of a State Street garage, just a block from the Santa Barbara waterfront.

The new company proposed to build a 10-passenger flying boat, an unprecedented design which called for slow and painstaking workmanship. During the summer a twenty-year-old architectural draftsman and part-time auto mechanic became aware of what was going on in the garage. John K. Northrop, son of a local contractor, was intensely interested in things aeronautical. Nevertheless, it is said that he walked past the factory again and again with studied casualness, before making up his mind to go boldly in and ask for a job.

The Lougheads put the shy towhead to work on the hull of the new flying boat, already called the F-1 model. By concentrated personal study, Northrop had mastered stress analysis. And, despite being younger than any of the shopworkers, he set to work successfully to design and stress the wings of what was at the time the world's largest seaplane.

It was a real monster. The F-1's upper wing stretched to a length of 74 feet, the lower to 47 feet; on booms to the rear was a triple tail. And the ship was powered by two 160-hp Hall-Scott water-cooled engines.

Construction of the big flying boat proceeded slowly. Allan and Malcolm flew the Model G on passenger and charter business to help pay their rent. One 60-mile flight gave the plane the distinction of being the first to hop the Santa Barbara Channel off the California coast.

Then the United States entered World War I, and it was hoped to sell the new F-1 to the Navy, but the flying boat was not completed until March 1918. With haste to have the big plane evaluated by the government, Allan and Malcolm, pioneer flyer Carl Christofferson, and a newspaperman, set out to fly from Santa Barbara to San Diego. The 211-mile journey to the Navy's North Island base was made in 181 minutes, and set a new nonstop over-water mark.

Riders overflow F-1 for cameraman in the heydey of $5 joy hops, but actual capacity was 10 including pilots.

Top company personnel with Curtiss HS2L-type seaplane built for the Navy: Malcolm Loughead in gun turret behind (left to right) Norman S. Hall, Anthony Stadlman, Burton R. Rodman, Allan Loughead, and John K. Northrop.

Naval authorities kept the F-1 in San Diego for several months. The Lougheads meanwhile got an order for two more seaplanes, to be built to the standard specifications of a Curtiss HS2L. In the interests of national defense, the company invested some $5,000 to better the basic design, but unfortunately was never reimbursed. The brilliant factory superintendent, Tony Stadlman, experimented with bulletproof fuel tanks for the flying boats, and young Jack Northrop was released from military service to work on them. Wartime employees rose to a top of eighty-five. Though completed too late to see any actual patrol service during the war, the pair of Loughead-built HS2Ls were duly accepted by the Navy.

When Allan and Malcolm got the F-1 back from Uncle Sam, they decided to convert her into a landplane: the F-1A. The flying-boat hull was replaced with a special teardrop nacelle, below which hung a tricycle landing gear. The fittings for the wire wing bracings were molded in streamlined shapes with the idea of reducing wind resistance. Test shapes were hung in a wide glass tube. A workman with a good ten-cent stogie was detailed to puff smoke happily into the tube. Intense and alert, Jack Northrop would sit and watch the cigar smoke flow around the varied shapes he had designed, making drawings and notes. In the end this crude wind-tunnel

Converted to wheels as the F-1A, the big ship is ready for 1918 coast-to-coast flight.

work resulted in the addition of 10 miles an hour to the speed of the F-1A.

In 1918 the Loughead brothers decided on an effort to focus public attention on their big plane: they dispatched the ship on a transcontinental demonstration flight. With O. S. T. (Swede) Meyerhoffer and A. R. (Bob) Ferneau as pilots, and L. G. Flint as mechanic, the heavy biplane got away from Santa Barbara just a few days after the Armistice. Fighting terrific winds and storms, the F-1A covered 415 miles in 6 hours and 10 minutes, made a forced landing on the desert at Tacna, Arizona, and then went on to Gila Bend to gas up. During the next takeoff a mesquite bush fouled a propeller and the big plane went up on her nose in a dry creekbed. Swede, Bob, and Flint escaped injury, but the damaged F-1A never got to the East Coast.

The faithful Model G, having often kept the little company solvent, was at last retired in 1918. With scant sentiment, the engine was sold and the framework of the Lougheads' first airplane was junked for scrap. The F-1, again fitted as a flying boat, took her place in the duties of taking passengers for rides from the beach at Santa Barbara.

The 1919 season for tourists was a brisk one, with flights at $5 a hop. Another source of income was the

Journey's end in Arizona: pilots and mechanic walk away but plane is sent home to Santa Barbara for rebuild—and change back to float-equipped F-1.

Malcolm (left) and Allan Loughead man the dual controls of their reconverted flying boat.

motion picture business. Mounted in the front cockpit, far out ahead, a rotating movie camera could record all manner of histrionics going on in the rest of the plane while in flight. One novel charter involved a wedding performed aloft—during which the best man became violently airsick.

By and large, the F-1 was an excellent ship, flying slow and steady, lazily droning back and forth above the California coast. In October 1919 the U.S. government chartered her for the use of King Albert and Queen Elizabeth of the Belgians while on their visit to southern California. Allan Loughead took Their Majesties on a long flight to Santa Cruz Island and back, during which the King flew the plane himself. The King was so impressed with the F-1 and her builders that he awarded Allan and Malcolm the Belgian Order of the Golden Crown.

Like the little Model G, the giant flying boat survived years in the air with only minor mishaps, and no injuries to passengers or crews in hundreds of hours of flying time. After barnstormers dropped the prices for passenger hops to as low as a dollar, the Lougheads sold the flying boat to a syndicate that intended to start an air service

Ad in 1919 uses views of four planes to plug versatility and hint at a buzzing assembly line.

Publicity debut for the S-1 at San Francisco's Civic Center, with film starlet Mary MacLaren.

to the amusement centers on Catalina Island. The venture failed to get airborne, however, and the F-1 lay sadly abandoned on the beach at Santa Barbara until idle vandalism reduced her to kindling.

Readying for postwar aeronautical expansion, the Loughead Aircraft Manufacturing Company sank $29,800 in what they hoped would prove to be the long-sought "poor man's airplane," a flying machine that would take the place of the automobile in every backyard garage. The company was not the first, and certainly not the last, who thought its brain child would be the answer to this will-o'-the-wisp envisioned by all aircraft manufacturers.

The Loughead bid was the S-1, a true revolution in aircraft design to which scant attention was paid when it was first introduced. It was only a tiny, single-engine craft—strictly a sport job for the individual flyer—yet its construction and design were far in advance of its time and offered a preview of things to come.

The S-1 was put together in a way that made it unique. The fuselage was built with the monocoque—from the French, meaning "single shell"—construction in which

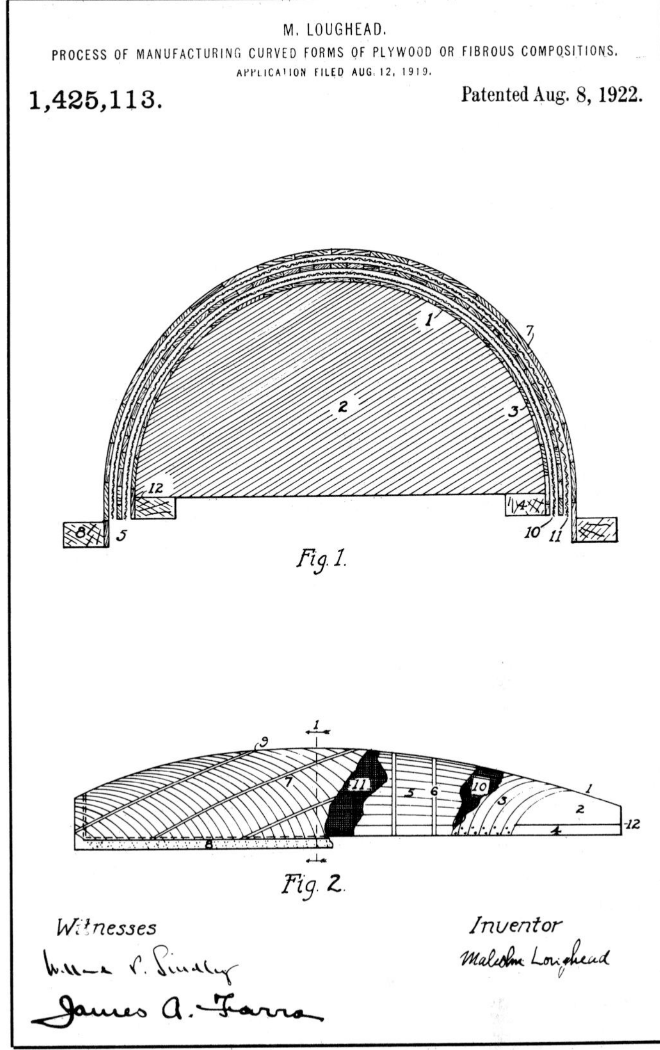

M. LOUGHEAD.
PROCESS OF MANUFACTURING CURVED FORMS OF PLYWOOD OR FIBROUS COMPOSITIONS.
APPLICATION FILED AUG. 12, 1919.

1,425,113. Patented Aug. 8, 1922.

Fig. 1.

Fig. 2.

Witnesses

Inventor

Original patent issued to Malcolm Loughead for the making of plywood fuselages in curved forms.

First successful molded shell, fitted to frame for S-1's fuselage. Unique monocoque process devised for the midget biplane was later used in construction of historic single-engine Lockheeds (see also Appendix).

the strength of the whole comes from the outside skin rather than from internal bracing. Around a framework of concentric hoops, sections of plywood covering were attached to give the fuselage the neat, smooth appearance of a tapered tube.

The idea of a wooden monocoque fuselage was not new, but the process developed to build the S-1 was, and in addition was both effective and valuable. Before 1919 the occasional assembly of this type of plane required the laborious application and gluing of each strip of plywood over the rounded outline form.

It was during their preoccupation with seaplanes that Malcolm and Allan Loughead, Jack Northrop, and Tony Stadlman thought out and patented a unique method of making fuselage shells. They used a concrete mold of the 21-foot length desired for the S-1. In this were placed three thicknesses of spruce plywood strips, alternately laid and well swabbed with casein glue, and the whole set in position by clamping a cover on the mold and inflating the rubber bag within it. Kept under pressure for twenty-four hours, the half-shells thus produced could be joined to make beautiful streamlined fuselages, with no outside cables and pulleys necessary.

To power the little dream ship, Allan Loughead and Stadlman designed a 2-cylinder, 25-hp, water-cooled opposed engine called the XL-1. It was mounted on the nose of the cigar-shaped biplane and offered next to no wind resistance.

Loughead-Stadlman engine delivered 25 hp, top 75 mph.

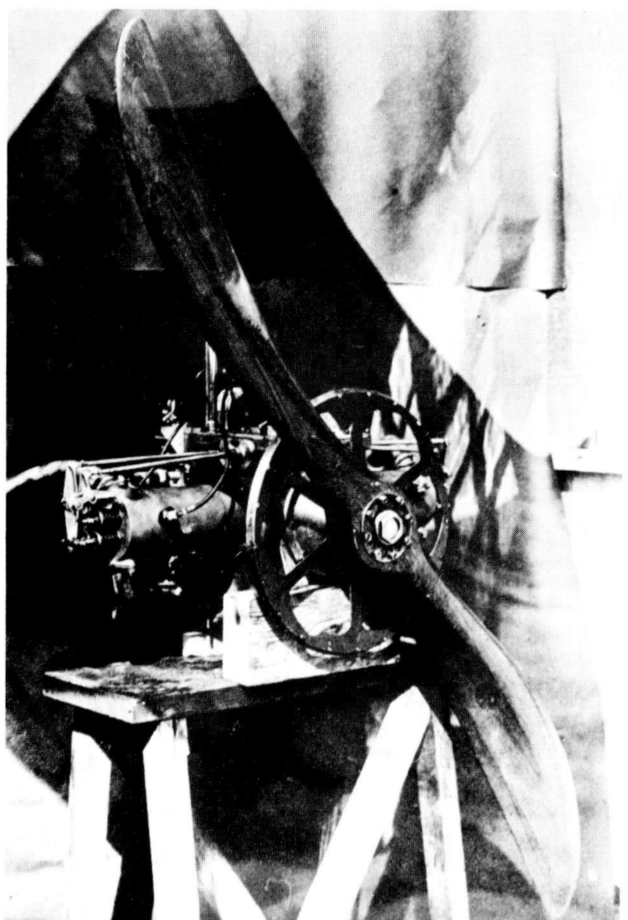

When it came to wings, Jack Northrop had a method for research as unusual as his cigar-smoke wind tunnel. He and his men collected barrels of dead fish, dumped them in a vacant lot near the waterfront; and there, oblivious to the stench, studied the braking action of the seagulls that came swooping down to feed. From Northrop's sketches came a lower wing for the S-1, which could be turned vertically to act as an air brake—a forerunner of today's widely used landing flaps. And, in order to accommodate the midget biplane in a garage, as promised, the wings could be readily folded back along the tapered fuselage.

The S-1 was test-flown at Redwood City, California, by a young flying instructor, Gilbert G. Budwig. The ship proved every bit as good as she looked. Budwig reported a 75-mph top speed, and fine handling in the air. The whole ship weighed only 790 pounds, and landed so slowly that the air-brake wing was seldom if ever employed.

Loughead Aircraft embarked on an extensive advertising campaign for the plane. Since the S-1 was only 21 feet long, it could be transported and exhibited practically anywhere. The plane that was "small, reliable, and economical" and "within the reach of every automobile owner" went to shows and public gatherings all over California.

And nobody bought one.

The reason for its lack of sales was simply poor timing. At another date and place a single-cockpit sport biplane with the unique features of the S-1 might have sold very well. But in 1919 the market for such a ship was nonexistent. Hundreds of war-surplus Curtiss JN-4s and De Havilland trainers were available, brand new, for as little as $350, and the Liberty engines to power them could be had for peanuts. Those who wished to continue their wartime piloting, or sample the joys of the air for the first time, went out and bought a new Jenny or DH, still in its crate.

Thus, despite its revolutionary design, imaginative construction, and great potential, the S-1 Sport Biplane was a glorious flop. Unable to find a commercial market, the Loughead Aircraft Manufacturing Company suspended operations in 1921 and its assets were liquidated.

For nine years the ingenuity and energies of the Loughead brothers—and for five, those of Jack Northrop and Tony Stadlman—had been expended on just three airplanes of original design and two built to government specifications. With a closed factory and no prospects, the chances that the four designer-manufacturers would ever build another airplane appeared exceedingly slim. Yet their efforts so far were just a start on what was to come.

Sleek and sporty, little S-1 had foldable wings.

3

FROM AN INGLEWOOD HAYFIELD

After the Loughead Aircraft Manufacturing Company of Santa Barbara closed its garage doors, the men involved went their separate ways.

Malcolm Loughead had already done spectacularly well, developing the hydraulic four-wheel brakes he'd installed on an old Paige roadster back in 1916. He moved to Detroit to be near the automobile manufacturers and set up a firm to produce the brakes he'd patented. Tired of being called "Log-head," Malcolm used the phonetic spelling of his name for the first time: his new business was the Lockheed Hydraulic Brake company.

It took patience and persistence to sell the auto companies on hydraulic brakes—"Suppose the fluid all leaks away?"—but the great advance was accomplished when Walter P. Chrysler introduced Loughead's invention to the auto world on the first Chrysler motorcar, brought out in 1924. More contracts brought public acceptance and soon Malcolm's brakes were a complete financial success.

Allan Loughead became associated with the California distributor of the new brakes. In addition, he was kept busy selling real estate in the burgeoning area around Los Angeles.

Jack Northrop went to work for Douglas Aircraft in Santa Monica, where he did design work on several models, including the Cruisers which the U.S. Army flew around the world in 1924.

Open for business: officers of the new Lockheed Aircraft Co., are (left to right) *general manager Allan Loughead, president Fred E. Keeler, vice president Ben Hunter.*

The clean lines and unique construction of the ill-timed little S-1 continued to fill the minds and imagination of both Northrop and Loughead. Occasionally they met and talked about getting together to produce a new plane. This time, they reasoned, it would be made bigger: not just a little personal sport craft, but a cabin ship, with ample room provided by the lack of interior bracing.

Northrop roughed out some tentative drawings for a pilot-and-4-passenger airplane. His concept was to make it exceptionally clean in appearance, commodious, and faster than anything available. It would be a ship with racing characteristics for the commercial field.

Loughead, as a pilot, contributed his practical experience and mechanical knowledge. Northrop, the visionary nonflying designer, felt that here was an opportunity for producing the aerodynamic dream of the decade.

There was no question that the unusual monocoque fuselage would be the base of the design. Built 6½ feet longer than the S-1, it would make the ideal shape for mounting a radial Wright Whirlwind engine. This power plant, the best on the market and already in general use, got 200 horsepower from its 9 cylinders.

Though Allan was afraid nobody would want to fly in a machine that did not incorporate visible means of external support, Jack Northrop's studies led him to hold out for the thick, internally braced, full cantilever wing already pioneered and used successfully by Anthony H. G. Fokker. The Flying Dutchman was already famed for his design of German combat aircraft before coming to the United States in 1922 to establish his own airplane factory. Northrop knew that, with care, he could adapt a Fokker-type wing, making one weighing scarcely more than a braced-and-cloth-covered fabrication, yet far stronger.

Financing for the new venture was accomplished in a roundabout manner. Loughead and Northrop first interested W. Kenneth Jay, an ex-Army Air Corps instructor from Iowa, who now made a living as an accountant in Los Angeles. Convinced that the proposed airplane would have a commercial market, the three put together a stock prospectus and went to see one of Jay's associates, Fred E. Keeler.

Keeler's line was brick, tile, and china; he knew little of airplanes. And for this proposed investment there was no finished sample which experts might examine and report on as to sales potential. Keeler could only judge the caliber and enthusiastic determination of the men who brought him the prospects of an unborn company which hoped to build a wonderful new type of airplane.

Fred Keeler leafed through the papers carefully and made up his mind. Then and there he offered to put up the entire $25,000 necessary to found a company and build a prototype. One thing that helped him decide was the known success of Malcolm's hydraulic brakes, in which he already had a well-paying investment. As a businessman, Keeler felt that the name Lockheed had already been widely advertised and accepted by the public. An airplane with such a name would be off to a good start.

Using $22,500 from Keeler and $2,500 from Allan Loughead, a Nevada corporation called the Lockheed Aircraft Company was formed in December 1926. In return for his investment and controlling interest, Fred Keeler became president. Allan was vice president and general manager and Ken Jay was secretary-treasurer of the new firm. To keep his fingers on the purse strings, Keeler made his lawyer, Ben Hunter, executive vice president of Lockheed; his assistant, G. Ray Boggs, also had a hand in the management.

Operations began in a small rented building near the corner of Sycamore and Romaine streets in Hollywood. Allan Loughead, who clung to his real estate work in order to make ends meet, appeared at the plant about four o'clock each afternoon. He kept tabs on progress and offered suggestions—some used and some not—

First Vega came out of this little Hollywood plant near corner of Sycamore and Romaine streets.

Sandbags test the 41-foot wing, whose long spars and reinforced ribs are covered with sheets of plywood veneer.

on speeding the project along. With Jack Northrop as full-time (and only) engineer, Tony Stadlman back as factory superintendent, and a dozen carpenters and helpers, it was like the old days in Santa Barbara. The little factory's sheet-metal walls began to reverberate with the buzz of saws, the tapping of tack hammers, the slap of casein glue on plywood. Nearly $17,500 went into the first Vega, including tools and equipment for the tiny factory.

Slowly the beautiful streamlined wooden airplane took shape. Jack Northrop did all the engineering, designing, drafting, and stress analysis involved. It was he who suggested "Vega" as the name for this first model. In addition to being short and easy to remember, there was a feeling of astronomical speed and distance in using the name of one of the brightest stars in the firmament.

While construction of the inanimate but lovely new Hollywood "star" proceeded, the flight that would make history and trigger the wholesale advancement of aviation took place. Charles A. Lindbergh landed in Paris, nonstop and alone from New York, on May 21, 1927.

The aviation boom was on. Only four days later James D. Dole, Boston-born head of the Hawaiian Pineapple Company, offered a $25,000 prize to the first flyer to cross from the North American continent to Honolulu. To be sure, there were already similar prizes on the boards for the first Dallas–Hong Kong and Paris-Cleveland flights. What gave Jim Dole's offer real momentum was a second prize of $10,000, and a starting date of August 12. Starving barnstormers and manufacturers, hungry equally for money and publicity, pricked up their ears at the news. This meant a race to Hawaii.

Lockheed's secretary, Ken Jay, found a buyer for the first Vega even before it was finished. He bumped into an old World War flying pupil, ex-Lieutenant John W. Frost of San Francisco. A debonair bachelor, Frost had been making a living in New York as a stockbroker and bond salesman. Now he was anxious to get back into flying.

Through a brother, Jack Frost had connections with the *San Francisco Examiner.* With an important event like the much-ballyhooed Dole Race coming up right in its back yard, it was unthinkable that the Hearst chain's original newspaper should not be taking an active part. The Frost brothers suggested that the *Examiner* buy the new Lockheed airplane as its own entry, with Jack to fly it.

Publisher George Hearst, Jr., an aviation enthusiast himself, was sold, but he drove a hard bargain: he got the Vega as an entry in the "pineapple derby" for only $12,000. Loughead, Jay and their associates knew the sale price represented a loss, but considered the prestige of selling to Hearst and the entry of their plane in the race to be well worth it.

All the officers and nearly everyone from the twelve-man factory turned out for the first trial flight of the Lockheed Vega. Following an American tradition, they chose their holiday, July Fourth, a Tuesday, for the auspicious occasion. With the wingless plane towed tail first behind a truck, they trekked cross-town to a large hayfield near Inglewood. Here, in what later became the southwest corner of the Los Angeles International Airport, the Vega was assembled.

Edward Antoine Bellande was chosen to fly the plane

Aviation's new star: prototype Vega is 27 feet 6 inches long, 8 feet 4½ inches high, with 200-hp Wright Whirlwind engine for 135 mph top speed. Handcrafted ship is all wood except for engine mount, tail cone, wire wheels, and fittings.

Vega arrives at Oakland, where (left to right) *race pilot Jack Frost takes over from Eddie Bellande, Jack Northrop, Allan Loughead, and Ken Jay. As the* Golden Eagle *with 2788 registration, plane sets intercity records.*

on its crucial first flight. An ex-Navy flight instructor from the Gulf coast of Mississippi, little Eddie Bellande was a barnstormer, skywriter, and crop duster, and had been testing new airplanes off and on since 1915.

Eddie ran up the 200-hp Wright J5C, tried the controls, and sent dust plumes eddying across the sun-drenched grass. Waiting out the heat of the day, he lifted the Vega off precisely at 4 P.M. She was faster than anything he'd ever flown and Bellande marveled at the way the plane responded to the slightest touch of stick and rudder. He was up for an hour, an unusually long first hop, lazily climbing, banking and swinging back over the heads of the anxious watchers again and again. Finally he touched her down, taxied up to the waiting men and cut the switch. Pushing back his goggles with a flourish, Eddie climbed out.

"Boys, she's a dandy!" he said. "A real joy to fly!"

On a second hop, it was fitting that Jack Northrop, who had conceived the airplane and had been in constant attendance as it took shape, should be its first passenger. His agile mind was already awhirl with minor improvements for Vegas to be produced in quantity, as well as entirely new low-wing and seaplane configurations.

Less than six weeks remained before the Dole Race

Jack Northrop earns honor of fitting crank to start the engine for Vega's maiden flight July 4, 1927. Wing was removed for tail-first haul across town to this hayfield, today part of Los Angeles International Airport.

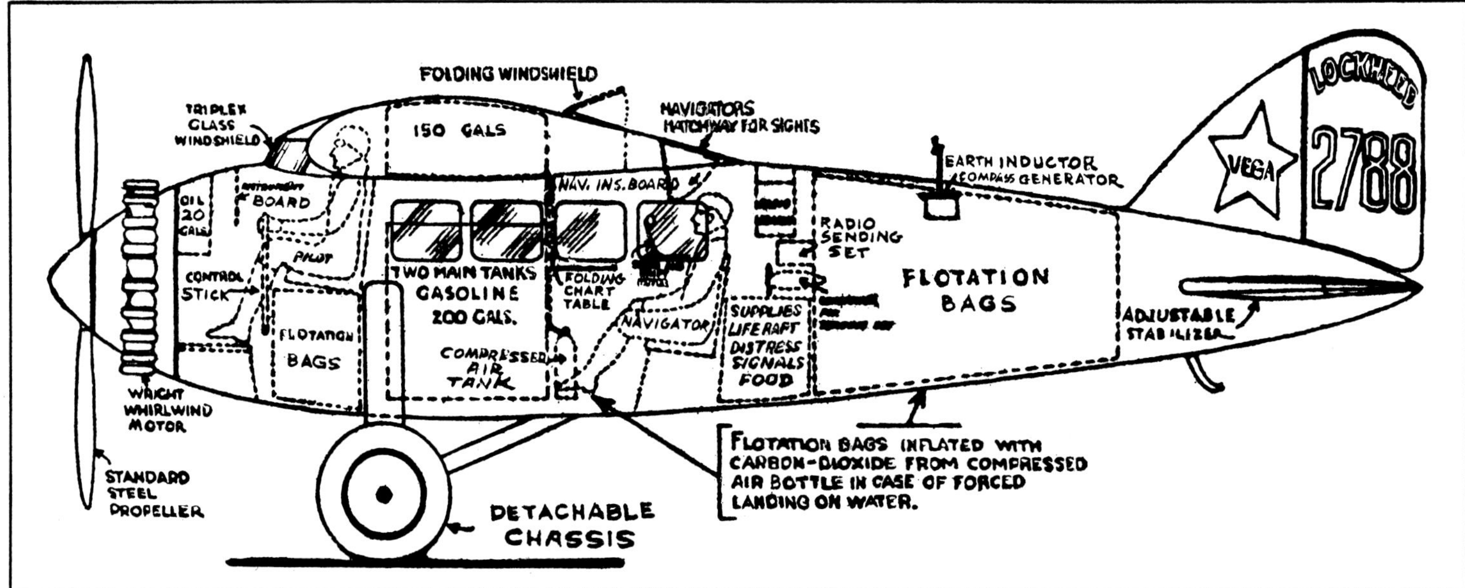

Hearst published this cutaway to show his racer's extra emergency equipment for the long over-water flight.

starting date. Eddie Bellande flew the Vega up to Oakland, and Jack Frost took delivery. Painted a bright orange with red trim and the first "star" trademark, the Lockheed was well christened *Golden Eagle* by the Hearst organization. In tests the new ship quickly proved itself the nation's swiftest commercial airplane. Frost flew it between Los Angeles and Oakland in as little as 3 hours and 5 minutes, and on subsequent trips established new records for various passenger and cargo payloads.

This first of the Lockheed series differed from later-model Vegas in that it had an open cockpit forward, and a triangular vertical fin. Also, because George Hearst insisted on every known safety precaution for the Oakland-Honolulu journey, many modifications were made for the *Golden Eagle* at the little Lockheed factory in Hollywood. The wheels and struts were made dropable to ease a possible forced landing at sea. Large flotation bags were installed in the wing tips, beneath the pilot's seat, and in the entire rear of the tubular fuselage. These were all connected to a carbon dioxide bottle and, by a special Northrop-designed nozzle, could be inflated in less than sixty seconds. If the gasoline was dumped and the empty tanks added to the flotation system, it would be possible to support over 8,500 pounds—nearly two tons more than the fully loaded weight of the airplane. In addition, the base of the fuselage was packed and padded with cork, and special rubber strips were prepared to seal every door and window crack. In the event of a ditching, it was believed that the downed plane could stay afloat for at least thirty days.

These preparations appeared more than adequate, but a rubber life raft was also provided, provisioned with food and water, and equipped with paddles and a 24-foot square of silk sail. A removable compass could be installed in the raft, and there was a variety of rockets, Very flares, and smoke bombs for attracting attention.

It was believed that the services of a competent navigator would be necessary for the flight because an error of as little as two degrees might cause the plane to miss the Hawaiian Islands entirely. To navigate for Frost, the paper hired twenty-four-year-old Gordon Scott, from Santa Monica, California. A friend of Jack Northrop's, South African–born Scott had been employed as an engineer at Douglas Aircraft, and the year before had navigated a racing yacht from California to Honolulu.

Frost took the *Golden Eagle* through speed runs and instrument checks at Oakland, while Scotty prepared his charts and passed his navigation tests before a National Aeronautic Association committee that had been given the task of supervising the race. To help Scott take sights, a special navigation hatch was cut in the Vega's fuselage just behind the trailing edge of the wing, complete with a folding windshield.

Though the Hearst entry was ready to go on the original race date, Jack Frost, in a gesture of pure sportsmanship, originated a "pilot's agreement" to postpone the event for four days. This would allow time for other flyers and a last-minute arrival to still qualify for the 2,439-mile over-water flight. Everyone agreed that the ex-broker was a real square shooter. A familiar figure in his bow tie and checkered white plus fours, Frost and young curly-haired Scott kept busy attending to the final details on their plane. At the last moment they decided to chuck a heavy radio transmitter and take only the receiving set.

Finally, on August 16, 1927, there were eight airplanes on the dusty, unfinished Oakland Airport, as ready as they ever would be to start the derby. Hell bent for Hawaii were two Travel Airs, two Breese monoplanes, a Swallow, a Buhl sesquiplane, a scratch-built Goddard, and the Lockheed. Their pilots included Arthur Goebel, Bennett Griffin, and Martin Jensen, all to become famous. Some had navigators along; and there was a lone girl passenger, attractive twenty-two-year-old Mildred Doran of Caro, Michigan. One Breese and the Goddard cracked up on takeoff. Bennie Griffin soon brought his Travel Air back with a hot engine, as did Bill Erwin with his Swallow.

Pilot Jack Frost and navigator Gordon Scott just before takeoff for Hawaii on August 16, 1927.

Of the four planes that actually left for Hawaii, only two would come wearily in to Wheeler Field north of Honolulu more than 24 hours later.

Frost and Scott's brightly painted Vega was the second plane to leave the field. The *Golden Eagle,* its tanks topped with 360 gallons of gasoline, lifted easily from the sandy runway, and at the boundary markers was 200 feet up. Climbing steadily, she swung out above the Bay toward the city beyond. Frost waggled his wings in farewell to the cluster of people waving from the roof of the *Examiner* building in downtown San Francisco. Then the plane was an orange speck above the Golden Gate, heading out toward the Farallons and the vast reaches of the Pacific Ocean.

The *Golden Eagle* was never seen again.

The ill-starred race was won by Arthur Goebel and William Davis, Jr., flying the Travel Air monoplane *Woolaroc.* Martin Jensen and Paul Schluter, who flew and navigated the only other plane to complete the hazardous trip, found it hard to believe that the *Golden Eagle,* with its superior speed, had not arrived long before their gaudy Breese monoplane *Aloha.* The red-white-and-blue Buhl two-winger piloted by Augy Pedlar and carrying Mildred Doran was known to be notoriously overloaded and underpowered. Race officials, though saddened, were not surprised when the ship did not turn up in Hawaii. But where were Jack Frost and Gordon Scott in their well-equipped Lockheed Vega, considered by many to be the pace-setter?

As the hours passed, it was evident to all that the *Golden Eagle* and the *Miss Doran* must be down. The Acting Secretary of the Navy, E. W. Eberle, authorized what was to be the greatest air-sea search in history up to that time: 540,000 square miles—from the Farallons in sight of the California coast to points 50-miles south of Diamond Head—were covered by destroyers, submarines, Coast Guard vessels, and the twenty-eight scouting planes of the carrier *Langley.* Their reports were all equally laconic: "No word. No sign."

In Honolulu, Jim Dole, distraught by the tragedy his well-meant offer had brought, offered $10,000 each for news of either missing airplane. In San Francisco, George Hearst, Jr., put up another $10,000 for word of the *Golden Eagle.* Both Denham Scott, brother of the missing Gordon, and Ken Jay of Lockheed, Frost's friend, went out on the *Langley.* For days they watched as her planes combed the empty waters of the Pacific.

It was a long, quiet drive back to Los Angeles for Allan Loughead, Jack Northrop, and Gordon Scott's sister, Sheila. There was very little conjecturing, though each was wondering what could have happened, for they all had the greatest confidence in the Vega and her crew.

What *did* happen?

The dangers of long overwater flights were only slightly known in 1927. There were always darkness, storms, and winds to contend with. Blind flying, out of visual contact with sky or sea, could cause even the best of pilots to misbelieve his instruments, and put his plane into the tight inadvertent downward maneuver so aptly called the "graveyard spiral."

The 110-mile cruising speed of the Vega with extra tailwinds as the goal was neared could have taken Frost and Scott far beyond the Hawaiian Island group, where their gasoline supply would have been exhausted. There was always the possibility of carburetor ice-up, even in the relatively warm air of the Pacific. The *Golden Eagle*'s radio should have been able to home in on the transmitter on Maui, but both it and the earth inductor compass protruding above the fuselage were far from foolproof. And there could have been errors in navigation, failure somewhere in the usually dependable Whirlwind engine, or an unknown weakness in the still new Vega. There were many, many opinions and theories, one about as valid as another.

No indication of the fate of *Miss Doran* was ever found, but tantalizing clues concerning the *Golden Eagle* turned up, enough to warrant further intensive investigation by relatives of Frost and Scott. Weeks later the radioless fishing schooner *William H. Smith* reported seeing "a piece of driftwood painted bright yellow" floating in mid-Pacific. Because the *Smith*'s captain had known nothing of the Dole Race, he let whatever it was he saw go uninvestigated.

Assuming that the *Golden Eagle* had gone into the sea, why didn't she float? Particular pains had been taken to keep her and her crew riding the waves. Even with a killing crash, wouldn't there have been floating debris from a wooden, cork-lined airplane? Perhaps there was, but by the time it had bobbed and been battered about in the ocean, or eventually come ashore, it might have been too small, and unrecognizable.

Rumors trickled in to Honolulu from various islands, reporting the hearing of an airplane engine, the sighting of "a yellow monoplane"—even reading the *Golden Eagle*'s license number, NX 913, on the wing. These were at first discounted because of the similar color and registration (NX 914) of Jensen's successful *Aloha*.

Harder to refute were the claims by seventeen witnesses from different places along the coast of the main island of Hawaii. They all reported sighting red and green Very flares on the slopes of 13,680-foot Mauna Loa, on both the nights of August 18th and 21st. Captain E. R. Block of the Army and stationed at Kilauea, had been so convinced that a plane was down that he and a sergeant had started on foot up the mist-shrouded volcano immediately after the flares were sighted. Unhappily, the sergeant suffered an attack of acute appendicitis, and the pair were forced to return to the post.

Denham Scott, with faith in both his brother's navigating ability and the worth of the Vega, went to Hawaii in 1928 and spent five months in further search. He talked to Marty Jensen, who, long after the race, was more than ever convinced that the *Golden Eagle* had reached Hawaii. Scott also learned that during the excitement and pressure of the immediate search, an Army plane had been sent to scout the big island; however the report that it had done so was in error. During each day of that period in August, the lava-strewn slopes of Mauna Loa had been entirely obscured by fog rolling in to meet the steam from its crater.

Doggedly, Scott quizzed the people who had spotted the arching, 30-second flares, and verified the accuracy of what they had seen by an elaborate set of tests of various lights, rockets, and flares sent up by a party located on the mountain. The searchers next endeavored to comb the area that seemed a common focal point of origin far up the volcano. Among almost impassable rocks they found dried beds of sirupy black basalt, interspersed by steaming cones and fissures in a landscape that might have been imagined by Dante. The molten lava from an eruption in 1926 was still cooling far below. A man walking on the thin shell could easily break through and tumble unseen into the suffocating fumes of a sulphur hole. In this ever-changing inferno, the wreckage of a 41 x 28-foot airplane could have promptly been obliterated. Denham Scott went home still convinced that along the 8,000-foot contour of Mauna Loa lay some hidden evidence of the lost airplane that would never come to light.

Nearly two years after the Dole Race, a last effort was initiated by Ezra Frost of New York, brother of the missing pilot. Using eleven Army planes and forty men from Luke Field, a 10-square-mile area was carefully photographed and a resulting aerial mosaic painstakingly scrutinized. If the lost Pacific flyers and their *Golden Eagle* ever lay on the slopes of Mauna Loa, by that time they had doubtless been mercifully buried under volcanic ash and the crater's lava flow.

Farewell look at the first Lockheed: note open cockpit forward, triangular tail, last-minute NX 913 license.

4

OVER POLAR WASTES

The sadness and sense of unexplained failure that followed the loss of the *Golden Eagle* lingered on until dispelled by new hopes and endeavors. A quirk of circumstances brought Lockheed an order from a determined man who knew what he wanted and liked what he saw.

In 1927 the explorer later known to fame as Sir Hubert Wilkins had neither his knighthood nor his famous beard. He was simply Captain George H. Wilkins, an energetic and imaginative Australian who, at thirty-eight, had already spent nearly half his life in travel and scientific exploration of the world's remote areas. In fact, the hold of the Arctic was so strong on him at this time that he owned only one conventional suit of clothes for his rare appearances in civilization.

Wilkins had been trying for two years to establish the worth of some of his theories concerning the region of the North Pole. As a scientist he wanted to learn more of Arctic weather and how it affected the rest of the world. The rumors of a land mass in the uncharted Arctic Ocean appealed to him as an explorer. And as an aviator he desired to demonstrate the advantage and practicality of trans-Arctic air transportation—not just a dash up to the pole and back, but a flight across the top of the world from North America to Europe.

Sponsored by Detroit businessmen and American newspapers, Wilkins had tackled the Arctic with teams of men and expensive equipment. He had flown four airplanes from primitive and fogbound Alaskan airfields,

Ski-shod Vega on step in a trial hop before the flight across the Arctic's "blind spot" in April 1928.

only to have his well-planned expeditions dogged by bad weather, pilot temerity, and a series of accidents. Since little of a nature to excite the public imagination had been accomplished, by the summer of 1927 the explorer's backing had evaporated, until his capital assets consisted of one whole Stinson Detroiter biplane and the parts of two smashed Fokkers.

Captain Wilkins's fortunes were at a low ebb as he sat at the window of a San Francisco hotel, mulling over his dubious prospects. A pilot himself, he had about decided on a solo trip in the old Stinson, a last attempt to cross the unknown ice and fly at least to Greenland. Then, as he recalled it:

". . . across my distant vision flashed the most efficient-looking monoplane I have ever seen. It was a fleeting glimpse, but I saw instantly and at a distance its distinctiveness. It had no flying wires; no controls exposed—nothing but a flying wing. To one who had been dreaming development of airplanes for eighteen years, the sight of this machine was the materialization of a vision. It gave me the thrill that another might experience if he saw his ideal woman in the flesh."

The "machine" was the *Golden Eagle*. After much search, the Captain found the ship at Oakland where it was being prepared for the Dole Race. He drove to Los Angeles and sought out the tiny Lockheed factory near Sycamore and Romaine streets, determined to investigate this dream plane further.

Though somewhat dismayed to find that the airplane he'd seen was the first and only one of its kind, Wilkins was much impressed with the monocoque construction process, and the skill and precision with which the wooden ships were being built. He met and liked Allan Loughead, and pored over blueprints, specifications, and performance figures with designer Jack Northrop.

The factory had its second Vega nearly complete and a third started. At hand too were Northrop's plans and mock-ups for the revolutionary low-wing, single-float seaplane later to be known as the Explorer, and his sketches for a parasol-wing job with open cockpit that would become the company's Air Express model. Yet more than ever Wilkins was excited by the possibilities of a Vega for his transpolar flight. His only problem was how to buy it. Wilkins's friends and former backers berated him for wanting to use a new and untried type of airplane. They pointed to the disappearance of the first Vega. But he was unswayed. He had deep faith that this streamlined beauty was to be his ticket to success.

Then he had a streak of luck. Two of the planes left over from his previous expeditions found unexpected buyers. The captain lost no time. He placed his order and deposit for the company's third Vega, already partly as-

Wilkins (left), Eielson and Vega No. 3. Rounded fin is the first built on an original, later was used exclusively.

sembled for use as a demonstrator.

Instead of acquiring a top-heavy staff for this new polar exploration, Wilkins decided to be his own business manager, mechanic, and general factotum. His only need, then, was to find the right man to pilot his Vega and so leave himself free to navigate, operate a radio, and make scientific observations and recordings. Wilkins had an old and trusted friend in mind, the Alaskan pioneer flyer, Ben Eielson.

Carl Ben Eielson was a lean, gray-eyed Norwegian-American from North Dakota who was by now considered the Arctic's foremost pilot. He'd gone to Fairbanks in 1922 ostensibly to teach school, but his real love was airplanes. Promoting a surplus Jenny, the ex-Army aviator had been the first to fly in an Alaskan winter, and he had also piloted Alaska's initial airmail service. Just about everybody in the territory liked Ben. He was an eligible bachelor who could be gay and companionable on the ground, but was steady, reasoning, and self-reliant in the air. And, like Wilkins, Eielson had both the vision to foresee Arctic air routes and the desire to establish them. When it came to steadfast purpose, the two made a great team.

Meanwhile the Lockheed woodworkers and mechanics were fitting the Vega to Wilkins's special requirements. It was powered by a Wright J5 Whirlwind engine, and had extra gasoline tanks in the wing and two in the body of the ship behind the pilot. There was no door to the cabin, just hatches to admit the occupants; and the windows were arranged to permit observation to the sides and down through the floor. Navigational readings and the performance of his short-wave radio would be good, Wilkins hoped, because the Vega's all-wood construction eliminated a good deal of metallic interference. To cope with deep snow he ordered a pair of metal skis—plus a spare set of wooden ones—stowed aboard against the time they would replace wheels for use on Arctic runways. Another feature was the runner attached to the rear of the fuselage: in case of a forced landing a portion could be sawed off and converted into a sledge.

The bright orange-and-blue monoplane was hauled through the streets to Rogers Airport, assembled there, and test-flown on January 9, 1928. As he had been for the *Golden Eagle*, little Eddie Bellande was chosen as test pilot for this Vega, carefully circling about the city for twenty minutes. Eddie landed, taxied the ship up to the expectant Wilkins and the men from Lockheed, climbed down, and patted the shiny fuselage.

"She's a pippin," he said, and the explorer's face lit up with a grin of anticipation.

Eielson arrived from the north the next day. "She looks all right," was his noncommittal verdict on the Vega. He tested the ship cautiously at first, but was soon flying her with confidence. He'd take off, climb, and then land at near-stalling speeds. Except for one forced landing in a plowed field due to a gasoline obstruction, the performance and load tests proceeded without a hitch. Out at Muroc Dry Lake, the Whirlwind-powered Vega took off with a load in 2,700 feet, and flew at a comfortable 134 mph.

Wilkins and Eielson were soon ready for their crack at the Arctic, and mid-March found the two men with their new Lockheed at Barrow, on the northern tip of Alaska. The temperature was 48° below zero, so the first procedure on landing was immediate draining of the oil. The trim, colorful Vega drew admiring comments from the handful of residents who trooped out on the frozen lagoon to greet and help, while the Eskimos fought among themselves for the privilege of carrying the flyers' gear.

For three weeks Wilkins and Eielson waited for good weather and prepared their rations, scientific and survival equipment, radio and airplane. Then, on the first attempt to get off, one of the metal skis broke. The flyers substituted the wooden pair and tried again. This time they ran out of runway, careened up the bank of the Barrow Lagoon, and came safely to rest on the snow-covered tundra.

Shifting operations to the adjacent and larger Elson Lagoon, Captain Wilkins hired every man and boy who came within hailing distance and set them to work in digging out a new takeoff spot. For five days the Eskimos shoveled snow and leveled ice hummocks with picks and saws. Finally a mile-long runway stretched along the shore of the Arctic Ocean. But it was only a scant fourteen feet wide.

Getting off on April 15th was touch and go. The track was still bumpy and undulating, and Eielson had the tough task of keeping the Vega straight. Thirty, forty, fifty miles an hour, the plane gathered speed. Peering aft, Wilkins could see the stabilizer swaying, just missing the snowbanks piled on either side. Too much rudder pressure, and a swing of a few inches one way or another would bring disaster.

The howl of the Whirlwind drowned the dry rattle of the skis. Sixty, seventy—and the tail came up. Ben Eielson kept his nerve and George Wilkins prayed. Then they were off, climbing smoothly to swing out over the forbidding polar sea.

Now began a long vigil for Leon S. Vincent, the Government Teacher at Barrow, who was trained in Morse code. Cradling the little radio receiving set which Wilkins had left with him, he listened all through the long hours of that April Sunday and far into the night. The hesitant tapping of the explorer reached back to Alaska:

"KDZ, KDZ. Are OK so far . . ."

Vincent picked up the messages every hour all through the evening. After 2 A.M. he could make out only a transmitter buzz, and by 4 o'clock even this had faded into silence. It would be weeks before he learned what had become of the daring men whose hands he'd shaken in farewell the previous morning.

Blasting along over the Arctic Ocean, Wilkins and Eielson were doing fine. Even in the night they were not without the sun to give them navigational bearings, for it never dropped below the horizon. The frigid air through which the Lockheed winged its way was around −45°. Beneath was a vast expanse of ice, its masses arranged by wind pressure and currents.

They could have headed directly over the North Pole, but scientific knowledge, not glory, was Wilkins's objective.

Across a 1,300-mile stretch, most of it never before seen or traveled by man, the aerial explorers found no indication of protruding earth beneath the Arctic ice. Wilkins was later to cable criptically: "No foxes seen"—a prearranged code message to the American Geographical Society to say that the so-called Arctic Land Mass was a myth.

Landfall for the flyers was Grant Land, Canada's northernmost reach. Flying at 6,000 feet, Eielson turned the Vega north and east again, over the roof of the world toward Norway's Spitzbergen.

The sturdy plane was aided by a stiff tailwind to round the northern tip of Greenland and fly on through piles of high-stacked clouds. By constant reckoning, computing, and changes of course, Wilkins continued the remarkable feat of guiding the airplane cross-longitude toward their destination. Eielson, cramped and stiff in the cockpit ahead, threaded the Vega through the massive cloud corridors.

After twenty hours in the air the lightened Lockheed reached Spitzbergen, the goal which Wilkins had been trying to attain for three long years.

The land did not greet the voyagers kindly. Spray from the open sea whipped high against the craggy coastal peaks, winds tossed and buffeted their fragile plane, and they were suddenly enveloped in a raging snowstorm. A patch of smooth, snow-covered land flashed past; dead ahead loomed a mountain. Eielson swerved in time to avoid it, and crabbed his way out over the ocean again. His windshield was clogged now with wet snow and frozen oil—he could see only by peering alternately out of the open side windows. In the back Wilkins dodged from pane to pane, writing directional notes to be passed up to Eielson who had barely time to read them. With gas running low, they had to land. And quick.

Desperately the pilot fought to bring the Vega back to shore, trying to find the little smooth patch again. Almost blindly, with scribbled directions from Wilkins, he came winging over it, turned into the blizzard, and settled on the snowdrifts. The skis touched and the Lockheed slid to a stop in barely thirty feet. Instantly Wilkins flung out the engine covers and an empty can, tumbled out himself, and struggled forward to drain the oil. Eielson sat numb for a moment, temporarily deafened from over twenty hours of the engine's roar.

After stamping snow around the skis to secure the ship, the men settled down to munch pemmican and wait for the storm to blow itself out. Their wait lasted four days. It was just as well that the charts were not detailed enough to show the name of this sea-locked landing place. Later they were to learn that it was called Doedmansoeira, or Dead Man's Island.

Leaving this snowy prison proved the most dangerous part of the Arctic flight. The flyers stamped and shoveled a downhill runway for the plane, but even with the Whirlwind revved up to full throttle, the Vega refused to budge.

Wilkins got out of his navigator's hatch behind the wing, and pushed. The plane slid, gathering momentum; though he clung to the step, he soon fell off. Eielson, unable to see to the rear, horsed the Lockheed skyward and wheeled out over the sea, only to spot the forlorn, parka-clad figure alone on the snow. He circled and plunked down in the drifts again.

For a second try, Wilkins slung out a short rope ladder he'd prepared back in Barrow. This time he ran clumsily alongside the ship as she began to slide, and leaped like a bareback rider to land on her fuselage. Clutching for a hold on the smooth, rounded shape, with the rope in his teeth he struggled to gain the open hatch. But Eielson, feeling weight in the back, gunned the ship. Just before the skis came bounding up on step, Wilkins realized his chances of reaching the hatch were slim. He slithered off the fuselage, but was struck by the tail and bowled over and over down the slope. Eielson, in the air, came around and landed again.

Winded and dazed, the explorer discussed the predicament with his pilot. By now they had only ten gallons of gasoline left in the tanks; still, they were reasonably certain that a settlement was close at hand. They determined on one last try at a takeoff. If it failed, Eielson would leave in the plane alone and Wilkins, with a tent, would camp until the pilot returned with transportation.

This time the weary flyers lifted the tail of the Vega into flying position on a block of snow. Then they dragged a log of driftwood up from the beach, with the idea of poling their plane like a boat.

Half in, half out of his hatch, Wilkins pushed and strained. Eielson rocked the Vega with her throttle wide open. For a full minute she hung, then with a lunge was free. The breathless captain tumbled into the bottom of the cabin, unable to answer the pilot's questioning shouts until the plane was airborne with both of them at last.

It took only a few minutes to cross the five miles of open water and pick out the radio masts of Green Harbour, a Norwegian mining settlement. With the landing of the Lockheed on the snow-covered shore, one of the

Safe arrival at Green Harbour, Spitzbergen, to win world fame and a knighthood—and a big kiss for Ben Eielson.

greatest flights in aviation—2,200 miles across the Arctic's intercontinental "blind spot"—had come to a successful conclusion.

In recognition of this achievement, Captain Wilkins was knighted by King George V. Ben Eielson received both the United States Army's Distinguished Flying Cross and the Harmon Award for the most outstanding aeronautical achievement of the year 1928.

The praise of both men for their Lockheed Vega, its dependability now well proven, was strong and sincere. All the faith, careful planning, and fine craftsmanship that had gone into the ship had at last paid off. Prompted by worldwide publicity given the Wilkins-Eielson flight, inquiries—and orders—came flooding into the office of the little California aircraft company. The pageant of Lockheed's renown had begun.

After their round of appearances before cheering crowds in Europe, Wilkins came away from Buckingham Palace no longer plain George, but Sir Hubert. Ben Eielson, ever gallant, later stated that his biggest thrill was a kiss from the pretty wife of the French Under-Secretary for Air.

Even before returning to the States, the conquerors of the Arctic laid plans to explore the other end of the globe. There was still land to be charted on the fringe of the Antarctic and much to be learned about the weather of this little-known continent. Commander Richard E. Byrd's expedition was being made ready at this time, and there was much speculation about a "race to the pole" between the two explorers. Sir Hubert assured the commander that his new Wilkins-Hearst Antarctic Expedition would be a modest one: he had no thought or intention of a flight over the South Pole.

Wilkins sent a tentative order from Europe for a second Lockheed airplane to be used in the Antarctic. Before leaving the company in June 1928, Jack Northrop had proceeded with drawings and preliminary arrangements for the low-wing, single-float seaplane with retractable outrigger pontoons. This revolutionary design—one he'd started at the time Wilkins bought his Vega—was now called the Explorer model in the flyer's honor. The fuselage was cut and work had begun before a final consultation between Sir Hubert and the designer brought out the possibility of landing amid pack ice. Therefore a high-winged monoplane would be preferable. The Explorer was temporarily shelved in favor of a regulation Vega joined by stiltlike bracing to twin floats; thus it became the first seaplane in the wooden Lockheed series.

Its companion, the veteran of the Arctic exploration, was also equipped with pontoons. In recognition of the publicity and business his great flight had brought to Lockheed, the company sold Sir Hubert his new ship at cost.

With two planes Wilkins needed a second pilot. He chose another veteran of Alaskan bush-flying: Joe Crosson, black-haired and smiling, with a bit of a mustache to hide his youth. Joe came down from Fairbanks in the summer of '28 for his first flight in a Vega.

The sea-going monoplane was launched from a wooden ramp off Terminal Island in San Pedro Bay. Allan Loughead came down to the harbor for the occasion along with Jerry Vultee, who had taken Jack Northrop's place as chief engineer. Tod Oviatt, also from the shop, donned his bathing suit and gave a hand to float the plane off into the salt water. Then Joe Crosson took the Vega on an easy run, lifting her gently off the tops of the little waves and making a great circle out over the Pacific.

By September 1928 the Wilkins party and their two Vegas were headed south by steamer. Again the explorer purposely kept his expedition small. In addition to himself, Eielson, and Crosson, there were only Orval Por-

Lockheed's first Vega seaplane is hauled ashore after test at San Pedro. Designer Gerard Vultee (center) *assists Wilkins's Antarctic Expedition ship.*

ter, a top-notch motor mechanic, also from Alaska, and a radio operator, Victor Olsen. At Montevideo, Uruguay, planes and personnel transferred to the Norwegian whaling factory ship *Hektoria* and were carried to the whaling station at Deception Island in the South Shetland group.

Olsen's radio messages about their progress were relayed to New York and there rewritten for public consumption by the Hearst news syndicate, which was sponsoring the expedition. Apparently to differentiate between the two Lockheed Vegas flown by the explorers, Hearst writers dubbed the planes the "Los Angeles" and the "San Francisco." Wilkins himself never named either.

Sir Hubert expected a good ice sheet on the bay of the

Seasoned bush pilot Joe Crosson (left), *down from Alaska to fly Wilkins's second Vega, which was completed as a seaplane by Lockheed's new chief engineer Gerard Vultee and sold at cost by Allan Loughead* (right).

—and he named it "LOCKHEED MOUNTAIN"

Illustration and headline from an ad whose text reveals, "Captain Wilkins chose a Lockheed for his polar expeditions by air because he knew 'it was the finest ship available.' "

U-shaped island, so he had the planes fitted with skis and slung ashore. The Vega from the Arctic exploration was the first complete airplane to touch the Antarctic regions.

But for the first time in fourteen years, the ice at Deception Island was unreliable. An unusually warm season had reduced it from a thickness of seven feet to a soft, unsafe honeycomb. The beautiful landing surface Wilkins recalled from previous visits was useless. Aboard the *Hektoria* the men waited for better weather in the form of a cold snap, but to everyone's amazement a mild rain fell, and the snow about the ski-shod Vegas melted away overnight.

The expedition members and a willing work party from the whaler set about building a runway on the bayside peninsula. It was like the strip at Barrow all over again; but here, instead of snow and ice, great chunks of cokelike volcanic tuff had to be cleared away. The strip was ready November 16, 1928. Wilkins and Eielson tried a short run. Because of the lack of snow, the first flight ever made over Antarctica was accomplished in a wheel-equipped airplane—again the faithful Vega that had served in the Far North.

Eielson in the older Lockheed, and Crosson in the new one, both flew short test hops, looking in vain for a better landing field. They even thought to dare the treacherous bay ice with a spot landing on a 300-yard stretch. Ben tried this and slithered on the wet and glistening surface far beyond the markers. The Vega crunched through the rotten ice and came to rest with her tail in the air and nose in the water. The whalers dragged the ship to safety and Orval Porter dried and cleaned the brine-washed engine. Joe Crosson later flew the ship on floats from an ice-free stretch of the bay, but seaplane operation from Deception Island was an extreme hazard, due to great flocks of sea birds that scavenged about the whaling factory.

Beset on all sides by unfavorable circumstances, Wilkins nevertheless set to work to enlarge his peninsula runway. The lava-banked strip, facetiously dubbed Hoover Field, was a zigzag gash on the slope, undulating over two small hills and punctuated with a couple of 20-degree bends. Bad though it was, the explorer and Eielson decided to use it December 20 in a try for at least one worthwhile flight. Ben was calm, as always, but he hardly opened the throttle of the new Vega until they passed the first dogleg. The Lockheed bumped and bounced down the first hill, plowed over a snowbank, lurched through a ditch, then turned to speed up the other hill and catapult into the air at the top. Somehow, Eielson kept her flying.

Heading south, they carried out a 1,300-mile flight along the shore of the Palmer Peninsula, penetrating deep to the edge of the Antarctic continent. Wilkins was

With the Antarctic Expedition (left to right): *Parker D. "Shorty" Cramer, first pilot; Sir Hubert Wilkins; S.A. "Al" Cheesman, second pilot; and Orval Porter, mechanic.*

able to map roughly, describe, and photograph some 100,000 square miles of hitherto unknown territory. It was the first time that new lands had ever been discovered from an airplane. He flew at 6,000 feet, plotting dozens of geographical features and naming them for his friends and financial backers. Among these were the Whirlwind Glaciers, after his redoubtable engine, and the Lockheed Mountains, for his airplanes. Then there were Capes Keeler and Northrop, for the president and former chief engineer of the Lockheed company. The first landfall on the continent itself became Hearst Land in honor of the newspaperman.

A falling barometer finally turned them back from the forbidding snowscape where crevasses yawned and a wheeled landing anywhere would be unthinkable. Flying with a tailwind, their last look at Antarctica proper was a prominent cape jutting out in the ice shelf. This Sir Hubert named "after my friend and companion, Carl B. Eielson." Wilkins's superb navigation brought them directly back to Deception Island, and Ben found a hole over the fog-shrouded base through which to bring the Vega safely down.

Time and weather permitted only one more flight that season. Dodging sea gulls, terns, and the petrels called "Mother Carey's chickens," Joe Crosson got the seaplane off the harbor and flew Wilkins on a shorter journey south to recheck a portion of the expedition's discoveries. Then it was time to get out of there before the winds and cold of winter set in. Planning to return in September, the men dismantled the two Lockheeds. The wings were stored in an iron shed of an abandoned shore installation; the fuselages, complete with engines and tail surfaces, were tightly wrapped in canvas and left to weather the Antarctic winter in the open.

Eielson and Crosson never came back to Antarctica. They returned to Alaska to found an airline, and Ben, while flying to the relief of the icebound fur ship *Nanuk* the next November, crashed on the shore of Siberia. After weeks of harrowing search, it was Joe Crosson who found the wrecked plane and the frozen body of Alaska's foremost Arctic pilot.

A new Wilkins-Hearst expedition had meanwhile left for Deception Island aboard *Hektoria* to take up where the earlier exploration had left off. Mechanic Orval Porter, whom Wilkins called "the backbone of the party," had signed on again, and the pilots were another pair of seasoned Arctic flyers. One was Parker D. Cramer, veteran of a round-trip flight from New York to Nome, plus an assault on the North Atlantic which had ended on the Greenland ice cap. From Ontario came a skillful Canadian bush pilot, Al Cheesman.

Expedition members and the crew of the *Hektoria* found the orange airplanes intact on the shore of Deception Island where they had been left. Winds had kept blizzards from covering them completely, though they still had to be dug from their snowy prisons. Sir Hubert examined the Vegas, found everything sound, and remarked that "plywood has its merits." With its engine lovingly ministered to by Porter, one of the planes was assembled and in flying condition within thirty-six hours.

All they needed was weather to fly in, but again the capricious Antarctic conspired against them. The above-freezing temperatures were as unusual as those of the season before. With the aid of the British Royal Research ship *William Scoresby,* the explorers set off down the west shore of Palmer Peninsula in search of better conditions. They took advantage of every possible spell of good flying weather, with the *Scoresby* ready to swing a Vega on floats off into the water beside her. The record was twelve minutes from deck tie-down to takeoff. Shorty Cramer got in a couple of flights with Wilkins and made one attempted ski-equipped hop from the melting ice beside the anchored vessel. Most of the flying fell to Al Cheesman, who proved an excellent man with float planes.

During the 1929–30 season the Wilkins-Hearst expedition flew 3,000 miles and charted some 1,200 miles of new coast. Flying from the research ship the explorer and his pilots stabbed toward the white wastes of the continent again and again, pushing back the frontiers of geographical knowledge.

By the time he was headed home on the *Hektoria,* Sir Hubert's agile mind had seized on the idea of further polar research by submarine. He was also anxious to get back to New York for a belated honeymoon. He and Cheesman left the whaler 125 miles off Uruguay, and flew in to Montevideo harbor. Then they went to Buenos Aires, where they wound up the affairs of the expedition in five days. The Lockheeds, which had flown at both ends of the earth, were sold to the Argentine government.

Down in Antarctica, the land beyond the Lockheed Mountains has been renamed the Wilkins Coast to honor its discoverer. The great explorer died in 1958, believing his original and most famous Lockheed Vega was in a museum in Buenos Aires, where the Argentines had promised to put it. However, a minor crack-up damaged the ship before the intention could be carried out, and through the years it simply rotted away in an airport boneyard. So by the time Harvey Lippincott, a Pratt & Whitney representative, discovered it after World War II, it was a sad and sodden mass of punk.

While Wilkins, Cramer, and Cheesman were mapping the Graham and Palmer coasts, Commander Byrd's expedition on the other side of the continent pushed inland from Little America and flew over the South Pole. A third aerial expedition from Norway combined business with land-scouting in still another Antarctic sector.

Norwegians had been using the Antarctic seas as whaling grounds for many years, and the work had reached the proportions of a stable industry. One of the larger companies, Bryde & Dahl of Sandefjord, Norway, conceived the idea of using aircraft to spot schools of whales: float planes with a good range could circle out from a factory ship and report the best grounds for the smaller killer-boats to head for. The Wilkins-Eielson Vega, shipped home from Spitzbergen via Oslo after its trans-Arctic jaunt, naturally attracted much favorable attention. Bryde & Dahl determined to have a similar plane for their whaling operations. With government approval, they hired two well-known Norwegian naval pilots—Captains Riiser-Larsen and Lutzow-Holm—to take care of the matter.

The pair did things with Scandinavian thoroughness. Lutzow-Holm journeyed to Burbank and personally supervised the rigging of a new Vega with a Whirlwind engine. He even brought along his own mechanic to learn every detail of maintenance for this American model, the first Lockheed to be sold outside the United States and Canada. Bryde & Dahl shipped the plane to the whaling grounds aboard the factory ship *Thorshammer* in the fall of 1929.

Riiser-Larsen and Lutzow-Holm apparently spent as much time in the Antarctic seeking and mapping new coastline as they did in hunting for whales. Operating from the small trawler *Norvegia,* the naval aviators winged their way from a hundred miles offshore to the Antarctic coast between Coats and Enderby lands. They left their plane bobbing in open water, skied the rest of the way to shore, and raised the flag of Norway. More reconnaissance flights were made in January and February 1930, during which the Norwegians discovered what are now Queen Maud Land and Princess Martha Coast. Their own names, like those of Wilkins and Eielson, were bestowed on prominent Antarctic landmarks and became parts of the map. Hjalmar Riiser-Larsen continued his explorations and later was head of the Norwegian Air Forces.

Bryde & Dahl next sent their well-traveled Lockheed on a cruise to hunt whales in Greenland waters. This was more the work for which it had originally been imported. Day after day the Vega was sent out to scour the frigid waters in search of telltale spouting. The local Eskimos

Norwegian Vega rests amidships between flights in 1930 to seek whales and new land in Antarctica.

The Viking, *here leaving with the MacMillan expedition of 1931, went on to many years of movie and charter work.*

christened the plane *Qarrtsiluni,* meaning "soul of the whale." On return to Norway the ship was sold. It finished out its days on photographic work, flown with skis. Still later the rugged Whirlwind engine from *Qarrtsiluni* had a further career as power for a propeller-driven sledge, reported as "the fastest in the mountains."

One more Lockheed must be mentioned for its use in Arctic regions. In the summer of 1931 the famous American explorer Commander Donald B. MacMillan acquired a slightly used Vega and took it on a survey expedition to the Labrador and Greenland coasts. Appropriately, the ship was called *The Viking.*

Pilot for this venture was Charles F. Rocheville, who had accompanied MacMillan and Commander Byrd to Greenland in 1925. Charley Rocheville had been employed in California as an aircraft designer, but the Depression and the lure of the North brought him back into active flying. Also along as cameraman was Glenn R. Kershner, with the bulky equipment for taking motion pictures with Multicolor, a technique involving four cameras. Howard Hughes was interested in this new process, a forerunner of color photography.

Without great fanfare Commander MacMillan, Rocheville, and Kershner flew the float-equipped *Viking* out of Rockland, Maine, headed north. During the summer, in Labrador and beyond, they mapped 1,500 square miles of previously uncharted land and explored some 50,000 miles of additional territory. The color film in the Multicolor cameras was reported as "beautiful," but because of projection difficulties was never released.

The expedition's Lockheed was sold to a Seattle businessman, and flown with both floats and wheels in the Pacific Northwest and Arizona. Today it is prominently displayed at the Ford Museum in Dearborn, Michigan.

5

COAST TO COAST

Herb Fahy in The Black Hornet.

Crossing their wide country from one coast to another has always had great appeal to most Americans. There have been (and are) records for making the journey by every means of conveyance from roller skates to space capsule. To accomplish the fastest trip from coast to coast in one way or another seems to be a primal urge.

Flyers have been no exception, and the records they set have been well publicized. As early as 1911, cigar-puffing Calbraith Perry Rodgers completed the very first transcontinental aerial journey in 84 days. Flying a Wright EX named *Vin Fiz* from Sheepshead Bay, New York, to Long Beach, California, he survived some seventy landings and numerous crashes to finish the trip.

Even the first nonstop flight across the nation took nearly 27 hours in 1923. Army pilots John Macready and Oakley Kelly plugged along in the blunt-nosed, wide-winged Fokker T-2, built specially to fly the 2,516 miles from New York to San Diego.

For a long time a nonstop effort from west to east was considered next to impossible. Though aided by prevailing winds, a plane would have to lift its heavy overload of gasoline high above California's coastal ranges and the Rockies during the first part of the trip. But by the spring of 1928 the Lockheed Aircraft Company had produced an airplane that could do it.

Interest in the *Golden Eagle* and Wilkins's transpolar Vega had put enough orders on the books of the tiny Lockheed factory in Hollywood to warrant moving to a new and better plant location. President Fred Keeler, through his connections in Burbank, found 20,000 square feet in a building already occupied in part by the Mission Glass Works. Burbank was only a small city, surrounded by farms, orchards, vineyards, and acres of gravel and vacant brushland. When the Lockheed Aircraft Company moved in and began operations there at San Fernando Road and Empire Avenue in March 1928, nobody dreamed that the fifty-man work force in the shabby brick building "down by the Turkey Crossing" would someday expand to some 80,000 employees all over the world.

The first plane built in the new plant was destined to make the Lockheed name synonymous with speed. Ordered by a well-to-do Santa Monica sportsman named Harry J. Tucker, it was a gleaming white Vega trimmed with red-and-blue funnel stripes. This was the first Lockheed to be fitted with the 9-cylinder 425-hp Wasp engine. With over twice the power of the Wright Whirlwind, it was made by the Pratt & Whitney Aircraft Corporation of Hartford, Connecticut. The combination of Wasp power plant and Lockheed airplane was soon to prove ideal.

Harry Tucker, originally from Long Island, was in the airplane-engine business himself, associated with inventor Al Menasco. Though Tucker was not a pilot, he was enthusiastic about flying, and with the purchase of the new Vega he was in the big time. Here was a plane that appeared well capable of breaking all manner of speed and distance records. Harry called his new Lockheed *Yankee Doodle,* a good name and one bound to catch the public fancy. All he needed was a pilot.

He found one in tall, handsome Arthur C. Goebel, still the toast of the Coast for winning the previous year's Dole Race to Hawaii. A Rocky Mountain boy with long experience in aerial acrobatics and movie stunt-flying, Art Goebel couldn't live forever on his first-prize money from the pineapple derby. One day he appeared at the ranch-house office in Burbank and leaned on the desk of Miss Marie Kelly, Allan Loughead's executive secretary and girl-of-all-work. Slightly deaf from the roar of airplane engines, Goebel announced to all within hearing:

"I'd give my right arm to fly a Lockheed!"

Art soon got his wish, and for free. They gave him a couple of ferry flights to check him out, and then Harry Tucker hired the famous ocean flyer to pilot his *Yankee Doodle.*

An accident in another plane put Tucker on crutches for a while and postponed his plans, but by June he was ready to try the west-to-east nonstop flight. Since Goebel was in Japan on a demonstration tour, Leland F. Shoenhair was the first to take the controls of the red-white-and-blue *Yankee Doodle.* Like so many other California pilots, Lee was Army trained, and had flown just about everything that could stagger into the air.

Shoenhair and Tucker made a valiant try at reaching New York. After a start from San Diego, they kept going as far as Harrisburg, only to find fog over the eastern Pennsylvania mountains blocking the way. Prudent Lee wheeled the Vega around and proceeded back to a landing at Columbus, Ohio. Even so, the time was excellent: only 17½ hours in the air.

While waiting for Goebel's return Stateside and good weather, Tucker had his plane retrimmed. Broad red-white-and-blue arrows replaced the funnel stripes down the sides of the ship, and big heavy Old English lettering proclaimed her to all as the *Yankee Doodle.* Harry's own name was on the cabin door. With Goebel back, another name was added just below the little side cockpit windows.

On August 19–20, 1928, the pair got the Vega off Mines Field at Los Angeles with a full 450 gallons of gasoline, enough to last the 2,710 miles to New York. Touching down at Curtiss Field on Long Island, *Yankee Doodle* became the first airplane ever to fly nonstop across the continent from west to east, and the first to make a coast-to-coast hop in less than 24 hours.

Watch in hand, his brown business suit scarcely crumpled, Art Goebel rose up in the confined cockpit to greet Frank Tichenor, publisher of *Aero Digest.*

"Good morning, Frank," he called. "I make it 18 hours

Arthur Goebel and Harry Tucker with Yankee Doodle, *the Vega that proved in 1928 that "Lockheed" meant speed.*

and 58 minutes from L.A.—and about time for breakfast!"

The hungry flyers also reaped financial rewards. In addition to supplying their gasoline and oil, The Richfield Company of California gave them $10,000 in recognition of their achievement. Commercial aviation had come a long way in five years. A stock plane had beaten the Army's specially built T-2 by almost eight hours. And the best time by train was practically three days.

Because *Yankee Doodle* was a standard Vega, Art and Harry carried their extra gas in five-gallon cans, packed in the cabin. Owner Tucker paid in hard work for the records his airplane set. He had to pump the gas by hand up into the wing tanks, where gravity flow would drop it to the engine. As a can was emptied, Harry chucked it out the door. Twice on his trips he lost the door in this maneuver—which naturally cut down on air speed, as well as setting up an air flow that threatened to suck the passenger out with the empties.

After their west–east hop, Goebel and Tucker tried the Lockheed in a couple of races. Then a personality clash between pilot and owner brought changes. Tucker had plans for successive attempts on speed, distance, and even altitude records. He wanted to set and break records, even his own, with no respite, and remarked that he had no intention of becoming a parrot, "the bird that talks most and flies the least."

Harry's ambitions brought him a third and final pilot: Captain C. B. D. Collyer, a lean Virginian. Missionary's son, former aviation cadet, airmail pilot and skywriter, Charlie Collyer had gained recent fame for a steamship-and-plane trip around the world in July 1928, and had participated in transcontinental races.

Collyer had flown just a Lockheed demonstrator, and that only once, when he took the stick of the sleek *Yankee Doodle* on October 24. Lifting her off Roosevelt Field at the bidding of his laconic new boss, he nosed the Vega west on another nonstop attempt. Most of the trip was made in fog, storms, and headwinds, and it took nearly 25 hours. Through the long night Charlie Collyer, aching and uncomfortable, wrestled with the controls to keep his course. His parachute straps chafed his back, and he vowed he'd use padding next time. In the cabin, Harry Tucker pumped gas, and left a trail of tin cans across the continent. For luck he carried a "mascot" contrived from a beribboned hot dog, with toothpicks for legs and tail.

When the men finally brought their Lockheed down at Los Angeles, Tucker was the first passenger, and his Vega the first airplane, to fly nonstop from coast to coast in both directions.

The Santa Monica sportsman could not rest on his achievements. He wanted to turn around, fly back, and try to better his own mark.

But time was running out for *Yankee Doodle*. On November 3, 1928, Collyer got the Vega over the coastal ranges and across the Mojave Desert. Nobody knows what happened after the record-seekers crossed the Colorado into Arizona. People in the mining camps south of Prescott saw the plane circling confusedly in the dark. Then the Vega came roaring wide open down rocky Crook Canyon, crashed, and scattered itself for half a mile through a forest of tall pines.

Yankee Doodle's existence was short, but she left an unerasable impression: "Lockheed" now spelled speed in the public mind.

In Burbank, Jerry Vultee and his men completed a new Lockheed model—the Air Express—in November 1928. Actually this ship was a complete rebuild of a parasol-wing original, designed by Northrop, that had had a brief existence earlier in the year. Put out as a mail-and-passenger carrier with the needs of airmail pilots in mind, the ship had a rear open cockpit. The plane had been tested and accepted by Western Air Express, but after a crack-up on its maiden flight was returned to the factory. Now the Air Express was put through further exhaustive tests under the guidance of the gifted Vultee, and received the coveted Department of Commerce "approved-type" certificate.

Like *Yankee Doodle* it was fitted with a 425-hp Pratt & Whitney Wasp engine, and was capable of great things in the line of fast flight. A further speed inducer was the fitting of a tubular Duralumin engine cowling. This special enclosure for radial engines had been developed by the National Advisory Committee for Aeronautics and first tested on the Wright J5 engine of an Army AT-5A. The Lockheed Air Express installation was both the first use of the NACA cowl on a Pratt & Whitney engine, and its first use on a commercial airplane. It gave the torpedo-shaped Lockheed a barrel nose and added some ten to nineteen miles an hour to its 161-mph top speed. Though considered strange in appearance at first, the cowl was quickly accepted and became a common sight on all types of radial-engined aircraft.

The Air Express was still an experimental job when the Lockheed company decided to exhibit it at an air show in New York. A good ferry pilot would have to be found, since this ship was a real speed queen. As luck would have it, the pilot was right there in Los Angeles, in need of transportation east. He was Army Reserve Captain Frank M. Hawks, a California flyer who'd been barnstorming and carrying oil-field payrolls in Texas and Mexico. Hawks was now working for The Texas Company, and had been flying the oil firm's new Vega.

Neither Hawks nor Lockheed's Ben Hunter was exactly averse to the idea of making the ferry trip a try to better *Yankee Doodle*'s transcontinental time. Like the speedy Vega, the Air Express had no special fuel tanks, and someone would have to go along with Hawks to pump gas from five-gallon tins, augmenting the two 50-gallon

Parasol wing, new NACA cowl are distinguishing features of the rebuilt prototype Air Express in which Frank Hawks and Oscar Grubb wrote a new coast-to-coast record in February 1929.

wing tanks. The someone chosen was a man with an unlikely name for an air hero: Oscar E. Grubb, the bespectacled superintendent of Lockheed's final assembly.

Seventy-five rectangular cans of Texaco aviation gasoline were packed into the tubular cabin of the red-and-silver Lockheed. Then Oscar Grubb was folded amid them, and the door shoved shut behind him. The plan was for Oscar to keep the wing tanks pumped full. Then he was to cut up the empty cans with tinsmith's shears and make more room for himself: the company wasn't taking any chances on losing the door by having him jettison them. Though claiming not to be superstitious, the superintendent's fellow employees wired a rabbit's foot to the shank of the Lockheed's tail skid.

Hawks and Grubb got off just at sundown on February 4, 1929. Near Flagstaff, Arizona, they climbed above the fogbanks and went barreling along at 14,000 feet. Grubb pumped gas. Swathed in his big raccoon coat, Frank Hawks sat warm in the cockpit, with no inkling that far below him was a seething meteorological cauldron of the winter's worst weather.

Toward midnight a sick cough erupted from the engine and Hawks's heart missed a beat. Frantically he switched from tank to tank. The gauges read EMPTY and the Wasp quit entirely. Frank squirmed down in his seat to peer into the dimly lit cabin ahead. Oscar Grubb was sprawled grotesquely on top of the gasoline tins, sound asleep. Exhaustion, high altitude, and the monotonous drone of the motor in his confined quarters had done him in.

Hawks's roar made up for the lack of noise from the stopped engine.

"Hey Oscar! Oscar! Give her some gas or get ready to jump!"

Poor Grubb came to and responded on the pump with frenzied efforts. Soon the motor was barking again on all nine cylinders, and the lost altitude was regained. On they went above the endless clouds, with only the moon and stars for company. Twice Hawks took a chance on dropping down through the soup in order to check some visual landmark with his compass. He made no claims to being an "intrepid aviator" and wasn't ashamed to admit he was downright scared. After daylight the first descent brought something that vaguely looked like Kentucky out of the murk below. The second got the cloud-dodging travelers a glimpse of the capitol at Washington. Over familiar terrain now, the Air Express burned up the skyway to New York and came around into the wind to land at Roosevelt Field.

Oscar Grubb was half dead when he fell out of the cabin at the end of the trip. Gasoline fumes from the sliced cans had sickened him, and rough air had com-

Allan Loughead and Frank Hawks (who plans to keep warm in Air Express cockpit) wait for gas cans to be taken aboard for the non-stop dash east.

pounded his nausea. With no clear recollection of the flight, he gasped:

"Never again, not for a million dollars!"

Hawks propped him up. "Here's your real hero," he told the milling reporters. "He's the one who made it possible."

Even with the detour by way of Washington, they had beaten the Goebel-Tucker record by over half an hour. The new NACA cowling had been proved to function perfectly.

After this flight and the resulting publicity, it was not difficult for Captain Hawks to talk The Texas Company into buying the record-breaker to add to its growing fleet of aircraft. Back at Burbank, Hawks had the Air Express repainted a brilliant red, with white trim and the big star that was the trademark of his company, and her new name, *Texaco 5*. A fuel tank was fitted in the cabin to take the place of a helper on long flights, and a radio receiver was installed. Frank Hawks had more records in mind.

Before he was ready, there were new contenders. The second Vega the Lockheed company had built, and its first to go into use as a company demonstrator, was sold to Bernarr Macfadden of New York, the magazine publisher. The lion-maned health faddist had been badly bitten by the flying bug, and this was the first of numerous airplanes (including five Lockheeds) he was to own.

After the Hawks-Grubb venture, Macfadden realized that his own ship, though not as high powered, was probably capable of a similar flight. He instructed his pilot, O. K. Bevins, to give a try. An excellent flyer and instructor from Kentucky, Okey Bevins did his best with the Vega in March 1929. Fouled sparkplugs brought him down in New Mexico, and bad luck dogged his subsequent journey eastward. Attempting to take off after a forced landing on a farm near Belle, Missouri, Bevins fractured both legs, and washed out the Macfadden Lockheed.

Next it was Harry Tucker's first pilot, Leland F. Shoenhair, who got himself a job and a Lockheed of his own to fly: the B. F. Goodrich rubber outfit's new Vega *Miss Silvertown*. In June 1929 Lee essayed the nonstop journey east, but was signaled to land at Cleveland because of fogbanks reported over Pennsylvania. Goodrich had bought the plane only the day before, and was taking no chances.

A few days later, Captain Frank Hawks, already established as transcontinental speed champion, was at it again. On June 27–28, 1929, Hawks made two unprecedented flights. Alone, he took the Air Express from New York to Los Angeles in a little over 19 hours.

Then, after a scant seven and a half hours of rest, refueling, repairs, and refreshment, the recordseeker was off again for the East. Except for a Pacific fogbank which called for spiraling his gas-laden ship up to 3,000 feet in order to clear Cajon Pass, the weather was almost ideal in both directions. But it was after dark when *Texaco 5* brought Captain Hawks back to New York with more records.

Roosevelt Field was America's best-known airport, but in 1929 it did not yet boast any boundary or obstruction lights. Hawks jazzed the hangars to announce his arrival, and confusedly selected the crossleg of the T-shaped runway. He came rolling in fast and ploughed straight into the heavy wire fence of an adjacent polo field.

Despite this mishap Frank Hawks had accomplished an unusual feat of courage and stamina: he was the first man to fly alone from coast to coast; and he did it in both directions within two days. In addition to bettering the times both ways, he set the first round-trip record. But the weary captain had no thought of triumph as he sat dejected and deafened in his red Lockheed astraddle the fense. Hauled out, he went fast asleep on his wife's shoulder.

With these new records to shoot at, Lockheed's own test pilot, Herb Fahy, tried the trip the following month, flying another Air Express. A company demonstrator, the

Bernarr Macfadden's entry for transcontinental nonstop honors is Vega No. 2, flown with early triangular fin.

ship was temporarily named *The Black Hornet* because of the experimental installation of a Pratt & Whitney Hornet Engine on its nose. This power plant developed 525 hp—100 more than the famous Wasp—but was heavier and used more fuel. Its increased diameter on the oval contour of a Lockheed also meant a corresponding reduction in speed to be overcome. Another innovation on this Air Express was the first installation of wheel pants, added to cut down wind resistance. These were squared-off, hand-beaten affairs, a forerunner of the spun-aluminum, teardrop fairings soon to be developed.

Fahy's record dash did not work out, even with these additions for extra speed. Spewing oil and smoke, the *Hornet* came down with a scuffed piston at Kiowa, Kansas. After repairs in Wichita, Fahy took her back to Burbank where she was sold to the General Tire & Rubber Company as an entry in the National Air Races of 1929.

Frank Hawks's nonstop transcontinental records were to outlive his *Texaco 5*, which made them. Attempting to take off from a muddy field at West Palm Beach, Florida, the captain caught a wheel on a parked ship and hurled his famous plane into three others. Fortunately this spectacular smash-up produced no fatalities, but the Air Express was a complete washout.

The slogan "It takes a Lockheed to beat a Lockheed" was not just boastful talk. When it came to fast transportation, the Vega and Air Express were undisputed leaders of the field. With increasing demand from individuals, business firms, and airlines, in two short years the Lockheed company had built over eighty airplanes. And in the early months of the fateful year of 1929, aviation in California was booming, along with everything else in the country.

The original founders of the Lockheed Aircraft Company chose this peak time to sell out. President Fred

Swinging the compass of Texaco 5, *to prepare for a batch of Hawks's solo records.*

Keeler had long ago realized a good return on his investment. Ray Boggs and Ben Hunter were organizing Nevada Airlines to fly passengers from Los Angeles to Reno, using Lockheed equipment. Only Allan Loughead was reluctant, feeling that the firm had a great deal of financial stability and was bound to go on to greater things. But, in July 1929, Lockheed assets and goodwill were acquired by a holding company, the Detroit Aircraft Corporation.

Detroit Aircraft was formed to knit an organization of airplane builders into a sort of "General Motors of the air." Edward S. Evans, prominent Detroit industrialist, was its head, and the board of directors included R. E. Olds and Charles F. Kettering.

The Michigan amalgamation controlled other aircraft manufacturers, such as Ryan and Eastman, and its diverse interests included the well-known Parks Air College in East St. Louis, the Grosse Isle Airport in Detroit, and companies to make gliders and metal-clad dirigibles. Some of the components were merely fond hopes, and the Detroit people soon found Lockheed to be the biggest and only profitable egg in their basket.

Production at Burbank was stepped up. There were grandiose plans for a new factory at Long Beach, an assembly plant in St. Louis, and research into new models and manufacturing at Detroit. To run their Lockheed operation, Detroit Aircraft sent out an able manager, Carl B. Squier. He was a most fortunate choice. A slim, dark-haired, friendly man, Squier had been a county-fair convert to flying in his native Michigan. As an Army aviator in France he'd come home with the Croix de Guerre. Then there'd been barnstorming and test-flying, and work with Stinson, Glenn Martin, and his own company, which made Eastman Flying Boats.

In addition to all-round managerial competence, one of Carl Squier's greatest abilities was salesmanship. He had friends and contacts all over the United States, and could sell just about anything that he believed in. After a few days in Burbank, he believed in Lockheeds.

The factory had been too busy to do much physical expansion, and despite the change in management the workers in the plant on the corner of San Fernando and Empire kept right on going. Monocoque fuselage shells continued to be processed in the concrete mold, and everybody pitched in with a can of tacks and a gluepot when one was ready to be mounted on its framework. Nearby were the assembly shop, the paintshop, and a drying shed aromatic with the wonderful odor of spruce plywood. Behind the factory stretched the so-called Lockheed Airport, a thin strip dotted with filled gopher holes and weed clumps, and bordered on two sides by the railroad embankments and telegraph wires of the Southern Pacific.

The ex-ranchhouse front office housed a little cubbyhole for the new general manager, and a four-drawer file cabinet contained all of Lockheed's records. The engineering department occupied what had once been a kitchen. Starry-eyed Jerry Vultee dreamed airplanes there, and his two draftsmen, Jimmy Gerschler and Dick Von Hake, transferred ideas and analyses to paper.

It was this three-man staff who produced the next Lockheed model, the low-wing, two-place Sirius, named for the bright Dog Star in the constellation of Orion. For a customer, Vultee and Squier had lined up the most famous flyer in the world—Colonel Charles A. Lindbergh.

The order came about casually. Lindbergh had been flying borrowed airplanes for some months, and wanted a ship of his own again. At the National Air Races at Cleveland he talked at length to Vultee. With the roar of the "pylon polishers" punctuating their conversation, Jerry took notes of the colonel's requirements and roughed out a preliminary sketch on hotel stationery. Later there was a conference with Carl Squier at the New York Athletic Club. The participants talked far into the evening and Carl came away with a diagramed tablecloth and various Lindbergh doodles on scrap paper to take back to California.

A great deal of secrecy surrounded the building of the first Sirius. For a long time it was purposely rumored as a special order for Edward S. Evans, president of Detroit Aircraft. The men in the factory learned the truth when a truck driver delivered a new 450-hp Pratt & Whitney Wasp engine, supposedly for "the Evans ship."

"Here's Lindbergh's motor," he boomed. "What kinda airplane ya gonna put it in?"

With the beans spilled, the factory prepared for a deluge of publicity. Every little movement of the Colonel and Mrs. Lindbergh was covered by the press in a reflection of mass acclaim and hero worship never equaled before or since. What they did, said, ate, wore—all were dutifully recorded; and if no statements were available, the harried reporters made them up.

As he had with his famous *Spirit of St. Louis*, Lindbergh wanted personally to see to the details of final assembly and tests of his new airplane. During the winter of 1929–30, he and Anne stayed with a business associate, Jack Maddux, in Los Angeles while the Sirius was being completed at Burbank. Every day the famous couple drove a back street and parked in the shade of a hangar beside the factory airstrip. Mrs. Lindbergh usually stayed in the big touring car while her husband busied himself about the plant.

After the initial feeling of awe at being associated with a celebrity wore off, the Lockheed crews found Lindbergh a warm, agreeable, friendly person. A perfectionist, he was interested in everything that concerned his plane. Hidden from the stares of the ever-present hero worshippers in the dark, tapering recess of a Vega fuselage, he might talk control-rigging for hours with a mechanic. Outside, assemblers Don Young, Firman Gray, or

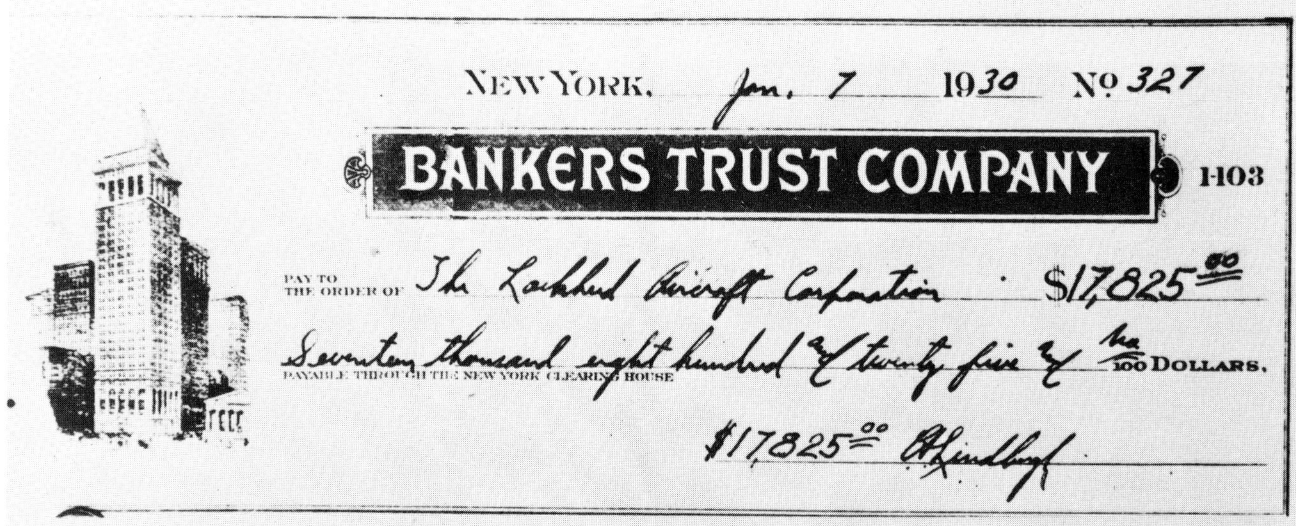

NEW YORK, Jan. 7 1930 No 327

BANKERS TRUST COMPANY 1-103

PAY TO THE ORDER OF The Lockheed Aircraft Corporation $17,825.00

Seventeen thousand eight hundred & twenty five & no/100 DOLLARS.

PAYABLE THROUGH THE NEW YORK CLEARING HOUSE

$17825.00 C.A. Lindbergh

Check that bothered Carl Squier doesn't include the $5,000 already deposited on Lindbergh's new Wasp engine.

Tod Oviatt would bring the patient Mrs. Lindbergh sandwiches and a cold soda from the lunchroom across the street.

The publicity had mixed blessings—and temptations. A Los Angeles dealer offered Carl Squier a brand-new Cord automobile if he could just get Lindbergh to *sit* in one long enough to be surreptitiously photographed. It was a tough proposition to resist.

Squier had an anxious time when it came to the final sale of the new Sirius. After cost considerations, countered by the tremendous publicity value, the Lockheed general manager came up with a price of $22,825 for the plane. The Lindberghs held a long discussion in a corner of the office. They seemed to be arguing. Carl suffered mental anguish. Had he asked too much and queered the sale? Finally the colonel came over with a check. Years later Squier asked his friend about the corner conference:

"Slim, what was all that talk you and Anne had in my office the day you bought the Sirius?"

General Lindbergh thought a minute and then laughed.

"Why, we were just deciding on what bank to draw the check!"

The beautiful low-winged Lockheed was famous even before it was finished. After its announcement, the company received orders for half a dozen sister ships, and was rushing these to completion at the same time.

As originally built, the black-bodied, orange-winged Lindbergh Sirius had two open cockpits with fixed windshields. At Mrs. Lindbergh's suggestion a sliding canopy was devised to cover both openings and provide more comfort and ease of communication. This was an unpatented Lindbergh-Vultee "first" that was to come into common use. Test-flying the new bird was an early job for Marshall Headle, an ex-Army and Marine flyer from Massachusetts, who was to pilot over three hundred Lockheed airplanes on their maiden flights.

On Easter Sunday 1930, Colonel Lindbergh was satisfied with his gleaming new airplane. Early in the morning he and Anne took off from Glendale for the East. They were bundled in bulky, electrically heated flying suits, kept warm by the current from a wind-driven generator. Casually the colonel announced that the flight was to be made at 14,000 feet or better, in order to test the advantages of the weather in the higher altitudes. Speeding along at an average of 171 mph, the pair just as casually broke the transcontinental record. Even with a fuel stop at Wichita, their elapsed time was 14 hours, 45 minutes, and 32 seconds. As copilot and navigator, Mrs. Lindbergh automatically set a women's record for coast-to-coast flight. Again, it had "taken a Lockheed to beat a Lockheed."

With the summer flying season coming on, the Lindbergh record was up for grabs. One man who stood a good chance of beating it was Colonel Roscoe Turner.

Deliberately flamboyant and a Southern gentleman (Mississippi via Virginia), Roscoe was always a keen competitor. He had been an ambulance driver, an army lieutenant, and a top movie stunt pilot. In 1930 the Turner attire was better known than his flying. He was always magnificent in appearance, and affected a uniform of his own design consisting of powder-blue tweed coat with Sam Browne belt, beige whipcord riding breeches, spotless boots, and all topped off by a white silk scarf and military cap with burnished wings. Though it was the subject of banter and jibes, Roscoe had good reason for his sartorial elegance. In his barnstorming days it had enabled him to win passengers and eat, while competitors in dirty overalls fought hunger pangs.

Colonel Turner had been flying Vegas for Nevada Airlines, but was looking for a more permanent connection.

First Sirius enjoyed instant fame because of its owner, but off-hand transcontinent records helped, too. Sliding cockpit canopies were later suggested by Anne Lindbergh and became standard equipment.

He had his eye on the Hornet-powered Lockheed Air Express which Herb Fahy had flown, the former *Black Hornet*. Its current owner, the General Tire & Rubber Company, had no competent pilot for it. Casting about in his fertile mind, Roscoe came up with a promotion idea for using the ship that was really a stunner.

He talked Earl B. Gilmore, head of California's Gilmore Oil Company, into buying the Air Express at a bargain

Pilot's-eye view of the Lindbergh Sirius instrument panel.

Charles and Anne Lindbergh, ready for Easter flight of 1930 (top), *and with TWA Vega, later.*

$15,000. Turner was to make record flights in it to advertise Gilmore products. The oil company used a big lion's head as their trademark, so to clinch the sure-fire proposition Roscoe acquired a five-month-old lion cub, and planned to fly him as a mascot.

In March 1930 *The Gilmore Lion* came into being. Painted cream with red-and-gold trim, it soon became a familiar sight at western airports and flying events. People flocked to see the Lockheed and its snappily dressed pilot. Gilmore, the lion cub, was a star attraction, too. He even boasted a specially made and tailored Irvin Air Chute, with a suitcase handle for ready carrying.

Turner and Gilmore did plenty of serious flying. Roscoe put his sights on the transcontinental record and, with his

And new idea: Roscoe with his brainwave Gilmore.

New owner, new paint job, new pilot: Roscoe Turner flies the former Black Hornet *to a new coast-to-coast mark.*

emergence on the national scene, many people who had never heard of California's Gilmore gasoline came to know Gilmore the lion.

On May 1, 1930, the flyer took his mascot and the Air Express up over Banning Pass to the east in an effort to beat Lindbergh's cross-country time. The plane was still fitted with the Hornet engine, and really gobbled the Gilmore gas.

Over New Mexico, Turner encountered strong headwinds and terrible flying weather. The lion cub got lonesome and tried to crawl up from the cabin into the busy flyer's lap. At one point Roscoe was sure they would have to jump, and only the thought of a lion floating gently down on some unsuspecting rancher drove him on. At a short stop in Wichita, the Lockheed was refueled while Gilmore happily devoured chunks of raw horsemeat. Still bucking winds, the pair made a stop for oil in Middletown, Pennsylvania. Then they ran out of gas before reaching Roosevelt Field on Long Island, and had to land short at Curtiss.

The Gilmore Lion missed that one, but two weeks later Turner and his furry friend roared into Glendale, California with a new east-west record of 18 hours, 42 minutes, and 54 seconds. They'd stopped only briefly in Wichita to replenish the needs of man, machine, and beast. Gilmore rode proudly home on Mrs. Turner's lap.

After the transcontinental triumphs of Lockheed's stock Vega, Air Express, and Sirius, the records began to be whittled away by smaller, specially constructed racing planes that, because of their high speeds, could afford several refueling stops en route.

For a while, exactly what constituted a coast-to-coast record was none too clear. Newark, New Jersey—conveniently and considerably short of Long Island—became a favorite Eastern terminus. There were nonstop, one-stop, and multistop records, with variations in passengers carried, payloads, directions, termini, and even the age group of the flyer breaking the record.

In June 1930 two well-known aviators from Detroit gave one of these variations to the transcontinental mark. They were William S. Brock and Edward F. Schlee, best remembered for their 1927 flight from Detroit to Tokyo, which included the first direct Atlantic hop from Newfoundland to London.

Billy Brock was an Ohio farm boy who had learned to fly with Glenn Curtiss when hardly out of knee pants. Cheerful, chubby Billy had graduated from flying mail, and had allied himself with Ed Schlee, a Detroit businessman. By the acquisition of the right corners, Schlee had built up a thriving chain of service stations, and his Wayco Oil Company held the Shell distributorship for southern Michigan. Billy taught Ed to fly, and gave him the itch to branch out into aviation. After their daring and successful flight, this pair added complete aircraft sales and service to Schlee's chain of enterprises. Their greatest *coup* was being appointed as a distributor for Lockheed in 1928.

For going on two years, the Schlee-Brock Aircraft Corporation sold Lockheed Vegas throughout the Midwest and handled the sales of dozens of airplanes. Business was excellent and Ed and Billy were kept on the jump, exhibiting and selling the speedy ships from New Mexico to New Jersey. For a while the lively Schlee-Brock organization was a tail that nearly wagged the dog. With a nation-wide distributorship and a subdealer setup, the Detroit-to-Tokyo flyers laid plans to take on the entire Lockheed factory output. They contracted for sixteen planes a month, and were ready to invest $3,000,000 in them.

This rosy financial bubble was pricked by the sale of Lockheed assets to the Detroit Aircraft combine, which had been put together right in Ed Schlee's home town. Detroit pulled the rug from under the Schlee-Brock distributorship, and set up its own sales organization. In July 1929, at the crucial time when there might have been a deal for mutual benefit, Ed Schlee lay in a Detroit hospital with a fractured skull. Standing on the wheel of a Vega, he had lost his balance and fallen into the whirling propeller.

Ed Schlee (left) and Billy Brock build a Vega and set a new record because they believe in Lockheeds.

Billy Brock tried to hold things together while his partner recovered from the near-fatal accident. After just a few months of operation, the little Canadian-American Airlines they were trying to establish in Minnesota went broke, and its assets went under the sheriff's hammer. Despite the change in their fortunes, the Detroit pair were still sold on what Lockheed planes could do. Perhaps another world flight, all the way this time, would put them back on top.

In the Schlee-Brock shops were all the parts to build a new Vega. All that was lacking was a fuselage, which was readily purchased from the factory. In the spring of 1930 Billy and Ed put together a Lockheed of their own. It was a beautiful ship, painted a deep red with cream-colored wing, tail, and wheel pants. There was much secrecy about what the plane would be used for, and the rumored world flight was not denied.

To test the long-distance capabilities of their Lockheed, Brock and Schlee chose to make a double transcontinental dash across the southern segment of the United States, from Jacksonville, Florida, to San Diego, California, and return. In the rash of Los Angeles–New York flights not much attention had been paid to this route, which is about 400 miles shorter.

Wearing his usual cardigan sweater and his "lucky" tan-and-white sport shoes, Billy Brock sent the shining Vega skimming off the beach at Jacksonville. In the cabin, Ed Schlee busied himself with a transmitter-receiver lent them for the flight by Powel Crosley, Jr., of the radio company. Though it had only 150-watt strength, it enabled the boys to keep tabs on local storm conditions and issue terse bulletins as to their own progress.

They had fine weather except for a whirling dust cone

This Sport Cabin Sirius with Jimmy Collins in the office couldn't crack the Lindberghs' time flying east.

over the Imperial Valley, and the Florida-California part of the trip went fine. It was the first nonstop flight ever made between those states. At San Diego, the flyers stopped only long enough to gas up and munch a sandwich. The return trip was much tougher than Brock and Schlee had anticipated, and they dodged thunderheads and bucked headwinds all the way. After an unscheduled fuel stop at Tallulah, Louisiana, the pair got back to Jacksonville in 31 hours and 58 minutes. This flight, made June 17–18, 1930, was a new elapsed-time record for a round trip across the United States.

Since high tide prevented his using the beach from which he had taken off, Billy Brock landed with near-empty tanks at the Jacksonville Municipal Airport. Like Frank Hawks a year earlier, fatigued with nearly two days and a night of transcontinental flying, the tired pilot misjudged his landing, rolled into a boundary fence, and put the Vega up on her nose. Brock and Schlee were unhurt, but the Lockheed had to be shipped back to Detroit for repairs. It was sold eventually to the Crosley Radio Corporation.

Famed test pilot Jimmy Collins made a try at the Lindbergh record on the Fourth of July 1930. He was ferrying a gaily painted red-and-white special Sport Sirius to its new owner, Walter Blumenthal of New York. Jimmy came tearing across the continent, but even flying alone he was far behind the Colonel's mark.

Then in August, Captain Frank Hawks, flying a small, racing Travel Air Mystery Ship, recaptured his cross-country speed title, and a plane built by Lockheed was not to hold the record again until the age of jets.

6

RACING TIME AND SPACE

Since they had a better-than-even chance to beat all competition, Lockheed monoplanes were entries in most of the racing meets of the late twenties and early thirties, particularly those on a national scale.

Primarily as competition for military and experimental aircraft, there had been a National Air Races held each year since 1924. The annual meet was staged in various cities, and brought manufacturers in contact with potential buyers, and also served as a proving ground for ideas and new designs.

More than that, the National Air Races were a great country fair of the air, where pilots, mechanics, builders, owners—everyone connected with the industry—could get together in a holiday atmosphere. Lasting friendships were made and renewed, and the midnight oil burned on beyond daylight in the hangars and sheds and tents where determined men and women labored to put more speed into their machines.

For the manufacturers and owners, a race winner meant more business. For the mechanics and ground crews it was the satisfaction of precision teamwork and the excitement of competition. For the pilot, seeking to make a name for himself and his plane, it was all these plus the thrill of public approval. Seldom did a racer ever come out with a profit, and many lost both their shirts and their lives. Still, the surging, screaming crowds, the sound of flat-out engines, and the smells of popcorn and hot motor oil brought them back each year. It was heady stuff.

The throngs which flocked each year to the National

Lee Shoenhair and Miss Silvertown *streaking in from Los Angeles in the 1929 National Air Races.*

Air Races reveled in the spectacles put on for their benefit. Like Romans watching gladiators in the Coliseum, they chose their favorite villains, their clowns, their heroes who could do no wrong. And, like the Romans, they came with just a taste for blood—and were often rewarded.

The NAR, as it was called, first had Lockheed airplanes in competition at its 1928 meeting, held at Mines Field southwest of Los Angeles. Due to the excitement over Lindbergh, and flying in general, more than half a million people were expected, and the committee rounded up cash prizes amounting to $80,000.

To alert national interest, the program included a number of On–to–Los Angeles races taking off from New York City, with different categories for planes of various engine displacements. The most appealing to adventurous pilots with flat wallets was an unprecedented nonstop race across the continent. At the time of the announcement only one airplane, the Army T-2, had ever flown all the way from New York to the West Coast without coming down to gas up.

Colonel William K. Thaw of Pittsburgh—World War flyer and commander of the famous Lafayette Escadrille, insurance broker and railroad director—believed that Lockheed's Vega would be the ideal plane to enter in the nonstop race. He ordered one through the company's Eastern distributor, Air Associates, Inc., of New York. It was to have special tanks, special bamboo-padded fuel lines, and a special engine: the 515-hp Hornet by Pratt & Whitney. This last would make it the fastest passenger airplane in America at that time. The ship was painted purple and gold, and cost the dapper colonel a neat $30,000.

Thaw chose to act as navigator for his colorful new sky-splitter, and installed Jack Morris, a Pittsburgh flying instructor, in the cockpit. The pair took delivery of the ship in Burbank, and got it back to New York barely in time to get ready for the big race.

Art Goebel and Harry Tucker had made the first nonstop west-east transcontinental hop only a couple of weeks earlier, showing that a stock commercial Lockheed could do it. Art and Harry had *Yankee Doodle*'s racing number, 44, already painted on, and considered their record flight a mere curtain raiser for the main event.

Thaw and Morris reasoned that they had nearly 100 more horses on the nose of their ship than had the Californians' Vega with its 425-hp Wasp. They took further heart when the veteran Goebel got lost on a simple trip to Connecticut, supposedly looking for Hartford's Brainard Field. (This was later suspected to be a hoax, perpetrated by the wily Goebel to mislead his competition.)

Then, at the last minute, publisher Bernarr Macfadden got a yen to fly in the race. It would help sell magazines. He negotiated with Thaw, offering $35,000 for the powerful purple Lockheed. This was difficult to resist, and the Pittsburgher sold with the proviso that he and Morris would still fly the ship. The bushy-browed physical culturist managed to get his new acquisition christened *True Story* on the eve of the race, but canceled plans to go along himself. It was just as well for him that he did.

The New York–Los Angeles Nonstop Air Race got under way from Roosevelt Field on September 13, 1928. In addition to the two Lockheed entries, there were two Stinsons, a Buhl, and four Bellancas, including the famed *Columbia* which had flown to Germany the year before. Well-known pilots like Nick Mamer, George Haldeman, Shirley Short, Emil Burgin, and "Boots" Le Boutillier were at their controls. As the afternoon sun stretched wing

William Thaw couldn't turn down $35,000 for his racing Vega, in 1928 the U.S.A.'s speediest passenger plane.

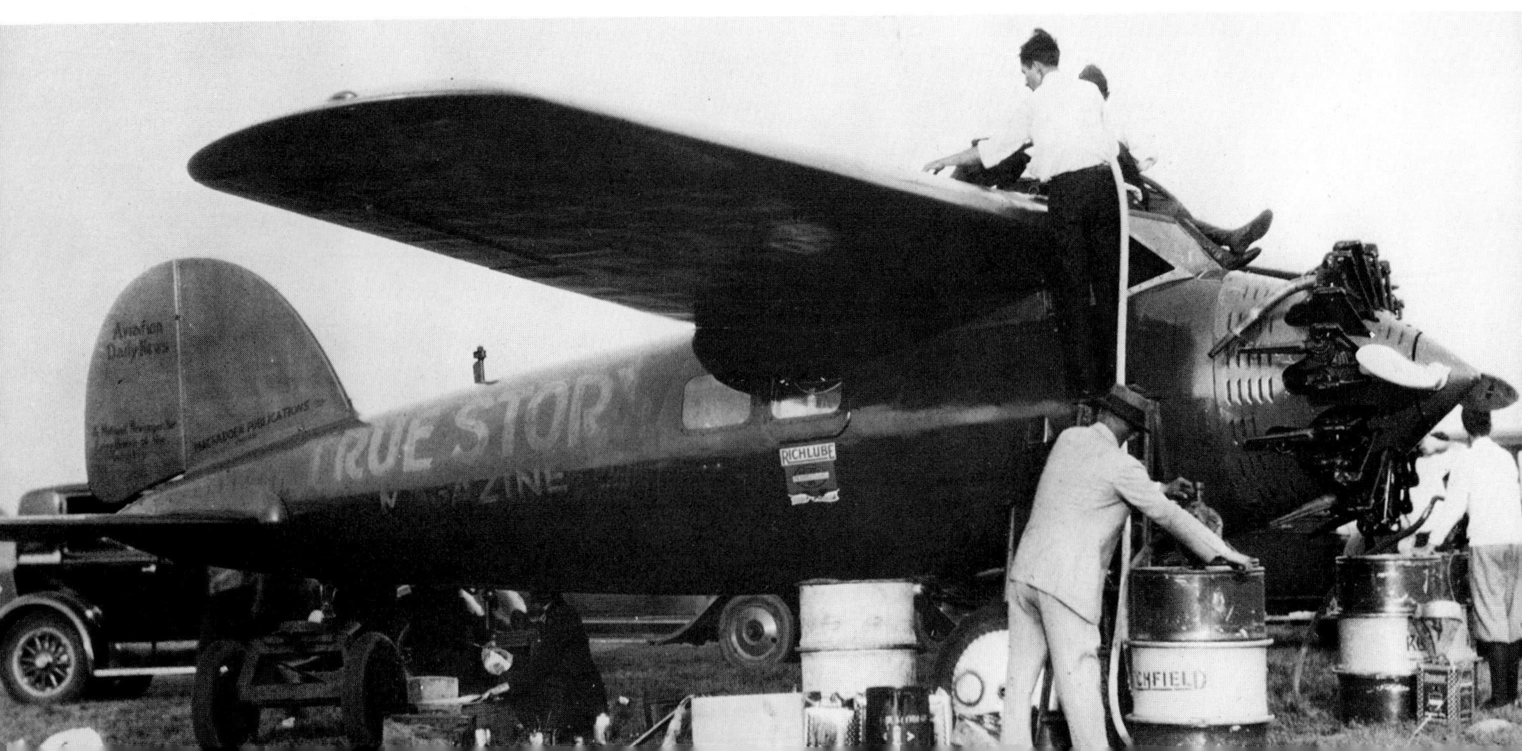

shadows into grotesque lengths, they took off, one by one.

Goebel and Tucker, in white shirts and brown business suits, acted as though they were hopping over to Teterboro for tea. But in no time Art had *Yankee Doodle*'s tail up and was off and away in the dusk.

The Thaw-Macfadden *True Story* was the last to leave. The blast of her Hornet ripped up a vast cloud of black dirt, nearly smothering the spectators as she turned about into the wind. With 650 gallons of gas on board there was some question as to whether the heavy racer would get off. But Jack Morris had *Yankee Doodle* to catch, and he didn't hesitate: of the nine ships in the race, *True Story* used the least runway, and her lights quickly disappeared into the night.

The first (and only) New York–to–Los Angeles nonstop derby was a bust. Next day found all nine contestants down and scattered from Pennsylvania to Arizona, and one far to the north in Wyoming.

After fighting exceptionally bad weather all night and all day, Art Goebel and Harry Tucker nearly made it. Then the door of the Lockheed blew off while Harry was pitching out gas cans. Art finally decided it would be smart to come down at Prescott, Arizona, to check a balky carburetor and make sure of the gas supply. Still game, the pair continued on to Mines Field with the wind howling and eddying through the cabin. There they taxied triumphantly up in front of the grandstand—disqualified because of their stop, but still the sole entry to complete the race.

Bernarr Macfadden's *True Story* didn't last out the night. South of Decatur, Indiana, an oil-line break dropped the pressure to zero, necessitating an immediate forced landing. Colonel Thaw propped open the cabin door and dropped out a parachute flare, illuminating a flat expanse of Hoosierdom. Jack Morris leveled off the Vega to set down. Just at the crucial moment the flare went out.

Blindly, Jack groped for the ground. In the dark the tail skid caught on a fence and the Lockheed went somersaulting end over end in a tearing, smashing pile-up. The engine and wings were torn completely off. Miraculously the men were somehow thrown clear in a heap together, and regained consciousness to the gurgle of gasoline pouring from the ruptured tanks. With dislocations and a fracture they lay for five hours on the hard, cold ground, until daylight and their feeble shouts brought help. Bernarr Macfadden's most expensive "true story" was a fast write-off, and Colonel William Thaw's bid for cross-country racing honors ended in a Decatur hospital.

Other On–to–Los Angeles, transcontinental races of 1928 were operated on a city-to-city, elapsed-time basis. A Lockheed Vega easily won the New York–to–California event in its C classification that year. The plane involved was *The Tester,* which belonged to Erle P. Halliburton of Duncan, Oklahoma.

A former oil-field truck driver who had invented a new and better method of cementing deep wells, tough and

Pilots miraculously survived Indiana crash.

Erle P. Halliburton and pilot Bob Cantwell with The Tester. *Car is a Lincoln, with 1928 California tags.*

wily Erle Halliburton's growing business took him all over the Southwest. His original Vega was the fourth Lockheed built and the first to be purchased for private use. Halliburton became so sold on Lockheed planes and their potential in business and commercial work that he started a Lockheed distributorship for his Oklahoma area. Entering a plane in the derby to Los Angeles was therefore good advertising.

The oilman's second Vega, *The Tester,* was flown by Halliburton's personal pilot, Robert W. Cantwell. Jockeying the bright-yellow Lockheed in the transcontinental journey was a breeze for Bob Cantwell, an ex-barnstormer from Texas. Competition in his class consisted of a Fairchild 71 and a Fokker Universal, both good airplanes but no speed packages. Cantwell and *The Tester* won each and every lap, clear across the continent. Counting local prizes given out along the way, Bob took in $6,155, a wristwatch, and a Mexican serape.

Arriving at Mines Field, Cantwell proceeded to show his work was not confined to cross-country piloting. The Oklahoma flyer entered the Unlimited Free-for-All 50-Mile Closed-Course Race against favored Art Goebel. The yellow *Tester* went flashing around the Mines Field pylons with the white *Yankee* in close pursuit. Cantwell's time was only 5 seconds faster than Goebel's, but it was enough to win. Erle Halliburton and the men at Lockheed were rightfully proud of the showing their planes had made in the races.

With his boss's blessings, Bob Cantwell was back with the Vega for the next year's National Air Races at Cleveland. The ship had been in use on the Oklahoma promoter's new SAFEway Airlines. Down at the outdoor shops in Tulsa, the SAFEway crew had waxed and polished the Lockheed to a fare-thee-well, and added the latest thing: the NACA cowl, developed late in 1928, which put another 12 mph into the Wasp-powered yellow racer.

Cantwell's competition was a brother airline pilot "on vacation" with one of his company's speedy Lockheeds. Jaunty Roscoe Turner flew in from the west with Nevada Airlines' *Sirius,* a regulation 5-place Vega with neat teardrop wheel pants in addition to its engine cowl—a considerable advancement over the 80-mph, little Timm biplane Roscoe had been flying the previous year. Turner and Cantwell fought it out in the Civilian Cabin Ship Race. Even without pants, Bob's ship delivered a couple more miles than Roscoe could get out of his, and Cantwell came roaring home a winner.

The elegant Turner bounced back two days later with an amazing performance in the big 50-mile free-for-all, a 1929 forerunner of the famous Thompson Trophy Race that Roscoe would one day dominate. Competing against special Army and Navy stripped-down racers, "America's best-dressed pilot" whipped his Vega around the triangular course with startling speed and verve. Roscoe finished behind Doug Davis's Travel Air Mystery Ship and an Army P-3A. But the experience of the race with Cantwell helped, and he upped his speed some 13 mph this time to take third and nose out the Navy entry, a Curtiss F6C6. The generals and admirals in attendance looked hard and long at Turner's stock airliner.

The nonstop derby from Los Angeles to Cleveland with its $5,000 prize proved a good drawing card that same year. There seemed little reason to believe that the trip would be as rigorous as 1928's in the other direction. The winner was to be decided on an elapsed-time basis and could arrive at any time during the ten-day meet.

All four entries in the race were Lockheeds. In the interests of pleasing the public, the judges decreed that a nonstop entry must arrive before 6 P.M. of any of the race days. If Roscoe Turner had not misjudged his time on this requirement, his cowled and panted Vega *Sirius* might have been in the money.

Sandy-haired, boyish Lee Schoenhair, who had twice previously flown Vegas nonstop to Ohio, piloted the Goodrich Company's *Miss Silvertown* once again on the long trip to Cleveland. He arrived early in the meet, while two other dark horses in the race remained in Los Angeles.

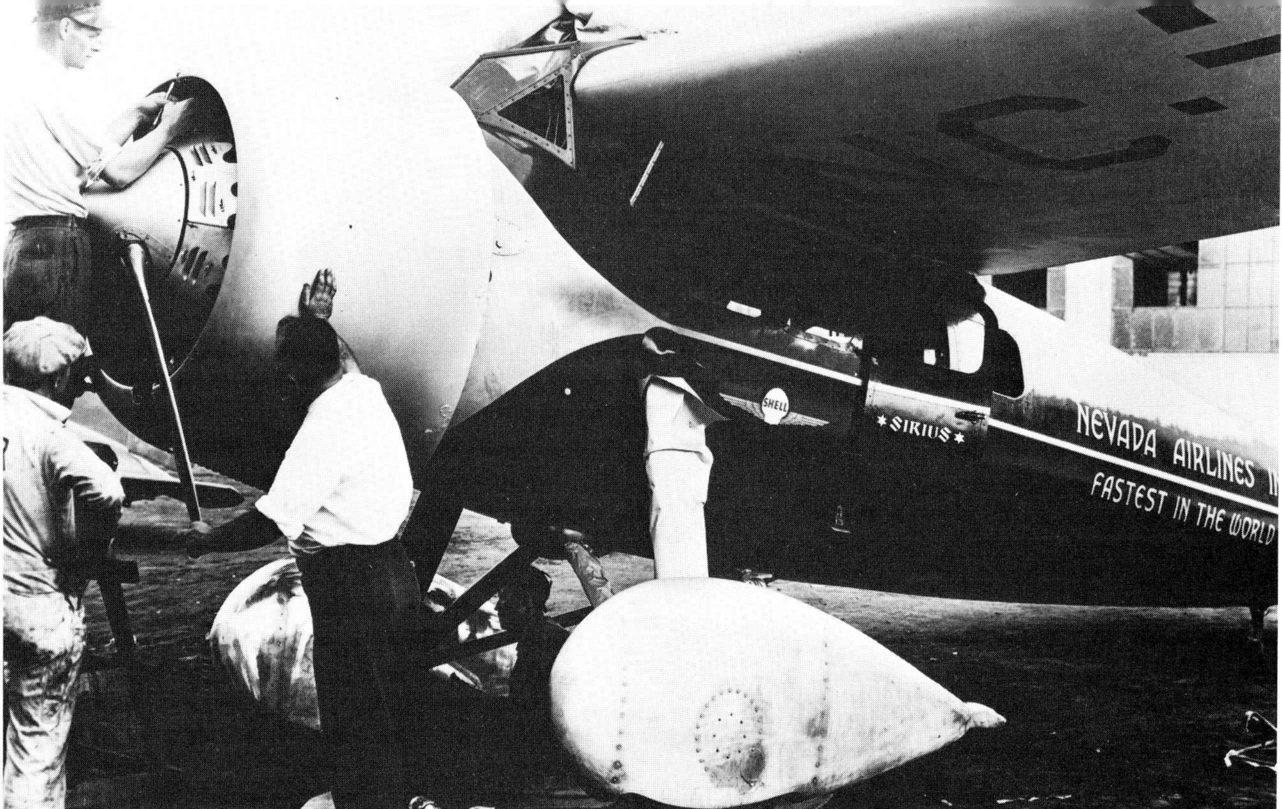

Roscoe Turner's Vega, Sirius, *gets the new NACA cowl and a pair of the earliest teardrop wheel pants.*

General Tire & Rubber Company had been trying for several weeks to get a Lockheed of their own to enter in the nonstop derby. Two Vegas, en route to Akron on ferry trips, had been destroyed in fatal accidents. In desperation the tire company officials dispatched their hired pilot, Henry J. Brown, to see if matters could be speeded up. Serious Brownie Brown was an airmail flyer on leave from his job with National Air Transport, and had precious little time for his racing assignment. On the way west he met Lockheed's test pilot, Herb Fahy, who was languishing in Kansas after an unsuccessful transcontinental record attempt with one of the company's demonstrators, an Air Express. It was this plane or nothing. Brownie and General Tire took title to the Hornet-powered, parasol-wing ship three days after the races had begun in Cleveland.

With 200 gallons in the wings and 350 in the fuselage, the hastily prepared *The General Tire* was a flying gas tank. Brownie got her off from Los Angeles in the dark and was soon flying eastward at full throttle. The course he had plotted lay over desolate territory, and the first landmark he could identify was Fort Leavenworth, Kansas. Fighting fatigue, the pilot was kept busy all through the long hours pumping gasoline to feed the hungry Hornet.

Even 550 gallons was not quite enough. Five miles from Cleveland Airport the engine began to sputter, and then cut out entirely. Brownie hunched forward in the open cockpit, watching his air speed and stretching his glide. He brought the big black Air Express straight in, floating silently down in front of the grandstand and over the finish line. The crowd cheered the mail pilot's out-of-gas, dead-stick landing and his announced time of 13 hours and 15 minutes—over half an hour better than Shoenhair's.

The two rubber company entries had arrived, but another contender remained on the West Coast, ready to make a bid for the race money. Quiet, popular John P. Wood had just bought a new Lockheed for his Northern Airways of Wausau, Wisconsin. A major in the Wisconsin National Guard, Johnny Wood was well known as winner of the 1928 Ford Reliability Tour, and had placed in two other transcontinental races. Now he was after the big one.

Because he intended to fly his new Vega for passenger and charter work later on, Major Wood elected to use the five-gallon-can method of carrying extra gasoline. Ward Miller, a young Lockheed mechanic, went along to handle this chore, squeezed in amid the gas tins. Communication with the pilot ahead was effected by a string on pulleys to which clothespinned notes were attached.

A missing engine spoiled Wood's and Miller's first attempt to fly to Cleveland and they landed in a bean field near Willard, New Mexico. Using a bottle of vinegar, a local Jack-of-all-trades freed a stuck valve and the men high-tailed their Vega back to Los Angeles.

After running in a new engine, the racers were ready for a fresh start. There was just enough time to reach Cleveland on Labor Day, the last day of the races. Taking off in the dark, Wood could see the flashes of a severe electrical storm far ahead, and put the Vega in a steep climb to get above it.

At about 3 A.M., when they were high above the dark and stormy California desert, the ship began to fall off in a spin, and Major Wood snapped on the dash lights to check his instruments. Feeling the pull of the plane and sensing trouble, Miller instinctively unbuckled his safety belt and unlatched the cabin door. He was expecting a note or sign from Wood to throw out a flare, but the signal never came. The last thing the mechanic remembered was a terrific crash that rammed him into the packed gas cans. His first thought was that they had hit a mountain.

"When I regained consciousness," wrote Miller later, "I was falling through space. I remember reaching for the rip-cord ring and getting a hold on it, but don't remember pulling it as I passed out again. I regained consciousness again for a minute or so and thought how quiet and peaceful it was. I passed out again and when I woke up I was lying out in the desert and the sun was just coming up."

Miller dazedly wandered in the desert for the better part of two days. He looked for Johnny Wood and the plane, but found only wooden rib fragments and a wing tip. Finally he stumbled on a blacktop road, got a ride into Needles, California, and led the continuation of the search by air. It was another thirty-six hours before a small plane from Phoenix came upon more scattered wreckage, and the body of Major Wood. The Vega had apparently been struck by lightning, which exploded the gas tanks.

After his providential escape, Ward Miller forsook aviation and went into the banking business. In Cleveland, Brownie Brown soberly accepted the derby prize, and was thankful for his own good fortune.

Still another Lockheed participated in the air races that year, a Whirlwind-powered Vega flown in the first women's air derby from Los Angeles to Cleveland. Its pilot was a thirty-one-year-old former social worker named Amelia Earhart. She had been carried across the Atlantic as an air passenger the year before, and was by this time the world's most famous woman flyer. As with Lindbergh, publicity attended all her movements, and of course extended to the aircraft in which she chose to travel.

Air Associates, Inc., Lockheed's distributor for the East Coast, sold her one of their Vega demonstrators to fly in the much-heralded "powder-puff derby" that summer. Together with Lieutenant Orville Stephens, an Army pilot on leave, Amelia flew it across the country and put down at the Lockheed factory strip for a routine check before proceeding to Clover Field in Santa Monica and the start of the women's air race.

After a year of hard knocks around New York City airfields at the hands of a variety of pilots, Miss Earhart's Vega was not exactly in the best of shape. Amelia herself called it a "thirdhand clunk." Lockheed's temporary test pilot, a stocky little man with a patch over one eye, had stronger language to describe it. Lockheed prudently decided to dismantle the offending ship, and replace it with a new demonstrator of their own.

The Earhart Lockheed was the biggest and fastest plane in the women's derby, and the hottest ship Amelia had ever flown. Carefully she lifted the light green Vega in and out of control fields along the way, with only a minor ground loop at Yuma, Arizona, to mar the journey. At each stop Amelia took in stride the hoopla that accompanied the progress of the petticoat pilots. To her mind the derby was important in proving her oft-reiterated statement: "Women can fly just as well as men." She came in to Cleveland in 22-plus hours, a happy third behind Louise Thaden's Travel Air and Gladys O'Donnell's snappy Waco.

Henry J. Brown (center) and the Air Express whose dead-stick arrival at Cleveland was winning time in the 1929 NAR.

NAR director Cliff Henderson greets Amelia Earhart after the first powder-puff derby. Vega is her second, turned in for the one she later flew across the Atlantic.

The little pilot with the eyepatch who had tested Amelia's "clunk" at the Lockheed plant in 1929, proved himself among the best in the next year's National Air Races in Chicago. He was Wiley Post, a former oil-field roustabout from Oklahoma. Wiley had learned to fly with the insurance payments from the accident which had cost him the sight of his left eye. Soon he had sold both himself and his services to Mr. Florence C. Hall, a well-to-do partner in Hall & Briscoe, Inc., dealers in oil-field leases. As "F. C." 's personal pilot, operating out of Chickasha, Oklahoma, Post took the oilman on both pleasure and business trips.

Enterprising Mr. Hall's first Lockheed was a beautiful new $20,000 Vega with special paint and lettering. Like the similar planes he later owned, it was named in honor of his daughter, Winnie Mae. Post flew this ship a few months and then sadly ferried it back to Burbank for resale when the Hall & Briscoe interests suffered a business lull. Along with the airplane, Wiley sold himself to Lockheed as an extra test pilot. In addition, he held a pioneer airline job in Mexico, being one of less than a hundred licensed flyers in that country. The first *Winnie Mae* went to Nevada Airlines and was renamed to become Roscoe Turner's racing *Sirius.*

With an improvement in business, F. C. Hall bought another Vega in the spring of 1930, and Post resumed his old position, with permission to fly the second—and most renowned—*Winnie Mae* in the coming races.

Again for the nonstop derby to Chicago the five entries were all Lockheeds. The pilots gathered at the factory in Burbank to check out their ships, working with good-natured rivalry to prepare them. Swashbuckling Roscoe Turner readied his cream-colored Air Express, last year's Cleveland derby winner, with Gilmore, his "man-eating chipmunk," tied and panting in the shade of a wing. Art Goebel blocked out all but one window in his Vega (the former first *Winnie Mae* and ex-*Sirius*) and packed the cabin with long-range tanks. Keeping very mum about it, Lee Shoenhair taxied down by the railroad embankment, and secretly doped the tanks of *Miss Silvertown* with a red fluid "called after some woman"—which turned out to be Ethyl. Everybody's friend Billy Brock affectionately patted the tail of his red-and-cream *New Cincinnati,* the veteran of his Jacksonville–San Diego record round trip.

"This is all you fellows will see on the way to Chicago," he announced cheerfully. Billy planned to tote Cincinnati announcer Bob Brown along, to broadcast from the Vega for the Crosley Radio Corporation.

Wiley Post was the only unknown in the nonstop event, which he proceeded to win with a time of 9 hours and 9 minutes. In a horse-race finish that delighted the crowd, Wiley managed to nose out Lee Shoenhair, who had left Los Angeles several minutes ahead of the *Winnie Mae.* In elapsed time it was Post, Goebel, Shoenhair, and Brock. Roscoe Turner and Gilmore finished last, but didn't mind because they were soon far more "lionized" by the crowd than were the winners.

Not evident to the Chicago spectators was the fact that the difference in time between Post, the winner, and

Winnie Mae *at the beginning of her fame, as an executive transport for oilman F. C. Hall.*

Roscoe, in fifth place, was less than fifty minutes. For a 1,760-mile trip this was certainly a good example of the long distance reliability of Lockheed airplanes.

A sidelight of the 1930 races was the winning of the $3,500 Seattle-Chicago derby by John Blum. Associated with Northwest Air Service of Seattle, Blum flew a Whirlwind-powered 5-place Vega, a plane which by that time was out of production and considered vastly underpowered.

The races came back to Cleveland in 1931, where they were to become an annual affair. The cross-country event this year was the first Bendix Trophy Race. It differed from former transcontinental competition in that the contestants were allowed stops to refuel en route, if necessary, and then go on. Nevertheless another contingent of long-ranging Lockheeds was made ready—but without regard for this new provision: their pilots scoffed at the idea of taking time to stop and refuel.

This year also saw Lockheed's new Orion competing. This was a fast cabin plane, brought out early in the season. It mounted the passenger facilities and the cockpit (up front like the Vega's) on a broad, low wing that housed a fully retractable landing gear. Lockheed definitely had the airlines in mind as customers for this stock plane with racing characteristics.

Of the old gang, only Art Goebel was still trying with his special Speed Vega. Harold S. Johnson had one of the new Orions to deliver in Chicago to his employers, Continental Airways. Known as "the man who looped the Ford Trimotor," Harold was a rugged individual. He made a practice of wringing out any plane he ever flew and finding out just what to expect of it before letting a passenger set foot in the aisle. He made no exception of the new Orion, and had several little refinements, such as extra stabilizer fairings, to add to her speed. Slow-talking, fast-flying Beeler Blevins of Georgia had another of the low-winged Orions, the property of Asa Candler of the Atlanta family who made Coca-Cola.

Wiley Post, a dark horse in 1930.

The five nonstop racers in 1930 all flew Lockheeds, and clocked in (left to right) Art Goebel, second; Roscoe Turner and Gilmore, fifth; Lee Shoenhair, third; Wiley Post, first; and Billy Brock, fourth.

Also in the starting lineup were three fleet Altairs, samples of the new low-wing, retractable-landing-gear job that Lockheed had evolved from the two-place Sirius. Captain Ira C. Eaker was flying an Army Air Corps command transport Altair with civilian registration. A handsome New York City stockbroker named James Goodwin Hall had a big yellow-and-black one he'd named *The Crusader;* the shield painted on its side was left blank, since the crusade was temporarily kept quiet. And then there was lanky Lou Reichers, pilot for the irrepressible Bernarr Macfadden. The aviation-bugged publisher was back with another entry, a 625-hp Cyclone-powered Altair with a gorgeous paint job of jet black with gold leaf.

The new multistop proviso tripped up this formidable array of talent and Lockheeds. Streaking to Cleveland in a tiny Laird biplane named *Super Solution,* Shell Petroleum's demon Jimmy Doolittle beat them all. Blevins, who took off just before the famous ex-Army major did, said that the little Laird overtook and passed his Orion over the Mojave Desert.

"Ah thought ah was flyin' backwahd," drawled Beeler.

Blasting along the 2,046-mile airway to Cleveland, Doolittle and his racer made two stops and still reached the races in 9 hours and 10 minutes. Johnson's Orion took over an hour longer, followed by Blevins, Eaker,

Goebel's Vega has long-range gas tanks for racing.

Art Goebel, who got fifth-place money in 1931 Bendix.

Capt. Ira Eaker's racing Altair sported piratical insignia.

First Bendix Race also brought out (standing left to right) *Lou Reichers, Jimmy Doolittle, Jim Hall, Beeler Blevins behind* (left to right) *Ira Eaker, Walter Hunter, Harold Johnson.*

Cross-continent hop was showcase for the new Altair, first to have wheels tuck in flush to the wing surface.

Goebel, and Hall. "Hard-luck Lou" Reichers, never noted for his navigation, "missed a few switches" of the railroad tracks he was following, and came down out of gas at Beatrice, Nebraska.

Knocked out of competition by a rash of racing planes that were little more than flying engines, the long-range, stock transport Lockheeds were withdrawn. During the next two years' NAR, they were conspicuous by their absence.

Later on there was an occasional Lockheed entry as a sporting gesture by a pilot or owner who was going to the races anyway. There was always a possibility that the favorites might be withdrawn or forced out, leaving an open field for slower entries to cop some ready prize money. Roy O. Hunt flew an Orion in the 1935 Bendix. Named *Sheridan,* the plane belonged to Wiley Post's old friend and backer, F. C. Hall. It was 64-mph slower than the flashy racers that won, but Roy nevertheless took fourth place and pocketed $1,000. The same year Amelia Earhart, just poking along in her "little red bus," picked up $500 expense money for fifth.

Much the same thing happened at the 1936 National Air Races, in Los Angeles. Sponsor Vincent Bendix offered an extra $2,500 to the fastest woman pilot completing the full transcontinental trip. When all the special and high-speed racers either were nonstarters or cracked up en route, the stock planes—and the women—took over.

With a predawn takeoff from Floyd Bennett Field in Brooklyn, perky little Laura Ingalls roared westward to disappear into the night. The Long Island girl piloted her new, gleaming black Lockheed Orion. Flying alone, as always, Miss Ingalls crossed the continent in 15 hours and 59 minutes. She placed second to a stock Beechcraft

Amelia's little red bus was up against speed packages but still came in fifth (Sheridan *behind tail fin).*

Laura Ingalls in her Auto-da-Fé *helps to make it Ladies' Day at the 1936 NAR with second place.*

C-17R flown by Louise Thaden and Blanche Noyes. Bendix and the race committee were both surprised and humble when the three girls who had supposedly flown "just for the ride" came trooping up to the grandstand for the trophies and top money.

The Lockheeds were not quite finished as Bendix Trophy contenders. In 1938 an aeronautical Jack-of-all-trades named A. Paul Mantz caught the racing bug. The famous movie stunt flyer had several ships in his Burbank hangar, but nothing in the long-distance flying category. He did know an example of Lockheed stamina, however, as a result of preparing Amelia Earhart's transpacific Vega in 1934. And, thanks to the vagaries of motion picture work and charter service, Paul had long ago learned to see potential in planes that others had written off as useless. Back in St. Louis was a seven-year-old, cracked-up airplane, the one and only Lockheed Orion to be built with a metal fuselage. The ship had begun existence as an Altair and then been converted to become Jimmy Doolittle's *Shellightning*. Mantz bought the damaged Orion and had it completely rebuilt, with a powerful Wright Cyclone engine to haul it. Various little streamlining touches added to her speed.

In both 1938 and 1939 the California pilot flew the revamped Orion in the Bendix Trophy Race. Using the upper altitudes and the greater 750 hp of his supercharged engine, Mantz bustled off to Cleveland and twice pulled down third place. The first year he was considerably slowed by encountering a high-flying hawk. The bird tore a hole in the front of the Orion's wooden wing and lodged in the trailing edge, giving Paul some anxious moments. In 1939 he recorded an average speed of almost 235 mph and reached Cleveland in 8 hours and 41 minutes. It was good practice for the postwar Bendix Races, which Mantz, flying a converted P-51 Mustang, was to win three years in a row.

When the California speed merchant retired his brilliant-red Orion to don battledress as an Army colonel, the single-engine Lockheeds had won and placed in National Air Races competition for over a decade.

"Who knows?" mused a Lockheed engineer recently; "if somebody could have figured out a back-to-back Twin Wasp installation, and been brave or foolish enough to fly it, they might have got 500 miles an hour and beat everything!"

Paul Mantz's converted racer—the sole metal-fuselage Orion ever built—has rugged new Cyclone to bring it in third in the 1938 and 1939 Bendix Trophy Races. It's the only Lockheed Orion still existing today.

7

SPANNING THE NORTH ATLANTIC

Reichers (left) and Macfadden with the gold-leaf Altair that, as Miss Liberty, almost reached to coast of Ireland.

The aviation world was aroused by the successful Lindbergh, Chamberlin, Byrd, and Brock-Schlee flights across the Atlantic in 1927. Soon all over the nation it was a rare hangar that did not shelter at least one budding transatlantic flyer. The prestige and supposed riches awaiting at the other end of the Great Circle rainbow to Europe were difficult to ignore. Veteran pilots, nonpilots, and plain publicity-seekers all succumbed to the lure. Destinations and avowed purposes varied, but the general idea was to get there, make a "first" or record of some sort, and return home to fame and acclaim.

In a rash of such transoceanic flight attempts, the participants ignored the fact that the North Atlantic is wide, cold, and unforgiving of mistakes. For a while, as many ocean-hoppers met with failure and death as with success. There were ill-advised and downright foolish efforts which had little hope of being carried to completion. But among them were well-planned and well-equipped attempts with a reasonable chance of getting across.

Such a venture was launched early in 1931 by Miss Ruth Rowland Nichols and Colonel Clarence D. Chamberlin, with the blessings and the aircraft of the Crosley Radio Corporation of Cincinnati, Ohio. Ruth Nichols was thirty years old, and had an overwhelming urge to fly. Blue-eyed and brown-haired, her gracious manner recalled her quiet Quaker upbringing in a well-to-do Rye, New York, family. Her background was a far cry from the rough-and-tumble world of flying which she had deter-

Ruth Nichols with Akita, *readied by Clarence Chamberlin for her transatlantic try in 1931, and* (below) *end of the flight near the runway at St. John, New Brunswick.*

minedly chosen as a career.

Already a government-licensed pilot, and a veteran of air tours and races, Miss Nichols was casually asked by Clarence Chamberlin to fly one of the airplanes he had designed. It was the start of a long association. The thin, quixotic Chamberlin, famed for his Atlantic flight to Germany in 1927, was by this time engaged in a complex round of aviation interests including design, manufacture, and charter flying out of Jersey City, New Jersey. Soon he had Ruth Nichols under his wing, and became her friend and most trusted technical advisor. Together they plotted a course of action calculated to put her across the ocean in Paris as the first of her sex to fly the Atlantic alone.

In endless confabs, Chamberlin and Miss Nichols concluded that an airplane with speed was a prime requisite for an Atlantic flight to be tried by a woman. It would cut down on both the hours of endurance required of the engine, and of the pilot herself. The fast Lockheed Vega, with its long cruising range, was their first choice.

The $20,000 price tag on a new Vega was far beyond the income of Miss Nichols, and Colonel Chamberlin's enterprises were never noted for producing more than a precarious living. In the name of sweet publicity for his radios, Ruth charmed Powel Crosley into the loan of his *New Cincinnati,* the homemade Lockheed with which Brock and Schlee had been breaking transcontinental records.

The speedy ship was the hottest thing that Ruth had ever touched, and she thought at first that the supercharged Wasp beyond her toes was going to pull itself right out of the motor mount. Soon she became familiar with the gleaming array of knobs and needles on the instrument panel, and knew how to manipulate both

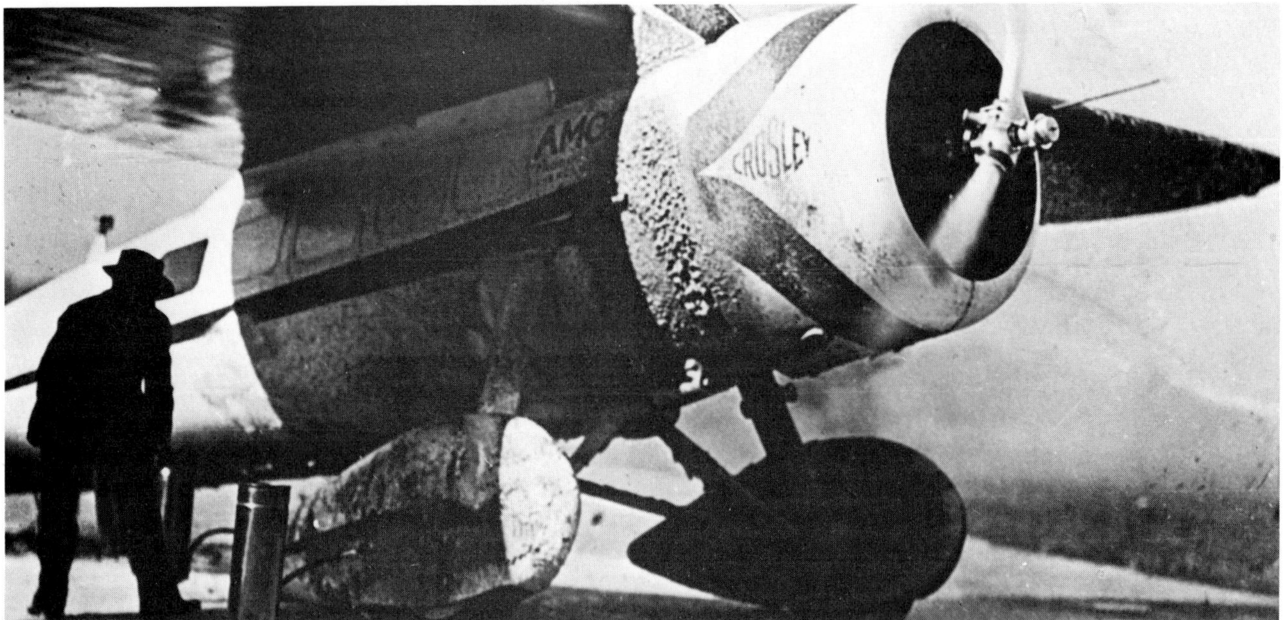

More trouble for Ruth: fire at Louisville puts Akita *out of the Atlantic running once again.*

stabilizer pump and throttle with one hand, while guiding the red-and-cream Vega to a landing with the other.

Step by step Colonel Chamberlin instilled confidence in his protégée and guided her in a progression of transcontinental, altitude, and speed flights that broke all previous records made by women. At last Crosley gave Ruth permission to fly the ocean with his plane.

Chamberlin and his work crew blocked out the windows of the Vega, put extra fuel tanks in the cabin, and installed a new artificial horizon and a directional gyro, plus the second Hamilton-Standard controllable-pitch propeller ever made. With this the pilot could change from a fast, biting pitch in takeoff to the normal one best suited for cruising. Resplendent in a new white-and-gold paint job, the Lockheed also had a new name: *Akita,* a South Dakota Indian word meaning "to explore."

After weeks of preparation and waiting for favorable weather reports, Ruth Nichols was at last ready to fly the Atlantic. Her plan was to jump off for Paris from the gravel airstrip at Harbour Grace, Newfoundland. Ruth and *Akita* left Floyd Bennett Field, Brooklyn, on June 22, 1931, with a planned intermediate fuel stop at either Portland, Maine, or St. John, New Brunswick. Unfortunately, Miss Nichols chose St. John, a field she knew only by hearsay. Hacked out of surrounding wooded hills and cliffs, the New Brunswick stopover was far too small for the fast Lockheed.

Miss Nichols slid the shiny white monoplane in over the trees and lined up for a landing with the setting sun a fiery glare in her eyes. Halfway down the runway the dazzle was abruptly eclipsed by the shadow of a high, wooded embankment dead ahead. Without a chance of stopping, Ruth gave the ship the gun and the Vega staggered up, clearing the cliff by inches, only to catch in the treetops and crash beyond. The motor doubled under and the cockpit burst wide open just ahead of the pilot's seat. Mechanically she cut the switch. Gas poured down the sides of the plane and hot oil boiled from the torn tank below her. Ruth crawled painfully out and along the wing, while an unfeeling news photographer snapped pictures and made no effort to help. By a miracle there was no fire, and gentle hands soon lifted the girl down from the wrecked plane.

Two days later, while Ruth Nichols lay in the St. John hospital with five broken vertebrae, Wiley Post and Harold Gatty made the Atlantic leg of their world flight, and the famous *Winnie Mae* became the first Lockheed airplane to span an ocean.

Colonel Chamberlin shipped the broken Crosley Vega back to Jersey City, and with insurance payments the plane was rebuilt to carry Miss Nichols for a new assault on the Atlantic. To prove that she could go the distance even though still wearing a steel corset because of her injury, Ruth flew *Akita* 1,977 miles nonstop from Oakland, California, to Louisville, Kentucky, on October 23, 1931. Next day bad luck struck again: the ship caught fire while being taxied. The girl escaped unscathed this time, but the Vega was reduced to a charred hulk. By the time the never-give-up team of Nichols and Chamberlin had rebuilt and readied the Lockheed a third time, the North Atlantic honors were snatched away by another woman, flying another Lockheed Vega.

The conquering lady was, of course, Ruth's friend Amelia Earhart. It had been four years since her Atlantic flight as a passenger in the Fokker seaplane *Friendship* in

New First Lady of the Air: Amelia Earhart.

1928. The slim, tousle-haired woman, now the wife of New York publisher George Palmer Putnam, had never been able to feel that she had rightfully earned all her acclaim. Wilmer Stulz had done all the piloting that time, she insisted over and over, and she had been "just a sack of potatoes." Since then, however, Amelia had gained all kinds of flying experience in a great variety of weather, and piled up hundreds of hours on a number of types of aircraft. One day in the winter of 1931 she simply turned to her husband over the breakfast table and asked him:

"Would you *mind* if I flew the Atlantic?"

Putnam never batted an eyelash. "Of course I don't mind," he replied; and with full confidence added, "I think it's an excellent idea."

Although she hadn't flown it a great deal, Amelia already owned an airplane ideally suited to the venture—her red-and-gold Lockheed Vega. Occasionally she flew it in her work of publicizing aviation and air travel. On a speaking engagement in September 1930, there'd been an accident while making a routine landing at the Norfolk Naval Air Station in Virginia. Coming in on the grass field, Amelia hauled back on the stick to keep the tail down.

Suddenly the triangular door behind her flew open. She tumbled half into the cabin and, struggling to recover control, clamped down on the brakes. The Vega went up and over in slow motion to smash on its back. Amelia and a passenger were pretty well shaken up.

She shipped the Lockheed for repairs to Detroit Aircraft, where it was given a new fuselage taken from one of their demonstrators. When it was returned to her, Miss Earhart promptly leased the plane to the Ludington Lines for passenger service between Washington and Norfolk. Ludington's air travelers had no inkling that the 6-passenger airliner that whisked them down for a holiday on the Virginia beaches would soon be part of a flight across the Atlantic.

Amelia Earhart announced her forthcoming trip to only a trusted circle of friends. In answer to "Why?" she simply replied: "For the fun of it," or "Because I want to." The grooming of the Lockheed was put in the charge of the famed Bernt Balchen, the husky, laconic Norwegian-American Arctic explorer who had gone with Byrd on an Atlantic flight of 1927.

Just as Clarence Chamberlin had done for Ruth Nichols, so Bernt Balchen readied Amelia's Vega and gave her the benefit of his own transatlantic flying experience. Balchen was soon to accompany Lincoln Ellsworth on an Antarctic expedition, so he was able to prepare the ship with none of the fanfare he would have elicited had it been known that the red monoplane was to be piloted by Miss Earhart herself. At Teterboro Airport in New Jersey the Arctic flyer and his men beefed up the Vega's fuselage, installed a new fuel system and extra tanks for a total capacity of 420 gallons, and put in a brand-new supercharged Pratt & Whitney Wasp engine.

The flight was under way before the public was aware that it had even been planned. Bernt flew the Vega to Harbour Grace, with mechanic Eddie Gorski in the cabin aft of the gas tanks, and Amelia catnapping on her rolled-up leather flying suit.

The predictions looked good for a flight to Europe the next day, May 20, 1932, and Amelia got off in the evening. She still had two hours when the glow of the setting sun could be seen—if she looked back, which she didn't. She flew high at 12,000 feet and, after four hours, headed straight into a black mass of clouds and storms. A weld on the engine's exhaust manifold began to burn through. Far worse, the altimeter quit.

Seeking to evade the storm, Amelia climbed above it, only to find ice piling on the Vega's stout wings and slush obscuring vision through the windshield. Carefully she groped down again, until the whitecaps of the turbulent waves below were visible in the darkness. If it had been a calm sea, she could easily have gone right into it, since she had no means of guaging her flight height with her altimeter gone.

Amelia flew on blind, between altitudes where ice formed and where she thought the ocean to be. She set her faith in her compasses, particularly the directional gyro, then the best blind-flying instrument available. Occasionally she sipped tomato juice, her only ration.

With the coming of dawn the clouds separated, and Amelia could see water again. There was also a long, dark shape far ahead that looked suspiciously like land.

Crowd in the Irish cow pasture doesn't agree that Miss Earhart's feat had "added nothing to aviation."

With the exhaust vibrating and no altimeter readings possible, the prudent young flyer decided to come down—just as soon as an airport or suitable landing spot could be found.

The mass on the horizon proved to be Northern Ireland. Soon Amelia was circling the green fields of Londonderry, searching for one not dotted with cattle or sheep. She touched the Vega gently down in a pasture near Culmore, 15 hours and 18 minutes out of Harbour Grace, and became the first woman to fly the Atlantic alone.

Farmer Pat Gallagher took her to a telephone five miles down the road. "I did it!" Amelia happily told her husband in New York.

There were still over a hundred gallons of gasoline in the tanks of the Lockheed, on which the Irish officials dutifully collected an import tax.

Forthright Amelia Earhart Putnam minced no words in her subsequent interviews: "This trip," she said, "was simply a personal gesture. That all-too-appropriate appellation 'a sack of potatoes,' probably as much as any other single factor, inspired me to try going it alone."

Always the feminist, she continued: "My flight has added nothing to aviation, but I hope has meant something to women in aviation. If it has, I shall feel it was justified; but I can't claim anything else."

America was proud of Amelia's candor. She was no longer a self-styled "phony heroine," but a great woman flyer.

Amelia Earhart was the first person, man or woman, to fly a Lockheed airplane alone across the Atlantic Ocean, but a week earlier, a newer, faster Lockheed with a lone male almost beat her to it. The man was Louis T. Reichers, flying the gorgeous Altair owned by publisher Bernarr Macfadden. Tall, thin Lou Reichers was an ex-Army flyer, barnstormer, and pilot-for-hire. His goggled visage and little black mustache were a familiar sight around the flying fields on the East coast, particularly in his native New Jersey.

It was Reichers, who taught Macfadden (after a long, hard struggle) to fly: the mercurial physical culturist obtained his license at the age of sixty-two in 1931. No matter what his competition and his associates thought about his egotism and ethics, they had to admit grudgingly that Bernarr Macfadden's love of all phases of aviation was sincere. The enthusiastic purchaser of many fine airplanes, the publisher had bought his Altair as the last of five Lockheeds (including two Vegas, an Air Express, and a Sirius) that he owned at one time or another. The Altair was a black plane with an unusual top surface of gold leaf, and the $32,000 it cost Macfadden could nearly have bought the entire Lockheed company at the time. Originally named *The Gold Eagle,* this ship is remembered by older factory employees as "the most beautiful Lockheed ever built." The gold leaf was applied in individual small squares, patted on by hundreds of cosmetic powder puffs bought and used just for this purpose. With a 625-hp Wright Cyclone engine the ship was a bit thirsty on gas, but great for speed.

To provide publicity for Macfadden, Lou Reichers proceeded to make a number of intercity record flights, as well as regularly showing up at air races and airport dedications. Lou was like so many pilots of the time in dreaming of transatlantic flight, and he found his visions to be in the realm of possibility when at the controls of

The Gold Eagle. Knowing that his food-faddist boss was nourished by publicity fully as much as by raw carrots, Reichers sounded out Macfadden on the subject.

The plan was to make a fast flight to Paris, refueling en route at Harbour Grace and at Dublin. The 2,050-mile Atlantic leg would be made in complete daylight, the first time that this was projected. Lou told the publisher that, with such a flight, he might even get his name in the Hearst newspapers, a possibility mighty appealing to Macfadden.

Perhaps with the fate of the early Pacific racer *Golden Eagle* in mind—but more likely to bolster the sagging circulation of *Liberty* magazine—the ship was renamed. In an Atlantic City ceremony that would gladden any public-relations man's heart, Governor A. Harry Moore of New Jersey rechristened the ship *Miss Liberty*, to the noise of popping flash powders and whirling newsreel cameras.

Officially disassociated from Macfadden Publications because of insurance problems, Reichers extracted a promise from "B. M." of a $10,000 bonus if he could cut Lindbergh's time to Paris in half, or better.

"What about navigation, Lou?" Macfadden asked. "No railroads out there to follow."

The pilot assured his backer that he'd get the best weather forecasts and use dead reckoning on his course. As to the possibility of failure, he shrugged: "I'll be unhappy, and you'll lose an airplane."

It was up to Lou to install extra tanks in the Altair, and make arrangements to have them filled to their total capacity of 465 gallons. One tank even occupied the rear seat, thereby quashing the rumors that Macfadden planned to go along himself. To give the adventure an authentic ring, it was announced that the trip was "in the nature of a survey flight to determine the feasibility of a transatlantic merchandise and messenger service." The eager pilot had a tough time keeping a straight face when this bit of nonsense was broadcast.

Of all days, the weather picture looked bright for Lou Reichers on Friday, May 13, 1932. Despite the wails of Macfadden's publicity boys, he left Newark Airport shortly after midnight, and reached Harbour Grace in a little over six hours. There he had to unload his jacket, which superstitious well-wishers had stuffed full to bursting at the last minute with good-luck charms.

In landing on the barren hilltop's dirt strip, the Altair kicked up a rock that lodged in the horizontal stabilizer. Lou spent an extra hour patching the hole with glue and sailcloth donated by local fishermen. Then he was off down the 4,000-foot runway, and airborne for Dublin.

The midnight start and the furious pace he was setting began to tell on Reichers, who was in an unheated cockpit and flying at 15,000 feet. Boring along through cloud peaks, he shivered continuously and uncontrollably, and rationed himself to a big swallow of hot coffee every half hour. He scarcely realized that he was suffering from oxygen depletion, and at last dreamily decided that it would be best to drop to a lower altitude.

The sun was beginning to set when Reichers brought *Miss Liberty* down through the gray clouds and tried to fly for a while in sight of the water. According to his calculations land should be in sight. Skimming his black-and-gold craft barely thirty feet above the whitecaps, Lou kept on for fifteen minutes, and then another ten. Suddenly there were rocks jutting up—ugly black ones flashing by right under the left wing. Startled and scared, the pilot put his ship into a steep climbing turn.

Lou wanted to find the Irish coast, but had no wish to barge into it full tilt. A rainstorm brought visibility down to nearly zero. With only an hour's gas, the would-be Atlantic speedster cursed himself for ever getting into such a mess. Sweating now, he climbed higher, searching for a hole in the cloudbank. When he found one, he was over water again. Lou looked for land, rocks, anything. Then, far off to the north, lights twinkled in the gloom.

It was a passenger liner, and *Miss Liberty* was soon circling over it. In the rain and dark Lou couldn't tell much about her, except that she represented help at hand, and he'd better make use of it. He was lost now, and he knew it: his gauges showed only twenty minutes left to keep flying.

Since the Lockheed was made of wood and nearly empty tanks would provide buoyancy, Lou still had hopes of getting out of the deal alive. Three times he made passes low along the dark water, blinking his lights in SOS signals while he flashed past the vessel. Sure that his presence had been announced, he slid the Altair toward the sea alongside the big ship. The tail touched, and she skittered on the water like a skipped stone. Yanking the throttle and tugging on the stick, Lou tried to peer ahead. The heavy nose of the low-winged plane plunged under the next wave and brought up short. With no time to pull in his head, the pilot's face smashed hard against the windshield and he was knocked cold.

It was half an hour before Reichers regained consciousness, ears ringing, head aching, and face bloody. Nose down and tail high, *Miss Liberty* floated on her broad wing, pitching, bobbing, sliding in the trough of the waves. The downed pilot could see nothing and felt abandoned until a searchlight stabbed out of the dark to bathe him in its brilliance. The ship was back to get him, and soon the creaking of oars announced the arrival of a lifeboat. In the heaving seas the boat would alternately tower above the plane, and then seem to sink far below it. Slowly the officer in charge maneuvered in close, and came within two feet of the cockpit where Lou was standing groggily. Beside them the flapping tail threatened at any moment to crunch down on the gunwales of the lifeboat.

"Jump! Goddammit, jump!" yelled the officer. "We can't hold here all night!"

Reichers jumped and was caught. Soon the liner loomed over the lifeboat, and in a few more minutes he was under sedation in the ship's hospital bay.

The Atlantic flyer could not have chosen a better ship to come down alongside. She was the *S.S. President Roosevelt*, less than two hours out of Cobh, Ireland, and bound for New York. Captain of the vessel was George Fried and her Chief Officer was Harry Manning, who was in charge of the lifeboat; both were veterans of other dramatic rescues in the North Atlantic.

"Son," said the ruddy-faced captain to Lou, "it's going to take seven days to get you back to where you left yesterday."

Reichers had been plucked from the sea seventeen miles south of Kinsale Harbour in County Cork. He had apparently been unknowingly skirting the Irish coast for at least sixty miles.

Lucky Lou got out of the adventure with only a broken nose. Macfadden met the *President Roosevelt* at the pier in New York and told the assembled press that, under the circumstances, his pilot had exercised fine judgment. A good sport over the loss of the beautiful Altair, his greatest joy was that his archenemies, the Hearst papers, carried Captain Fried's full report of the rescue of Reichers. They failed to mention the publisher's name, but they did print the words *Miss Liberty*, and this was enough to delight Macfadden.

Lou Reichers was right about the floating qualities of the wooden Lockheed. Two days after her ditching, the derelict was sighted still afloat about thirty miles out in the Atlantic off Fastnet Light. The sun gleaming on the gold leaf attracted the Swedish steamer *Crown Prince Olaf* to the scene. Her crew spent half an hour trying to salvage the waterlogged plane, but finally left *Miss Liberty* to be slowly swallowed by the sea.

Previous to the journeys of Reichers and Amelia Earhart, one of the most unusual transatlantic flights on record took place in the summer of 1931. The trip itself was comparatively uneventful, but the circumstances surrounding its conception and execution ranged from political intrigue to comic opera.

After World War I, the defeated Austro-Hungarian empire was dissolved and Hungary itself dismembered. Under the Treaty of Trianon the little country lost 71 percent of its territory and 63 percent of its population, emerging as a ghost of its former greatness, and contained in a flat, defenseless central plain. Hungarians were uprooted and separated from ancestral homes and land, with many coming to America.

Though good citizens, the deeply patriotic and religious Hungarian-Americans had a common cause in protesting the Treaty of Trianon, and at gatherings it was always a prime topic of conversation. Many people talked, but one young man felt strongly enough to dream of a novel protest. He was Sandor Wilczek, better known by his adopted name, Alexander Magyar.

Magyar came from the tiny village of Bataszek, and had been a pilot for the Hungarian Air Force during the closing days of the war. With his home disrupted as a result of the hated treaty, he came alone to America in the early 1920s and found work in Windsor, Ontario. Doggedly, Sandor clung to his love of flying, but it was difficult for an alien to find real work, particularly when local pilots were living from hand to mouth. Nevertheless the Hungarian, with 4,000 hours, managed to line up an occasional student to teach, and a charter job now and then when he could afford to rent an airplane. Coaxing a battered Canuck out of some Canadian pasture, his mind kept going back to his great idea.

Transatlantic flights were the big news of the day. They had been undertaken in the name of goodwill, in the needs of big-time advertising, and purely for fame and fortune. Why not, reasoned Magyar, make a flight as a great gesture to focus attention on the wrongs that had been done to Hungary?

Often jobless and usually nearly broke, the young flyer lived with Dr. William Molnar, a Windsor clergyman. One evening he broached his plan to the good doctor, who advised seeking inspiration from the Bible. Using the time-honored device of opening the Book at random, the minister's finger pointed to the words: "These things ye shall do." It was sign enough for Alexander Magyar. Immediately he set about making his idea a reality.

Starting with the neighborhood Hungarian-Canadian social clubs, Sandor earnestly outlined his grand scheme and asked for modest donations to set it in motion. Soon the tall, hawk-faced flyer with the eloquent brown eyes was making impassioned pleas at bigger gatherings across the river—which is also the Canada-U.S. border—in Detroit. The idea was brought to the attention of Monsignor Elemer Eordogh of Toledo, head of the Hungarian-American Clerical Society, and Franz Prattinger, editor of the Detroit Hungarian-language newspaper. Both endorsed it; and the word spread nationwide.

In England the obscure Hungarian flyer found an unexpected ally in Lord Rothermore, owner of the London *Daily Mail*. Because of his interest in the plight of the little nation and his editorials in regard to the Trianon division, the British viscount was sometimes called "the uncrowned king of Hungary." Rothermere joined forces with the Canadian-American movement by offering $10,000 to the first pilot to succeed in a nonstop flight from the North American continent to Budapest.

The biggest windfall came from Emil Salay, owner of a large sausage factory in Flint, Michigan. The fifty-eight-year-old meat packer had promised his father, formerly a cavalry officer, that someday he would "do something for Hungary." This was his chance, and he put up

$22,000 toward purchase of a suitable airplane with which to make the flight.

By this time a sizable committee, composed of clerics and businessmen, had been formally organized in Detroit, and was bent on promoting the Hungarian-American Ocean Flight. The original plans called for a nonstop Detroit-to-Budapest jaunt, with refueling in the air over Newfoundland. To make the trip, the committee selected a Detroit-Lockheed Sirius, a sister ship of Colonel Lindbergh's famous transcontinental record-breaker. There was no question of a name for the ship: it was to be called *Justice for Hungary.*

In the shuffle to fill the cockpits of the 2-place, low-wing Lockheed, the committee almost ignored Alexander Magyar, who had thought up the flight to begin with. For a while it didn't look as if he was going, and first reports announced the crew as Colonel Eugene Czapary and Captain Stephen Grosschmid. Then Alexander's friends got him back on the inside track.

Magyar was still a lieutenant in the Hungarian Air Corps Reserve, and so suggested having as his copilot his old friend and flying instructor, Captain George Endres. A native of Perjamos, Hungary, the thirty-four-year-old Endres had been decorated many times during the war, but was best known for a daring escape from a Siberian prison camp back to his own lines via Sweden. His family had settled in Cincinnati, Ohio, before the war, and George was the only member to remain in Hungary. When the invitation to participate in the politically inspired flight came from America, Endres was quick to accept.

Magyar and Endres went to California to take delivery of the new Sirius in August 1930. It was black, with white trim and red wings, and the colorful Hungarian coat of arms was emblazoned on the vertical fin above the Lockheed trademark. Both pilots needed considerable familiarization with the ship, and Magyar even took a refresher course in navigation and the flying of larger planes at Parks Air College in East St. Louis, Illinois. Soon the September storms commenced on the North Atlantic air lanes, and it was too late to risk the long over-water flight.

In order to meet extra expenses, and to give the average Hungarian-American a sense of participation in the much-publicized journey, thousands of postcards were prepared and sold at a dollar apiece, to be carried on the *Justice for Hungary* to relatives and friends in the old country. It was not unusual to find Magyar and Endres themselves hard at work selling cards at charity bazaars and street fairs in the Detroit area. During the winter, ownership of the Lockheed passed to the man who had the greatest investment in it—Emil Salay, the meat packer.

With the 1931 Atlantic flying season, Magyar and Endres were ready to go. Captain Endres was senior in age and rank, so he occupied the front pilot's cockpit,

Justice for Hungary (below), *with Magyar* (left) *and Endres, had a special mission.*

One of the airmail cards the flyers hustled to raise money for the Hungarian flight was bought and sent to Lord Rothermere, who promoted the project with news stories and a $10,000 prize.

with Lieutenant Magyar navigating from the rear. By now they were both confident of flying the red-and-black Sirius anywhere, in any weather. Since Lord Rothermere's prize offer specified a flight "from the North American continent," they decided to refuel at the familiar way stop, Harbour Grace, Newfoundland.

After days of waiting at Roosevelt Field, New York, Endres and Magyar simply got "tired of lying around." Against the advice of the famous Dr. James Kimball, head of the United States Weather Bureau in New York, the flying partners left for Newfoundland on July 13, 1931. Kimball had predicted fog off Cape Breton; the Hungarians found it right where he said it would be, and nearly missed their destination.

"Doc was right," said Magyar at Harbour Grace. "We won't move again 'til he says 'go.' "

Two days later the Atlantic weather expert flashed the word and the flyers piled into the Sirius. She was already loaded with 635 gallons of gas, a 150-pound radio, and 32 pounds of mail. At the last minute Newfoundland postal authorities blocked the posting of five hundred additional letters "because of the political nature of the trip." The flyers made a low takeoff to the west, circled back over Harbour Grace, and headed out to sea beyond Conception Bay.

Magyar and Endres were helped by westerly winds, but found a solid cloudbank below their speeding airplane. Except for a short stretch off the European coast they never saw the Atlantic at all. A bad three-hour storm buffeted the plane and knocked the earth inductor compass out of whack. Despite this, Magyar managed to navigate by the stars, and the radio set proved of immense help in establishing bearings from unseen ships on the ocean below. Their landfall was a railroad station in the north of France, and then it was touch and go as to whether the dwindling gasoline supply would take the Lockheed all the way to Budapest. Radios reported sighting the Sirius over Germany, Linz, and then Vienna. In Budapest 180,000 Hungarians jammed Matyasfold Airdrome, eagerly awaiting the arrival of their countrymen.

High over the Danube Valley the *Justice*'s engine coughed and spluttered. Magyar tried to hand-pump a few more cupfuls of gas to the starving cylinders. Endres stretched the Lockheed's glide. There were only a few more miles to cover. Over familiar home ground, the pilot finally chose a highway on which to put the Sirius down in the dusk. Two plodding farm carts blocked the road; he swerved—and landed in an adjacent field of stumpy rows of maize. The flight "to do something for Hungary" had brought Magyar and Endres 3,229 miles from the bleak shores of Newfoundland to a spot near Bicske, only fourteen miles from Budapest.

Taken immediately to meet Hungarian Premier Count Bethlen and his Cabinet, the tired aerial voyagers had to disappoint the people who waited at the airdrome. Later the pair were triumphantly carried through the city to the cheers of thousands. Their welcomers included Admiral Horthy, Regent of Hungary, as well as their backer, Emil Salay, who had made the trip from America to be on hand to greet them.

Out in the corn field near Bicske the faithful *Justice for Hungary* was garlanded with great streamers of fresh flowers as long columns of men, women, and children filed reverently by to gaze at "the wonderful airplane that had flown from America." Later the slightly damaged Lockheed was dismantled and carried in a colorful procession into Budapest. It was a wild and happy time for Hungary, a nation which had so little cause or occasion for celebration.

True to his word, Lord Rothermere awarded the $10,000 prize to Endres and Magyar. To him, and to all the people who had contributed their pennies and dollars, the Hungarian-American Ocean Flight had accomplished its avowed purpose in calling world attention to the hated Treaty of Trianon.

With the noble deed accomplished, it was a sad anticlimax to find the participants arguing over the profits. The details were never made clear, but by September Alexander Magyar had resumed his original name of Wilczek and was challenging six brother officers to sword duels for alleged defamatory statements.

Several weeks later Emil Salay was reported to be planning to reimburse himself from the profits of the venture, with the surplus to be divided between the flyers. To this Magyar agreed, while Endres claimed he alone was entitled to a share. Hot Hungarian blood boiled, and a new duel between Magyar and Endres was scheduled for October 26. Only the pleading of the Hungarian Aviation Society called off a meeting on the field of honor between the erstwhile partners. The next day, romance replaced rapiers, and Magyar was married in Budapest to Gisela Puskas. It may or may not have been significant that the bride's former husband was a New York fencing master.

Together with Emil Salay, Alexander Magyar (or Sandor Wilczek) finally returned to America, in November. This time he came as a bona fide immigrant under the quotas, content at last to have accomplished his inspired mission for Hungary.

In Budapest, George Endres somehow kept control of the *Justice for Hungary*. The following May he flew the Sirius down to Rome for the Congress of Transatlantic Flyers called by General Italo Balbo. Banking steeply while coming in for a landing, Endres apparently ran into a small whirlwind, sideslipped, and crashed. Both the Atlantic conqueror and his radio operator, Captain J. Pittay, died in the flaming wreckage. The accident cast a pall of gloom over the congress. General Balbo and Il Duce himself walked in the Endres-Pittay funeral procession, and over 100,000 Hungarian mourners met a special train returning the martyred national air hero to Budapest.

To court the goodwill of Hungary, Mussolini soon made an elaborate presentation of a new plane to replace the demolished *Justice*, and it was used to make some of the special mail-carrying flights that had been planned for Endres. Named *Star of Savoy*, the gift was a squat and stubby biplane, nothing at all like the sleek Lockheed that Endres and Magyar had flown from America.

The Hungarian government commemorated the Sirius on two sets of postage stamps. Today the battered Wasp engine, salvaged from the Rome crack-up, is still on display in a Budapest museum. This and some small pieces are all that remain of the fruition of one patriot's determination to do something for his country.

The success of the Hungarians inspired other national groups to sponsor ocean flights that would link America with their former homelands. There were projects to fly to Italy, Portugal, Sweden, Spain, Poland. One of the better-equipped and -financed ventures was a goodwill nonstop flight from New York to Kaunas, the capital of Lithuania. This was first tried in July 1933 by Captain Stephen Darius and Lieutenant Stanley Girenas, using a special Bellanca monoplane named *Lituanica*. The pair got across the Atlantic all right, but some 400 miles short of their goal they ran into heavy weather over Germany and crashed fatally in a forest near Kuhdamm.

The deaths of Darius and Girenas was the occasion for national mourning in Lithuania. In the United States their sponsors felt that something should be done to complete the flight and give the country a place in the aeronautical sun. A new American-Lithuanian Trans-Atlantic Flight Association was formed in Chicago to set plans in motion. The committee chose Felix Waitkus, a twenty-eight-year-old Chicago plumber's son of Lithuanian descent, to make the flight. Waitkus had attended the University of Chicago, and won his wings with the U.S. Army Air Corps at Selfridge Field in Michigan. A lieutenant in the reserve, he ran a flying school at Kohler, Wisconsin, with his

Felix Waitkus gets aboard his heavily laden Vega, hoping to cover the 4,500 miles to Lithuania in 30 hours.

Lithuanian stamp celebrates Waitkus and his transoceanic flight of September 1935.

father-in-law, Anton Brotz. The association replaced the lost Bellanca with a good used Lockheed Vega from California's Shell Oil Company. Waitkus and Brotz readied the ship at the Kohler field, blocking out windows and installing extra tanks in the cabin in place of the standard seating arrangements. With a new, white paint job, trimmed with orange, she became *Lituanica II.*

Waitkus's Vega was not ready to leave Floyd Bennett Field on Long Island until September 21, 1935—rather late in the season for a long-distance flight, especially when loaded with 700 gallons of gasoline and a thousand special airmail letters. Dressed in a leather jacket and jaunty beret, the lieutenant lifted the Lockheed off the concrete runway and headed east in his bid for transatlantic honors.

Waitkus and *Lituanica II* met more than just the seasonal storms over the North Atlantic. There were headwinds, rain, and fog. Much of the way he flew on instruments, with no outside bearings possible in the vast misty whiteness of day and the dark blackness of night pressing all around him. Like other ocean flyers, Waitkus flew high until ice formed on his wings, then low until it melted off. By dawn on the second day Felix was sure he was across the Atlantic. But he was also certain that he could never make it to Kaunas.

When patches of Ireland at last appeared through the fog beneath the speeding Vega, the Lithuanian-American pilot decided it would be wise to come down, refuel, and then go on. He came winging in over the Sheefry Hills of County Mayo and selected what appeared to be a good level pasture near the village of Ballinrobe. Weary from fighting the elements, Waitkus slipped the white Lockheed in for a landing. A wing caught and plowed up the ground, the landing gear crunched off and the ship skidded to a stop on its belly. In the sudden silence the dazed pilot listened quietly to an Irish weather forecast being broadcast especially for his benefit. A few minutes later he was breakfasting at the nearby farmhouse of Paddy Walsh.

Felix Waitkus finished his flight to Lithuania in a special plane placed at his disposal, so the trip was adjudged a

Lituanica II *cracks up in Ireland—but plane ended its career in Soviet Russia.*

success inasmuch as he really got there. The damaged Lockheed was repaired and shipped from Ireland to Kaunas, where it was purchased by the Lithuanian Air Ministry. With the communist takeover of the country in 1940, the *Lituanica II* is thought to have been taken to Moscow to be evaluated by Soviet aeronautical experts. There is a remote possibility that portions of the last wooden Lockheed to fly the North Atlantic may still be in existence somewhere behind the Iron Curtain.

On this side of the Atlantic, there is no question as to the whereabouts of Amelia Earhart's first ocean-hopping Vega. A little over a year after her flight from Newfoundland to Ireland the ship was purchased for $7,500 by Philadelphia's Franklin Institute. Transferred in 1966 to the National Air and Space Museum, and somewhat darkened by age, the red-and-gold monoplane was cleaned and refurbished for exhibit. Today it is the oldest Lockheed airplane in existence.

Built in 1928, Amelia Earhart's Vega added a record coast-to-coast flight to its honors before she sold it in 1933.

8

ACROSS THE PACIFIC

The enthusiasm for flying across the Atlantic was never matched by flyers who even idly contemplated a similar conquest of the North Pacific: the 4,500-mile trip over fog-shrouded and storm-lashed waters appealed to only a handful of hardy aviators. To stimulate interest, therefore, the air-minded Tokyo *Asahi* (Morning Sun News) offered a $25,000 prize for the first nonstop flight, either way, between Japan and America.

Airplanes were improving by 1929, but a single-engine ship capable of lifting the nearly 1,000 gallons of gasoline necessary to go the distance would have to be specially built. A Tokyo flight would also require some good, solid financial backing; and, even in such boom times, the green stuff had to be carefully promoted. Fortunately an angel was available in the person of John Buffelen, a Tacoma, Washington, lumber tycoon who wanted to put his town on the Pacific air map.

Genial John Buffelen and the Tacoma Chamber of Commerce had a man to fly to Tokyo. All they needed was a suitable airplane.

The pilot on whom the lumber city's committee pinned their hopes for world recognition was Lieutenant Albert Harold Bromley, a twenty-nine-year-old Iowa flyer with Army training. Boyish, taciturn Bromley had put up $2,000 of his own money for the venture; with more cash assured, he began to make the rounds of the West Coast's aircraft factories.

It was at the Lockheed plant in Burbank that the lieu-

Robbins and Jones headed for home after missing their tin goose on Vega's second try to get to Tokyo.

The man who tried the hardest to hop the Pacific.

tenant found the experimental "seaplane" that designer Jack Northrop had started for Hubert Wilkins. There had been little or no engineering done: it was merely a fuselage with the camber cut away to accommodate a lower wing. Bromley had to exercise considerable vision to see this dusty wooden shell as a finished airplane capable of flying him from Tacoma to Tokyo. But after talking to chief engineer Jerry Vultee, his enthusiasm was aroused, and he ordered the plane completed to his specifications for the long-distance attempt.

Within a few months Vultee and the factory crew had assembled the original Explorer model, Lockheed's first low-wing airplane. Its extra-long wing was broad and straight, with no dihedral angle—like the high wing of a Vega but at the base of the fuselage. A single cockpit, well to the rear, accommodated the pilot. The ship was painted the standard international orange.

Test-flying the special job was carried out from the long flat surfaces of Muroc Dry Lake, some sixty miles north of Burbank. On one run of nearly a mile, Lieutenant Bromley got off in the new monoplane with 8,500 pounds, an unofficial load record for the times. Jerry Vultee experimented during the tests with three types of vertical tail surfaces on the ship, settling on a compromise of rounded fin and squared-off rudder, used only on this particular airplane.

Satisfied with her performance, Bromley flew the big Explorer nonstop to Tacoma, where a special takeoff ramp was being readied at Pierce County Airport. In the presence of 10,000 cheering onlookers the gleeming orange Lockheed was christened *City of Tacoma* by Clasina Madge Buffelen, the small daughter of the flight's backer.

A tail wheel was substituted at the last moment for the conventional skid, to give the Explorer an even better chance of successful takeoff from the unpaved runway. With favorable weather predictions from the Aleutians and the Kuriles, and with plane and engine in the best possible shape, the chosen pilot was ready to start the longest over-water flight ever attempted by man.

On Sunday, July 28, 1929, the *City of Tacoma* was poised atop the wooden ramp designed to give a boost to her take-off run. Harold Bromley, his goodbyes said, climbed in and listened carefully to the sweetly ticking Wasp ahead. The ship was in flying position, her tanks topped off full at 902 gallons. Gassing-up had already taken place—during the cool of the morning. It was this little overlooked detail that brought disaster.

As 20,000 onlookers quieted to watch, the Explorer rolled slowly down the ramp, gathering speed. At the bottom there was scarcely a jar, and Bromley thought that his last worry was over. Then a splatter of gasoline hit the windshield. With tail down, plus natural expansion, the fuel bubbled from the tank breathers atop the fuselage in a steady spray, fogging the view ahead. Building up speed, the pilot peered over to the side of the shield, only to have his goggles coat up with fuel. Desperately he brushed them back. A thousand feet further on the tail lightened at the 60-mph pace, but the stinging spray of gas was blinding Bromley. He could feel the ship wobble from the runway, swerving to the left. Then the right wheel crumpled on the rough ground, the wing followed, and in a moment the heavily loaded Lockheed was perched on her nose in a cloud of dust.

Harold Bromley leaped out as the ship careened to a stop. Gasoline gushed from the shattered wing and cracked fuselage. The massed and screaming spectators, converging on the wreckage, swept aside police, National Guardsmen, and a barbed wire fence. By some miracle there was no fire, and order was quickly restored. The lieutenant, very low in spirits, did not offer any alibis.

"Nobody is to blame but myself," he said. "I can do it if they'll give me another chance."

John Buffelen and the Tacoma committee assured the flyer that financing for a new airplane was certain. In Burbank the Lockheed factory worked like mad, and a new *City of Tacoma* was completed in a little more than six weeks. Innovations on the second version included dropable landing gear and a metal-sheathed belly skid along the bottom of the fuselage. Jerry Vultee was still experimenting with tail surfaces, and this Explorer was

Bromley's three Explorers (from top down): *first has conventional fin and rudder; second, a rebuild, with rudder that flapped; third looks more like a Sirius, but still has lone cockpit and wide wing, plus 2-degree dihedral.*

fitted with an overhung, counterbalanced rudder. With no wind tunnel, he had to "cut and try." Unfortunately, it was one of the talented designer's few bad guesses.

Test pilot Herb Fahy took the ship up for a trial hop on September 18, 1929, and quickly discovered a dangerous tail flutter. Three times he circled the Lockheed field at low altitude to show the engineers how it flapped. As they watched, the offending rudder whipped loose and fell practically at their feet, followed by the fin itself. Herb went into figure-eight contortions to control the uncontrollable. Off the east end of the runway the Explorer dipped under some wires, swished through the branches of a pepper tree, nicked the corner of a bungalow and came to inverted rest in a back yard. Fahy, lucky this time, crawled out with only a broken elbow and bruises.

Back at his drawing board Vultee had meanwhile designed the successful low-wing Sirius for Colonel Lindbergh. The third plane built for the Tacoma-Tokyo flight still retained the greater wingspread and single cockpit of the Explorer, but had a larger, Sirius-type fin and rudder. Two degrees of dihedral were given the wing for better flying characteristics.

While waiting for his successive airplanes to be completed, Harold Bromley made ends meet with odd jobs of check-flying for Lockheed, and work piloting Vegas for Corporación Aeronáutica de Transportes, S.A., a Mexican airline that ran from El Paso to Mexico City and Brownsville to Mazatlán. Then in May 1930 the Pacific hopeful was back at Muroc Dry Lake for tests of the third *City of Tacoma.* Bromley did all the preliminary check flights himself. It looked like this Explorer was the plane in which he'd finally be heading for Tokyo.

On thin financial ice, the Detroit-Lockheed management did not have the funds to cover Bromley's insur-

Three endings (from top down): *hot gas foils takeoff of* City of Tacoma *No. 1; fancy tail comes off in test hop to dump No. 2; check pilot Ben Catlin dies when heavily loaded No. 3 trips and burns.*

ance for a full-load test. The crucial flight fell to their own new check pilot, big, friendly Hugh W. "Ben" Catlin, who was covered until May 25.

At daylight on the day before the deadline the Explorer was readied with 900 gallons of gas in her tanks. Ben Catlin *had* to fly her, even when a leak in a gas tank delayed his takeoff until the heat of the day. Harold Bromley drove to a prearranged position a mile down the shimmering lake bed: if the *City* was not off the ground by that point, the test pilot was to pull the dump valves. A mere half a mile ahead, the twelve-foot embankment of the Santa Fe Railroad angled across the long level expanse of Muroc.

Ben gunned the Lockheed and got rolling into the wind. Apparently riding a ground cushion, he whipped by Bromley's car with the tail wheel still touching, and resorted to bounce technique to clear by inches the railroad embankment on beyond. Floundering through the air, the *City of Tacoma* made a half-roll to land on her nose. The engine tore off on impact and the rest of the plane skidded on its back another hundred yards. Fire blazed around the hot exhaust stacks and licked up the trail of gasoline to the fuselage. Ben Catlin came walking out of the flames a human torch, only a hundred feet from the horrified Bromley rushing to the rescue. Whispering that he had been unable to reach down to trip the dump valves and mumbling apologies "for wrecking the ship," the test pilot died that evening.

Shaken by this dismal chain of events, the Tacoma Chamber of Commerce sought a fourth and final airplane for Lieutenant Bromley from another manufacturer, and any hopes of a Lockheed being the first plane to span the North Pacific appeared very dim indeed.

Still the Tokyo *Asahi*'s $25,000 prize was there to be claimed, and in addition some Seattle businessmen had put up another $28,000 for the first flight "from fifty miles of Tokyo to ten miles of Seattle." Like the Japanese newspaper's offer, this was interpreted to mean a flight in either direction, and by 1931 there were a score of new aspirants in Tokyo and Seattle, hoping to win either prize—or both. Among them were two flyers from Fort Worth, Texas. They were Reginald L. Robbins, a shy twenty-eight-year-old ex-barnstormer, and Harold S. Jones, a Chicagoan who had built a fortune in oil. The Texans proposed an excellent method of going the distance: they intended to be refueled in the air, en route.

Drawling Reg Robbins was no stranger to the operation of aerial refueling. In 1929 he and a partner had held the airborne endurance record, circling Forth Worth for 172 hours. The Tokyo flight would simply be extending the method as needed to cover the great distance. Bachelor Hank Jones had a yen, and the money, to participate in the flight simply as a sporting venture.

The pair purchased Erle Halliburton's old record-breaking Lockheed, *The Tester*, and renamed her *Fort Worth*. On the theory that it would consume far less gas, they proceeded to install a 220-hp Whirlwind engine, replacing the ship's original 425-hp Wasp. Painted white, with only a yellow panel for identification on the upper wing, the Vega was soon to be seen at refueling practice over the Texas plains, with the gas hose dangling from a big Ford Trimotor flown by Nick Greener and James J. Mattern.

The Robbins-Jones attempt to fly to Tokyo got off from Boeing Field in Seattle on July 8, 1931. Robbins was mistaken for a visiting cowboy, and was only let through the crowd when he insisted, "Man, ah'm goin' to ride in that ship to Tokyo!"

The *Fort Worth* made a long takeoff with her low-powered engine, skimming the housetops of south Seattle in the darkness of early morning. All day long the flyers plugged to the northwest, to be met in the evening by the refueling plane over Fairbanks, Alaska. The headwinds were terrific, cutting their speed to a little over 70 mph, but Jones managed to complete the transfer of 200 gallons of gas.

Proceeding down the Yukon Valley, Greener and Mattern maneuvered their Ford above the white Lockheed three more times to pass down the precious fuel. The critical point came at Nome, where the last contact was scheduled to be made. But the *Fort Worth* was buffeted by williwaws, and Reg Robbins just couldn't keep her steady beneath the lumbering "tin goose." The hose would come tantalizingly close, only to be swung by a howling gust away from Hank Jones's outstretched hand. Taking on the full 425 gallons they'd need was impossible, and the weary Texans landed at Solomon, Alaska. This first nonstop flight from Seattle to the Nome area required nearly 27 hours. Ironically, the weather a hundred miles farther on was reported as clear, with a tailwind blowing all the way down the Siberian coast to Japan.

Robbins and Jones flew back to Seattle for another try. The Whirlwind engine was a mistake, they decided, since it took so long to cover distance that the advantage of low fuel consumption was nullified. They reinstalled their Wasp, expecting better maneuverability in refueling as well.

The second attempt was made less than a month later, with both engine and speed coming up to expectations. The Texans refueled satisfactorily over Fairbanks and proceeded toward Unalakeet on Norton Sound. Somewhere in the fog and clouds they outflew the Ford carrying Nick Greener and Jimmie Mattern—who became lost themselves after taking off for this second refueling.

Balked again, Robbins and Jones gave up thoughts of Tokyo and came back for a landing at Fairbanks. It was the end of another dream of hopping the Pacific. The flyers returned to Fort Worth prizeless. But Jimmie Mattern had acquired a taste for long distances: a year later he would be off on his first try at flying around the world.

Before the 1931 season was over, Clyde Pangborn and Hugh Herndon won the $25,000 *Asahi* prize with their flight in a Bellanca monoplane from Japan to Wenatchee, Washington.

The crewcut head of Harold Bromley appeared once more on the transpacific scene before the northern route became the realm of commercial aviation. No man tried harder to achieve a successful flight. After his bad luck with the three wrecked Lockheed Explorers, Bromley had essayed a west-east hop from Japan in 1930, flying a big Emsco monoplane. He'd been driven back by winds and leaking exhaust gases after thirty hours above the ocean.

Two years later the never-give-up lieutenant was in the picture again, flying a Lockheed Vega equipped with a 240-hp Guiberson Diesel engine, an experimental power plant manufactured in Dallas, Texas. With 600-gallon tanks, special dropable landing gear, and a belly skid, the Vega was made ready. Bromley was tired of being made the butt of jokes about his nonsuccess, and once more had Tokyo in mind as a destination. On May 31, 1932, he herded the Lockheed nonstop from New York to Los Angeles, an unofficial distance record for diesel-powered aircraft. But the very next day the Seattle businessmen withdrew their $28,000 prize offer and Harold Bromley never did get to fly across the Pacific as a pioneer pilot.

With a dreary record of failure in North Pacific attempts, Lockheed airplanes waited another two years before being vindicated by two triumphant flights across the South Pacific, the first from west to east. It was fitting that the initial eastward journey above the "Great South Sea" should be made by the man whose name was already synonymous with blazing sky trails in the Pacific—Australia's great airman, Sir Charles Kingsford-Smith.

Smithy—as all his friends called him—had been a Royal Air Force pilot who returned to his homeland "down under" after World War I, determined to get into commercial aviation and to prove the feasibility of air travel.

Though he made others, Kingsford-Smith's Pacific flights brought him his greatest renown, particularly the original journey over the sea between California and Australia. The hop west to Hawaii had been made several times when Smithy and three companions did it in 1928; but when they continued on to Suva and Brisbane in the second hand Fokker *Southern Cross,* the feat captured the imagination of the whole world. Later he went on to circumnavigate the earth, to break the London-Sydney record, and to establish his own airline at home. To the people of Australia and New Zealand, he personified the spirit of aviation, even before his accomplishments had brought him a knighthood.

Thus when a great air race from London to Melbourne was announced in 1934, Smithy naturally felt it was a national challenge: the race should be won by an Australian. He was getting old for air racing—thirty-eight—but this would be a wonderful climax to his career in the air before he settled down to flying a desk. Chief financial sponsor of the race was fellow countryman, Sir MacPherson Robertson. A contraction of his name was given to the event, which became known over the world as the MacRobertson Race. Robertson also wanted to see an Aussie win, and made funds available for purchase of Kingsford-Smith's plane. Additional money for the ship came via public subscription.

Kingsford-Smith shared the Commonwealth spirit of his various backers and therefore would have preferred a

Built for projected Paris hop, Special Sirius was crashed by Capt. George R. Hutchinson, later became Kingsford-Smith's Altair, Lady Southern Cross.

Kingsford-Smith's blue Altair as she appeared Down Under before her name was changed to Lady Southern Cross.

British airplane. But when it was found that nothing suitable would be ready in time, he turned to American manufacturers. There were howls of criticism from advocates of "buy Empire" when their national hero chose a Lockheed Altair with which to enter the race.

His Altair was four years old, having originally been built for an abortive New York to Paris flight by George Hutchinson, and then bought and flown for pleasure by movie director Victor Fleming. Completely rebuilt at the Lockheed factory, the ship was equipped with an early application of power landing flaps. Painted a light blue with silver trim, she was named *Anzac* by Kingsford-Smith in hopes that she would put up a good show for the "diggers" of Australia and New Zealand.

Haste was necessary if he was to participate in the race. The passengers of the S.S. *Monterey* had to forgo deck sports for one voyage when the Lockheed was sent from California to Sydney as deck cargo, lashed to the liner's tennis court. As the fastest airplane ever seen in Australia, the Altair created a sensation on arrival. There was a slight delay when the government forbade use of the name *Anzac*, so she became instead the *Lady Southern Cross*. Then Kingsford-Smith was flying her, breaking intercity records all over the continent. On one Sydney-Brisbane run he gave his famous transpacific Fokker *Southern Cross* a four-hour start, caught up to her en route, and set down in Brisbane ahead of the old veteran.

Smithy and his personable navigator, Captain P. G. (Bill) Taylor, set off for England and the race with high hopes, only to discover at Cloncurry, Queensland, that the aluminum NACA engine cowl was cracked in a dozen places. While a new ring was being fashioned, time ran out for the would-be racers to arrive at the starting line in Britain, and Kingsford-Smith was forced to withdraw as an entry in the MacRobertson classic. With a feeling that he had let down his backers and Australia itself, he commented ruefully: "A nation's hero may often become a nation's whipping boy overnight."

His decision to make the hitherto untried Australia to California flight stemmed from a desire to rehabilitate himself in the eyes of his countrymen. Since the Lockheed had been bought for the race in which he had been unable to compete, the only thing left to do was to take the plane back to the United States, sell it, and return the money to the people who had contributed.

With these thoughts, Smithy and Bill Taylor took off from Brisbane on October 20, 1934, bound for Suva in the Fiji Islands. The tricky thing at the first stop was to land on the 300-yard green turf of the Albert Park Sports Oval, which Smithy, using full flaps, accomplished in half the distance. Then the flyers hopped over to mile-long Naselai Beach, the only spot in the islands from which a heavily loaded plane could possibly leave.

The first attempt to take off from the smooth, gently curving beach almost brought an end to the flight. There was a mean crosswind to contend with as the *Lady Southern Cross* slowly gathered speed and Kingsford-Smith got her tail up. Nearing 60 mph, she started to edge toward the water. With bursts of throttle, Smithy tried to hold the Altair, but the wind had her tail and she swiftly slithered across the wet sands and plunged into the sea.

In an instant the pilot had the engine full out in a shattering roar. Water from the whirling propeller went sluicing back over the Altair as the ocean swirled around her undercarriage and reached the trailing edge of the wing. Skillfully, Australia's greatest airman kept his ship slowly rolling through the softening sands, fighting to come around to the beach and pull her out of the water. Only a moment's hesitation would have seen the plane hopelessly mired and a certain victim of the incoming tide. Helped by Fijian police and willing onlookers, the Lockheed inch by inch gained the level ground above the reach of the waves.

A new takeoff at dawn a few days later was entirely successful, beginning the 3,150-mile over-water journey to Honolulu. No one had ever flown this stretch of ocean before except Kingsford-Smith himself. Bill Taylor's superb navigation kept the *Lady* on continuous course, and the terse radio reports of the pair gave their changing position as they traveled north and east. Using minute coral islands as checkpoints, Smithy and Taylor flew all day. The sun set on nothing but water and a tiny speck in the vast Pacific skies—the blue Altair.

Night brought storms and flying by instruments through torrents of tropical rain. Smithy climbed to 14,000 feet and fumbled for the landing-light switch to get a look at the barrage of water. Suddenly he felt that something was wrong. The needle of his bank-and-turn indicator swung over hard and stayed here. The ship was unaccountably spinning.

The pilot pressed both feet on one rudder pedal, braced and straining until he thought his back would break. He felt searing anger at himself for being unable to do one of the first things a beginner is taught: recovery from a spin. Motor throttled back, the Altair spiraled down eight thousand feet before Smithy was able to regain control. Then, even with the engine full out, the plane would not regain speed or height. Inexorably she dropped through the stormy night, closer and closer to the water. Kingsford-Smith forced himself calmly to survey the instrument panel, and—then he had it. The flaps were down!

In turning on the landing lights, he had accidentally hit the switch of the motor that controlled the flaps. The drag had thrown the ship into the spin and was still braking her. Trouble located, the pilot abruptly halted the aerial struggle and the Wasp immediately stopped laboring, and carried them on once more.

The Hawaiian Islands were the 400-mile-wide target as the big blue monoplane came up on Lanai in the morning sunshine. Changing course, the *Lady* was soon over Diamond Head, then Honolulu, and proceeded to a smooth landing on the green grass carpet of Wheeler Field. With traditional Hawaiian hospitality, Smithy and Bill were soon garlanded with leis.

After repairs to a cracked oil tank and a leaky fuel system, carried out under direction of the United States Army Air Corps, the Lockheed was ready for the final leg of the long flight. On November 3–4 she flew the last 2,400 miles. The speedy Altair brought them to the California coast nearly two hours ahead of their estimated time of arrival. When the *Lady Southern Cross* topped the hills of San Francisco to drop down on Oakland Airport she was the first airplane to fly from Australia to the United States, and Kingsford-Smith the first man to wing his way across the Pacific in both directions.

A second unprecedented conquest of the western seas took place only two months later. Not content with her Atlantic laurels, Amelia Earhart yearned to be the first woman to fly the Pacific. Her old Lockheed hung in Franklin Institute at Philadelphia, but she had a later and almost identical Vega, complete even to her favorite color scheme of deep red and gold.

With this plane, Amelia had in mind a solo flight from Hawaii to the California mainland, something that had never been done before. She turned to a new man for technical assistance: A. Paul Mantz, whose main work at the time was supplying and flying all types of aircraft for the movies, and who was to be a winner of Bendix Races in years to come. A master of all things aeronautical, the knowledgeable Mantz took over the preparation of Miss Earhart's Lockheed.

P. G. Taylor (left) and Sir Charles Kingsford-Smith on the Lady's wing to receive cheers on arrival from Honolulu.

A woman to fly the Pacific alone and two men to help her do it (left to right): technical advisor Paul Mantz; Amelia Earhart; publisher George Palmer Putnam, her husband.

Ocean-hopping pilots of Lockheed Vegas faced an instrument panel similar to this.

The powerful Wasp engine that had powered her across the North Atlantic two and a half years earlier, had been removed before her famous Vega went on exhibit, and was now in her new ship. Additional new features were a propeller with controllable pitch, rubber-encased metal fuel lines, and an inflatable rubber boat.

With no desire to repeat the scary time she'd had over the Atlantic, Amelia insisted on the installation of *two* altimeters on her instrument panel, which also contained an array of just about everything developed to further all-weather flying—except perhaps a robot pilot. Other additions were a two-way radio telephone and an extra fuselage tank.

Amelia Earhart reported later that, compared to the trouble-ridden solo hop from Newfoundland to Ireland, her flight across the Pacific was a joyride. Though a lengthy tropical downpour had drenched the Army's Wheeler Field, the weather east of Hawaii was reported favorable. On January 11, 1935, America's "first lady of the air" climbed aboard her Vega and ran up the faithful Wasp. It sounded perfect, and she nodded to a bedraggled soldier to slosh over and pull the chocks that held her wheels.

Considering the added weight of 520 gallons in the extra fuselage tank, Amelia made a wonderful takeoff. Tail high, the Vega tore down the runway, spewing up cataracts of red-brown mud. Plane and pilot were off in 3,000 feet, less than half the length of the field. Circling over slopes covered with sugar cane, the pilot climbed among the clouds that dotted the late afternoon sky. She would have clouds and fog all the way, but no storms.

Miss Earhart's was the first civilian long-distance flight made with two-way radio telephone equipment. She broadcast her position, or just odd bits of thought that popped into her head, and was entertained in turn by Station KFI of Los Angeles. Among other messages was one from her husband, George Palmer Putnam. He just told his wife to talk a little louder.

Amelia Earhart flew through a night of stars that seemed to rise out of the sea and hang just outside her cockpit window. The new sun soon flared obliquely into her dark sun glasses, and from its position she knew she was on course. Three hundred miles out from San Francisco she spotted a Dollar liner, lined up on its wake, and was tickled to see that all three of her compasses checked with it exactly.

Landfall for Amelia's red monoplane was Pillar Point on the California coast. Pulling up over a notch in the hills, the whole beautiful expanse of San Francisco Bay lay below her. The Vega sailed over San Mateo and sat down on Oakland Airport just 18 hours and 16 minutes out of Hawaii. This time there were cheering thousands to greet the famous woman flyer. Amelia Earhart had become the first person, man or woman, to fly this 2,408-mile stretch of the Pacific Ocean alone.

Oakland turns out to salute a girl and a single-engine wooden monoplane 27½ feet long.

9

GIRDLING THE GLOBE

The idea of setting a record for round-the-world travel originated with French novelist Jules Verne, the top science-fiction man of his day. Verne's imaginary Phileas Fogg accomplished the feat in 80 days. What seemed the impossible in fiction became reality in 1889 when *New York World* reporter Nellie Bly actually went around in 72 days using ground and sea transportation.

With the advent of the airplane, it was in the cards that the record would eventually be whittled down to computation in hours. Four Lockheed Vegas were involved in dashes for globe-girdling honors, and the successful contender became the most famous Vega of all.

The first American to plan a record try completely by airplane was John Henry Mears, a fifty-year-old New York stage producer. Spectacled, balding Mears did not look the part of an adventurer, but getting around the world in the shortest possible time had been his hobby for two decades. As a young man, back in 1913, he'd brought the record again to America, with a trip of a little under 36 days, a mark that stood for thirteen years. When it was finally lowered to 28 days in 1926 by Edward S. Evans and Linton Wells, Mears and Captain C. B. D. Collyer retaliated in 1928 by setting a new record of 23 days, using a folding-wing Fairchild monoplane for all but the two big ocean hops, which they made by steamship. Mears and Collyer were the first Americans to wangle permission to fly clear across Soviet Russia in their own plane, and their negotiations made it easier for others

Mears got a crack pilot, equipped his Vega to cope with everything except old-fashioned bad luck.

who followed to do the same. Charlie Collyer lost his life in a transcontinental speed record attempt the same year.

After only a year the new Mears record was snatched away in 1929 by the big German dirigible *Graf Zeppelin*. John Henry, chafing and fretting, vowed that round-the-world honors would be returned to America. Between theatrical chores he began to make plans for a complete circumnavigation of the globe by air, including the conquest of both the Atlantic and Pacific oceans.

It was a real challenge, and the energetic theater man jumped into it wholeheartedly. He spent hours poring over maps and charts, mastered navigation problems, and learned to operate a little 50-watt radio transmitter. Early in 1930, with his own resources and additional financial backing from friends and newspapers, Mears was ready to go ahead.

The veteran globe-trotter chose as his plane a new Lockheed Vega, a beautiful maroon, cream, and silver job which was duly christened *City of New York* by the wife of the city's mayor, James J. Walker. Big rippling American flags graced both sides of the ship's fuselage, as did the great seals of the world's largest city. Before the $21,000 plane left Burbank she was given a rear navigation hatch and a Pioneer earth inductor compass. Special fittings were added to accommodate the floats that would be installed in Siberia for the switchover to seaplane operation across the Bering Straits to Alaska. Less practical, but notable among his publicity assets, was Mears's mascot, a pert little white Sealyham terrier, Tailwind II, a gift from movie star Mary Pickford.

John Henry Mears and V.I.Pup.

Since Mears was a nonflyer, the greatest problem of his proposed global journey seemed to be the choice of the proper man to occupy the front cockpit. At first John Henry had hopes of obtaining Commander Byrd's well-known Arctic and Antarctic pilot, Bernt Balchen. When that did not work out, he hired Fred Melchior, a Swedish flyer on leave from the Junkers Corporation of America, but technical delays caused the flight plans to drag on and Melchior had to return to his job as chief pilot for the German concern. Mears finally took on Henry J. Brown, the handsome airmail pilot who had won the 1929 National Air Races nonstop derby from Los Angeles to Cleveland, flying the General Tire & Rubber Company's Lockheed Air Express. Brownie took over the controls of the *City of New York* and proceeded to become thoroughly acquainted with her handling.

Early on the morning of August 3, 1930, John Henry and Tailwind piled in among the gas tanks, radio, food, and equipment in the cabin, and Brownie taxied the big red Lockheed out on Roosevelt Field for takeoff.

"See you all in fifteen days!" called Mears.

Even with the human and canine load, plus 338 gallons of gasoline, Brown made a record takeoff: the official timer clocked the *City* as airborne in 30 seconds. With beautiful weather, the trip to the Atlantic jumping-off place, Harbour Grace, Newfoundland, was accomplished in speedy time. The next leg, spanning the ocean to Dublin, Ireland, would be the first crucial one.

Yet, after all the meticulous planning, fine weather predictions, and auspicious start, the *City of New York* was not to be the first Lockheed airplane to circle the globe, or even to fly the Atlantic. Making haste to be on their way to Ireland, Mears and Brown elected to take off a half hour before dawn. The feeble light showed little of the tricky gravel of the Harbour Grace runway, and Brownie made his run diagonally in order to take advantage of a southwest wind. Halfway down the field the thundering Vega lurched into rough ground and a tire blew. Bumping along, the ship tore through brushwood and piles of stones, shedding her landing gear, wing tips, and most of the fuselage bottom before slamming to a stop.

Both Mears and Brown climbed out of the battered wreckage unhurt, but, in the confusion, little Tailwind II disappeared. John Henry seemed more concerned over his missing dog than the loss of his plane and the abrupt conclusion of his global dash. It was two days before the frightened mascot was found in a salt marsh and returned to his relieved and beaming master.

Despite the accident and financial loss, the theater

man's spirits gradually revived, and he began to make new plans to crack the round-the-world record by air. At the Lockheed factory a duplicate Vega was built for him in the spring of 1931. It was identical to the first *City of New York*, except for the application of Detroit Aircraft's wire-braced Hi-Speed landing gear. For his companion this trip, Mears planned to have Vance Breese, then Detroit-Lockheed's ace test pilot. The Vega was painted and ready when the world flyers received a crippling blow to their plans. For some obscure reason the Soviet government refused permission for a new Mears flight across territory of the U.S.S.R. With his trip made impossible, John Henry Mears never took delivery of the second *City of New York*, and went back to being a sedate member of the theater world. His Lockheed became the plane in which Amelia Earhart made her Hawaii-California flight and chalked up subsequent new records.

With Mears out of the running for 1931, the glory road around the world was wide open. Plans were announced by a number of well-known flyers, but the equipment, the international connections for supplies, and the money to swing it were all beyond the reach of most.

An exception among them was little, one-eyed Wiley Post. Like Mears, he was determined to beat the record world flight of the *Graf Zeppelin*, and prove that airplanes, not dirigibles, were the true transports of the future. Wiley had the backing of his boss, Oklahoma oilman F. C. Hall, and he had the use of Hall's personal plane, the sleek white Lockheed Vega *Winnie Mae*, which Post had flown to victory the previous year in the Los Angeles–Chicago nonstop race.

However, despite all his prowess as a pilot, the stocky thirty-one-year-old Oklahoman had never made an over-water flight, and knew only elementary navigation. In setting out to fly around the world, he needed a man along to plot his course. Wiley knew just the one he wanted: a Los Angeles navigation instructor named Harold Gatty.

Dark-haired, serious Gatty was about the same size as Post, but slimmer and three years younger. He hailed from Tasmania, and had attended the Royal Australian Naval College before putting in several years as a navigator on the merchant ships that plied the Pacific. Emigrating to the United States in 1928, Gatty set up a small school to teach navigation to flyers from a sailor's viewpoint. His talent for aerial plotting brought him to the attention of renowned Lieutenant Commander Philip V. H. Weems of the U.S. Navy, who used Gatty theories and calculations in setting up his famous Weems System of Air Navigation.

Art Goebel and Mrs. Charles A. Lindbergh were among the intense little Australian's distinguished pupils, and he laid out transcontinental and transocean courses for flyers like Roscoe Turner and Harold Bromley. As a release from humdrum classes, Gatty was always ready to fly with the pilots he tutored. Bromley induced him to go along on his unsuccessful Japan to Tacoma flight attempt of 1930. Far out over the Pacific the cockpit of Bromley's big Emsco monoplane was flooded with fumes from a leaky exhaust ring. Both Harolds were lucky to survive the struggle to get back to Japan alive. Yet only a few months later Harold Gatty agreed to try to fly around the world with Wiley Post. His thirst for adventure, like Post's, was unquenchable.

Preparations went on for six months, with every last inch of the *Winnie Mae* and her Wasp power plant gone over and double-checked by Lockheed, Pratt & Whitney, and Wiley Post in person. Everyone who ever knew him remembers how Wiley really loved the *Winnie Mae*, and how the slow-moving, laconic Oklahoman always came alive when he was in or around the white, blue-trimmed Vega.

To train himself for the long hours at the controls, Post practiced never sleeping the same hours on any two days of the week. He always said that breaking himself of the habit of regular sleep was far more difficult than piloting an airplane around the world. And for comfort in the sleepless hours to come, Wiley pulled out the straight-backed metal bucket seat of the Vega, and replaced it with a nice roomy armchair.

F. C. Hall cheerfully footed the bills for the extra tanks and alterations that went into the *Winnie Mae*. Before long she had to have a restricted license and the oilman couldn't even ride in his own airplane.

To obtain the proper credentials and permissions, Post and Gatty personally visited the Washington embassies of all the nations over which they expected to fly. Since Russia was not represented in 1931, they negotiated with Moscow through the Amtorg Trading Corporation of New York, and received assurance that the Soviets "would not deter" a flight across their territory, nor would they officially recognize it. All the bills for gas taken aboard in the U.S.S.R. were paid in advance through Amtorg.

After weeks of waiting, Wiley Post and Harold Gatty got away from Roosevelt Field, Long Island, at five o'clock on the morning of June 23, 1931. They flew directly to Harbour Grace, where they stopped only for lunch and to gas up. It was there that Gatty discovered he'd brought only a dollar with him, which quickly went for sandwiches. His account of Post warming up for the Atlantic takeoff gives a typical description of his companion:

"Wiley let the motor roar out its defiance to the 1,900 miles or more of open water which lay beyond the tranquil harbor. He cocked his one good ear to the tune of the exhaust, and his one good eye was glued to the tachometer."

With the benefit of perfect planning, the *Winnie Mae*

Oil streaks on the cowl signal a new record as Harold (left), *Wiley, and* Winnie Mae *pause for a rest.*

proceeded to cross the ocean with no trouble, the first Lockheed airplane to fly the Atlantic. For Wiley Post, who the day before had thought Long Island Sound was quite a stretch of water, the Atlantic seemed endless. Much of the flying was blind because of fogs and clouds; Wiley sat out the long hours, just watching the instruments and keeping the ship straight and level. Occasionally Gatty, busy with his directional calculations and readings of the drift indicator he had invented, would voice a command into the speaking tube—"A little more to the right, Wiley"; or, "A little more to the left."

They flew through the night and into the day, and when Harold's figures showed they were across, Wiley ducked the plane down through the soupy fog and found a darker shadow emerging as land. He put the Vega down on the first airport he saw, the Royal Air Force's Sealand Airdrome in Cheshire, near Liverpool—just 16 hours and 17 minutes out of Harbour Grace, and having flown right over Ireland to England. Since it was constructed for speed, it was not surprising that the Lockheed made the fastest Atlantic crossing up to that time.

Post was so pleased at being across all that ocean that he had to clear his thoughts to remember that the *Winnie Mae* still had to fly on around the world. Hopping on to Hanover and Berlin, the pair got their first sleep in the hotel at Tempelhof Airdrome. Drowsy Wiley thought the noisy reception by the Germans more tiring than flying the Atlantic.

The next day's thousand-mile flight to Moscow was made in nearly ceiling-zero weather. Armed with maps for visual ground reference, Post and Gatty hedgehopped across Poland, East Prussia, and into Russia. High winds and rain, added to no visibility, obliged Post to go on instruments again, with precise instructions from Gatty in the back. Finally the Soviet capital city loomed up on the flat horizon through breaking clouds.

In contrast to the cheering crowds in Berlin, there was only a handful of people at October Airdrome to welcome the American flyers to Moscow. Representatives of an international cultural group took them in tow and insisted they sit down to a formal, nine-course, four-hour dinner. Since the June dawn arrives over the Kremlin at 2 A.M., Wiley and Harold got only about two hours' sleep before plunging on toward the East.

The next three days saw Post and Gatty and the *Winnie Mae* winging their way across four thousand miles of the U.S.S.R. Sometimes they followed the Trans-Siberian Railroad, but for the most part Harold was always kept busy fixing the Vega's exact position and calling the turns of course up to Wiley.

Post fought lack of sleep and the monotony of continuous flight, but he never complained. Plunked in his armchair, he had trained himself to think only of the task at hand, and did it. Gatty suffered mainly from a ravenous appetite, which he was ashamed to admit to his stoic companion.

After nipping across a corner of Manchuria, Wiley thought it might be well to stop for the night and refuel at the Siberian outpost of Blagoveschensk. Oil flares dimly outlined the water-covered field. As usual in landing, Post admonished Gatty to crawl as far back in the tail as he could, and to "hang on like hell!" Mushing down, the Lockheed settled on the inundated airfield, whisking up spray like a seaplane. Mud filled the pants and quickly clogged the wheels. Only Wiley Post's delicate touch kept *Winnie Mae* from doing a fast flip as she slithered and slowed. Trying to keep her going toward a patch of dry ground proved impossible, and the left wheel sank into the sludge—along with Wiley's heart.

Gatty jumped out of the cabin into mud a foot deep and ascertained that the Vega, though bogged, by a miracle was in one piece and upright. While waiting for the arrival of a promised tractor, hungry Harold got in a meal, a hot tub, and a nap. When he got back to the airfield with a basket of food for Wiley, he found that the pilot had slogged out to the mired Lockheed and was sound asleep in his chair. Over twelve hours went by before the ground dried sufficiently to release the *Winnie Mae* from the mud. The tractor never did come from the collective farm, so the task was finally accomplished by two droshky horses and a score of grunting, very wet, and dirty Siberians.

Airborne again, Post and Gatty began to think that perhaps with luck they could win through to New York in even less time than they'd hoped. At Khabarovsk they paused for over twenty-four hours to renew their strength with food and sleep, and to check over the Vega after her grueling hours in the air and her encounter with Siberian mud.

On the longest jump of the flight, nearly 17 hours, they boldly struck out for Alaska. Hail and rain impeded progress, and Gatty discovered that the Russian maps were very hazy as to the exact locations of mountain peaks, to say nothing of their elevations, and Post remarked that "the country was wild enough to scare Dan'l Boone." Beyond the international date line through the Bering Straits the pair had the novel experience of living over again a day just past.

With their landing on the sandy beach at Solomon, Alaska, the flyers were back on U.S. soil. Here again the flight was nearly ended. While taxiing for takeoff, the *Winnie Mae* stuck in the soft sand, her tail lifted, and the whirling propeller smacked the ground. Anxiously, Post jumped down to survey the bent propeller tips, and then proceeded to straighten them with a wrench, a broken-handled hammer and a big, round stone.

The engine was still hot when Harold Gatty swung the mended prop to prime it. The Wasp backfired and the flat side of the blade caught him on the shoulder. Bruised and momentarily dazed, the plucky navigator got up and resolutely climbed back aboard the Vega. Soon the ship was off the shifting sands of Solomon and following the Yukon River up to Fairbanks. Here, while weary Post and aching Gatty snatched four hours of sleep, Alaskan Airways mechanics installed a new propeller they happened to have in stock.

On the homestretch now, the pair set out for Edmonton, Alberta, dodging Alaskan mountains and then blasting for hours through a prairie downpour. Blatchford Field at Edmonton was thoroughly soaked. Looking down, Gatty said a little prayer: "Oh God, not Blagoveschensk again!"

Wiley set the Vega down and, without pausing, half taxied, half flew her to the concrete hangar apron. By this time the eyes of the world were on Post, Gatty, and their *Winnie Mae*, for the flight's progress was being reported on hourly radio bulletins. Busy flying around the world, the men were not prepared for the public reaction that burst over them at Edmonton. In the turmoil of photographers, radio announcers, reporters, and official greeters, somebody stuck a microphone in front of the pilot, whose mind was already occupied with thoughts about mud-soaked airfields. "Say something, Mr. Post!" came the entreaty.

"I'm tired of sitting down," grunted Wiley.

"We're tired and we're dirty," added Harold, "and not much to look at, anyway."

They rested while Edmontonians worked all night to clear a suitable paved runway for the *Winnie Mae*. They took down all the electric cross-wires on the two-mile concrete stretch of Portage Avenue that leads from airport to city, and hauled the Lockheed over for takeoff.

In the dawn light, Post let the Wasp out and charged full tilt down the street. He'd never seen anything like it, and got a new idea of ground speed as curbstones, hydrants, and light poles flashed by the wing tips. Then the white monoplane lifted and was off in a climbing turn over the city, bound for New York.

After a brief stop in Cleveland, Post and Gatty landed the *Winnie Mae* back at Roosevelt Field late in the evening of July 1. When they climbed out, pandemonium let loose, and the bone-weary and disheveled men were nearly mobbed by a seething, cheering crowd, a spontaneous demonstration of acclaim that reflected the relief, joy, and admiration of Americans everywhere.

It was the greatest thing since Lindbergh. The majestic *Graf Zeppelin* was just a poky old paddle wheeler. Wiley Post, Harold Gatty, and *Winnie Mae* had flown around the world in only 8 days, 15 hours, and 51 minutes.

The excitement that followed the Post-Gatty achievement naturally brought new contenders for the record. Most of the flyers who planned hops across the Atlantic, either on paper or in actuality, now added vaguely, ". . . and I'll probably fly on around the world."

Clyde Pangborn and Hugh Herndon tried, but their Bellanca was much slower than a speedy Lockheed. After delays in crossing Siberia they turned from plans to fly around the world and made the first successful, and prize-winning, flight from Japan to the United States.

Owners and pilots of Lockheed planes looked longingly into the possibilities of breaking round-the-world records, but usually gave up the idea when they found out how much money, careful preparation, international

Time out from the limelight to get a fresh paint job and the legend of her achievements—so far.

string-pulling, knowledge, and real stamina would be required. Any detailed study of what Wiley Post and Harold Gatty did always produces even greater respect for their abilities.

But one determined pilot tried twice. He was James J. Mattern, a handsome young daredevil from San Angelo, Texas. Only twenty-six, Jimmie Mattern had been a football player and dance-band drummer, and was a graduate from the Army Air Corps's Kelly Field. His wide grin and wavy dark hair were familiar to Hollywood's stunt-flying fraternity, and later to early airline passengers who droned across the plains of Texas. When San Angelo's Cromwell Airlines quietly folded, Jimmie acquired the company's best ship, a Lockheed Vega, and used it for charter service out of Fort Worth. The long-distance bug had really bitten him in 1931 as a result of being pilot of the refueling plane for the almost-successful Reg Robbins–Hank Jones flight to Tokyo.

A lieutenant in the Reserve, Mattern met Bennett Griffin in Fort Worth while both men were putting in some training time. Bennie Griffin was an Oklahoma City pilot who'd made a good try in the Dole Race to Hawaii in 1927, but had been forced back to Oakland with an overheated engine. He still wanted to vindicate himself with a record flight of some kind, and by teaming with Mattern and the Lockheed, the chances looked good.

It took only ten minutes for the two Reserve officers to agree on making a round-the-world flight, but the actual preparations took ten months. Mattern and Griffin found themselves the heads of a business enterprise—soliciting funds, arguing over contracts, and musing about fuel deposits, visas, and permits. The thorny question of flying over Russia was settled with a $1,500 advance to the Soviets, for which they were to furnish gas, oil, and aid to the world flyers at selected landing spots. Most of the financial backing came from oilmen in the Southwest who saw in Mattern, Griffin, and their Vega a sporting competitor to their friend F. C. Hall and his *Winnie Mae*, being flown by Wiley Post.

Christened *Century of Progress* in honor of the upcoming World's Fair in Chicago, the blue-and-white Lockheed was carefully prepared for her journey. Installation of a rear cockpit in the fuselage just aft of the trailing edge of the wing, containing a duplicate set of instruments and controls, made this the first and only dual-controlled Vega to take to the air.

Jimmie and Grif got away from Floyd Bennett Field on Long Island at 5 A.M. on the morning of July 5, 1932. Nearing Newfoundland, they ran into real pea-soup fog and lost three hours looking for a hole through which to get down and land at Harbour Grace. They refueled and then Mattern, not wishing to tarry, got the Vega rolling and took off into another fogbank. Out over the Atlantic the boys spelled each other at the controls, and kept going east either through the fog or above it.

Mattern and Griffin never saw the ocean, but they spanned it in the record time of 10 hours and 50 minutes, a mark which stood for six years. Wistfully they passed up a landing in England to bore through more fog over the North Sea and continue on to Berlin. This, too, was a record: the first direct flight from America to the German capital. At Tempelhof they took a brief rest, wolfed down a couple of steaks, and set out again.

Despite the speedy beginning, the *Century of Progress* never reached her next scheduled stop. Post and Gatty had been plagued by hellish weather beyond Berlin, but

Century was beating the Post-Gatty time when a hatch started the trouble that ended this way.

Mattern and Griffin went bombing along toward Moscow, by the light of a full moon. Then, without warning, the metal-edged hatch over Jimmie's head tore loose and went hurtling back against the tail of the ship. Fighting to control the damaged stabilizer, Mattern searched for a landing place. Below was a broad field with scattered haystacks that looked as good as any. He brought the Lockheed in for a fast landing to keep control. She touched, rolled, and then the wheels sank in the soft ground to flip the plane over with a splintering crunch. The marshy field in which the Mattern-Griffin flight ended so abruptly was at Borisov, a few miles inside the U.S.S.R.

Everybody else says they did fine: bandaged Jimmie (left center) *and Grif get congratulated during a stop in Germany on their way back home.*

Shaken and soaked with gasoline, the men crawled out of the torn and twisted Vega and surveyed the wreckage.

"Twenty-five thousand dollars gone, and failure—all because of a loose hatch," muttered Jimmie. Then reaction set in, and he and Bennie were both violently sick.

The flyers considered their attempt a flop, but European cities gave them great ovations and receptions in recognition of their fast Atlantic flight to Berlin. With their fee already in hand, the Russians even undertook to crate up the smashed remains of the *Century of Progress,* and return them to the United States.

Jimmie Mattern had a new idea for the next year, but he kept it very secret. He found some new money in Chicago and hired Fred Fetterman, known as "the best man on Lockheeds in the East," to work in a hangar at Floyd Bennett Field to rebuild the wrecked *Century.* The damaged wing was mated with the fuselage taken from a Vega, one of three so-called Stanavo Eagles owned and flown by the Standard Oil Company of New Jersey. The striking paint job it once wore was the inspiration for a new version, applied with artistic detail to the rebuilt *Century:* a giant, glowering red eagle was outlined on both sides of the blue fuselage, with his painted pinions spread over the white wings and his fearsome talons reached out to grip the wheel pants.

The trusty Wasp engine from the original *Century* was supercharged now and tuned fine by Pratt & Whitney. Also installed on the beak of the red-white-and-blue bird was a Hamilton controllable-pitch propeller to swing. Into the cabin and wings went special tanks, including two that had formerly served the *Winnie Mae,* and some from Amelia Earhart's transatlantic Lockheed.

Meanwhile, to a trusted few, Jimmie leaked his big secret. This year there would be no Bennie Griffin to check his navigation, spell him at the controls, or give him cheerful repartee. The tall Texan was going to attempt the first *solo* flight around the world. This was the reason for his months of roadwork and calisthenics, to prepare himself physically, and for the hours spent studying advanced navigation so he could find his way around the globe.

Mattern dropped into the *Century*'s cockpit on June 3, 1933, for another one of those dawn takeoffs. The reporters nearly went wild when they finally learned that Jimmie was going alone, and would attempt to get off with a gross weight of 9,150 pounds. Firing up the Wasp, Jimmie taxied out on Floyd Bennett with 701 gallons of gas aboard. He poured on the coal, eased more than four and a half tons of wood, metal, and gasoline into the sky, and streaked into the northeast.

Out over the Atlantic for a second time, Jimmie encountered the perils met by his predecessors. Ice formed on his wings. To get rid of it in a hurry he put the Vega in a power dive, and down she went, gathering momentum with the load of sleet. At 2,000 feet he gingerly tried to level off.

CRACK!

With a report like a cannon, the thin plywood covering on one wing split from spar to spar. Jimmie sat frozen, expecting the whole wing to tear off at any moment. Now he was down on the deck, flying blind about three hundred feet above the fog-shrouded, black water. The ice began to melt away. After five minutes the rigid pilot decided the wing was going to hold.

Dawn brought some relief, but the *Century of Progress* wasn't across the Atlantic yet. Mattern got her back up to 6,000 feet—only to have the engine quit. In the sudden silence he frantically pushed and pulled the throttle, steadily losing altitude. Perhaps leaning the mixture might have made the Wasp backfire, but Jimmie didn't think of it. He just couldn't think of anything. Eight hundred feet above the ocean she did backfire, all by herself. Falter—backfire—then the revs started and the engine took hold. Once more Jimmie Mattern was sure his heart had stopped completely.

Fighting to avoid more fog and storms, the flyer found himself edging north of his original planned course to Paris or Berlin. Finally he identified a rugged strip of coast as Norway and started in search of Oslo. Shaken and unable to compute his navigation tables properly, the exhausted Texan landed at Jomfruland Island on the shore of the Skagerrak. Somehow he put the Vega down safely on a boulder-strewn beach.

For several hours Jimmie Mattern, curled up sound asleep in a lighthouse keeper's cottage, did not know, or care, that he had just flown 4,100 miles, a new solo nonstop distance record, and completed the first direct air trip from New York to Norway.

The Mattern grin and the fierce new Century *in 1933.*

Horses hauled the grounded Lockheed to a better stretch of beach, and a revived Mattern left for Moscow after a short stop at Oslo. In the Russian capital he patched his split wing. He also discovered the cause of the heart-stopping engine failure over the Atlantic: a tiny piece of straining felt had temporarily clogged the gasline.

Jimmie had three hours of sleep and took off at midnight for Omsk, thundering over the Urals in an inky storm with lightning snapping at his wing tips. His tired body was temporarily refreshed by a sauna bath at Omsk, but the pace was beginning to tell on both man and airplane. The quick succession of 1,800-mile solo hops was too much.

In his own recollection, Mattern's flight soon became a vague series of landings, takeoffs, and accidents. There had been a damaged shock cord at Omsk. Next, on the way to Chita, a gasline broke, and Jimmie nearly passed out from the fumes. In the ensuing forced landing he damaged the *Century*'s tail, and had to wait while Siberian mechanics were sent to fix it—using iron rods and shoe boxes, all carefully glued in place with a fabric of old shirts. On the next hop of 2,000 miles the fagged-out pilot was unable to concentrate enough to find the way to Khabarovsk; he decided to put the ship down in the Amur River and call it a day. Mattern piled pillows around his head to reduce injuries and brought the Vega in over a low, treeless island in midriver, fully expecting to ground loop in the soft sand. Surprisingly, the ship touched and rolled to a safe stop. Trembling with relief, Jimmie crawled out and fell fast asleep on the ground.

He awoke to find himself surrounded by curious Siberians who had crossed to the island in rowboats. They appeared delighted by the presence of this mechanical eagle, which had dropped in, and arranged a supply of tractor gasoline and crude oil to speed Mattern on his way. Clanking and belching smoke, the ill-used Wasp managed to haul Jimmie and the Vega on to Khabarovsk.

At the Siberian jumping-off place for Alaska, Mattern was restored with food and sleep and heartened by his continued, and phenomenal, good luck in the face of mishaps. Jimmie was already well behind the Post-Gatty time, but still had hopes of setting a solo record that would be difficult to top. He took off for Nome at 4 A.M. despite adverse weather forecasts. Sure enough, a solid wall of icy clouds 800 miles out turned him back the whole weary way to Khabarovsk and the need to make a fresh start.

On their second try the Vega and its game pilot got across the Sea of Okhotsk, over the badly mapped Siberian mountain ranges, and within four hours of a return to the American continent. Then, over the desolate Arctic tundra near the Anadyr River, the oil lines froze and the luck of Jimmie Mattern's solo world flight finally ran out.

His crash the previous year had him still worried about flipping over, so Mattern tried an unorthodox maneuver. He flew the faltering Vega, wide open, close to the ground and knocked off the landing gear. Then he belly-landed the ship on the frozen tundra, sliding along like a toboggan till the engine was forced back and buckled under as she stopped.

Except for a sprained ankle, Jimmie was safe and in good shape. But with only three chocolate bars to eat, his situation on the deserted plain soon became desperate. For a few days he lived in the wrecked Lockheed. Then he hobbled down to the wide Anadyr River in hopes of rescue. He fashioned a grass hut, insulating it with his maps, and slept fitfully on the warm ashes left by his fires until the frost seeped through again to wake him. Thousands of mosquitoes swarmed about him.

For food, Mattern at last shot a duck, only to have it stolen by gulls while he went back to his plane for an engine cylinder to use as a cooking pot. A muskrat proved almost inedible, as did some eggs he found. Seeking to move to a better position from which to attract attention, the stranded flyer made a raft from driftwood, lashed by control cables from the Vega. It soon capsized in the icy water and floated away. When Jimmie tried to dry himself his clothes caught fire and he had to jump again into the frigid river.

A second makeshift raft finally floated the determined Texan to an island in midstream. On his fourteenth day alone he built a fire which caught the underbrush and soon swept the entire island. Smoke and flames at last attracted a family of Eskimos who were making their annual trip down the Anadyr, and Jimmie was saved. The hungry pilot had been dreaming of orange juice and a salad, but was very happy to partake of dried fish. The Eskimos took him downriver with them, fascinated by the zipper of his heavy flying suit. It was July 5 before they reached the Bering Sea trading post of Anadyr, and the world learned that Jimmie Mattern was alive after all.

There were still complications in getting the lucky flyer

The eagle Vega bites the dust on Arctic tundra, and this time no parts get shipped home to be used again.

Never-say-die Jimmie Mattern takes tea with friends while he waits for a Russian lift to Nome.

back to American soil. He had friends with planes in Nome, but the Soviet government insisted that one of their own flyers should be allowed to bring Mattern out of Siberia. They dispatched a crack Army pilot, Sigmund Levenevsky, clear across Russia from the Black Sea with a seaplane to fly Jimmie over to Nome. While waiting for Levenevsky, Mattern and an English-speaking Russian went back the eighty miles up the Anadyr River and salvaged the engine and instruments from the wrecked *Century of Progress*. They were crated for shipment to New York, via Moscow, but Jimmie never saw them again.

Mattern breezed into New York City on July 30, 1933, fifty-seven days after he'd left in the other direction. He was flying a borrowed Lockheed, the metal Stanavo Vega, painted like Jimmie's *Century* to resemble an eagle. It was en route from Toronto that Mattern made the first international radio broadcast from an airplane.

While Jimmie Mattern of Texas was preparing for his solo effort, Wiley Post of Oklahoma got back in the limelight with the *Winnie Mae*. The famous Vega now belonged to Wiley, as its generous owner, F. C. Hall, had given him title. Post announced that he proposed to fly around the world again—this time alone.

Jimmie Mattern trained himself rigorously with early morning roadwork and calisthenics. Wiley's physical preparations consisted of his own peculiar methods of sleep training, or "un-training." When told how Jimmie was hardening up his muscles, Post wryly remarked that the muscles Mattern was hardening "weren't the ones he was going to sit on during a solo trip around the world." The quiet Oklahoman would often go on all-night fishing excursions with congenial company and a couple of bottles of beer.

Post certainly had a high regard for Harold Gatty, but he decided to dispense with a navigator for the 1933 attempt. The available charts of Russia were practically useless, and much of the long trip would be seat-of-the-pants flying at low altitudes anyway. Wiley intended to put his faith in something new: the Sperry Automatic Pilot. This little black box, developed by gifted inventor Lawrence Sperry, would faithfully hold a plane on course, even while the pilot catnapped.

Installing the automatic pilot in the confines of the *Winnie Mae*'s cockpit was no mean feat, and at one time six men from the Sperry plant were crowded into the Vega, twisted like pretzels as they conducted careful ground tests of the device. A directional radio, lent by the U. S. Army, was another valuable asset. And to reduce lubrication problems, Pratt & Whitney service representative Ray Peck hooked up eighteen pieces of copper tubing with grease fittings, so the pilot could grease the engine's rocker boxes directly from his cockpit seat. Post had a fuel and advertising agreement with Socony-Vacuum Oil for this trip, and the firm's Flying Red Horse trademark appeared on the repainted *Winnie Mae*.

Jimmie Mattern had gone, been lost, and finally reported safe by the time Post was satisfied that his Lockheed was ready to fly. On Saturday morning, July 15, 1933, he lifted the *Winnie Mae* off Floyd Bennett Field in just 29 seconds, using only 1,900 feet of runway in "the best takeoff ever seen of any Atlantic flyer."

Pratt & Whitney's Lionel Clark, who had been handling Wiley's plane and preparations as well as his engine, was ready to go to bed for two days. "And there was Wiley,

The P&W modified Wasp C, now displayed with Winnie Mae *in the National Air Museum, powered the Vega throughout her entire career of record-making flights.*

Post ready in July 1933: Winnie Mae *has a cabin full of solo equipment, new lower hatch.*

bright as a daisy, starting out to fly around the world!" recalls Clark.

Partly by dead reckoning, and partly by tuning his radio to a special broadcast put on by a London radio station, Post shot up to Newfoundland, across the ocean, and on to Tempelhof Airdrome in 25 hours and 45 minutes. Wiley and his Lockheed Vega were the first man and airplane to fly nonstop from New York to Berlin.

Using the autopilot, Post had plans for a global circuit in just five hops: Berlin, Novosibirsk, Khabarovsk, Fairbanks, and New York, with maybe a stop in friendly Edmonton "if he was tired." He made the first one all right, but had to compromise on the rest. All the way, it was a 15,596-mile trip.

Violent storms forced the one-eyed pilot to land in both Königsburg, Germany, and again at Moscow. The Sperry pilot, good as it was, conked out twice, leaving the flying over the great Russian hinterlands strictly up to the wonderful Post stamina. It was finally repaired by Siberian mechanics at Irkutsk, who also soldered a leaky oil line while the Oklahoman snatched a few hours of sleep. After waiting out a rainstorm, Post roared into Khabarovsk ahead of schedule. It was amazing, but he began to see that he had a chance not only to establish a solo record, but to beat his own mark, the one set with Gatty two years before.

Wiley headed up the Siberian coast toward the Bering Strait with his autopilot functioning perfectly. The faithful Wasp droned on and on, and the white, blue-winged Vega passed high above forbidding mountains, seas, and Arctic tundraland, her human pilot nodding but confident.

The interior of Alaska was a jumble of mountains and streams that were hard to identify. Which was the Yukon? Wiley circled and peered, and at last made out a landing strip beside some radio towers. He came around, lined up on what passed for a strip—it was only 700 feet long—and set the Vega down. The *Winnie Mae* bounced, rumbled along, shed a wheel pant, cracked her landing gear, and went up on her nose in the gravel.

It looked like the end of Wiley Post's solo trip around the world. The controllable-pitch propeller had dug in and was bent beyond repair. The place where Wiley had come down was Flat, Alaska, a remote mining camp.

All the miners in Flat wanted to help. They put Post to bed in the radio shack and made temporary repairs to the cracked landing gear. Then they relayed a message to Fairbanks asking for more-specialized aid. It was veteran bush pilot Joe Crosson who got the word, found an old fixed-pitch propeller, then flew it to Flat along with two mechanics to help install it while Post slumbered. They worked all night removing the bent prop and installing the substitute. Joe led *Winnie Mae* in to Fairbanks for a stopover, then Wiley was off again six hours later.

The weather on the Alaskan-Canadian border gave Post and his plane one last punch. The clouds hung low, the rain came down in sheets, and pilot and autopilot flew blind for seven hours. As it had on his flight with Gatty, mud awaited him at Blatchford Field in Edmonton. There Wiley took a rest, guarded by Mounties as he lay with an icepack on his head, which ached from high altitudes. The Vega was fueled and trundled over onto Portage Avenue, for a repeat of his touch-and-go departure two years earlier. Soon he was flashing past light poles again for another takeoff down the street, straight toward the city.

Late that night the Lockheed and Wiley Post touched down at Floyd Bennett Field in New York, to be greeted by a thunderous reception.

The unbelievable had happened. The little man with the white eyepatch, all alone, had piloted a single-engined airplane all around the world in just 7 days, 18 hours, and 43 minutes. Racing over wide oceans and broad continents, Wiley Post and the *Winnie Mae* had cut twenty-one hours off their previous record, and gained for all time a place among aviation's immortals.

10

LONGER, FASTER, HIGHER

It was a certainty from the first that Lockheed planes would be used to establish other types of records in addition to those for long-distance and transocean flying. During the routine use and testing of the ships, there were many opportunities that could not be ignored.

Not long after the establishment of the factory in Burbank, the Lockheed company had a persistent visitor. Out of a job, and enamored of the speedy streamlined ships that were regularly appearing at the shop doors, ex-Army pilot Herbert J. Fahy hung around the front office for weeks. Short, wavy-haired Herb was a fine fellow, but nobody knew much about his flying ability. Allan Loughead occasionally gave him short check hops and ferry jobs just to keep him off the doorstep. Fahy undertook every such chore with enthusiasm.

With production increasing, Lockheed couldn't go on using the part-time services of airline pilots like Larry Fritz or Dole Race winner Art Goebel. A regular factory test pilot was needed to make first flights, demonstrations, and an occasional sales junket. Herb Fahy's doggedness finally won him the assignment.

The former lieutenant turned out to be a pretty good choice. In addition to his persistence and growing experience, he had another asset useful to Lockheed publicity. This was his wife, Claire, a "pert and comely aviatrix," in the language of the twenties. As The Flying Fahys the couple attracted attention both to themselves and their demonstrator wherever they flew. Dark-haired, bouncy

Lee Shoenhair after he and Miss Silvertown *flashed over a Florida beach to cop six world speed marks in 1930.*

Mrs. Fahy was quite likely the first woman to take the controls of a Lockheed Vega.

A test pilot, with big things ahead, Fahy had high hopes of joining the ranks of the transatlantic flyers and globe-trotters. Though this was not to be, Herb did establish a mark unique in Lockheed history: over May 28–29, 1929, he chalked up a world's solo endurance record, made without refueling.

Using a stock Whirlwind-powered Lockheed rigged with auxiliary tanks, Fahy talked the ever-willing Richfield Oil Company of California into supplying his 435 gallons of gas. In return they got a pair of RICHFIELD—THE GASOLINE OF POWER decals slapped on the fuselage where they would show up nicely in news photographs.

Herb liked to fly in old sneakers, a beat-up jacket, and a green celluloid eyeshade to shield his wide brow from the encroaching California sun. In this outfit, and packing sandwiches and coffee, he climbed aboard the stock demonstration Vega at Los Angeles Metropolitan Airport.

The takeoff was tricky, for the ship's 41-foot wing had to lift a total of 5,888 pounds. After that, all the test pilot had to do was to set the Vega level and circle around and around the Los Angeles County landscape—and keep awake. This went on all day, all night, all the next day. Fahy ate lightly and sipped his java sparingly. The night hours were of course the worst, particularly when the navigation lights of the plane failed and the pilot continued on in the dark. He stayed well above and away from the hills, always keeping the airport lights in sight. With daylight, the hours dragged and the Whirlwind engine droned on and on, and Herb's eyes fought to stay open under their shade. Jubilant watchers below cheered and signaled as the orange Vega passed the old official mark and continued its endless circling for more than an hour beyond the unofficial record. At last, and with its gas tanks nearly empty, Fahy set the Lockheed down.

Herb's eyes were just slits when he cut the faithful Whirlwind and clambered out. In chic flying togs, Claire Fahy broke through the crowd to hug the record-breaker. He'd been airborne, all by himself, for 36 hours, 56 minutes and 36 seconds.

Though he coaxed dozens of Lockheeds aloft on their maiden flights, the endurance test was the high point of Herb Fahy's career. He tried unsuccessfully for the transcontinental record in Lockheed's Air Express *Black Hornet;* he talked about a flight from New York to Rome. Then he and Claire were going to fly around the world in less than the twenty-one days required by the *Graf Zeppelin.* But, as for so many such projects, financial backing was not forthcoming. The Flying Fahys kept on with their jobs —Herb flying Lockheeds for Detroit Aircraft and Claire demonstrating Eastman Flying Yachts for another branch of Detroit's loosely knit amalgamation of aircraft companies.

Weary Herb Fahy blinks in the sunlight as helmeted wife, Claire (right of propeller), *rushes to greet him after his nearly 37-hour endurance flight in May 1929. Fahy died in crack-up of Sirius demonstrator the following year.*

In a hazardous profession, it was inevitable that Herb should have his share of crack-ups working for Detroit-Lockheed. He twice escaped unhurt when Vega demonstrators were washed out, and miraculously suffered only a broken elbow in the crash of the second Explorer *City of Tacoma.* Then tragedy struck at last on April 25, 1930. Demonstrating a brand-new Sirius, Herb and Claire tried to get off from a rough field at Roscommon, Michigan. The low-winged plane struck a brush pile, nosed over, and crashed on its back. Claire Fahy was uninjured, but Lockheed's first chief test pilot died in a hospital without regaining consciousness. Mrs. Fahy was killed later the same year, when the engine of her Waco Taper Wing stalled on takeoff at Tonopah, Nevada.

Not so attractive to the public as competitive racing, but important to engine and aircraft manufacturers, were speed trials against time. Speed tests for a certified world's record were costly and exacting projects because they meant close supervision by qualified observers and timers who were accredited by both the National Aeronautic Association (NAA) and the fifty-three-nation Fédération Aéronautique Internationale (FAI). Official timers were supposed to receive a $25 fixed fee, but many dedicated persons donated their services in order to be on hand where aviation history was being made.

Many American pilots got their first experience with the metric system during time trials. Bags of sand for the loads were weighed out in kilograms on approved scales; exact courses were carefully measured in kilometers. Special watches were used, and barographs installed in the airplanes to affirm that the runs were made at specified altitudes.

Leland F. Shoenhair, chief pilot for the B. F. Goodrich Company, scanned some of the hundreds of records on the international books and decided to give the United States a better representation. Lee had in mind the speed records with various exact payload weights held by a British De Havilland Hound and a French Nieuport-Delage. Goodrich's Vega, the Wasp-powered *Miss Silvertown,* should be able to do better than the existing marks of almost 160 mph set by the European airplanes.

As a good straightaway course for his attempt, NAA picked a stretch of Atlantic coastline between Mayport and Saint Augustine, Florida. It was already a favorite spot for automobile speed trials, for its long, level beach measured the prescribed 50 km, or approximately 31 miles.

Shoenhair came down from Ohio in the white, blue-trimmed Lockheed, its supercharged Wasp engine tuned and ready for the speed runs. Officials sacked out bags of white Florida sand, and stowed 550 kg (1,102 lbs) around the center of gravity in *Miss Silvertown's* cabin. Then, delicate stopwatches in hand, they manned pylons at the ends of the beach, and kept in touch by telephone.

The rubber company's pilot blasted the Vega around five laps of the course. Despite the drag of an unlatched cabin door, he set two world's speed-load records on February 18, 1930. Four more marks fell two days later when the sandbags were increased to 1,000 kg—over a ton. Lee's best times were an average speed of 185.452 mph for 100 km (62 miles) carrying 500 kg, and 175.997 with 1,000 kg.

Flying the shoreline route straight and level, back and forth, Shoenhair urged every ounce of speed from the Vega, flashing over the heads of the timers for over four hours. People on the beach at Jacksonville thrilled to the sight of the bullet-shaped Lockheed tearing along just a few feet above the sand, engine roaring wide open.

"Here he comes!" they yelled; and, almost in the same breath, "there he goes!"

Lee flew back to Akron with the successful speed-load time trials in the bag and resumed his routine duties as pilot for the Goodrich company. Lockheed, Pratt & Whitney, and the United States all had six new world's records to boast of—and did.

In the meantime, America's "first lady of the air," Amelia Earhart, was not resting in her efforts to put women in aviation on an equal footing with men. In November 1929 she was in California, and welcomed her first chance to fly a Vega with the greater horsepower of the Wasp engine.

The factory put at her disposal a cowled and panted demonstrator just two days out of the shop. This was a gleaming white Vega Executive model, complete with chemical toilet and stenographic equipment. Amelia rev-

Amelia Earhart with the man to satisfy—NAA timer Joe Nikrent. Satisfy him she did, as the drawing and headline of a Lockheed advertisement (bottom) *indicate.*

AMELIA EARHART—
"first lady of the air"
Flies a Lockheed-Vega

eled in the pep of the 425 horses up front, and it was easy to get her to try to beat the existing women's speed record of 156 mph.

With bespectacled Joe Nikrent of NAA to time her, tousle-haired Miss Earhart whipped the spotless Vega around an abbreviated 3-km course at Los Angeles Metropolitan Airport, averaging 184.17 miles an hour. It was Amelia's first official record as a pilot, and her elation is reflected in her otherwise matter-of-fact logbook: "Speed run, 197 mph on one leg. Hooray!"

The following June, America's best-known woman flyer got another crack at the international records for women. She went to Michigan to fly the first Duralumin-fuselage Vega turned out by the assembly shops of Detroit Aircraft, testing a new NAA course near Grosse Isle Airport south of the city. The sun got in Amelia's eyes during the first trials: she whacked a bird and then missed a pylon. The next day brought better results.

Though not as fast as the wooden Lockheed she'd flown at Los Angeles, the metal job performed admirably with varied loads and distances, and set up three more records for Miss Earhart—who was now, without question, the world's speediest woman.

Brown-haired, blue-eyed Ruth Nichols wasn't blessed with either the instant fame or the financing Amelia acquired so readily, but she was just as determined to make her mark. Friendly competition between the two began during the Women's Air Derby of 1929, and for a while both girls were out after any and every record they could establish. Amelia's publicity was ready made, and sponsors sought her out. It was different with Ruth: though it went against her quiet Quaker instincts, Miss Nichols had to court the headlines in order to attract financial backing. Her situation was emphasized by the legend below the cockpit of her Vega, *The New Cincinnati*: THIS SHIP IS LOANED TO MISS RUTH NICHOLS BY THE CROSLEY RADIO CORPORATION.

In their forthright efforts to set records, make "firsts," and "beat Amelia," Ruth and her brilliant aeronautical advisor Clarence Chamberlin thought of all the angles. Spring of 1931 found them preparing the Crosley Vega for Ruth's projected transatlantic flight, and they needed to know just what the ship would do. They were constantly testing such innovations as adjustable-pitch propellers, high-compression pistons, bigger and better superchargers, all in addition to other special gear.

The Earhart speed record loomed large as the one to beat. Colonel Chamberlin devised new wire-braced landing gear for the *Cincinnati* and fitted the Goodyear Airwheels with small, close-fitting wheel pants. To avoid all possible drag, even the door handle and the shoe on the tail skid were removed. The souped-up Wasp engine, with an injection system of pure oxygen, was rated at 600 hp. Tuned to top shape, both engine and airplane responded promptly to the slightest whim of the woman in the pilot's seat.

The level land near Carleton, Michigan, had by now been established as the official NAA site for speed runs. Early on the morning of April 13, 1931, Ruth Nichols made her record try with the powerful Crosley Lockheed. To mark the beginning and end of the 3-kilometer course, two big white sheets had been spread, still warm from the bed of one of the yawning officials. Electrical instruments were used, and the requirements entailed sweeping over the timers at the 500-foot level, with round trips to offset any help from a prevailing wind.

Four times Ruth dived her ship with wide-open throttle to gain maximum speed, leveled off above the trees and tore along the straight course from bedsheet to bedsheet. The plane rocked and swayed in the bumpy post-dawn air, and the woman flyer had to grip the stick with both hands and her knees to keep the red-and-cream Vega on a steady run.

The results were heartening: 210.685 mph—over 25 mph better than Amelia's record of the previous year. Miss Earhart did not attempt to regain her speed title, as she had recently acquired a husband, the use of a new autogiro, and more dreams of conquering oceans.

A month before breaking Amelia's speed mark Ruth Nichols had set a different type of record with *The New Cincinnati*. This was a high-altitude flight, which took place on a bright windy day in March.

To combat subzero temperatures expected in the upper atmosphere, Miss Nichols wore an outfit that was colorful both inside and out. Consensus had it that she was attired in: long underwear, a green sports skirt, four sweaters ranging in color from old rose to lavender, and a heavy borrowed flying suit of reindeer hide; with finishing touches of a tartan muffler, fur-lined flying helmet with badger flap, beige wool hose, two layers of wool skating socks, reindeer-hide socks with the fur turned inward, beaded reindeer boots and mittens—and, finally, a parachute. The general effect was that of an extremely well-padded Eskimo.

Churning a special 10½-foot propeller, Ruth jumped the Lockheed off the tiny Jersey City Airport with a run of just 92 feet. With only 50 gallons of gas aboard, in 1 minute flat she was up to 2,200 feet and making a turn over the skyscrapers of New York. The Vega climbed and climbed, heading west above the New Jersey hills. Fighting a vicious headwind, Ruth was soon far above the clouds, with familiar landmarks blotted out far below. She was fairly comfortable until she reached 20,000 feet; then her clumsy clothing could not keep out the chill from the −50 degree temperature just outside the little cockpit windows. Also, her oxygen equipment was primitive: she simply stuck a tube in her mouth, and gulped from a steel tank strapped to the wing outside. Soon her tongue lost all sense of feeling.

Ruth bundles up for high altitudes in 1931.

Nearing the top of her climb, Ruth shot new life into the stuttering Wasp with a stream of pure oxygen to the carburetor. The engine coughed, cleared, and the Lockheed shot up another 500 feet. With the two-ton plane literally hanging on the prop, the sky above turned the darker blue of the stratosphere and the altimeter quivered at 30,000 feet.

Six miles up, the engine suddenly quit cold—out of gas. Numb and light-headed, the girl frantically fumbled for the reserve tank switch while the Vega plummeted down like a lead weight. Dizzily she pushed the throttle open, and to her relief the Wasp caught and roared again. Now it was a matter of getting down to earth before the precious five-gallon reserve supply was exhausted.

Ruth dived through the deep cloud layer, peering for New Jersey. She emerged into sunshine—and a wide expanse of open ocean. Despite the Lockheed's 200 mph, and a continuous westward heading, the angle of ascent had been so steep, and the headwind so strong, that the ship had been, in effect, traveling backwards at forty miles an hour! The same head-wind had gobbled up the gas at an alarming rate.

The bemused pilot searched the seascape in every direction, and with relief made out the tall spires of lower Manhattan in the distance dead ahead. In a few minutes the concrete canyons were echoing as the Vega thundered low, squeaking across the Hudson, the ferry slips, and the ridge to a straight-on approach to the Jersey City field. Ruth slipped in over the wires and rolled to a stop.

Miss Nichols's tongue was so stiff from cold as to seem frozen, and after Mrs. Chamberlin peeled her out of some of her gay padding she found it hard to stand alone. Coffee and conversation, however, brought her back to normal. The official record was checked out as 28,743 feet: *The New Cincinnati* had taken her higher than any woman had ever flown before.

Still another superlative remained for Ruth to achieve. Six months later she flew farther than any woman had flown before. Jacketed upright in a steel corset she had been wearing since her Atlantic flight crack-up in June, the spunky woman got her rebuilt Lockheed off the airport in Oakland, California. She headed high over the Rockies on a tougher route than any plotted for previous transcontinental attempts, and came down some 1,977 miles east, at Louisville, Kentucky, 14 hours later.

Back in Jersey City, Clarence Chamberlin was experimenting with an older Lockheed Vega of his own, a Christmas present given him by Mayor Karl Van Wagner of Teaneck, New Jersey, and G. Frank Croissant of New York. The famed transatlantic flyer fitted the ship with a 225-hp diesel engine on loan from the Packard Motor Company. The diesel was dependable and rugged, but it had an alarming tendency to blow out its glow plugs, used in igniting the fuel. Whenever this occurred, there would be long plumes of black smoke streaming back along the side of the Vega. Startled spectators below often dashed wildly to the nearest phone with a report of an airplane "on fire" or "being shot down." Colonel Chamberlin usually referred to the experimental craft as his "flying furnace," but he christened her *Miss Teaneck*.

While her Crosley Vega was being reconstructed, Ruth Nichols often flew the diesel job, and once took it on a Midwest speaking tour. She reported that seven out of ten instruments were jarred out of kilter by the pounding Packard up front. The odor of diesel fuel permeated both cockpit and cabin, so that both the luggage and the lady herself were always slightly redolent of the oil fields. Happily, Ruth possessed both a sense of humor and a strong stomach. Fingering her slim pocketbook, she overcame her distaste for the smelly engine when totting up her expenses for the trip: the flying furnace had hauled her some three thousand miles at a fuel cost of just $15.12.

One of the first things Colonel Chamberlin tried with his Christmas present was to see how high it would go. The diesel-powered Lockheed climbed nearly 3 miles in 16 minutes, and on January 24, 1932, he got her up to 19,393 feet over Floyd Bennett Field on Long Island. Three Sundays later Miss Nichols braved the clatter and odor of the Packard. Pointing the sooty cylinders skyward, she topped Clarence by nearly 2,000 feet, and returned to earth with a new American altitude record for diesel-engined aircraft—21,300 feet, the best for both men *and* women.

Ruth thought little at the time about the height she'd reached with the flying furnace. But her new recognized mark of 19,928 feet was duly filed by the Fédération Aéronautique Internationale.

Today this offbeat achievement is the only unsurpassed official record still in the name of the much-admired Ruth Nichols, and the only one still held by a Lockheed Vega.

Another famous flyer was also interested in the high altitudes—not just for brief visits, but as a place where air travel of the future might be easier. Wiley Post, after two record-breaking trips around the world, was still flying his veteran Vega *Winnie Mae* in 1934. He also took on experimental chores as an occasional mail pilot for TWA.

For a while, Wiley contemplated competing in the MacRobertson Race from England to Australia in 1934, and even filed his entry. But the lure of the great spaces "up where the air is thin" proved a greater challenge. Post worked with Goodrich Rubber engineers on an altitude suit that would keep him alive at heights above 50,000 feet. By today's standards of G-suits and pressurized clothing for Mercury astronauts, it was a clumsy affair, resembling a diver's equipment with laced, clumping rubber boots and a clamped-on tank helmet. Wiley planned to keep it inflated with pressure from the engine blower and a mixing tank of liquid oxygen between his feet. Heating elements were sewn into the suit to keep the flyer warm.

The outfit looked so weird, with little Wiley peering dubiously through the circular face plate, that it was only natural for the reporters to call the getup Post's "man from Mars" suit. Primitive as it was, it set the pace for future use of pressurized clothing for fighter pilots, and was another contribution to aviation for which Wiley Post received far too little credit.

In 1934, Italy held the world's altitude record with an official mark of 47,352 feet. Sponsored by the Pure Oil Company, the little Oklahoman with the eyepatch went

Diesel-powered "flying furnace" is long gone, but unique record made by Ruth Nichols in 1932 still stands.

Ruth Nichols hopes to add more records to Akita's list after rebuild by Chamberlin with wing 14 inches lower, belly skid, and bubble cockpit, but one-of-a-kind "sunken-wing" Vega, cracked-up November 1932, never flew again.

after it, with his attempt billed as one of the features of the Chicago World's Fair then in progress. Over South Bend, Indiana, at 42,000 feet the supercharger quit completely, and no record was established.

Back in Oklahoma, Post next found a backer in oilman Frank Phillips, and the *Winnie Mae* acquired the PHILLIPS 77 AVIATION GASOLINE decals she still wears today. Twice more Wiley tried his suit and ascended to the dark-blue heights. The first time the prop control froze at 51,000 and the "man from Mars" could nose the Vega no higher. On the second try the altimeter froze, but the barograph recorded an unofficial 55,000 feet.

Post really wanted to know not only how high the regions of the upper air could be penetrated, but also what speed a plane might obtain in flying cross-country at those altitudes. Even a five-year-old Lockheed might be faster than more powerful, modern ships if flown in the substratosphere.

Remodeled at Phillips Field in Bartlesville, Oklahoma, the well-traveled *Winnie Mae* was shorn of struts and teardrop wheel fairings, and fitted with dropable landing gear. A tough metal belly skid was attached to the bottom of the fuselage. The big Wasp engine which had twice flown around the world was modified with an additional supercharger, a rear-end blower, and the first pressurized ignition system.

Washington's Birthday 1935 found Post and the *Mae* at Burbank ready to make a try at the transcontinental nonstop speed record, cruising at substratosphere height. After takeoff, Wiley released the landing gear, hurtled upward, and went speeding along in the silence inside his space suit, unable to hear anything except his own heartbeat.

Barely forty miles out, the engine began to heat up and the oil pressure dropped. Wiley, his good eye fixed anxiously on the instrument panel, began swearing fervently. Feathering the prop to a horizontal position with a special crank, he looked down to locate a proper place to skid the Lockheed in on her belly.

Below stretched Muroc Dry Lake, the vast, thirty-mile stretch of featureless flatland where so many planes have been test-flown. H. E. Mertz, proprietor of Muroc's

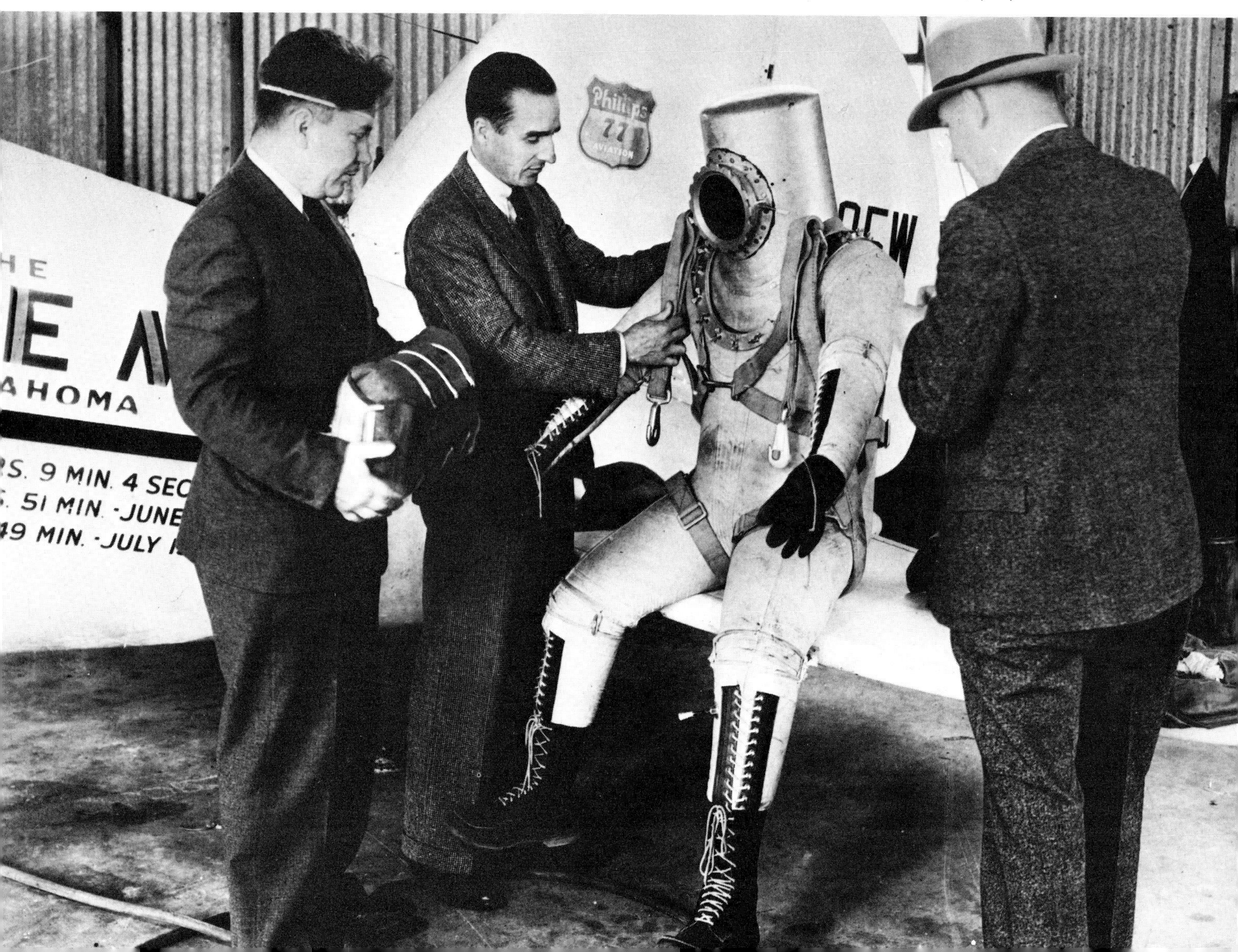

Wiley Post (left), *helping to harness his "man from Mars" suit, has no idea he'll give a holiday driver fits.*

Path gouged by Vega's new skid after dead-stick landing on Muroc Dry Lake in February 1935. (Right) Post leaves dropable landing gear at Los Angeles on third stratosphere attempt.

general store, was spending the holiday out on the lake with the unique four-wheel sail car he'd made from an old Franklin auto chassis. Alone, with the dry lake bed stretching to the horizon in every direction, he had stopped to adjust the jib boom of his sail. Intent on his work, Mertz neither saw nor heard Post's skillful belly landing downwind. Wiley, unable to release his helmet, climbed out of the ship, padded softly up behind the storekeeper, gingerly tapped him on the shoulder. Mertz straightened up, glanced around, and then with a startled yell "took out straight across the lake." Looking back as he ran, the frightened man recognized the famous *Winnie Mae* and slowed down. Finally he sheepishly returned to help perspiring Wiley Post out of the scary suit.

With motives that were never discovered, persons unknown had dumped over two pounds of emery dust and filings in the manifold intake of the Wasp engine. Wiley Post, who didn't think he had an enemy in the world, felt rotten about it, and so did the entire flying fraternity.

Carrying a special load of mail for Transcontinental and Western Air, Wiley tried three more times for a coast-to-coast record. His best flight, on March 15, 1935, took him 2,035 miles to Cleveland in 8 hours and 4 minutes. He would have knocked an hour off the transcontinental record if he'd been able to continue at the pace he set, but the oxygen supply had been miscalculated and Post had either to come down or die. He skidded the Vega in on the grass alongside the airport runway.

Another attempt in April got him as far as Lafayette, Indiana, where the supercharger let go at 33,000 feet. A final assault on the record brought Wiley only to Wichita, where for the last time the graceful *Winnie Mae* was inelegantly but expertly slid to earth on her belly.

Wiley Post had led the way to using the thin air of the substratosphere. With a normal top speed of about 192 mph, the *Winnie Mae* had been flown at speeds of 340 mph and more in the then-unknown regions high above the earth. Space experts today think that Wiley, without his realizing it, quite probably was the first to hit the powerful current now called the "jet stream." And Post's cross-country stratosphere experiments are considered as a more lasting contribution to aviation progress than his history-making flights around the world.

11

SHRINKING THE WORLD

Many international flights now regularly flown by daily airliners were not even attempted until the 1920s, and what is today's routine scheduled trip was then a pioneering adventure. The "first" trip accomplished by air from one place to another was always front-page news, and the early Lockheeds figured prominently in this phase of aviation development.

Strongly nationalistic, Mexico was struggling in 1930 to support and promote flying and air travel. Gringo flyers from the States still manned its infant airlines, and only one military flying school provided the country with native-born pilots. Misfortune dogged the Mexican army's efforts toward aerial recognition.

Captain Emilio Carranza, "Mexico's Lindbergh," had crashed to his death in a New Jersey thunderstorm while attempting a New York–Mexico City flight in a replica of the *Spirit of St. Louis*. Colonel Pablo Sidar, with a specially built Emsco monoplane, fell into Costa Rican seas on an attempted Mexico City–Buenos Aires flight. It remained for a small, dapper Mexican Air Force colonel named Roberto Fierro to redeem faith in his country's pilots.

The thirty-three-year-old Fierro was one of Mexico's first military aviators and he had ten years of service in the Army. Using money raised by public subscription, he ordered the third Sirius model to be built by Lockheed. It was destroyed in the fatal accident that killed the company's test pilot, Herb Fahy; so the colonel took a later ship of the same series.

June 1930: young Col. Roberto Fierro's Sirius, which he and Capt. Arnulfo Cortes fly nonstop to Mexico City.

Pure white with gleaming red trim, Fierro's Sirius was named *Anahuac*, an Aztec name for the "land of herons," an ancient lake now occupied by Mexico City. The colonel had plans for a 10,000-mile goodwill flight to South America and across the South Atlantic to Europe. As a starter he wanted to complete the important New York–Mexico City nonstop flight, on which his friend Captain Carranza had lost his life.

Cool, cautious, and conservative, Fierro and his pilot-mechanic Captain Arnulfo Cortes flew the shiny new Lockheed in easy stages to New York. After days of patient preparation, the pair took off from Roosevelt Field on June 21, 1930. With clockwork precision the Mexican flyers ticked off the miles down through Virginia, Alabama, Louisiana, and Texas, successfully avoiding a severe electrical storm that was sweeping in from the Gulf. Their *Anahuac* reached Valbuena Field at Mexico City in 16 hours and 35 minutes. Ten thousand happy Mexicans turned out in the rain to greet the pilots with shouts of "Viva Fierro! Viva Mexico!"

Enthusiastic well-wishers carried the army flyers inside a hangar where President Ortiz Rubio waited to congratulate them. *El Presidente* proclaimed that Roberto Fierro and Arnulfo Cortes had done a great thing for Mexico but prudently banned their flying on to South America and Europe. "Our country needs its good sons," he said. The record-making Sirius was put in service as a command ship for the Mexican War Department. Eventually the grateful government gave it to Colonel Fierro, and he flew it for several years as his personal transport.

And 32 years later: model of white-and-red Anahuac *stirs memories for General Fierro at his desk in the capital of Mexico.*

Built during the same period as Fierro's *Anahuac* was another low-wing Lockheed designed for the use of Art Goebel, the rugged veteran of both the Dole Race and transcontinental record flights. Art's plane was not a Sirius, but a single-cockpit Explorer like the planes built for Harold Bromley's proposed Pacific flights. Her eight tanks would hold 800 gallons of gasoline.

Goebel announced plans for an assault on the nonstop transcontinental record and a Paris to New York flight later in the summer. He named the blue-and-yellow ship *Yankee Doodle*, reminiscent of the previous Lockheed he'd flown to fame.

Despite her capabilities, the Explorer did not satisfy the famous distance flyer, and he never took delivery. She went instead to the Pure Oil Company of Chicago, to be flown for advertising purposes. Repainted and rechristened *Blue Flash*, the low-wing Lockheed was flown by a hired pilot, Captain Roy W. Ammel.

An ex-Army flyer and Chicago building materials broker, slight, balding Roy Ammel had kept drifting back to aviation after various business ventures. For his Pure Oil assignment the captain went to California to take delivery of the big Explorer. Fire damaged the ship after a forced landing at Gila Bend, Arizona, and a crew from the factory under Don Young had to come out and disassemble it for shipment back to Burbank. It was September before Ammel and the *Blue Flash* reached New York, with plans for the first solo flight direct to Rome. Lockheed's ace troubleshooter Don Young was again retained by Pure Oil to speed Ammel on his way, and there was even some talk of stowing the curly-haired little mechanic in with the gas tanks. But the fall weather over the Atlantic did not cooperate, and after weeks of waiting, Captain Ammel decided to make a lone visit to the Army base where he had once been stationed: France Field in the Canal Zone.

The first nonstop flight from New York to Panama came off on November 9–10, 1930. The Explorer loaded with 703 gallons of gas, Ammel got the ship off the runway at Floyd Bennett Field in 2,000 feet and headed south. He flew the blue plane by beacons, the sun, and dead reckoning all the way, fighting winds that kept blowing him off his course until he guessed he'd flown "about a thousand miles extra." Struggling to keep awake on the 24-hour, 35-minute journey, the Captain sang to himself and lifted his seat to keep his head out in the slipstream. After the battery in the *Blue Flash* ran down, he read his instruments with a pocket flashlight. The leather flying suit which had seemed so snug and comfortable in New York nearly smothered Ammel as he approached the tropics. In the close confines of the cockpit he took nearly an hour to worm out of it. He was

Built for long-distance flying, Art Goebel's Yankee Doodle *became Roy Ammel's* Blue Flash.

Roy Ammel and fan before Blue Flash *gets off to Panama.*

extremely happy to see the shores of Panama rise out of the Caribbean and to set the Explorer down on France Field.

A return flight to Chicago brought disaster. Transferring to the longer, unfinished airfield at Anton, Ammel found that the uneven terrain differed considerably from the concrete of Floyd Bennett Field back in New York; but he tried a takeoff anyway. The *Blue Flash* skidded on a wet spot, dug her nose in the earth, and reared up to crash on her back. Luckily there was no fire, for Roy Ammel, unconscious but not seriously injured, had to be chopped out of the wreckage. The New York to Panama hop was his one and only flying venture on a national scale.

Another pilot whose appearance in the aviation news was nearly as brief as Ammel's was James Goodwin Hall, a well-to-do, thirty-four-year-old New York City stockbroker. Handsome Jim Hall's mission was to publicize the work of The Crusaders, a national organization engaged in helping to end the federal prohibition against liquor.

During the summer of 1931, Jim and his flashy yellow-and-black Lockheed were very much in the public eye, dashing from city to city on record-shattering flights. The ship was one of the first Altairs, a low-winged speed package with retractable landing gear. It was named *The Crusader* and carried the anti-Prohibition group's big shield emblem.

Hall first beat Roscoe Turner's 1930 Canada-Mexico mark, flying the Vancouver–Agua Caliente route in 7 hours, 48 minutes, 31 seconds. Next he clipped 46 minutes from Frank Hawk's New York–Havana record. Covering the 1,400 miles nonstop in 8 hours and 35 minutes, Hall subsisted on only two oranges. He was handed a

Cuban cocktail when he climbed out at Havana.

"This alone was worth the trip," remarked Jim gratefully. "How about another?"

The Crusader's aerial protests against the dry laws continued with new records set for the New York–Chicago, New York–Montreal, and New York–New Orleans trips. Hall usually took one of his broker friends along for the ride. In order not to offend militant drys during participation in the National Air Races, he temporarily painted out the slogans urging an end to Prohibition.

The cometlike career of James Goodwin Hall's yellow racer came to a disastrous conclusion on September 21, 1931. The flying broker planned a record flight to Detroit and attendance at the American Legion convention, taking as a passenger Peter J. Brady, a well-known New York banker and civic leader. Immediately after lifting off from Floyd Bennett Field, Hall found himself in thick fog. He could not believe that the *Crusader*'s bank-and-turn indicator was functioning properly: it indicated level flight, yet the Altair was obviously in a screaming power dive.

Before bailing out himself, the pilot stood up in the cockpit and turned to help Brady. At that instant the plane pierced the lowest layer of fog above Staten Island and plunged straight into a house. Brady was instantly killed, and a housewife in her garden burned to death. Jim Hall's parachute, which he never touched, was torn partly open on a brick building as he was catapulted across two rooftops to alight unhurt in a churchyard 150 feet away.

During the period in which Hall flew, lanky Lou Reichers in another Altair was warming up for his transatlantic flight attempt. In October he and his boss, Bernarr Macfadden, missed setting a new Newark-Washington record by just three minutes. The following April, Lou made the first nonstop flight from Montreal to Havana. Both the weather and the Altair performed perfectly on the trip, and Lou checked off landmarks on his Rand McNally road maps with monotonous regularity. He set *The Gold Eagle* down on General Machado Airport just 9 hours and 3 minutes from Canada.

Reward for a man with a mission: Jim Hall welcomed by a long cool one as he arrives from dry New York.

Record-setting paces in Latin America had already been set by a Lockheed Vega. Wishing to show how closely the two continents could be linked with business and commercial exchange, the Foreign Advertising and Service Bureau arranged for the use of Standard Oil's best

"The most beautiful Lockheed ever built" gleams for Lou Reichers before Montreal-Havana hop in 1932.

White and McMullen pose in civvies with their white Vega, which Mattern later flew in "eagle" trim.

Stanavo Vega, and the services of two good Army pilots, Lieutenants Will W. White and Clement McMullen.

On February 14, 1930, this pair left Newark for Buenos Aires, setting new time records on every single leg of the trip. Spelling each other at the controls, they covered 6,780 miles in a little over 5 days, making only six stops en route. White and McMullen were the first to pilot a Lockheed over the hump of the Andes. On arrival at Palowar Field in Buenos Aires, they were acclaimed as "the Eagles of the North."

Early in 1932 another Lockheed made the South American circuit in 23 days. She was the special, modified Orion *Spirit of Fun* owned by Hal Roach of movie comedy fame. The modifications consisted of a nose six inches longer than a standard Orion, slightly more dihedral to the wings, and a retractable tail wheel. Anxious to try out his new white-and-red speed queen, Roach, accompanied by producer Arthur Loew, made a whirlwind business trip to Buenos Aires and back. They traveled so fast that some of the customs formalities at various airports were neglected and had to be straightened out long afterward.

Stocky James B. Dickson, the Hal Roach pilot, got to know the Orion's capabilities in short order during the Buenos Aires trip. On return to the United States he set a transcontinental record for passenger-carrying, winging *The Spirit of Fun* from Newark to Los Angeles in a flying time of 14 hours and 49 minutes. Soon Roach and Metro-Goldwyn-Mayer Studios were planning an even greater journey for their Lockheed—a round-the-world trip covering five continents.

The *Spirit* was shipped to China by steamer. Rather than disassemble her, Jim Dickson flew the Orion down to San Pedro and landed on a blocked-off street near the Matson docks. Then he taxied up to a crane that slung the plane aboard ship as deck cargo.

From Shanghai, carrying MGM vice president Loew and his secretary Joseph Rosthal, Dickson piloted the Orion on an unprecedented eight-day flight over uncharted airways to Johannesburg, South Africa. Wishing to view the famous Victoria Falls in Rhodesia, the party flew there on November 17, 1932. South African flyers marveled at the streamlined Lockheed, the cleanest, fastest ship they'd

White-McMullen goodwill flight ends at Palowar Field after 51½ hours' total flight time from New York.

ever seen. Though it had flown from China with no trouble, they wondered out loud as to its ability to get off, heavily loaded, from the sandy Victoria Falls airdrome.

Dickson did not heed the warnings. Before climbing into the cockpit he remarked that he "hated to leave the place"—and his words were prophetic. Bogged in heavy sand, the Orion's wheels barely left the ground. She clipped off eight trees, lost a wing, and crashed in the brush on her back. Dickson was killed outright, but Loew and Rosthal escaped with only burns from the cans of tetraethyl lead that were carried to dope the plane's fuel.

The well-appointed after section of the fuselage was relatively undamaged, and was acquired by Terence Spencer, a Victoria Falls aviator-garageman. Spencer was keen on converting it into the superstructure of a launch to be used by a native chieftain in Barotseland. The spectacle of a Lockheed from Burbank ending up as a state barge for a primitive African chief is intriguing, but the fuselage of the Orion rotted away in storage before Spencer could accomplish the conversion. Jim Dickson is buried in Livingston Cemetery, and the propeller from the Orion marks his grave.

From Shanghai to Johannesburg in Spirit of Fun *(left to right): Joseph Rosthal, Arthur Loew, and pilot James Dickson.*

It was an Englishman who first broke African and European cross-continental records with a Lockheed. He was thirty-one-year-old Lieutenant Commander Glen Kidston, a wealthy British sportsman and a prominent auto and motorboat racer. After an early retirement from the Fleet Air Arm, he surveyed the progress of British civil aviation and found it much in want of speed and modernization.

Kidston ordered a Lockheed Vega from America, a special job with long-range gas tanks and all the latest radio equipment. One of the Detroit-built Vegas with Duralumin fuselage, the ship was sent to England by steamer and erected at Croydon Airdrome.

Commander Kidston and his personal pilot Owen Cathcart-Jones were both delighted with the American monoplane. On tests, its performance was better than they had believed possible. Just to try out the Vega, they hopped over to Paris with five people aboard, and set a new speed record of 72 minutes.

Kidston was so enamored of his Lockheed that he wanted to share it. He demonstrated the ship to various British manufacturers and tried to solicit their interest. His idea was to manufacture Vegas in England under license

The Lockheed Glen Kidston bought to inspire the British: his 5-place, metal-fuselage ship is the only Vega DL-1 Special model ever built. After his death, it entered MacRobertson Race as Puck, *ending with the RAAF in World War II.*

Ready for London-Capetown record (left to right): *radio operator T. A. Vallette, Glen Kidston, and Owen Cathcart-Jones.*

from Detroit-Lockheed. He was certain that the planes would be eagerly bought by fast commercial air services both in Britain and on the continent. Though the commander was persuasive and ready to back his beliefs with a tremendous cash outlay, he got only the cold shoulder from British manufacturers who during that period "simply could not entertain the idea of building an American airplane under license."

The English flyer determined to show just how insular and backward his country was when it came to promoting commercial aviation: he and Cathcart-Jones would go after the London-to-Capetown flying records.

Glen and "See-Jay" got off from Netheravon Field on March 31, 1931, and proceeded to fly to Capetown in just 6 days and 11 hours. On the first stages to Cairo they carried T. A. Vallette, a wireless operator on loan from the Marconi Company. His place was taken at Cairo by mechanic G. W. Hills. Because of the careful advance preparations, most of the flight went off with strict precision. No night flying was attempted; most nights mechanic Hills worked into the small hours, servicing the engine during that time to beat the tropical heat.

In Southern Rhodesia the English team of record-seekers was nearly stopped. The airfield at Bulawayo is situated at an elevation of 4,300 feet, and there, with a light wind and a heavy load, Kidston had a ticklish time leaving the ground. The Vega went tearing straight through a three-wire fence and barely cleared some high-tension wires beyond. Two hours later the engine suddenly quit without warning. The commander looked around and proceeded to bring the ship to a dead-stick landing on the only clear spot of country in miles. Again he flew through a wire fence, snapping off an iron post as well. The Lockheed slewed to a halt on an incline among huge anthills.

While Hills worked to locate the engine trouble, Kidston and Cathcart-Jones straightened a bent propeller. Then with the aid of Boer farmers they leveled anthills and cleared boulders for a precarious takeoff. Tired but triumphant, the English flyers finally reached Capetown with two full days lopped off the old record.

Glen Kidston had proved the worth of American-built air transport. Within a day he was forming a company to operate internal airlines in South Africa, using Lockheed equipment, and his propositions to build the speedy American planes in England were still pending. What might have been came to nothing a few weeks later. Kidston, on a business trip to Durban, was killed when a wing of his borrowed Puss Moth tore off and the plane crashed in the desolate Drakensberg Mountains.

Capable Cathcart-Jones continued occasionally to fly the white-and-black Lockheed, when it was shipped back to England after the death of its owner. In one test, with British aircraft inspection officials aboard, he flew the Vega at 205 mph in level flight. Another time, with a *Daily Herald* reporter, he beat a telephone call from Croydon to Hanworth. Covering the distance in 4½ minutes, the two taxied up to the hangar just as the call was put through.

Like other pilots, See-Jay had his troubles with the Vega's cockpit door. One day he ferried Sir Philip Sassoon, British Under Secretary of State for Air, from Birmingham to Lympne in a record 40 minutes. As the ship taxied up to the line, Sir Philip suddenly opened the door behind him to give instructions. The startled pilot lost all his trouser buttons in the scramble to regain control, and had difficulty in keeping his pants up during the ensuing public ceremonies.

For three years, work for the Lockheed was administered by a trust set up by the Kidston family, and consisted of charters and trips with the few pilots qualified to fly her. One of these was Miss Marsinah Neison, the youngest woman in England to hold a commercial flying license. Occasionally Miss Neison could be found at the controls of the high-performance Vega, shepherding RAF officers and a couple of British peers from one airbase to another—a creditable feat at the age of nineteen.

Early in 1934 the MacRobertson Race from London to Melbourne was announced, a classic sporting event which has never been equaled in aviation history. It was thought that transport aircraft with good long-distance performance would be the sure key to success in this great contest, and American planes were hurriedly sought as entries. By August, no less than nine single-engine Lockheeds were entered. Prepared to compete were Wiley Post, with his world-famed *Winnie Mae*, and Sir Charles Kingsford-Smith, with his blue-and-silver Altair. Another Altair was to carry Ruth Nichols, and further entries included Orions to be flown by Laura Ingalls, Frank Rose, Russ Thaw, and Harry Lyon. French pilot Michel Détroyat announced intentions to compete with a specially built Orion on which he had planted a powerful Hispano-Suiza radial engine.

To this formidable array was added the Kidston metal Vega. When it came right down to the race deadline, none of the others competed, and this was the only Lockheed in the race. Sold to an Australian, H. C. Miller, the London to Capetown veteran was named *Puck*, and manned for the race by two other Australians, Jimmy Woods and Donald Bennett.

Woods and Bennett made a good try, but their lack of knowledge of American-made hydraulic shock absorbers literally tripped them up. The landing gear on the Lockheed had been malfunctioning, and nobody knew how to fix it. The Vega's old pilot, Cathcart-Jones, had troubles of his own, flying a new and untried De Havilland Comet in the same race. The Australians took off regardless, and successfully reached Marseilles and then Athens. At Aleppo, pilot Woods brought the Lockheed in, with navigator Bennett crouched in the tail. *Puck* came down, the ground came up, and over she went as the undercarriage collapsed. Bennett was flung the length of the plane, and crumpled like an accordion against the door. He got off with three broken ribs; Woods suffered a nasty cut on the forehead. Bent and broken in the Syrian dust lay the sole Lockheed bid for the MacRobertson first prize of nearly $50,000. The speed classic was won by C. W. A. Scott and T. Campbell Black in one of the three De Havilland Comets specially built for the long race.

The England to Australia air lanes were always fraught with danger. In 1935 they claimed the life of Australia's greatest airman, Sir Charles Kingsford-Smith. A veteran of the route, Smithy decided to try to lower the record just once more. He wanted to show that his Lockheed Altair *Lady Southern Cross* might well have been a winner in the MacRobertson Race from which he had been forced to withdraw.

Kingsford-Smith refused to fly the Altair across the Atlantic to England, and had it shipped by boat. On his return to business in Australia, he planned to sit behind a glass-topped desk and leave the flying to others. "The England-Australia record attempt will be my farewell long-distance flight," announced Sir Charles, "and certainly the last in my faithful old ship."

Smithy and his old associate Tommy Pethybridge left Lympne Airdrome in Kent to make their bid in November 1935. On the seventh they got off from Allahabad, India,

Michel Détroyat tries his Orion in France with the 575-hp Hispano-Suiza substituted for the original Wasp.

and nosed out over the Bay of Bengal north of Rangoon. C. J. Melrose, another Australian flyer, reported that he sighted the Altair heading into a raging storm about 150 miles from shore and only 200 feet above the ocean. Smithy, Tommy, and the *Lady Southern Cross* never reached Singapore.

Reports of flares seen in the lonely Mergui Archipelago, and planes flying low over the jungles of Siam were all investigated by the RAF, which mounted a fruitless sea and air search. Two years later N. M. Andrews, an English sport fisherman from Moulmein, found a floating wheel and tire bobbing in the Andaman Sea, off Burma. The B. F. Goodrich Company identified the tire by its serial number. Lockheed's vice president, Carl B. Squier, examined the condition of the remaining portion of the retractable landing gear. He had only one question, which would never be answered:

Why had Kingsford-Smith, the veteran transoceanic flyer, been attempting a wheels-down landing at sea?

On the distaff side, Amelia Earhart did things with her Lockheeds in addition to flying across the Atlantic and Pacific, and setting women's records for speed. Three months after her flight to Ireland she was back in California ready for another "first." On August 24, 1932, she flew from Los Angeles to Newark in 19 hours and 5 minutes. Hers was the first solo flight nonstop from coast to coast by a woman. Though perhaps not so dangerous, the 2,448-mile overland trip was greater than any of her ocean flights, and it was her longest time alone in the air.

With her transatlantic Lockheed hanging in Franklin Institute's Hall of Aviation, Amelia gave her newer Vega a good tryout in July 1933. Even with a couple of stops, she cut down her own time from California to New Jersey by nearly two hours.

Amelia was officially invited to visit Mexico after her momentous Pacific flight, and made the trip in April 1935. Leaving Burbank with a night takeoff, America's

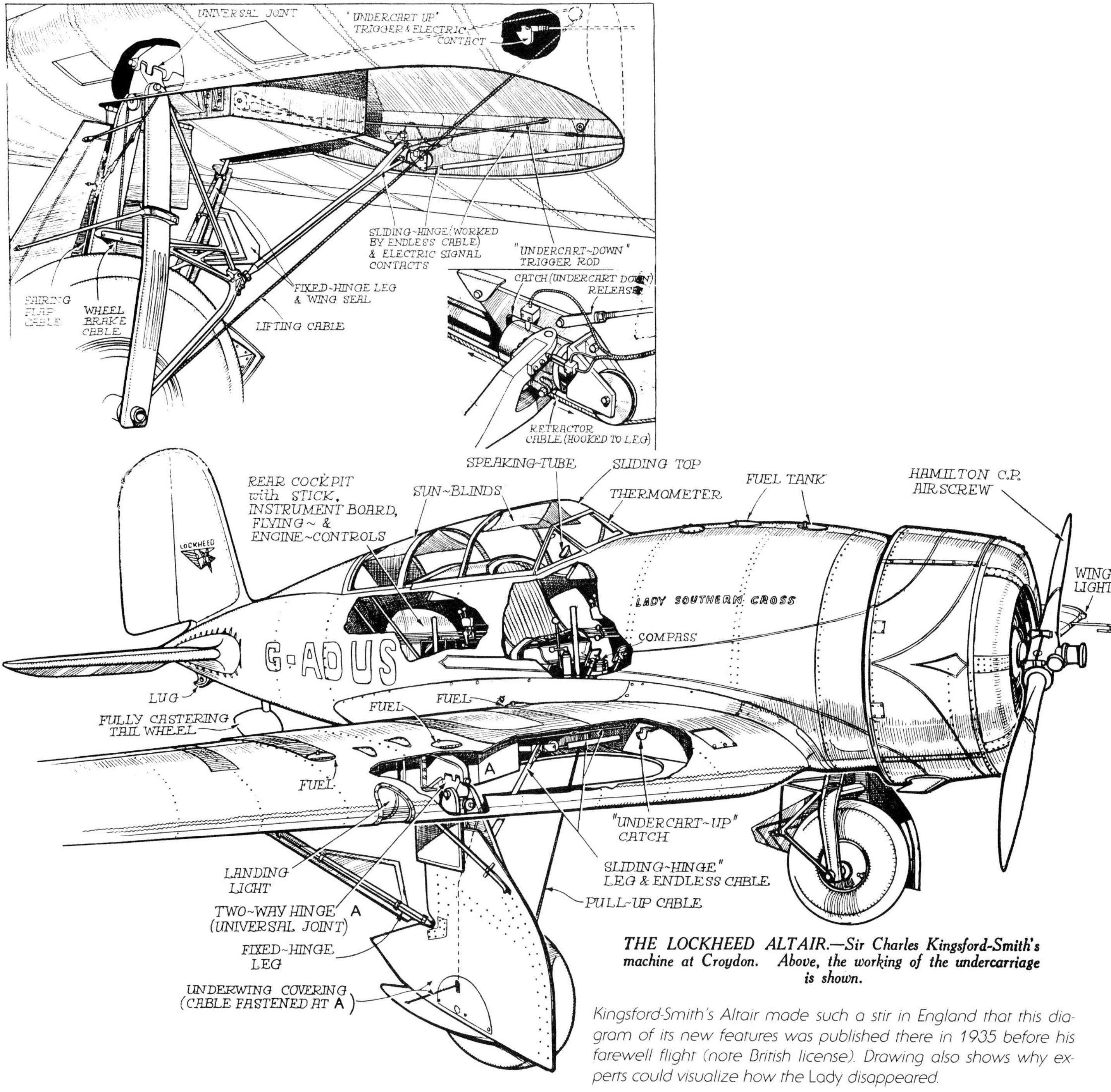

Kingsford-Smith's Altair made such a stir in England that this diagram of its new features was published there in 1935 before his farewell flight (note British license). Drawing also shows why experts could visualize how the Lady *disappeared.*

top woman pilot herded her trusy "little red bus" south over the Gulf of California, flying in the moonlight. Morning found her in a maze of mountain tableland between Guadalajara and Mexico City, not exactly certain of her location. A high-flying bug lodged in Amelia's eye, causing Zitácuaro to be indistinguishable from Zumpango on her charts. With blurred vision, she dropped down to ask directions near the town of Nopala. Cowboys and villagers pointed the way to Mexico City with signs and voluble Spanish. Arrived in the capital, Amelia had a happy time on her flying visit, decked out in a blue-and-silver mariachi outfit topped by a flowered white sombrero.

Officials were aghast when she proposed to make an unheard-of journey: the first nonstop flight from Mexico City to New York. In the thin air a mile and a half high at the Mexican capital, her heavily loaded plane "just could *not* take off," they told her. This made Amelia all the more determined. She conferred with Charles Baughan, who had been flying Lockheeds in Mexico since 1929. Baughan, locally known as Pancho Pistoles, thought she could get off if a longer field were available. As in Hawaii, the Army was gallantly ready to aid a lady: Mexican soldiers filled holes and leveled sand hummocks to prepare a three-mile runway on the dry bed of nearby Lake Texcoco.

At 4 A.M., May 9, 1935, with 470 gallons of gas in the Vega's tanks, Amelia got rolling. She refuted the dire predictions by using only a little over a mile of lake bed. Tearing along until the ground speed built up to over 100 mph, the Lockheed simply flew itself into the air.

Despite—or perhaps because of—the admonition of Wiley Post, who told her that flying over the Gulf of Mexico was "too dangerous," Miss Earhart cut directly across the 700 over-water miles between Tampico and New Orleans. She streaked north, in constant radio contact with the cities below. Though asked to land in Washington, Amelia droned on into the night to Newark, where her husband and a noisy crowd were waiting to welcome her.

Amelia's red-and-gold Lockheed Vega had once again taken her on a precedent-shattering trip, connecting two great cities. This was to be her last "first" with it. She next acquired a later-model Lockheed, the twin-engine plane in which she disappeared over the Pacific in July 1937.

The Earhart Vega was sold and used for charter, passenger-hopping, and movie work. Named *Record Breaker,* it was a familiar sight at airports in southern California and Nevada for several years, and many people can truthfully say: "I once flew in Amelia Earhart's plane."

Finally, on a ferry flight east in 1943, the ship caught fire at Wilson Field in Memphis, Tennessee. It was completely destroyed in twenty minutes.

With the exception of the *Winnie Mae,* the best-known wooden Lockheed was Colonel Charles A. Lindbergh's low-wing Sirius. The colonel and his wife flew it more than four years and its appearance as both a land and seaplane became etched on the minds of the majority of Americans.

After breaking the transcontinental speed record in April 1930, the Lindberghs used the Sirius as their personal transportation. In addition, the colonel flew it on business trips in connection with his work for Transcontinental Air Transport and Pan American Airways.

He was continually seeking the best performance from the plane. In August he installed a Wright Cyclone engine in the ship, upping the horsepower to 575, 125 hp more than the original Wasp. He was very interested in the development of fully retractable landing gear, and would probably have had his Sirius converted to an Altair had he not had another type of flying in mind for the low-wing Lockheed.

Pan American, for whom Lindbergh acted as a technical consultant, had ambitious ideas for expanding its services. The company had long-range plans to establish routes across both the Pacific and Atlantic oceans. Pan Am envisioned an airline of flying boats to begin with, which meant that all favorable landing spots, sheltered anchorages, and the best places to establish bases should be investigated, preferably at firsthand. International complications made such a survey a delicate as well as difficult matter.

Charles and Anne Lindbergh drop in at the Navy's seaplane base at Washington before start for the Orient.

Colonel Lindbergh, known and admired all over the world, was without question the ideal man for the job. He was a thorough researcher, and in all things aeronautical his valued opinions could be relied upon. Moreover, flying his own airplane and with his wife as copilot, he was bound to be welcomed and assisted anywhere and everywhere.

The Lindberghs' first survey flight in 1931 took them north to the Orient, and is vividly described in Mrs. Lindbergh's fine book of the same name. A set of big, shiny Duralumin Edo floats were installed on the black-and-orange Sirius because the greater part of the flight was to be over oceans, rivers, and lakes—following a great circle route up through Canada and Alaska, and down the island chain of Japan to China.

Pan American had cached gasoline and supplies at prearranged way stops, and wired money ahead for such purchases in Siberia and Japan. Colonel Lindbergh checked and weighed every bit of equipment before storing it in the forward baggage compartment of the Lockheed, and so careful were his calculations that not one superfluous item—either routine or emergency—was taken along.

Anne Lindbergh not only acted as copilot but also learned Morse code and the operation of the plane's radio. She was shaky and uncertain at first, but after mastering the intricacies of master oscillator and power amplifier proved a good hand at the key and earphone.

Following a flight to Washington for last-minute papers, passports, and clearances, the couple got away from Flushing Bay, Long Island, on July 29, 1931. Their route took them to Maine, then Ottawa and on north to the bleak shores of James Bay. Canadian bush pilots tried to persuade them to take the established airline route to Aklavik, but the colonel insisted on seeing what the shores of the Hudson Bay, Baker Lake, and Amundsen Gulf had to offer in the way of landing spots for a visiting seaplane. As it had for Wilkins and Eielson three years before, the entire population of Barrow turned out to welcome the famous flyers to Alaska, and tendered them a "thanksgiving dinner" in August.

The flight on to Nome found the Lindberghs held back by fog and darkness. They landed on Shishmaref Inlet on the north coast of the Seward Peninsula, dropped anchor in three feet of water, and calmly crawled into the forward baggage compartment to spend the night.

After Nome came the Kamchatka Peninsula and then the Japanese islands of the Kurile group. The Lindberghs' radio welcome to Japan was gracious, but the weather was just the opposite. Over Shimishiru To, a dark curtain of fog and storm clouds blocked passage south and then edged around to envelop the speeding monoplane from the rear as well.

With wireless advice to turn back and land at Buroton Bay, the flying colonel swung the Sirius about. Wind whistled back around his wife as Lindbergh slid back the cockpit hatch, slipped on helmet and goggles, and heightened his seat for better visibility. The wind flattened his face as he bent his energies to getting the ship down in one piece. Anne buckled her seat belt a little tighter.

Twice the pilot dived the Lockheed down the steep slope of the drowned volcano which encloses Buroton Bay, knifing between fog and mountain. Twice the bay was obscured and Lindbergh had to open the throttle and zoom up out of the dark pocket into the reassuring sunshine above. Then he flew back to nearby Ketoi Island and tried his tobogganing technique on *its* volcanic cone. Skimming down the slope over bushes, rocks, and a fifty-foot cliff, the skilled pilot set the seaplane down in the rough water, the pontoons skipping from wave to wave as she slowed and settled in their troughs.

After plowing through seaweed, Charles and Anne anchored and slept on the swell of the open sea in the lee of Ketoi. Difficulties with a wet engine and discharged battery obliged the plane to be towed by a Japanese naval vessel into Buroton Bay. With another unforeseen overnight stop on a small lake on the island of Kunashiri, it was August 26 before the husband-and-wife flying team reached Tokyo's Kasimigaura Naval Base.

Though Lindbergh scheduled the surveys to continue on the Asian continent, disastrous floods had swept China by the time the couple arrived. They offered their services to the National Flood Relief Commission and put the float-equipped Sirius to good work in surveying the damage done by the rampaging waters, particularly those of the mighty Yangtze. Operating from Nanking, the Lindberghs flew doctors and medicines to isolated outlying towns. Then they moved upstream to Hankow to operate from the British airplane carrier *Hermes,* whose planes were also flying mercy missions.

On what was to be a final trip to report on flood conditions, Colonel and Mrs. Lindbergh left the *Hermes* in their usual manner, sitting in the Sirius as, its engine idling, the plane was slung overboard by the ship's derrick. However this time there was just not enough slack to detach the hoisting hook. In vain Lindbergh tried to gun the ship, fighting the current while the taut cable tugged. Something had to give.

Like the blade of a huge water wheel, the plane's wing dipped—and the Lockheed tipped slowly over on her back. Charles and Anne Lindbergh leaped into the swirling Yangtze. Quickly hauled into a lifeboat, they looked back to see their faithful plane upside down in the yellow water, but still held by the derrick cable. They fully expected to see the plane go to pieces in the grip of the pounding river. Still the tough plywood fuselage held together, even though half cut through by the steel cable. Righted in a three-way tussle using the *Hermes,* the river, and a launch from an American gunboat, the sturdy Sirius was finally hoisted to safety aboard the British vessel.

With the trip brought to an unforeseen conclusion, the Lindberghs returned to the United States aboard a steamship. The Lockheed went back to Burbank for repairs.

Two years later another survey trip for Pan Am took America's best-known flying couple on a complete circuit of both North and South Atlantic transocean routes. Their Sirius was not only completely restored by the factory, but now had its third, and even more powerful, engine, a 710-hp Wright Cyclone, on which was mounted a Hamilton controllable-pitch propeller. Instead of the original orange, her wings and tail were now red.

Colonel and Mrs. Lindbergh left Flushing Bay, Long Island, on July 9, 1933, and headed across New England to Maine. For a short distance between Halifax and Newfoundland the transatlantic veteran piloted his red-winged Lockheed over the same air lane he'd pioneered with the *Spirit of St. Louis* back in 1927. Then, with the Pan American Airways survey ship *Jelling* for comforting support in the seas below, the Lindberghs turned north to explore the coastal anchorages of Labrador and Baffin Island.

Greenland, the world's largest island, came in for special attention. The flying couple skirted nearly 2,000 miles of its fjord-indented south coast, recording harbor details, currents, winds, and weather. Twice they flew across the vast Greenland icecap, and discovered two hitherto unknown ranges of high mountains.

Charles and Anne had always referred to their plane as *the* Sirius, since it was the first of its model to be built by Lockheed. But at Angmagssalik, on Greenland's east coast, the well-traveled seaplane finally received a real name. Perched on the wing of the ship as it rode at anchor below the little settlement of red houses, a young Greenlander laboriously painted it on the fuselage: *Tingmissartoq*, Eskimo for "the one who flies like a big bird."

The Lindberghs proceeded over Denmark Strait to Iceland, on to the Faeroes, Copenhagen, Stockholm, and Helsinki. Soviet Air Force plans escorted the visitors to a landing at Leningrad, and then, over a prescribed route, to Moscow.

Well aware of Lindbergh's prowess as a flyer, the Russians arranged for him to land in the heart of the city, on a short stretch of the winding Moscow River, between two iron bridges. On one side they erected a grandstand, and a park on the other was jammed with watchers. The colonel sized up the situation, made a few passes over the old red walls of the Kremlin, and let down. He whiskered just over the top chord of the first bridge, sideslipped steeply, then straightened out to go spanking along the river with plenty of room ahead. The crowds cheered, and Lindbergh's famous grin greeted the Red dignitaries.

The Lindberghs successfully cleared the Moscow bridges in their takeoff for other European capitals. A landing at the Les Mureaux Naval Base on the Seine resulted in a much quieter reception than young "Slim" Lindbergh had received on his previous visit to Paris.

It was November now, and on what should have been a routine flight the famous couple tried to pierce the foggy mists of central Europe.

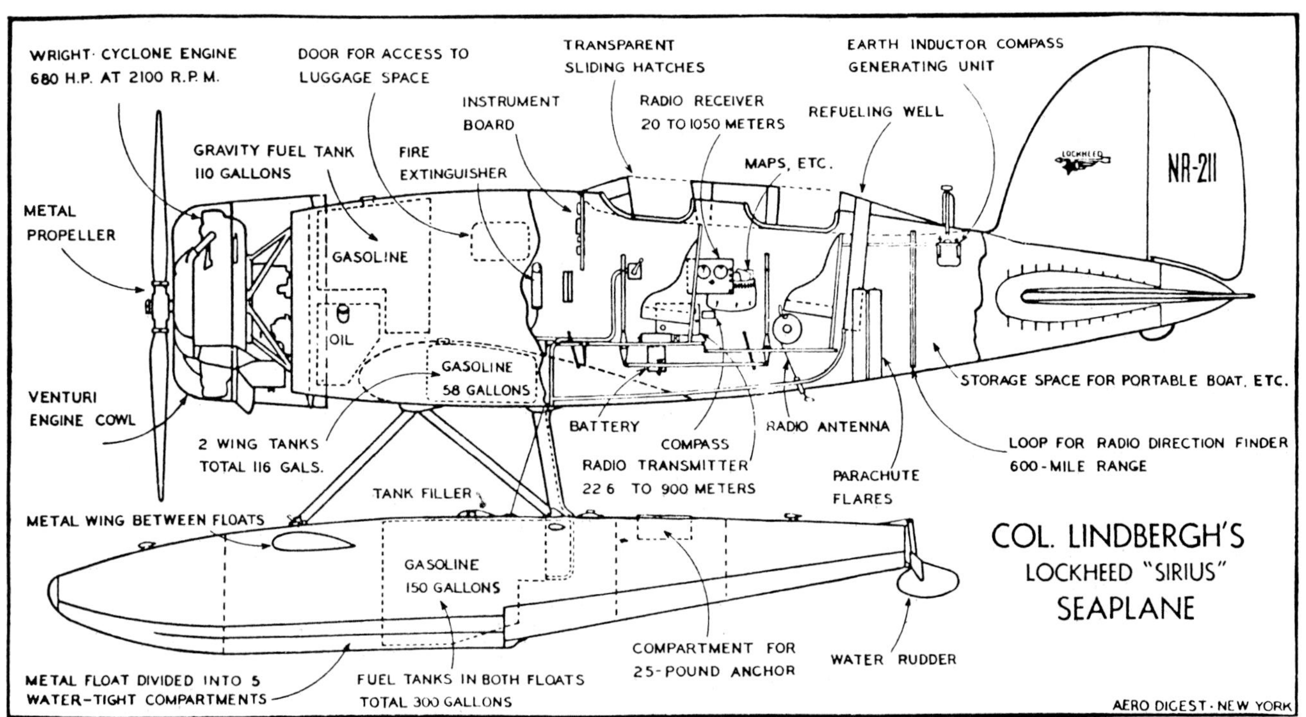

Clear skies and sunshine finally greeted the aerial travelers in Portugal. Still after data to help establish future airlines, Colonel and Mrs. Lindbergh inspected the harbors of the Azores, the Canaries, and the Cape Verde Islands.

The couple had hoped to cross to South America from the French transatlantic seaplane base at Santiago in the Cape Verde Islands. But the hot, dry tradewind blew relentlessly day after day. With the rollers coming in from the open sea there would be no chance of getting off the water with enough gasoline to reach Brazil. The Lindberghs returned to the coast of Africa.

At Bathurst, in the British colony of Gambia, the *Tingmissartoq* was made ready for the long jump to South America. Again the wind played an all-important part in the flight; but here on the coast, instead of an abundance of it, there was barely enough to help the loaded seaplane even to get up on step.

Three times the Lindberghs attempted to leave Bathurst, twice in the dawn and again at midnight. Fully loaded, and with a near-dead calm, the plane refused to leave the water.

The colonel was determined not to cut down his margin of safety by carrying any less fuel, but instead took other drastic measures. Broiling and half suffocated in the cabin, he spent an entire day removing an unused reserve tank by cutting it apart with tinsnips. Then he picked out other things to leave behind: ropes, anchor, tools, and all the bedding and flying suits. For personal gear he kept only the clothes on his back, and Anne had just a single extra shirt. He discarded ruthlessly until the plane was lightened by over 150 pounds.

On December 6, 1933, Charles A. Lindbergh once again made a direct flight across the Atlantic. It was 2 A.M. and Bathurst harbor was bathed in moonlight as he taxied the Sirius out on the bay.

With the Cyclone turning out full power, and the exhaust stacks sparking, *Tingmissartoq* raced to free herself from the glassy bay. In the light of the wing-tip lights the spray sparkled, and then ceased as she struggled clear of the water and rose into her true element.

For just short of sixteen hours the plane bored through the empty tropical skies. With the moon and stars, then flying blind through clouds, the colonel kept his course. Anne was at constant vigil with the radio, sending and receiving, and relieved as the signals from South American stations grew more distinct and readable. With daybreak came good weather, ships below for contact, checkpoints like the volcanic cone of Fernando de Noronha to keep the reckoning correct. Finally the low green coast of Brazil appeared in the haze ahead, and the Lindberghs dropped down to land on the river southwest of Natal.

Lindbergh next decided to vary his trip north, deviating from the regular Pan American route for a thousand miles of flight up the Amazon River to Manáos, and then on over llanos, jungle, and mountains to Trinidad. It was not until December 19 that the Lindberghs completed their ocean circuit with a safe landing on the chilly waters of Flushing Bay beyond the towers of Manhattan.

They had flown 30,000 miles over four continents, pioneering international air routes that would soon see use in both peace and war. Within a decade, great armadas of aircraft would be winging over Greenland and the Cape Verdes, speeding to the aid of the hard-pressed Allies in England and Africa. And their courses were made safer by the work of a dedicated couple who had first shown the way: Charles and Anne Lindbergh.

And the *Tingmissartoq?* The famous airplane, fully equipped, was presented to the American Museum of Natural History in New York, where it hung for many years from the ceiling of the Hall of Ocean Life. Later the big red-and-black seaplane went to the Air Force Museum at Fairborn, Ohio, and is now a major exhibit of the Smithsonian's National Air and Space Museum in Washington, D.C. It is the only Lockheed Sirius still in existence.

Lockheed built the eighth and last of their Air Express model on special order early in 1931. The white, single-cockpit, parasol-wing monoplane went to the Atlantic Exhibition Company of New York. This outfit had been formed with the intention of promoting the first New York to Paris flight by a woman. With Ruth Nichols and her Vega cracked up in New Brunswick and out of the running for a while, Atlantic Exhibition had a reasonable chance of getting a woman flyer to Paris—and realizing a sizable chunk of change from advertising publicity in the process.

For their pilot, the promoters chose young Laura Ingalls, the daughter of a socially prominent New York family. Miss Ingalls had studied music and language in Paris and Vienna, and been a pianist, ballet dancer, nurse, and secretary before discovering her grand passion: flying. Laura was one of the first women to earn a transport pilot's license. She also shocked her family with determined aerial acrobatics, considered unbefitting a young lady of her background. After having made 980 continuous loops in her DH Gypsy Moth over Muskogee, Oklahoma, and 714 consecutive barrel rolls over St. Louis, this diminutive fireball was in a class by herself, and competition to be reckoned with by both men and women.

Flying out to Burbank to take delivery of her new ship, Laura excitedly picked out the Lockheeds on the field below, and buzzed the factory in sheer exuberance. Her Air Express was a real beauty. It was rigged with eleven tanks to hold a total of 650 gallons; it had special speed landing gear; and all the cabin windows were blocked out. Subdued but not awed by the 450 straining horses up front, Laura carefully piloted the Lockheed back to New York. Always one to want to know every last detail

Laura Ingalls and the Air Express with which she won the Harmon Trophy for her solo circuit of South America.

concerning the construction and operation of her planes, the "society aviatrix" poked and pored over every inch of it. She asked questions until she knew all about the Air Express, sometimes to the exasperation of the Lockheed crews who were completing it, and the Long Island mechanics who readied it for flight.

Weighing less than a hundred pounds, Miss Ingalls was said hardly to disturb the center of gravity while flying her Lockheed. Garbed in a white coverall, jodhpurs or trim slacks, with her dark hair tucked up under a jaunty beret, Laura cruised up and down Long Island. She checked and rechecked instruments and fuel consumption, and mastered the techniques of blind flying with an instructor from Colonial Airways.

Coping with leaks delayed installation of gas tanks in the white Lockheed, and the proposed flight to Paris was not made in 1931. Amelia Earhart Putnam's solo Atlantic flight the next spring defeated the original plans made for Miss Ingalls. The next year the doll-like flyer acquired the Air Express herself, and proceeded to do credit to her long training in it.

Between February 28 and April 25, 1934, Laura Ingalls became the first flyer, man or woman, to complete a solo flight around the South American continent. Touching twenty-three countries, it was also the longest solo air journey made by a woman up to that time.

On March 21, Laura poked the cowl of the Air Express up to 18,000 feet and nosed through the Uspallata Pass of the Andes between Santiago, Chile, and Mendoza, Argentina. It was the first time that an American woman had flown over this formidable range in her own plane. Laura reported the Andes crossing as "gorgeous—a magnificent joy ride!" But her complete circuit of South America took careful, skillful flying. The 16,897-mile journey won Miss Ingalls a Harmon Award as the outstanding American woman flyer of 1934.

Her South American trip gave Laura the necessary experience in foreign air travel to prompt her to enter 1934's most exciting aerial event, the MacRobertson Race from England to Australia. With a legacy left by an aunt, Miss Ingalls ordered a brand-new Orion from Lockheed, and went out to Burbank to see to its construction and preparation. The Ingalls Orion was a gleaming black, with red-and-gold trim. Laura named it *Auto-da-Fé*—Portuguese for "act of faith"—and painted a cross-and-crescent insignia below the cockpit.

The ship incorporated all the latest in equipment: a supercharged Pratt & Whitney Wasp engine, Hamilton controllable-pitch propeller, landing flaps, Sperry Gyropilot, and a Westport radio compass and receiver. Laura's studies ranged from reports of landing techniques as practiced by pilots who'd flown Orions, to the reading of a battery hydrometer. The girl was so anxious to keep tabs on construction that she even climbed the plant fence on Sunday for an off-day review of progress.

It became impossible to enter the unfinished plane in the race to Australia. Instead, when she finally took delivery, Laura set her sights on the one significant American women's distance record left to be claimed, the first nonstop coast-to-coast flight from east to west.

Twice the tiny girl in the big black Orion set out, the first time to be forced down by a duststorm at Alamosa, Colorado, and the second by engine trouble at Indianapolis. On the Fourth of July, 1935, her foot was burned by a carelessly thrown firecracker, but a week later things looked good for a third attempt. In the dawn at Floyd Bennett Field, Laura slid into the cockpit of the *Auto-da-Fé* and latched the hatch. At 5:30 A.M. she roared off down the short runway and raced the sun across the continent. The record was hers 18 hours and 19 minutes later as she rolled to a stop in Burbank. And she'd beaten Frank Hawks's old solo time as well.

Not content with being the first woman to fly westward alone and nonstop across the nation, Laura Ingalls was determined to better Amelia Earhart's record time in the other direction. She came rocketing back to New York on September 12, 1935. Though delayed in starting by tire trouble, Laura burned up the sky with the black Orion. She arrived over the city lights only seven minutes behind the existing men's speed record. Watchers at Floyd Bennett saw the Lockheed as it "circled the Rockaways, came back over the field, circled once more over Jamaica Bay and Fort Tilden, cut over the ocean and then came back for a landing." All the fancy passes were just Laura showing her happiness at breaking the record. This flight beat the Earhart nonstop record of 1932 by 5½ hours, and Amelia's two-stop time by over three.

Laura Ingalls flew the *Auto-da-Fé* for another year and with it placed second in the 1936 Bendix Race to Los Angeles. Then the Orion was sold for use in the Spanish Civil War, and Laura went back to more sedate flying in a standard Lockheed Vega.

The special Ingalls Orion was among the last of the wooden series to leave the production line at the Lockheed factory in Burbank—as were two Altairs, both of which saw years of service in Japan.

The two greatest Japanese newspapers were (and are today) the *Asahi Shimbun* (Rising Sun News), and *Mainichi Shimbun* (Daily News). *Asahi* was a pioneer in promoting aviation and put up the $25,000 prize for the first nonstop Pacific flight, the one Harold Bromley tried so hard to make. The competing *Mainichi* determined to provide some aeronautical news of its own. In 1932, through the Okura Trading Company of Tokyo, the newspaper imported a fine new Lockheed Altair. There was a slight delay in delivery when the wing of the unassembled ship washed overboard from the freighter which was transporting the plane to Japan. Lockheed produced a new one in short order. The ship was put together and used for newsgathering and the transportation of publishing officials.

In 1935 *Mainichi* planned a goodwill flight from Japan to the Philippines to congratulate the first president of the Republic, Manuel Quezon, on his assumption of office. Piloted by Seizan Okura, the Altair also carried flight engineer Tokushi Fuse, and goodwill ambassador Fukuichi Fukomoto was tucked in amid the mailbags full of special letters. Carried out between November 10–26, 1935, this was the first flight between Tokyo and Manila and return. It was also timed to connect with the first regular San Francisco–Manila run of the Pan American Airways *China Clipper*.

A Japanese custom was to write autographs and goodwill messages on the fabric of traveling aircraft. The Lockheed's sleek sides and tail surfaces were covered with such scribblings, and in Manila the Japanese colony all went carefully over the plane to see if possibly Aunt Suki had sent a message. Over 4,000 more conventional letters were mailed to be flown on the return trip, which went by way of Okinawa.

Following this successful junket, *Mainichi* ordered another Altair to be flown to Manchuria in connection with the establishment of the Japanese puppet state of Manchukuo. Fumio Habuto, in charge of the newspaper's extensive aviation section, also wanted to fly the new ship on a goodwill trip to Siam, but such was the red tape

Mainichi Shimbun's *goodwill Altair* (top), *which cracked up 18 months after round-trip Tokyo-Manila flight, and* (below) *its sister ship, destroyed by USAAF raid in 1944.*

and rivalry between *Mainichi* and *Asahi* that the flight never came off. Decked out in colorful paint jobs, and with the star-and-bars *Mainichi* trademark on their tails, the two Altairs were put to work flying newspapers and mail from Tokyo and Osaka. They also took reporters all over the country for on-the-spot coverage of important news events.

The original *Mainichi* Altair came to an untimely end in 1937 when it tangled with a smokestack on approach to Itami Airport in Osaka. The remaining Lockheed had ten years of useful service with the newspaper, and nearly survived World War II. In the autumn of 1944 it was parked in a hangar at Tokyo's Haneda Airport when USAAF bombers came over. All hell broke loose, and in the language of a Japanese eyewitness "*the Mainichi* Altair was seriously demolished, leaving only its imperishable name on a page of the commercial aviation history of our country."

The Lindberghs' survey trip of 1933 had been the only flight across the South Atlantic by a wooden Lockheed. Their float-equipped Sirius crossed from east to west. Two years later another Sirius made the journey in the opposite direction.

The airplane involved was originally the property of Casey Lambert of St. Louis, and later flew as The Texas Company's *Texaco 16*. How it came into possession of the Cuban Navy is something of a mystery, but it turned

Menéndez in cockpit of Cuba's 4 de Septiembre *in 1936.*

up in Havana late in 1935. On January 9, 1936, the five-year-old Sirius got a new name. In a solemn ceremony Esther Gonzalez, daughter of the Naval Chief of Staff, broke a bottle of champagne over the propeller hub and christened the plane *4 de Septiembre*, the date honoring one of Cuba's sudden changes of administration. The tail of the ship bore the star and stripes of the Cuban Naval Forces.

Within a few days good-looking young Lieutenant Antonio Menéndez y Palaez was assigned to fly the Lockheed across the Atlantic on the first west–east trip to link Cuba with her old mother country, Spain. The lone pilot sealed off the rear cockpit to show that the long trip would be a solo venture.

Menéndez accomplished the flight in a little over a month.

He first headed the cowled and panted Sirius across the Caribbean to Venezuela and then on to Trinidad. A leaky gas tank delayed him at Port of Spain, and there were Latin protestations when he discovered he had forgotten his passport on arrival in Brazil. With the difficulties soothed by the Cuban consul, Menéndez proceeded to whisk the *4 de Septiembre* across the South Atlantic. He crossed from Port Natal to Bathurst, Gambia, in a little over seventeen hours on February 10, 1936. Flying up the African coast the navy pilot reached Seville, Spain, four days later.

In May, Menéndez returned to Cuba by boat to find himself a national hero. Twenty thousand people thronged the Havana waterfront to greet him, as well as a Cuban gunboat, five whistling merchant vessels and numerus launches. The colorful Lockheed Sirius which had linked the two Spanish-speaking nations also returned to Cuba and was kept as an historic aircraft until 1945, when it was destroyed in a hangar fire.

By 1936 ocean flying was becoming commonplace, and flyers were hard put to find a place to make a first flight to. Colonel Clarence Chamberlin, an old-timer when it came to Atlantic hopping, talked some of essaying a nonstop jump from New York to Rome, using his Lockheed Altair *Miss Stratosphere*. But he never got started.

Little Portugal had yet to be connected with the New World by air, a fact which set a tall, dark, upstate New York pilot to thinking and planning. He was Joseph Costa, a twenty-seven-year-old Portuguese-American barnstormer and charter pilot, who operated out of Big Flats Airport near the glassworks town of Corning. Costa's mother was still in Portugal, and this gave him an extra incentive to fly across the Atlantic.

In 1936 Joe acquired a good used Lockheed Vega for his proposed trip: one of the one-time Stanavo Eagles flown by the Standard Oil Company of New Jersey. Even dimes and nickels came hard during the middle thirties, but the popular pilot's friends and neighbors contributed toward expenses. They also held a variety show called the "Flight Frolic," and a "Costa Dance" to raise additional funds.

Joe beefed up his Vega's landing gear, installed extra tanks, and blanked out four cabin windows. In honor of

Joe Costa finds more friends and fun than records.

They helped to make it one small world: chance meeting at the Lockheed factory in 1935 gives (left to right) *Amelia Earhart, Wiley Post, Roscoe Turner, and Laura Ingalls a professional look at* Winnie Mae*'s faithful Wasp.*

Corning, she was named *Crystal City,* and bore a Portuguese cross on her tail.

Costa's plan was for a flight from Corning to Harbour Grace, Newfoundland, and then on to Portugal. He'd even decided to take along his father as a passenger, but just when things were ready the State Department quashed the whole project because of the Civil War raging in Spain. Undaunted, the lanky flyer requested clearance for South America. He figured that if he could get to Rio de Janeiro, the Brazilian authorities would let him fly the South Atlantic and on up to Lisbon.

In November 1936, Joe climbed the Vega's side and eased his six-foot frame down into the cockpit. Watchers in Corning last saw the white *Crystal City* as Joe wagged her wings and headed south. Things went well until Costa reached the Caribbean. Flying over the Dominican Republic a gas leak brought him down, and the suspicious Dominicans clapped him in jail. Clearance by radio from Puerto Rico brought release. Joe made temporary repairs to the gas line by rubbing soap into the crack and tying his handkerchief around it. He winged on to San Juan, keeping a wary eye on his emergency handiwork.

Cruising along the island chain, Costa soon made Pará, Brazil. After a visit with an uncle he took off on January 15, 1937, for Rio de Janeiro, with hopes of approval and clearance for his South Atlantic attempt.

The *Crystal City* never reached Rio. Flying in a tropical downpour, getting low on gas, and with darkness closing in, Joe picked a landing spot on a ridge near the village of Conceição do Serro. He brought the Vega in all right and had slowed to about 40 mph when the right landing gear hit an anthill and ripped off. The wing dipped, caught, and the plane skidded along to a jarring stop. Costa's head banged the instrument panel, and it was two hours before he regained consciousness, rousing to the twin sounds of driving rain and dripping gasoline. Nearby villagers soon found him, but with roads impassable, it was a month before Joe could be flown out by the Brazilian government. The would-be Atlantic flyer removed the Vega's engine and instruments during his wait, and they were eventually shipped back to Corning. The rest of the Lockheed was hauled to the village as a local curiosity.

Though big Joe Costa's bid for flying fame and fortune ended in a Brazilian anthill, he gained a host of new friends on his South American journey. He was the *last* man to set out to fly the Atlantic in a Lockheed Vega.

12

AIRLINERS AT HOME

The nation's infant airlines lost no time in adopting Lockheeds as ready-made transports. Here was an airplane that would snugly enclose its passengers in a cocoon of wood and neat leather upholstery; there was no chance of a stray foot punching through the fabric. To be sure, they would not be as commodious as the "giant" 14-passenger Ford Trimotors just coming into prominence. But with their thoroughbred look, the Lockheeds were bound to attract potential air travelers.

The very first Lockheed "airliner" had a brief but eventful career. This was the original Air Express model, developed late in 1927 and built during the next winter. The company felt that there was a market for fast, open-cockpit mail planes, with a place for four passengers if they could be enticed to ride along. Western Air Express, flying mail on the government's Contract Air Mail Route No.4 between Los Angeles and Salt Lake City, was a logical prospect.

However, it would obviously be necessary to rework the Vega into something that veteran airmail flyers would endorse.

WAE's pilots were accustomed to flying from a cockpit to the rear of an airplane, and using a radiator cap or a rocker arm up ahead to determine longitudinal attitude. They objected to flying from a position in the extreme front end, where the Vega had its office. Lockheed's Air Express was the answer, and developing the model was 100 percent the responsibility of chief engineer John K.

Charles Lindbergh with the Air Express, which he tried a few days before its first—and last—flight for WAE.

Feature of a late-winter exhibition is the new parasol-wing "Lockheed mail & passenger monoplane" designed for Western Air Express, shown with experimental fin and notice it would be in service after March 10, 1928.

Northrop. He raised the wing a foot and a half above the fuselage on cabane struts of streamlined tubing in order to provide the desired forward visibility.

In addition to the pilot's cockpit aft, there was room for a good stack of mailbags in the cabin, and/or four paying passengers. Experiments were made with a triangular fin such as appeared on the first two Vegas and the original Explorer, but it was discarded in favor of a rounded one with greater area and better lateral stability. On this fin was the familiar WAE Indian arrowhead insignia of the airline, and the new ship was named *Air Express.*

The new parasol-wing job was fitted with a 410-hp Pratt & Whitney Wasp engine, the second application of this famous power plant to a Lockheed.

The ship was given exhaustive tests by both manufacturer and the airline. In June 1928 Colonel Lindbergh, who had come West to pick up a new plush Ryan Brougham at San Diego, made a special trip to test-hop the Air Express from Vail Field at Montebello, California. Though he requested no publicity, the presence of the magic name "Lindbergh" was not kept entirely silent, and the colonel was quoted as saying, "It is a wonderful plane and answers the need of commercial flying in a splendid way."

It was Lindbergh's first flight in a Lockheed-built airplane. The contrast between it and the Ryans he'd been flying must have been very evident. That same day C. N. (Jimmy) James, pioneer Western Air Express pilot, flew the colonel's new Brougham and recalls that it was "about as stable as trying to stand on top of a ten-foot rubber ball!"

With pilot Fred Kelly I, Western Air Express dispatched the new ship on its first scheduled flight on June 6, 1928. Will Rogers, always an indefatigable air traveler, arranged to go along to Salt Lake accompanied by Dr. L. D. Cheney.

The maiden flight came to grief at the very first stop, Las Vegas. On landing, the ship hit a supposedly sunken concrete marker in the center of the field, did a fast flip, and slid to a stop on its back. Rogers, Cheney, and Kelly tumbled out, shaken but unhurt.

The humorist and his pilot continued on in a relief plane and Lockheed quietly trucked the damaged aircraft back to Burbank. It was completely rebuilt, but Western Air Express never retook delivery of their namesake airplane. Instead, the reincarnated prototype became Frank Hawks's famed record-breaking *Texaco 5.*

Another West Coast airline had been started by Jack Maddux, a successful Los Angeles automobile dealer. He had a dozen Ford Trimotors on the San Francisco–Los Angeles–San Diego runs of his Maddux Air Lines; they flew some 350,000 miles in 1928. But there were already travelers for whom the novelty of flying was not enough. They wanted real speed.

Eddie Bellande and Larry Fritz, who had test-flown the first Lockheeds, earned their bread and butter toting passengers in the Maddux Fords. Maddux and his pilots reasoned that there would be additional revenue in charter work. In cases where extreme speed was a factor, what better ships could be added to the fleet than a couple of the slim, trim products from the neighboring factory in Burbank?

Maddux bought its first Lockheed Vega airliner in July 1928 and another one in August. Soon the bright-orange monoplanes were a familiar sight on the airways out of Los Angeles. Movie people chartered them for trips to the

First Vega in airline service, this workhorse was used for charter/overflow by Maddux in 1928, carried cargo for Air Express, flew for Capitol, then hauled Varney payloads in the West, Mexico, and Texas until 1937.

desert resorts or up in the mountains to Big Bear. The governor of Baja California, Mexico, was a frequent customer; and once a Los Angeles broker and his party were sped east to Kingman, Arizona, to catch a Santa Fe train for New York.

The Wright Whirlwind-powered Lockheeds had space for only four people, yet it was sufficient to prove their worth as overflow ships for a sold-out run of the big Fords. Taking off well behind a "tin goose," the Maddux Vegas would cruise sedately along up to San Francisco, throttled down so as not to pass "big brother" en route.

There were mishaps of course, as with any new airplane subjected to the rigors of daily service for hire. Probably the fastest replacement the Lockheed plant ever did was a job on a Maddux Vega. Test pilot Marshall "Babe" Headle brought the plane in late one afternoon for a routine check. He thought that perhaps it "shook a little." On landing, it was discovered that the entire forward end of the fuselage was broken off and hanging by only one motor-mount brace. Everybody, particularly Babe, gulped—and then set to work. The factory happened to have an identical fuselage in stock, even to its fabric painted the international orange. Working all night, the crew dismantled and burned the old shell. They reinstalled landing gear, empennage, motor, and interior trim on the new one. Next morning the rebuilt Vega was back flying on Maddux Air Lines.

Clarence Wood dropped the other Maddux Vega into a sandhole while taxiing to the hangar at San Diego. The ship nosed over and "busted in half just aft of the passenger compartment." Shipped back to Burbank, the rigging crew at Lockheed again produced and installed a new fuselage in short order. After another minor accident, and use as a company demonstrator, this early Vega survived a decade of transcontinental and local service, flying for five other American and Mexican airlines.

Elsewhere in the country, dreams of speedy service between hitherto distant cities occupied the minds of businessmen caught up in the aviation boom. Little one- and two-plane outfits blossomed out all over the map. Some would prosper and grow to merge in the expanding national network. The greater portion would operate with high hopes for a few months or perhaps a year, and then quietly suspend service and sell off their equipment—provided their creditors hadn't taken it already.

Erle Halliburton, Lockheed's midwest distributor, had a Vega on demonstration in the 6,300-mile Ford Air Tour of June–July 1928. It proved to be such a sensation at every grassy way stop that pilot Bob Cantwell had difficulty to keep from selling it en route. The successful buyers, two North Dakota businessmen, got delivery of the ship right after Cantwell finished out the Ford Tour. On September 17, 1928, using their Vega and a Ryan cabin ship, A. W. Hugh and D. H. Bartholomew commenced a daily-except-Sunday service between Minot and Bismarck, North Dakota, calling their line International Airways, Inc. Cecil Shupe was their chief pilot and Carl Ben Eielson and Lee Shoenhair also flew briefly during its short and sporadic career. Since Western Air Express's mail plane made only a partial trip, and Maddux's operations were more in the nature of standby and overflow flying, the Vega of little International Airways was probably the first Lockheed in regularly scheduled airline service.

Universal Air Lines, one of the predecessor companies of today's American Airlines network, purchased two Vegas the same month that International got its start.

Continental Air Express flew passengers from San Francisco to Los Angeles speedily, and went broke almost as fast.

These were used on the passenger route from Chicago to St. Louis via Peoria and Springfield; the company's fat-bellied, mail-carrying biplanes flew direct.

On the West Coast was Santa Maria Airlines, Inc., under the direction of G. Allan Hancock, owner of an oil company. Captain Hancock was the man who backed the 1928 flight of Kingsford-Smith from California to Australia. His interests were wide, ranging from yachting to chamber music, but aviation was his pet enthusiasm. His Santa Maria Airlines flew a 4-passenger Vega on a daily run to Santa Barbara and Los Angeles. When not in use on the line, the ship was available as a trainer at the Hancock Foundation College of Aeronautics in Santa Maria.

A more ambitious California line was Continental Air Express, which began flying two routes from Los Angeles to San Francisco in 1928—one via Bakersfield and Fresno and another via Taft and Coalinga. Their Vega, together with a Fokker and two Kreutzer Air Coaches, was repossessed by the finance boys after less than two years' operation.

Airline operations of greater magnitude were soon to begin. Erle Halliburton wasn't satisfied to be just a cementer of oil wells and distributor of airplanes. Early in 1929 with his cousin, J. C. Halliburton, he organized an airline to serve Missouri, Kansas, Oklahoma, and Texas. They called it Southwest Air Fast Express; it was no accident that its initials were S.A.F.E.

Larry Fritz, who had successfully flown Fords and Lockheeds for Maddux in California, was brought to Tulsa as operating vice president of the new line. SAFEway Airlines—the other of its unofficial designations—began business on April 2, 1929, flying five new Ford Trimotors between St. Louis and Dallas via Kansas City, Tulsa, Oklahoma City, and Forth Worth. Halliburton's personal airplane, the bright-yellow Vega named *The Tester,* was pressed into service for use in carrying overloads on the Ford runs. Within a month Southwest Air Fast Express put on three more brand-new Vegas and four additional Fords. The big trimotors from Detroit were the accepted passenger airliners of the period, but Lockheeds were

Erle Halliburton, boss of Southwest Air Fast Express, and (right) Jimmy Wedell of Wedell-Williams Air Service.

employed when speed was a prime consideration. Erle Halliburton and his backers did well with the combination.

SAFEway's base of operations was Tulsa, then one of the world's busiest airports. The line had no hangars at first: all maintenance work was done out in the open, and during dust- or rainstorms the planes were staked out and tied to automobiles. Halliburton's ambitious air network was run by a highly concentrated, well-organized group of dedicated personnel, to whom overtime meant nothing when a job had to be done. In addition to Larry Fritz and chief pilot Bob Cantwell, there were Maurice Marrs, Ray Beindorf, Frank Morton, Frank Glenn, and Jimmy Haizlip to fly the Fords and Vegas. Merrill Grix was chief engineer, and Bob Arnold, John Forbes, and Ed Zehring kept the ships flying. Everything was daylight operation, with the ground crews sending a telegram to the next airport advising that a plane had left.

One of SAFEway's most lucrative sidelines was the "Sunday afternoon business" at Tulsa Airport. From dinner to dark, two or three Fords and all four Vegas were kept busy flying five-minute scenic hops over the city at $5 a head. The money they took in helped keep the budding airline in solvency.

In addition to their own Vegas, Halliburton and S.A.F.E. crews maintained other Lockheeds such as the Independent and Marland Oil jobs,and a blue-and-white plane called *Winnie Mae,* owned by an F. C. Hall of Chickasha, Oklahoma. One of the new airline's best customers was Will Rogers, who had a home in Claremore. The humorist-cowboy-turned-actor liked to fly as much as possible. He would often charter a Vega to transport himself and a party of friends to places like Los Angeles, Mexico City, or Chicago. Unlike the Fords, which bore the company name, S.A.F.E.'s Lockheeds were unmarked "businessman's specials." In addition to the boss's yellow job with the barrel-shaped NACA cowl, there was a red Vega, a blue Vega, and a tan Vega, each with neat leather upholstery to match.

Despite the volume of business and a tight operation, Southwest Air Fast Express became increasingly aware that it couldn't survive without an airmail contract to subsidize its passenger traffic for a while. Erle Halliburton tried, by joining forces with Robertson-Universal of St. Louis, to obtain the "southern transcontinental route" from the Post Office Department. There was an involved you-buy-me-or-I'll-buy-you deal, and finally SAFEway was sold to the American Airways group then forming, for a cool $1,400,000.

Southwest Air Fast Express had operated for eighteen months with no accidents or injuries to passengers or personnel. A record like that gave good indication that air travel was here to stay.

At the same time that SAFEway was flying its first planes across the Oklahoma flatlands, a new kind of transport service was being established up in the northwest corner of the United States. Using the region's myriad bays, rivers, harbors, and lakes as landing fields, it was to be an airline on floats.

In the spring of 1929, Joseph L. Carman, Jr., bought a new Wasp-powered Vega on pontoons, to add to the fleet of landplanes at his Seattle aviation school. Named *Juneau* and sent to southeastern Alaska, the Lockheed soon brought in a steady income. Swinging high over the steep-sided landlocked inlets, it ferried men to mining camps, supplied food to isolated settlements, or brought trappers' furs "outside" for sale.

At this time the Alaskan canneries were plagued with thefts from their widely scattered fishtraps. Canners contracted for the *Juneau* to fly a varying route over the trapsites. Any noncompany boat seen near a trap was reported. Fish poachers could never tell when the burnt-orange Vega would come thundering around a headland and swoop out of the mist to spot them. Thefts soon dropped to zero.

Carman's Lockheed was also used by the Alaska-Pacific Salmon Corporation and the Nakat Packing Company to transport their officials, and to act as a courier between canneries and their small boat fleets. When a school of fish was sighted offshore the sturdy Vega would be dispatched with a strange, hastily prepared load: dozens of bottles rolled clinking on the floor of the cabin, each tightly corked and enclosing a message advising the proper course and rendezvous for a probable good catch. Alaska-Pacific and Nakat fishermen learned to hail the *Juneau*'s arrival with hearty waves and whistles, for the bottle messages meant more dollars in the hind pocket when they next made port.

The fishery work and the revenue it brought in were all fine, but Joe Carman had other far-reaching ideas. On April 15, 1929, the *Juneau* made the first nonstop flight betwen the mainland of the United States and the then territory of Alaska. Piloted by Anscel C. Eckmann, with Robert E. Ellis as copilot, and mechanic Jack Halloran, the Vega made the 940-mile hop from Seattle to Juneau in 7 hours and 48 minutes. Steamship travel between the same two points required three and a half days.

That same day Carman launched a new company: Alaska-Washington Airways, designed to give Alaskans a new link by air to Stateside. There was no reason why almost everything going to and from Alaska couldn't be moved by airplane. During the new outfit's first five months the *Juneau,* on scheduled operations, charter, and fish patrol, carried more than 1,500 passengers and took in an average of $44 an hour for the company. The fare to Juneau was only $105, which could be produced by many an old sourdough anxious to get back to his chosen land.

Encouraged, Carman expanded Alaska-Washington Airways in all directions. Seaplane operation in the Pacific

Northwest had the advantage of putting aircraft at a dock only minutes from the heart of the cities to be served. Alaska-Washington established a Seattle-Tacoma-Olympia line, a triangular service to Vancouver and Victoria in British Columbia, and added ports of call like Ketchikan, Wrangell, Sitka, and Skagway to the Alaskan route. In addition, a subsidiary flying Vegas on wheels served Wenatchee, Ellensburg, Yakima, and Pasco in central Washington.

Over a three-year period Alaska-Washington and its subsidiaries were the owners of a real fleet of Lockheed Vegas. They bought seven—bright and new from the factory—and had a couple of Fairchild 71s and a Stinson Detroiter as well. Like homing gulls the shiny orange Vegas would come winging in to Seattle at night, and sit bobbing in the sparkling waters of Lake Union off the company's ramp on Roanoke Street. Next morning would see them thundering along at 2,000 feet above the island-dotted waters of the famous Inside Passage, while passengers bound for Alaska peered out in awe at a constant panorama of snow-capped mountains, icebergs, and glaciers.

Its float equipment, colorful advertising, and the scenic terrain over which it flew made Alaska-Washington a true glamour line. The route was good and met a growing need. But overexpansion, competition, and the first blows of the Great Depression had to be dealt with. The workhorse *Juneau,* literally worn out and hence unairworthy, was returned to the Lockheed factory. Its replacement was accidentally destroyed on the day of delivery. Two other new Vegas were burned and washed out after only a few months of service. The four that remained when the line went into receivership in 1932 were sadly auctioned off.

Nevada Airlines, Inc., is another name little known today. Organized in 1929 to fly from Los Angeles to

The you-name-it-she'll-do-it Vega (below) that made the nonstop flight from Stateside to Alaska in 1929, and (left) *how the artist dramatized AWA service by giving* Juneau *an Air Express parasol wing and rear cockpit.*

Reno, it also operated a route from the divorce capital to Las Vegas. Among its officers were former Lockheed executives Ben S. Hunter and Ray Boggs of Los Angeles. Nevada's manager of operations was the incomparable Roscoe Turner, just beginning to make his name synonymous with speed.

Roscoe organized the line, flew its planes, publicized it every chance he got. Nevada's backers supplied four Vegas powered by Pratt & Whitney Wasp engines. With a 3½-hour run for the 475 miles beween L.A. and Reno, Turner was certain the schedule could be stepped up. "Nevada," proclaimed Roscoe, "will be the fastest airline in the world." There is little doubt but that it was.

The flamboyant manager of operations chose the oldest of his four Vegas to streamline and make into a showpiece for attracting attention and business to the airline. This was the first of F. C. Hall's *Winnie Maes*, the one flown briefly by Wiley Post and sold back to the factory during a period when the oilman had no need for it. When Roscoe Turner flew the ship, it was the *Sirius*, and had the first cowl and pants to be sported on a Vega used as a commercial transport.

This was before Turner had acquired Gilmore the lion, but his fondness for mascots was asserting itself. He carried a rabbit's foot, a teddy bear, and a live turtle on his flights, and a likeness of the turtle adorned the tail of the airplane.

Roscoe maintained far from a turtle's pace in promoting Nevada Airlines. Just to prove that full transcontinental passenger service was feasible, he flew the *Sirius* from Los Angeles to New York in 19 hours and 53 minutes, with four stops en route. Behind him in the cabin sat a police lieutenant, a navigator (the then-unknown Australian named Harold Gatty), a mechanic, and a reporter. Even with this load of four and the turtle, the plane made the trip only a couple of hours behind the existing nonstop record set earlier in the year by Captain Frank Hawks's Lockheed Air Express.

At Cleveland in September 1929, Turner placed third in the closed-course, 50-mile event of the National Air Races, and the name of Nevada Airlines was spread by newspapers and movie newsreels from coast to coast.

Back out West, Reno was popular as a resort, and big-name stars of the movies flew up with Roscoe and his fellow pilots in the 4-place, star-named Vegas, proud to be traveling on the "Fastest in the World." Box-office luminaries like Loretta Young, Joan Bennett, Clark Gable, and Fred MacMurray hopped up to Reno, not necessarily to shed a spouse. Still, since many of the customers had in mind the tossing of a ring in the Truckee River after their decrees were awarded, Nevada Airlines got the nickname of The Alimony Special. Among the other pilots was "Little Jack" O'Brien, decked out like Roscoe in a uniform complete with Sam Browne belt.

During nearly a year of operation, Turner's pioneer effort put air transport in the public eye, flew nearly a thousand miles a day, never had a forced landing, never hurt a passenger. The closest they came to recording an injury was the time an irate wife chased her husband into a Vega. As he cowered behind a seat she pummeled him with an umbrella and berated him for losing a bundle at the gaming halls in Reno.

If it had not been for the financial crash of 1929, the Fastest Airline in the World might have kept going and expanded into the big time. It quietly folded, though, and Lockheed reluctantly repossessed Nevada's speedy little fleet. Roscoe Turner went on to greater flying achievements.

While Nevada's pilots were winging their way to Reno and Las Vegas, Texas Air Transport established a healthy mail and express business flying from Fort Worth to Waco, Houston, and Galveston. Since there was an occasional passenger who could be stowed with the mailbags, the company bought an Air Express complete with NACA speed cowl.

T.A.T. had better luck with the ship than Western Air Express had with theirs. The plane suffered an accident at Big Spring, Texas, and had to have a new fuselage,

Irrepressible Roscoe Turner finds space to plug Christmas for a California newspaper in 1929, decorates the tail of his streamlined Vega, Sirius, *with the likeness of a mascot that belies his ship's—and his airline's—record.*

Wedell-Williams bought Lockheed's last Sirius. It later served Delta Air Lines as a mail carrier.

but Texas Air and its successors—Southern Air Transport and American Airways—kept it flying on Southwest air routes for several years.

Late in 1928, Allan Loughead and Norman S. Hall started out on a 2,500-mile sales trip into Oklahoma and Texas with the hope of selling a couple of Vegas to wealthy oilmen. One result of the trip was the order for the first *Winnie Mae* from F. C. Hall of Chickasha, Oklahoma. Piloted by E. L. Remelin, the salesmen made a stop at San Angelo, Texas, where they met Carl G. Cromwell, another well-to-do oil operator. Cromwell was so struck with the Vega demonstrator that he bought it on the spot. The Loughead party had to catch a train back to Burbank.

A year afterward, Cromwell started an airline with two Stinsons and his Lockheed. He soon bought another. The ships flew daily routes out of San Angelo to Dallas, San Antonio, and Big Spring. It was on this line that Jimmie Mattern, as chief pilot, got to flying Vegas. Later, when tight money caught up with Cromwell Air Lines, Jimmie found himself in possession of a Lockheed in lieu of back wages. It was to be his chance to emerge on the national scene.

Flying out of St. Louis to Fulton and Jefferson City, Missouri, Gentry Shelton operated a one-plane, twice-a-day schedule for a few months in 1930. The flyer and his ground crew were occasionally chided about their small operation. "Whaddaya mean, one-horse airline?" snorted a Shelton mechanic after one of these jibes. He pointed to the Wright Whirlwind engine on the nose of the company's Vega. "We've got two hundred and twenty of 'em!"

Down in Louisiana a lean Texan had become a partner in one of the nation's largest privately owned flying services. Quiet, unassuming James R. Wedell wasn't shy, but he was more at home with planes than with people. Like Wiley Post, Wedell had the use of only one eye, but he could fly like a demon in anything with wings.

In 1927, fate put Wedell in contact with Harry P. Williams, a millionaire lumberman, and the virtual ruler of the town of Patterson, Louisiana. The Williams mills made jobs for everyone in Patterson, and "Mister Harry" saw to it that the town was run according to his wishes. Among other things, Williams enjoyed playing policeman. A benevolent despot, he'd arrest a man for a real or fancied violation and let him sweat out the possible stiff fine or jail sentence. In the end Williams would usually pay it himself.

This avocation put Harry Williams in contact with barnstormer Jimmy Wedell, down on his luck and caught with a decrepit flying boat on a remote bayou, and accused of smuggling hooch. Jimmy talked his way out of that one, then went on to sell Mister Harry on the wonders of air travel. Before he knew it, Williams had his own plane, and Wedell, as his personal pilot, was teaching him to fly it. Soon this strangely matched pair went further, and a hangar and shops rose on the shore of Bayou Tèche near Patterson.

Wedell-Williams Air Service was a major enterprise for the place and times. Combining Williams's money and labor pool with Wedell's designing genius and practical flying knowledge, the Louisiana partners were involved in nearly every phase of aviation. They kept over a dozen airplanes of various makes busy with a flying school, aerial photography, amphibious work, and charter service. The special Wedell-designed low-wing racing monoplanes built in Patterson became world famous.

Not the least of Wedell-Williams Air Service enterprises

Looking forward in the cabin of a typical 6-passenger Vega, a favorite of early airlines.

was their airline. This began with flights from New Orleans to Shreveport and was later extended to Dallas and Fort Worth. Another route flew from the firm's own field near the Crescent City to Houston, with a way stop at little Patterson, a town of 3,000 people.

To fly the line, Wedell-Williams bought four new Lockheed Vegas plus a fifth that they purchased in parts and assembled themselves. For a "piney woods" shop that could turn out champion racing planes, putting a Vega together was a snap. Still later, the partners bought a new Sirius, the last of the fixed-gear, low-wing twin-cockpit jobs to come out of the Burbank factory.

Even without the subsidy of a mail contract Wedell-Williams Vegas plied back and forth on fast schedules between New Orleans and Texas for several years.

Harry Williams autocratically decreed just how the business and shops should be run, and things got done. Jimmy Wedell was free to dream up and build fast aircraft, and to win races and break records with them. He always signed autographs and letters "Speedily Yours." If there was ever any time during slack seasons for other run-of-the-mill flying chores he'd cheerfully take them on, from an airline run to a student hop. On December 27, 1933, Jimmy flew Mr. and Mrs. W. B. Trammell and their infant daughter from Houston to Baltimore. Baby Sue Trammell was suffering from a brain disease and needed immediate surgery at Johns Hopkins Hospital. Wedell made this winter mercy flight in the face of fog and blizzards, arriving at the Maryland city in the middle of the night.

Had it not been for tragedy, there is no telling how far Speedy Jim Wedell and Mister Harry Williams might have gone in the flying game. As it was, both partners were killed in successive flying accidents. The firm was purchased and liquidated in 1936 by Eastern Air Transport, and most of the Lockheed Vegas from Patterson went to work in Mexico.

Running at right angles to Wedell-Williams's routes were the Bowen Air Lines out of Fort Worth, Texas. Head of this company was Temple Bowen, already a familiar figure in the transport field as an operator of Southwestern bus lines, and of the original Texas Air Transport. Bowen's routes were flown, spokelike, in four directions: to Tulsa, Oklahoma City, San Antonio, and Houston, with Dallas and Fort Worth as a hub.

From the start, Bowen battled for traffic with American Airways, which flew parallel routes. His method of competition was to lower rates and put on faster planes than those of his big rival. Soon four new white-and-red Lockheed Vegas bearing the line's flag emblem were winging north and south out of Fort Worth. To entice Texans to the air lanes the passenger fares were reduced to railroad levels. The folding leather seats all began to be occupied on every trip.

American had the Post Office business, and advertised: "Fly with the Air Mail!" Bowen countered with a letter slogan: "Fly *past* the Air Mail!" His Lockheeds could do it, too. American's crews were under orders not to wait even sixty seconds for the competing planes at junction points. But if a Bowen pilot just missed a connection, he'd simply go tearing by a lumbering AA Ford or Stinson Trimotor and be waiting patiently at the next stop.

Seeking even more speed, Temple Bowen bought the first two Orions to come off the production line at Burbank early in 1931. With their fully retractable landing gear, the new ships were the fastest transports in the sky.

Lockheed's first Orion is checked out before delivery to Bowen Air Lines in spring of 1931. Prototype was initially called a "Sirius 6-passenger cabin plane" and an "Altair Model D" (note fully retractable landing gear).

Soon the Texas promoter was running eighteen daily scheduled flights over his four routes, covering 4,500 miles a day. Bowen's was the first 175-mph passenger service in air history, and again Lockheeds were flying the fastest scheduled airline operation in the world.

But the accelerated pace was not enough. Unhappily, though he offered to carry mail at half the rate per mile his rivals received, Temple Bowen could not match the financial backing that kept American Airways in the air. The Bowen lines never did get a mail contract, and by 1935 another "world's fastest airline" was only a memory. During four years of flying Lockheeds, Bowen had suffered only one passenger accident: the original Orion was washed out at Tulsa with no fatalities. The remaining ships were sold to various owners and other airlines in the Southwest and Mexico. Temple Bowen's own Lockheed Sirius, converted as a mail and cargo carrier, flew briefly for Delta Air Lines when that line won the Deep South mail contract that Bowen coveted but never gained.

The other Southwestern carrier with a Lockheed fleet was Braniff Airways, Inc., of Oklahoma City. Taking up where SAFEway had left off, the new and struggling enterprise was launched by a forty-six-year-old Oklahoma City insurance and real estate man, Thomas E. Braniff.

With his younger brother, Paul, a World War I pilot, and two wealthy friends, Braniff went into business with Vegas in 1930. Soon he was expanding, and running his B-Line clear from Wichita Falls, Texas, to Chicago via Oklahoma City, Tulsa, Kansas City, and St. Louis. On the local scene Braniff's three-trip daily shuttle service between Oklahoma City and Tulsa was a popular feature. Bowen made connections with Braniff and provided a good deal of through traffic.

Like Temple Bowen's line, Braniff's had no mail contract, and was in stiff competition with American Airways. It has been said that the company was held together by the "courage, conviction and persuasiveness of Tom Braniff." For six years he served as president and general factotum with no salary. A loyal cadre of employees stuck with the company during the doldrums of the Depression. Sometimes they would go out and sell ad-

American had a fleet of six Orions. Contemporary planes in the background include (right to left)*: Bellanca, Pilgrim, Stinson, Boeing 247, and Lockheed Vega.*

This metal Vega had already worked for Bowen, Stanavo, and Central Airlines before coming to Braniff in 1934.

vance airline tickets to get some take-home pay.

Unlike Bowen, however, Tom Braniff bought no new airplanes. All but one of his Lockheed Vega fleet were purchased second- or even sixth-hand. Fully reconditioned in the Braniff shops, they functioned as adequately as Bowen's factory-new ships; and cost much less. Braniff flew its schedules with grim determination, and was one of the very few nonmail-carrying "independents" to survive the lean years.

This persistence paid off. Early in 1934 the Post Office Department canceled the airmail contracts because of alleged collusion among major carriers, refusing to allow them to bid again under their former names, and using U.S. Army Air Corps planes to fly the mail during the hiatus before new contracts were let. Among the successful new bidders was Braniff, awarded a new Chicago–Fort Worth mail run. The "payless, canned-bean-dinner days" of the B-Line were over. It put on two more used metal Vegas and, with the purchase of an additional route from Dallas to Houston, Corpus Christi, and Brownsville, Braniff Airways could advertise itself as extending from the Great Lakes to the Gulf.

Though increased traffic warranted putting on 10-passenger, twin-engine Lockheed Electras in 1936, one of the original little fleet of Vegas was kept on standby for another four years. All told, the B-Line had eleven of them, plus a metal Vega on lease from Detroit Aircraft.

Mid-Continent Airlines had much the same background and a story parallel to that of Braniff. In 1928 it was the thought of a young flyer in Sioux City, Iowa, to provide air service between his home town and the Min-

On hand to speed B-Line's first mail flight, May 17, 1934, are brothers Tom Braniff (left) *and Paul Braniff* (right). *C. R. Smith* (far right), *longtime head of American, takes delivery on an AA Orion from Lockheed's Lloyd Stearman.*

neapolis—St. Paul region. Backed by his father, a prosperous creamery executive, A. S. Hanford, Jr., commenced operations on his aerial short line.

After four years of modest operation, Hanford's Tri-State Airlines, Inc., still flew just the one round trip a day to and from the Twin Cities, using two secondhand Vegas. Expansion came gradually and, like Braniff, the Hanford line was saved from oblivion by the acquisition of not one, but two, mail contracts after the cancellation troubles of 1934. Soon Hanford's Lockheeds were wafting letters clear from Chicago to Winnipeg, and from Kansas City to Bismarck, North Dakota. Before long they absorbed Rapid Air Transport, which had an Omaha—St. Louis route.

The Hanfords, father and son, did not let the new prosperity go to their heads. They cannily procured more Vegas and built up a small but competent organization to keep them flying. Jack Seay, a longtime employee, recalled that he was hired simply because he had some experience with plywood and could patch holes or cracks in "the pickle barrels," as the doughty Lockheeds were dubbed by the ground crews.

After the younger Hanford's death in a sport plane accident, A. S. Hanford, Sr., continued in active operation of the airline, using a fleet of four Vegas and three Fords. Two-way radios for mail and night operations were installed in the planes, a difficult job to do in the close confines of the tapering, thin wooden tail of a Lockheed. At least one grunting and cussing mechanic discovered that he had stuck his foot clear out through the side of the plane.

In the course of procuring and rebuilding his various Vegas, the elder Hanford met Thomas Fortune Ryan III, a young financier from San Francisco. Ryan was involved with the reorganized Lockheed company in California, but he was really more interested in airlines. In 1936 he joined the renamed Hanford Airlines at their base in Kansas City and took over operation of the Midwest network. Steady respectability attracted additional capital from other investors. With Tom Ryan at the controls, Hanford's airway became Mid-Continent Airlines in 1938, and went on to become a major carrier before merging with Braniff in 1954.

Weathering the Depression was no cinch for a struggling air transport company. Many hardly got off the ground. The year 1931 was a particularly bad one for the smothering of infant airlines. There was W. E. Wethee's Midland Air Express, for instance. With George Halsey as chief pilot, he set two Vegas to winging the long miles from Kansas City to Cheyenne, Wyoming, and north to Sioux Falls, South Dakota. Empty seats at that time made the routes appear unprofitable. Chicago-Detroit Airways flew two rebuilt Vegas on their short line a few months, and gave up. Then there was Continental Airways, connecting Chicago and Washington with high-speed schedules and the services of top pilots like Harold Johnson and Russ Mossman. Added to mounting deficits and overexpansion, Continental had bad luck: both their almost-brand-new Lockheed Orions were destroyed in a Chicago hangar fire.

Misfortune also struck the New York, Philadelphia & Washington Airway Corporation, better known as the Ludington Lines. This efficient and tightly operated commuter service between the big Eastern cities was run by Eugene Vidal and Paul F. "Dog" Collins, both A-1 air

Ill-fated Continental Airways gets a boost when delivery flight of this Orion wins second in 1931 Bendix Race.

transport men, while the purse strings were held by the air-minded Ludington brothers of Philadelphia. Seeking to step up their schedule with a 68-minute nonstop Washington-Newark service, Ludington put on a new Orion, only to lose it in a disastrous crash after only a few weeks' operation. For the remainder of their two years' competition with the bigger, mail-carrying Eastern Air Transport, the speedy runs on the Ludington Lines were handled by Consolidated Fleetsters, plus Amelia Earhart's transatlantic Vega on lease.

Two sister ships of Ludington's Orions had gone to another Eastern line, Pittsburgh Airways. This company—organized by Jim Condon, ex-U.S. Navy, and former barnstormer Ted Taney—was a pioneer in flying passengers across the forbidding hump of the Alleghenies.

Condon and Taney had ambitious plans for their new subsidiary, New York & Western Airlines, with a route from New York to Pittsburgh via Camden and York. In addition to the bright new Orions, they leased the first three metal Vegas to be assembled by Detroit Aircraft, with option to buy. Business languished despite this formidable array of equipment, and NY&W ran for only five months. The Detroit organization, already in receivership, was stuck with five somewhat-used airplanes.

Philip H. Philbin of Denver took over the ex-Pittsburgh Orions the next summer for his recently formed Air Express Corporation. This was a new idea in transport—an exclusive air freight line operating coast to coast. In addition to the pair of Orions, Philbin picked up Midland Air Express's three Vegas, one a veteran that had begun service with Maddux Airlines in 1928. Under the direction of Vance Breese, Air Express's operations manager, all five Lockheeds were rebuilt in Detroit. Windows were blocked out and the Vegas were fitted with an extra-streamlined special Speed Gear.

The silver express fleet was put to work on the transcontinental airway, flying lobsters to Los Angeles and fresh flowers back to New York. Famed transpacific flyer Clyde Pangborn was an Air Express pilot, along with Jess Hart, Russ Mossman, Harry Van Liew and "Chief" Bohan. They worked in relays with the Orions to lower the transcontinental transport record three times until it stood at 13 hours and 50 minutes.

Phil Philbin's freight line was a preview of things to come in the expanding air transport picture, but a few years ahead of its time. Without funds to continue operations during the bank holiday of 1933, the Air Express Corporation went out of business.

On the West Coast the name of Walter T. Varney was well known in the airmail business. Son of a San Francisco advertising billboard executive, Varney stayed in aviation after World War I and operated a successful flying school and charter service out of San Mateo, California. In 1926 his pioneer 460-mile route from Elko, Nevada, to Boise,

Philbin's #104 offers overnight hops from N.Y.C. to L.A.

Idaho, and Pasco, Washington, had been the first contract carrier to get the U.S. mail into the air.

By 1931 Varney was back in Oakland with a small line to Sacramento and an exclusive agency to sell Stinson airplanes. He had sold his mail routes in the Pacific Northwest to United Air Lines—and was suddenly a millionaire. A great one for entertainment and free spending, Walter Varney might have settled down to enjoy his money then and there. But the Cord-controlled Century Pacific Airlines set up their own ground units to service the Stinson Trimotors they'd begun flying in California. Motor tycoon Errett Lobban Cord, of the Auburn Automobile Company, also owned Stinson Aircraft, and Varney was angry at this interference in "his" territory.

"We'll get the fastest commercial plane on the market," he told Franklin Rose, his young and trusted assistant, "and fly circles around their damn Stinsons!" And they did.

The Varney Speed Lines were born when the veteran operator sat down and wrote out a check for six Orions. Frank Rose, as president and general manager, took the order and flew down to Burbank. To Lockheed's Carl Squier and his tiny staff, floundering with absentee management from Detroit, the $100,000-plus check was manna from heaven. (Later, in much the same way, Varney was to help buy the whole nearly defunct Lockheed Aircraft Corporation.)

Sparkling white with red trim, the Varney Orions were six of the most beautiful airplanes ever to launch a full-fledged airline practically overnight. The sleek ships were named for winds from all four points of the compass, plus *Winter* and *Coast*. The advertised schedule was Oakland to Glendale in 1 hour and 58 minutes. Passengers were given a shiny new dime for each and every minute it took over that to reach their airport destinations. The flight time to Sacramento was 22 minutes, with the same offer. Some of the pilots were Monte Sharpe, Joe Taff,

(Continued on page 128)

DOMESTIC (U.S.) SCHEDULED AIRLINES USING

Name	Base of Operations	Years Operating Early Lockheeds	Types
Air Express Corporation	New York, N.Y.	1932–33	3 Vegas, 2 Orions
Alaska Air Express, Inc.	Seattle, Wash.	1933–36	1 Vega
Alaska Airlines, Inc.	Anchorage, Alaska	1944–46	1 Vega, 1 Orion
Alaska Air Transport	Juneau, Alaska	1936–42	2 Vegas
Alaska Coastal Airlines	Juneau, Alaska	1942–58	2 Vegas
Alaska Southern Airways	Seattle, Wash.	1933–34	2 Vegas
Alaska Star Airlines	Fairbanks, Alaska	1942–46	1 Vega, 1 Orion
Alaska-Washington Airways, Inc.	Seattle, Wash.	1929–32	7 Vegas
American Airways, Inc.	New York, N.Y.	1930–35	4 Vegas, 6 Orions, 1 Air Express
Arrowhead International Airlines	Duluth, Minn.	1929–30	3 Vegas
Bowen Air Lines, Inc.	Fort Worth, Texas	1930–35	6 Vegas, 2 Orions, 1 Sirius
Braniff Airways, Inc.	Oklahoma City, Okla.	1930–39	11 Vegas
Canadian-American Airlines, Inc.	St. Paul, Minn.	1929–30	2 Vegas
Capitol Airlines, Inc.	San Bruno, Calif.	1933–34	2 Vegas
Central Airlines, Inc.	Pittsburgh, Pa.	1934	4 Vegas
Chicago-Detroit Airways	Chicago, Ill.	1931	2 Vegas
Continental Air Express	Los Angeles, Calif.	1928–30	1 Vega
Continental Air Lines, Inc.	Denver, Colo.	1937–41	1 Vega
Continental Airways, Inc.	Chicago, Ill.	1931–32	2 Orions
Cromwell Air Lines	San Angelo, Texas	1929–32	2 Vegas
Hanford Airlines, Inc.	Sioux City, Iowa	1932–38	6 Vegas
Inland Air Lines, Inc.	Casper, Wyo.	1938–41	2 Orions
International Airways, Inc.	Minot, N. Dak.	1928–31	1 Vega
Irving Airways	Juneau, Alaska	1936	1 Vega
Maddux Air Lines, Inc.	Los Angeles, Calif.	1928–30	2 Vegas
Mid-Continent Airlines, Inc.	Kansas City, Mo.	1938–42	2 Vegas
Midland Air Express, Inc.	Kansas City, Mo.	1931–32	2 Vegas
Middle States Airlines	Akron, Ohio	1929–31	2 Vegas
Nevada Airlines, Inc.	Los Angeles, Calif.	1929–30	4 Vegas
New York, Philadelphia & Washington Airway Corp.	Washington, D.C.	1931	1 Orion
New York & Western Airlines, Inc.	Pittsburgh, Pa.	1931	3 Vegas, 2 Orions

SINGLE-ENGINE LOCKHEED AIRCRAFT 1928–58

Evolved to/Acquired by Present Company	Remarks
	Express only
Alaska Airlines, Inc.	
Alaska Coastal—Ellis Airlines	Merged 1939 to become Alaska Coastal Airlines
Alaska Coastal—Ellis Airlines	
Alaska Airlines, Inc.	
	Also briefly operated Inter Citair Airlines, Wenatchee, Wash. (1930)
American Airlines, Inc.	Used various ones over different periods
	Combined 12/29 with Canadian-American Airlines
Braniff International Airways, Inc.	Plus 1 Vega leased only (1931)
	Capitol Speed Lines, Inc. (1934)
United Air Lines, Inc.	
Continental Air Lines, Inc.	
Braniff International Airways, Inc.	Also called Hanford's Tri-State Airlines, Inc.; n/c to Mid-Continent Airlines (1938)
Western Air Lines, Inc.	
Trans World Airlines (TWA)	
Braniff International Airways, Inc.	
	Plus 1 Vega leased only (1931); also called Ludington Lines
	Also called Pittsburgh Airways, Inc.

DOMESTIC (U.S.) SCHEDULED AIRLINES USING

Name	Base of Operations	Years Operating Early Lockheeds	Types
Northern Airlines, Inc. (N.D.)	Minot, N. Dak.	1928	1 Vega
Northern Consolidated Airlines	Anchorage, Alaska	1948–52	1 Vega
Northwest Airways, Inc.	St. Paul, Minn.	1933–35	3 Orions
Pacific Alaska Airways	Fairbanks, Alaska	1934–36	1 Vega
Rapid Air Lines Corporation	Omaha, Nebr.	1933–34	1 Vega
Santa Maria Airlines, Inc.	Santa Maria, Calif.	1928–29	1 Vega
Shelton-Jefferson Airways, Inc.	St. Louis, Mo.	1930–31	1 Vega
Southwest Air Fast Express	Tulsa, Okla.	1929–30	4 Vegas
Texas Air Transport, Inc.	Fort Worth, Texas	1929–32	1 Air Express
Transcontinental & Western Air, Inc.	New York, N.Y.	1931–37	4 Vegas, 3 Orions
Universal Air Lines	Chicago, Ill.	1928–31	2 Vegas
Varney Air Service, Ltd.	Alameda, Calif.	1931–34	1 Vega, 6 Orions
Varney Speed Lines, Inc. (Southwest Division)	El Paso, Texas	1934–37	5 Vegas
Washington–New York Air Line, Inc.	Washington, D.C.	1929–30	2 Vegas
Wedell-Williams Air Service, Inc.	Patterson, La.	1930–36	5 Vegas, 1 Sirius
Western Air Express	Los Angeles, Calif.	1928	1 Air Express
Wyoming Air Service, Inc.	Casper, Wyo.	1935–38	3 Orions

FOREIGN SCHEDULED AIRLINES USING

Name	Base of Operations	Years Operating Early Lockheeds	Types
Aerovías Centrales, S.A.	México, D.F.	1934–36	3 Orions
Cía. Mexicana de Aviación	México, D.F.	1936	2 Orions
Commercial Airways, Ltd.	Edmonton, Alta., Canada	1929–44	1 Vega
Corp. Aeronáutica de Transportes, S.A.	Torreón, Coah., Mexico	1929–33	10 Vegas
Líneas Aéreas Mineras, S.A.	Mazatlán, Sin., Mexico	1937–44	11 Vegas, 1 Orion
Líneas Aéreas Occidentales, S.A.	Burbank, Calif.	1934–35	2 Vegas, 4 Orions
New York, Rio & Buenos Aires Line	New York, N.Y.	1930	2 Air Express
Pan American Airways, Inc.	New York, N.Y.	1930–32 1935–36	2 Air Express 2 Orions
Pan American–Grace Airways, Inc.	New York, N.Y.	1930–35	2 Vegas
Swiss Air Transport Co., Ltd.	Zurich, Switzerland	1932–35	2 Orions
Transportes Aéreos de Chiapas, S.A.	Tuxtla, Chiapas, Mexico	1935–42	5 Vegas

SINGLE-ENGINE LOCKHEED AIRCRAFT 1928–58

Evolved to/Acquired by Present Company	Remarks
Northern Consolidated Airlines, Inc.	
Northwest (Orient) Airlines, Inc.	
	Subsidiary of Pan American Airways
Braniff International Airways, Inc.	Also called Rapid Air Transport; absorbed by Hanford Airlines (1934)
American Airlines, Inc.	Also called S.A.F.E. or SAFEway Airlines
American Airlines, Inc.	Became Southern Air Transport (SAT), then American Airways
Trans World Airlines (TWA)	Also leased 1 Altair (1931) and 1 Vega (1934–35)
American Airlines, Inc.	
	N/c to Varney Speed Lines, Inc. (1933)
Continental Air Lines, Inc.	N/c to Varney Air Transport (1935), to VAT, Inc. (1936), to Continental Air Lines, Inc. (1937)
	Plus other Vegas leased; also called United States Air Transport, Inc., Washington Flying Service
Western Air Lines, Inc.	
Western Air Lines, Inc.	N/c to Inland Air Lines, Inc. (1938)

SINGLE-ENGINE LOCKHEED AIRCRAFT 1929–49

Evolved to/Acquired by Present Company	Remarks
Pan American World Airways, Inc.	Subsidiary of Pan American Airways
Pan American World Airways, Inc.	Subsidiary of Pan American Airways
	Later Canadian Airways, Ltd. (1931)
	Called C.A.T.
	Called LAMSA; then Líneas Aéreas Mexicanas, S.A. (1944–49) and operated by United Air Lines, still LAMSA
	Called L.A.O., Mexican operation by Varney Air Service
Pan American World Airways, Inc.	Operated in Argentina; called NYRBA; bought out by Pan American Airways (1930)
Pan American World Airways, Inc.	Air Express used in Argentina; Orions used in Mexico
Pan American–Grace Airways, Inc.	Chilean operation; called Panagra
Swissair	Central European operation
	N/c to Cía. Aeronáutica Francisco Sarabia, S.A. (1939)

Doug Fairbanks, Mary Pickford, and the Maurice Chevaliers add glitter to Varney's heyday. Note the boarding ramp behind them, which the line was one of the first to offer as a luxury touch for air travel.

Orion's performance and Frank Rose's expert handling add up to a sale to King Carol of Romania.

(Continued from page 123)

Avery Black, Vic Hoganson, Jack Evans, and Freddie Hammer.

Varney had grown up to appreciate the value of advertising and publicity. His public relations department was Warren Burke, who had served in Hollywood and knew how to work most of the angles. Movie stars like Arlene Francis, Maurice Chevalier, Jane Wyatt, and Constance Cummings were induced to ride in Speed Line ships and were well photographed doing so; nameless starlets had hair-pulling battles for the chance to climb the wing of an Orion and pose prettily. Burke's pictures often splashed the Varney name in newspapers from Lubec to Los Angeles.

This was an airline whose like had never been seen before, a bright spot in a depression-stricken industry. Cord's Century Pacific operation withdrew from the field in a rout. Flushed with success, Varney bought out Capitol Airlines, his only competition on the run to Sacramento. Next came acquisition of the Air Ferries, which linked the cities of the Bay area. At 5 P.M. a tired businessman could be whisked by amphibian from San Francisco's downtown Ferry building across the Bay to Oakland and be in Los Angeles in ample time for a dinner engagement. And a spotless Graham-Paige sedan would deliver him to the door at either end of his trip.

The glamor of Varney's Speed Lines couldn't last. In March 1933 the *East Wind,* groping for the Oakland field

One of Central Airlines' hastily acquired fleet of used Vegas, and (right) Varney Air Transport Vega. Continental Air Lines used one on standby until 1941.

in rain and sudden overcast, smashed blindly into two houses and killed fourteen people. The public's reaction to the disaster did much to nullify flamboyant news-spreads of happy Varney air travelers.

Varney always had a deal in the offing, and made a contact with King Carol to promote a possible Romanian national airline. Frank Rose, in Europe with the *West Wind* to prepare for the 1934 MacRobertson Race to Australia, was shuttled off to Bucharest to demonstrate the Orion and its capabilities to the king. After some struggles with protocol the California pilot took His Majesty for a lengthy hop, and sold the Lockheed on the spot. Unfortunately the airline never materialized, and soon afterward a Romanian army pilot clobbered the ship on a mountain north of Bucharest.

A better proposition was Varney Speed Lines' Southwest Division. This was established in El Paso, Texas, when the line finally picked up one of the canceled airmail contracts in 1934. Under Lewis H. Mueller and Avery Black, the Southwest Division operated one round-trip a day from El Paso to Albuquerque and Pueblo, Colorado. They flew three very much used Vegas, and carried only nine passengers in the first fifteen days of operation. Luckily the mail subsidy of 17 cents a plane-mile kept the sturdy old pots percolating, and before long two more Vegas were added.

It is ironical that of all the Varney enterprises, its little Southwest Division was the only one to survive and grow of itself. Named successively Varney Air Transport and VAT, Inc., its Vegas were gradually replaced by larger twin-engine equipment. Though the famous name of Varney has vanished from the air transport rosters, that little fleet of Lockheeds became the nucleus of equipment for today's Continental Air Lines.

Bowen, Varney, and a foreign airline were flying the Orions with success. The growing major networks could not afford to overlook this speedy low-wing transport that was being turned out in Burbank. They had been leary of the ship's retractable landing gear, which originally was a mechanical wind-up affair. But then Lockheed engineers got the bugs out of it and it became a simple matter of "about 18" shots of the hydraulic pump, with signals to indicate whether FULL UP or FULL DOWN. By '33 the big airlines were willing to trust the Orion and the new managers of Lockheed who were building it.

First to buy was Transcontinental & Western Air. With people like Colonel Lindbergh, Jack Frye, and Larry Fritz in the management, TWA knew the planes and had already acquired considerable experience with Vegas. Four of these, bearing the big Indian-head-and-arrow trademark, or just plain TWA, were already employed on various schedules, supplementing the airline's bigger Fords and Fokkers. They had bought a used wooden Vega and, after a trial lease, finally purchased the first three Detroit-Lockheed metal jobs, which had already seen service with New York & Western. Also leased for a short period was the one and only Altair DL-2A, a fast open-cockpit mail and cargo carrier. This experimental job was belly-landed in TWA service at Columbus, Ohio, in October 1931. Returned to the factory, it was converted to an Orion as Jimmy Doolittle's famous *Shellightning*, and is still in existence today.

The order for the faster Orions put TWA in a better competitive position for the expanding, faster mail schedules on its central transcontinental routes. Three of them, based at Pittsburgh and Kansas City, flew mail in relays from Newark to Los Angeles, along with Northrop Alphas and parasol-wing Consolidated Fleetster 20As.

TWA pilots who checked out in wooden Lockheeds, metal Northrops, and the wood-and-metal Fleetsters thought the Orion the most stable and the easiest to fly. They voiced doubts, however, about the Orion's retractable landing gear, which the two competitors did not have. With a cruising speed of 205 mph, though, the Lockheeds were by far the fastest.

Motor trouble seemed to curse TWA's Orions. After only

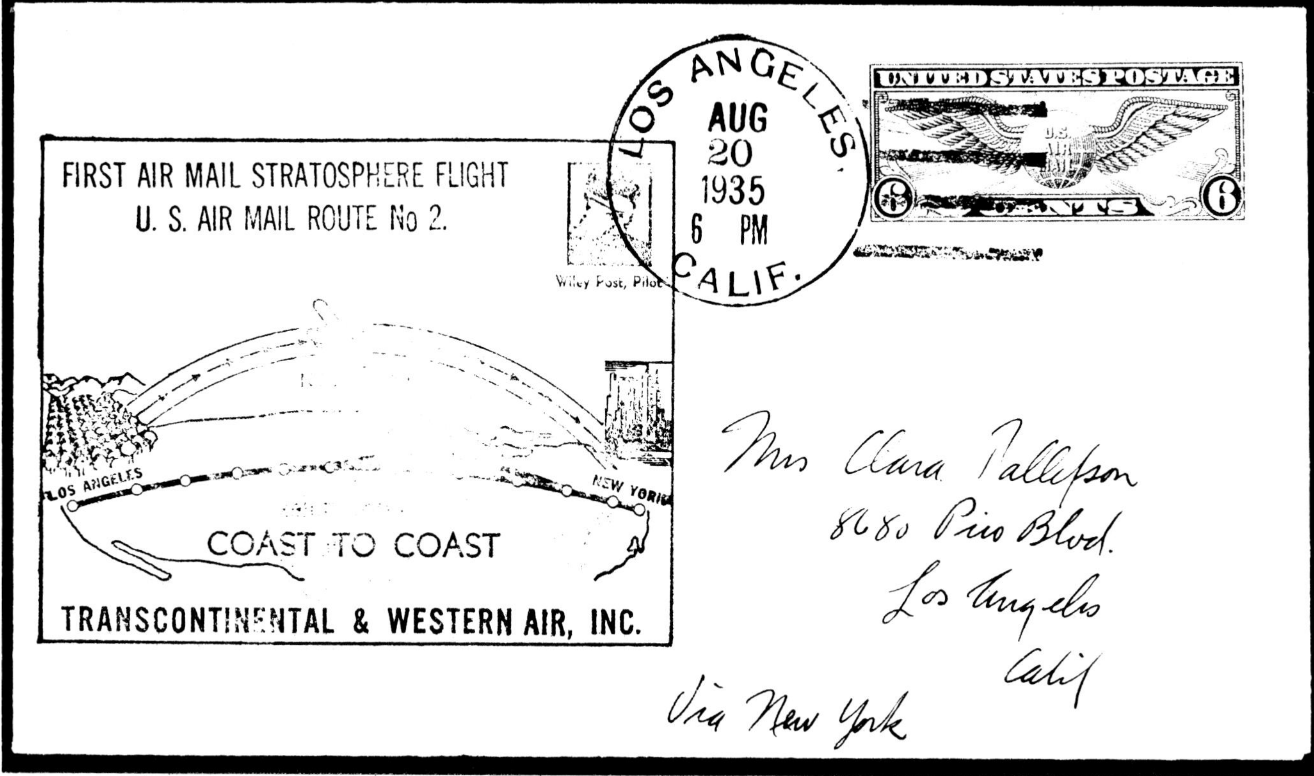

Transcontinental & Western Air still used wooden Vegas, jazzing up their first ship with a speed ring half-cowl (top) and hiring Wiley Post to carry mail like this on Winnie Mae's great stratosphere experiments in 1935.

two months' service, the first one dropped into the Missouri River when a gas line clogged on takeoff from Kansas City; pilot E. J. Noe was killed. The second suffered engine stoppage within sight of the Albuquerque Airport. Pilot H. H. Holloway slid the ship to a stop on the desert with wheels retracted. That Orion was repaired and put back to flying. It finished out a rough three and a half years of service with dozens of pilots on the transcontinental mail routes.

During this period, Wiley Post was flying his famous *Winnie Mae* for TWA during the course of his experiments with travel in the stratosphere. When he decided to retire the faithful Vega and obtain a newer plane, he bought Transcontinental & Western Air's third Orion. Fitted with the wing of Pure Oil's old Explorer named *Blue Flash,* it was the ship he flew to Alaska with Will Rogers.

American Airways had their order for Lockheed Orions on the books soon after TWA's. They had six built and delivered by September 1933. Painted AA's color scheme of blue with orange trim, they were an attractive fleet.

This Orion ended as a Spanish warplane, but here, in AA trim, it's a cargo carrier with windows blocked out.

American put them to various uses as either mail-and-cargo carriers, 5- and 6-passengers jobs, or a combination of both. They flew the long mail routes such as Atlanta–Los Angeles, Newark–Fort Worth, and Cleveland-Nashville.

After only two months' service, one American Airways Orion came to grief near El Paso. Pilot J. G. Ingram was only 800 feet up after takeoff when he felt a sudden jar and discovered the plane was on fire. Standing erect in the smoke-filled cockpit, he managed to tug out and toss off several mailbags before his clothes began to burn and he took to his 'chute. He suffered injuries as a result of such a low-altitude jump, but felt worst about the dog he had to leave behind, howling in the cargo bay of the doomed airplane.

The Orions were kept busy for a year, and then it seemed that the State of Tennessee was a jinx for American to fly mail over. Within seven weeks in the winter of 1934–35, the line lost three of its Lockheeds. One cracked up in Memphis. A second, 150 miles off course in the fog-shrouded Cumberlands, smashed into the top of Big Pilot Mountain near Sunbright, Tennessee, killing pilot Russell Riggs. Pilot John W. Johannpeter jumped safely from a third Orion and the ship came plummeting down in a farmer's yard near Shiloh Battlefield.

The remaining two American Airways Orions were sold when Civil Aeronautics Authority edicts successively discouraged further use of single-engine passenger equipment on major networks. One saw another decade of service in the Rocky Mountains and Alaska; the other found oblivion in the Spanish Civil War.

Before the CAA rulings, a procession of Orions came out of Burbank to fly for major carriers. Northwest Airways of St. Paul got in line with an order for three of them for its new Northern route. The Orions proved ideal for NWA's high-speed service between the Twin Cities and Seattle.

Lockheed incorporated the latest special features in these Orions, the last to be purchased originally for airline work. Powered with 550-hp Pratt & Whitney Wasp engines, they could climb at a rate of 1,450 feet per minute. In addition, Northwest's ships had the first wing flaps to be installed on a Lockheed airplane. With them, landing speed was cut to between 55 and 60 mph, enabling a payload increase of some two hundred pounds.

The Northwest Orions were painted white, with a black wing and broad black arrow trim and the NWA insignia in red and gold. Passengers who luxuriated in the folding leather-covered seats found the planes quiet and smooth to ride in, the wood and thick upholstery acting as insulation against motor noise and vibration. The Orions flew from St. Paul on west with full loads.

In the summer of 1934, NWA pilot R. L. Smith, flying an empty Orion from St. Paul to Chicago, set a new transport record of 2 hours and 40 minutes between the two cities. Once, when a pigeon was sucked into an air scoop, the resulting dead-stick landing with flaps was carried out safely. Northwest had good performance and no trouble from their Orions, and went on to purchase a new fleet of twin-engine Electras from the revitalized Lockheed company.

One NWA Orion went to a charter line in Texas, and the other two, with an ex-American Airways job, were acquired by Dick and Joe Leferink's Wyoming Air Service, Inc., of Casper, Wyoming. Starting as a short line, Wyoming flew south to Denver and Pueblo, and north to Billings, Montana.

In 1937 it picked up another mail-flying contract to serve the Black Hills region and east to Huron, South Dakota. Under Wyoming, the colors of the NWA Orions were reversed, and became glossy black with a starburst on the cowls. Among other WAS pilots were Jerry

Wing flaps, Wasp S1D1 power plants mean bigger payloads for the Orions on NWA's run to Seattle in 1933–35.

Brooder, Ken Turner, and Bob Garrett. The company became Inland Air Lines in 1938, and two of the fast black Lockheeds with their dependable Wasp engines flew the lonely plains routes until the early 1940s.

The cancellation of airmail contracts in 1934 brought many changes in the lines crosshatching the U. S. air map. In addition to the emergence of Braniff, Hanford, and Varney's Southwest Division into the letter-toting picture, there was Central Airlines of Pittsburgh, Pennsylvania.

Central was really the reincarnation of the old bankrupt Pittsburgh Airways. Jim Condon and Theodore Taney were running things again, backed by John and Richard Coulter, sons of a Greensburg, Pennsylvania, coal magnate. With the coveted mail contract secure, Condon hired out-of-work pilots from some of the purged bigger airlines and set about building up a fleet to fly the route from Washington to Detroit. As a stopgap measure the line bought four secondhand Lockheed Vegas.

Central's Vegas came from some odd sources and needed considerable remodeling to become mail and passenger carriers. One was Margery Durant's old *Ariel*, veteran of many miles of domestic and foreign vagabonding. Another was Stanavo's metal Vega, which "never did quite fly straight." From Detroit came two: the *Miss McAleer* of the polish company, and the *News*'s former photo- and news-gathering ship.

Operations manager Ted Taney was an early martyr to the growth of Central Airlines. In September 1934 a Vega was chartered to carry a load of tear-gas canisters to Providence, Rhode Island, for help in quelling riots stemming from New England textile strikes. Taney personally flew the assignment. Meeting dirty weather over the Alleghenies, he was forced to jump, and lost his life when his parachute failed to open.

Central had to start business in a hurry to get the mail going after the period it had been flown by the Army planes. From humble beginnings with small remodeled single-engine Lockheeds, the line eventually became Capital Airlines, a top competitor for Midwest and Eastern traffic until its merger with United in 1961.

As the United States struggled through the Depression in the mid-1930s, the major airlines began to acquire bigger, twin-motored transports. Their expanding loads and passenger traffic warranted the new Douglas DC-2s and DC-3s, Boeing 247Ds, and Lockheed 10 Electras. The older, smaller planes that had kept the schedules on the network were relegated strictly for mail and express hauling, or for standby use. Gradually they were pulled off the runs and sold to smaller operators, or to companies outside the then forty-eight states. Many went to Alaska, a vast territory where flying was the sensible—often the only—way to get back and forth. Alaskan bush pilots liked a well-proved, dependable airplane with plenty of wingspread and a slow landing speed. Most of their "fields" were scarcely that: just sandbars, or strips of gravel nestled between mountains. The flyers really preferred biplanes, or the wide-winged, pokey Fairchilds, Pilgrims, and Bellancas. But they did get a few Lockheeds, and put them to good use.

After Alaska-Washington Airways' valiant but short-lived effort to put service to the Territory on a permanent basis in 1929–32, a number of small bush-flying services and one-man airlines sprang up. Nick Bez of Seattle took over a couple of Alaska-Washington's Vega seaplanes and some of their routes, to start Alaska Southern Airways. His line was succeeded by Pacific Alaska Airways, a stepchild subsidiary of big Pan American.

Pan Am wanted the Alaskan operation as a preliminary to a direct transpacific route. They procured the services of one of the region's best bush pilots—rugged, dark-haired Joe Crosson—who had flown in both the

Despite four major crack-ups, Mirow Vega flew in Alaska for nine years.

Arctic and Antarctic. With a hodgepodge fleet of castoff aircraft, Crosson did the best he could as division manager, but was glad to standardize eventually on Lockheed's new twin-engine Electras. Pacific Alaska's remaining old float-rigged Vega went to Texas and then to further service in Panama, far from the Land of the Midnight Sun, where she had always flown.

Another hard-bitten Lockheed that flew over Alaskan terrain for a decade was a Vega brought north in 1935. This was a former Shell Oil ship that had been "practically washed out." Rebuilt, the plane was purchased by Hans Mirow, an ex-oiler from a German freighter who had learned to fly, and picked Nome, Alaska, as a good place to make a living at it.

Only because it was cheaper to have it repaired than to replace it, the Mirow Air Service Vega survived nearly ten years of rugged Alaskan bush-flying and airline service, mounted alternately on wheels and skis. The month of April seemed to be a poor one for this airplane. Every other April, from 1936 to 1940, the Mirow Vega was badly cracked up, and just as regularly sent "outside" to be rebuilt. The boys in the woodshop at Northwest Air Service in Seattle got to know intimately each gore and diaphragm of the Lockheed's body.

One of Mirow's pilots was Jack Jefford, comparatively new to the Territory, but a pioneer in precision and instrument flying in the Arctic. Jefford flew the Vega in 1939 to guide the icelocked steamer *Columbia* to a clear channel and bring in the miners and summer supplies for Nome's short trading season. This was accomplished by circling the vessel as she slowly nudged her way among icebergs, guiding her with directions sent by a homemade broadcasting set. Because the Lockheed was on wheels, Jefford kept her out over the jagged icepacks for as much as seven hours at a stretch during this mission; and if the throttled-down Wasp had ever taken a notion to quit, there would have been absolutely no possible landing place. Nome was grateful when the *Columbia* arrived safely, but the modest Jefford dismissed the feat as just another job.

Mirow's Vega went eventually to the larger Alaska Airlines organization and flew until 1944. Her last accident made impossible any further rebuilding down in Seattle. Gordon MacKenzie, a Vega pilot since Alaska-Washington Airways days, brought her down beside the South Fork of the Kuskokwim River after motor trouble and fire at 1,800 feet. Skillfully sideslipping onto a willow-covered sandbar only 300 feet long, MacKenzie threw the burning plane broadside against the saplings. The four passengers and pilot scrambled out unscathed.

Still another Vega flew in Alaska for nearly a quarter of a century. Formerly part of Phil Philbin's old transcontinental express fleet, she was fitted with floats instead of the Hi-Speed landing gear, and set to work in 1933 by Alaska Air Express. Flying out of Seattle up the channels and bays of the Inside Passage to Juneau and Anchorage, the silver Lockheed was later painted white and named *Nugget*.

In 1936 the Vega went into regular freight-and-passenger service with Alaska Air Transport of Juneau. Sheldon Simmons, founder, president, and manager of the company, was her principal pilot, and the ship went with him when he became co-manager of the new Alaska Coastal Airlines three years later.

Now painted blue-black with bright yellow trim, Shel Simmons's Vega was a familiar sight on Alaska Coastal routes in the southeastern arm of the Territory. By June 1954 she had flown approximately 1,200,000 miles. Wearing out the original Pratt & Whitney Wasp C Engine, this work-horse Lockheed went on with a new Wasp Jr. In 1952 her strong broad wing held up the collapsed roof of a Sitka hangar, and the stanch ship was later ferried

Why the early airlines wanted Lockheeds: Nugget *still sleekly efficient after twenty-five years of rugged service. When the Vega crashed in 1958, it was then the oldest—and last—of the single-engine series to work as a scheduled carrier.*

by air to Juneau for minor repairs. By the end of 1957 she had logged some 13,496 hours: the oldest, the last, and the only Lockheed of the single-engine series still flying for a regularly scheduled air carrier.

The end for this veteran of the skyways came on January 15, 1958. Flying "trip 40"—a southern circuit out of Juneau—the Vega was totally destroyed in a crash on the shore of Kadashan Bay across from Tenakee, Alaska. In the course of a forced landing, Captain Fred B. Sheldon was killed and two passengers seriously injured. Investigation showed the probable cause of the accident to have been wholly avoidable: The airplane had simply run out of gas.

13

AIRLINERS ABROAD

Foreign air service operators kept an eye on all developments in the United States as aviation boomed after 1927—and none more sharply than the Canadians.

The Dominion, with its vast distances, was waiting to be knit together with air routes. One bush pilot in particular realized that flying over the Canadian plains and Northwest Territories called for no ordinary aircraft, but required fast and powerful ships that could get men and goods to far-distant places in a hurry. He was Captain Wilfred R. "Wop" May of Edmonton, Alberta.

May was already famous for his service in World War I with the RAF and for trail-blazing flights over parts of the Canadian wilderness that no other pilot had ever dared attempt. By 1928 he had organized Commercial Airways, Ltd., with Victor Horner as a partner.

Wop and Vic bought a Lockheed Vega in February 1929, and proudly ferried it from Burbank to Edmonton. It was a far cry from the little open-cockpit Avians and Moths they'd been using, for it could carry four passengers or a good payload behind the Wright J5 engine. Swooping in low over Blatchford Field, Wop treated the watchers to a demonstration of power and speed. "It's like a giant orange cigar!" exclaimed one spectator.

The orange cigar had work to do. On May 21, Wop flew her on the first official airmail flight from Edmonton to Grande Prairie near the western border of the prov-

This heavy-duty ski installation got Canada's first Vega on and off airstrips across the prairie provinces and up to the Dominion's Arctic shores for 15 years. Plane had CF-AAL registration until it went to Nicaragua.

Schlee-Brock ship drones north over Minnesota in 1929. Vega later flew for Hanford, ended in Mexico in 1943.

ince. Commercial Airways had the contract to do it every Tuesday. Next came a government subsidy for carrying mail clear to the shore of the Arctic Ocean. From Edmonton to Aklavik in the Northwest Territories is 1,800 miles. The route had hardly ever been flown in the short midsummer season, yet Commercial was to inaugurate service to the Arctic in December.

After long preparation and careful planning, Wop May and his pilots—Cy Becker, Idris Glyn-Roberts, and Moss Burbidge—were ready. They used three new red Bellancas and the orange Lockheed on skis. From Fort McMurray, Alberta, to Aklavik they worked in relays to haul five tons of Christmas and philatelic mail, with thirteen stops on the frozen bays and lakes along the Mackenzie River route.

Staked down on some windswept inlet, the engines of the planes were shrouded with heavy tarpaulins. Oil would be quickly drained and the skis jacked up to prevent their freezing to the ice. The parka-clad flyers of the route often slept wiith perishable medicines and registered packets snug, but lumpy, in their bedrolls. In the morning came the chore of boiling up motor oil over a balky wood stove, and heating the cylinders of a Whirlwind in far-below-zero temperatures. This would have to be accomplished under a tarp with a blowtorch in one mittened hand and a fire extinguisher ready in the other.

Operating what was then the most northerly and longest scheduled airmail route in the world took guts, good planes, and money. Wop May and his Commercial Airways outfit had all three. They ran their Arctic airline for eighteen months, and it was only the financial failure of their backers that put the company on the auction block, to be bought and eventually absorbed by the larger Canadian Airways system.

During its long Canadian service, Wop May's Vega achieved many "firsts." As a feature of an air meet, May made an early morning start and flew two passengers 800 miles east, recording them as the first men ever to eat breakfast in Edmonton and lunch in Winnipeg.

One novel charter service involved special delivery of ice cream. Frozen and packed by an Edmonton dairy, the perishable sweet stuff was whisked north in the Lockheed to market in subarctic towns, where it sold well to settlers, miners, Indians, and Eskimos during the short but warm summers. And when Commercial Airways was allowed to issue their own special semi-postal stamps for use on the mail runs, it was the Lockheed Vega, first of the cabin-ship fleet, that was portrayed.

Perhaps due to the low horsepower of its Wright power plant, Commercial's Lockheed did not prove very satisfactory on floats—but it flew thousands of miles on wheels and skis. Canadian Airways later transferred it to the Manitoba area, operating it out of Winnipeg to cover routes to the Flin Flon mines and Sioux Lookout. After an unusual record of fifteen years in airline service, the ship was sold in 1944 for still more bush-flying in Central and South America with famed barnstormer Jimmy Angel.

Two other airlines with Canadian connections operated briefly during this period. Both were a part of the expanding Lockheed distributorship of the Schlee-Brock Aircraft Corporation of Detroit, Michigan. Detroit-to-Tokyo flyers Ed Schlee and Billy Brock were interested in more than just selling and servicing the stream of new Lockheeds pouring out of Burbank. They figured that the planes could be put to good use hauling passengers in places that lacked air transport.

Their first subsidiary was Arrowhead International Airlines, flying from Duluth, Minnesota, to Port Arthur, Ontario. With a float-equipped Vega, Billy Brock flew the first trip of this over-water route on September 11, 1929. Almost simultaneously Schlee-Brock acquired Canadian-American Airlines, Inc. This outfit flew from St. Paul–Minneapolis up to Winnipeg, Manitoba, with way stops at Saint Cloud, Alexandria, Fergus Falls, Fargo, and Grand Forks. It was a 4-hour trip, compared to 15 hours by train.

Within a few months both lines were combined under the name of Canadian-American, and five new Lockheeds were put on to fly the routes. Special oildraulic skis were mounted on the Vegas for the winter trips. With the exception of Alaskan runs, this was probably the first use of skis on a regularly scheduled American passenger airline.

Jolly, rotund Billy Brock, as president and operations manager of Canadian-American, proudly proclaimed that the thousands of miles of level terrain made C-A "the safest airline in the world." Said Billy, "There's an emergency landing field on each side of every fence!"

Canadian-American Vegas buzzed over fences and the frozen coastline of Lake Superior for a few months and then were quietly flown away for sale to new owners. Capital to maintain Schlee-Brock's multiple operations had simply vanished.

Though specially designed for fast mail-hauling, the Lockheed Air Express was late in coming on the market. Therefore, in addition to the prototype flown by Western Air Express and Texas Air Transport's job, only two others of this model saw airline use. These were bought in January 1930 by an outfit with both a long name and a long route: New York, Rio & Buenos Aires Line.

NYRBA had the mail contracts to fly from Miami all down the east coast of the South American continent. It was a seaplane operation, using big Consolidated Commodore flying boats, the Lockheeds, and the somewhat more commodious Consolidated Fleetster 17s and 20s—all equipped with pontoons.

New York, Rio & Buenos Aires flew its smaller planes on the mail routes of Brazil and Argentina. Among their pilots were Howard C. Stark, who pioneered airline instrument flying; Eddie DeLarm, the Cherokee Indian aviator; Bill Grooch; and N. C. Browne. The line was absorbed by the growing Pan American Airways system after nine months of operation. Pan Am stored the single-engine planes in Argentina and later sold and junked them.

Over on South America's west coast was another American mail carrier, Pan American–Grace Airways, flying from Cristobal, Canal Zone, to Santiago, Chile. In 1930 Panagra bought two Lockheed Vegas from Robert E. Funkhouser's Washington–New York Air Line. The ships had been used in lowering the Washington-Newark flying time to 1½ hours, but with increased business Funkhouser needed airplanes that could carry more passengers.

Panagra's green-and-silver Vegas were put on the Chilean sector of the 1,900-mile route between Lima, Peru, and Santiago. With the addition of the Lockheeds, Pan American–Grace's Foreign Air Mail Route No. 9 became both the world's longest and fastest airmail route. The Chilean government reserved passenger service to its own National Air Line, so Panagra planes and pilots flew the long, lonely stretches with no load except mail—up and down the barren coast of Chile once a week, with five full days of flying.

One of Panagra's pilots was Robert C. Reeve, later famed for flying over Alaska's bush and glaciers, and still later head of Reeve Aleutian Airways. Based at Arica, Chile, Bob Reeve flew the Santiago run without a radio and precious little in the way of instruments. In a Vega or the slower Fairchild 71, he'd cruise along, munching bananas and perusing magazines and newspapers from the States. When the weather closed in, he'd fly thirty or forty miles out over the Pacific, where there was always at least a 100-foot ceiling and no jutting mountains.

Reeve blew a tire and wrecked a Vega at Santiago in January 1931. Panagra's loss was ultimately Alaska's gain: He took this excuse to resign and head for the Far North. The other shiny-cowled Lockheed at Santiago was kept in standby service until 1935, a tiny predecessor of Panagra's fleet.

European development of commercial aircraft was snail-slow compared with progress being made on this side of the Atlantic, so it was natural for transport lines to heed the streamlined, well-designed planes turned out by American builders.

In 1931 two competing companies in Switzerland combined to form a national airline, Swissair. Interested in obtaining new high-speed equipment for fast schedules, they sent Balz Zimmerman—one of their two directors—to the United States to look around. Zimmerman listened to the blandishments of many eager manufacturers—then ordered two Orions, to be powered by Curtiss-Wright Cyclone engines. These red Lockheeds were the first American transport planes ever exported to Europe, and so tapped a market U.S. aircraft manufacturers have been supplying ever since.

Crated and shipped to Zurich via Antwerp, the Swissair Orions were put on the express flights to Munich and Vienna in May 1932. Their run to Vienna was 100 km/ph faster than anything then flying on the continent, and Zimmerman and his pilots regularly clipped minutes off the advertised schedules. "Der rote Orion" was the sensation of the European flying season that year.

Another famed Swiss pioneer aviator, Walter Mittelholzer, was the other director of Swissair, and used the Orions for some fast survey flights in 1933. First was a

Only known Air Express on floats. Named Maraca, the NYRBA Line registered her in Brazil for just a month in 1930.

Panagra mail carrier at Santiago before its crack-up.

"The Red Orion" is chosen for stamp to commemorate 25th anniversary of Switzerland's airmail service.

direct Switzerland–North Africa flight—Zurich to Tunis and return via Rome—all in 8 hours' flying time. Then Mittelholzer flew the Lockheed 4,500 km to Naples, Athens, Istanbul, and Belgrade, returning via Ravensburg, Austria, and establishing city-to-city speed records all the way.

Demonstrations like these showed what American planes could do, and set European carriers to buying U.S.-built equipment. The practical Swiss put the Orions back to steady, fast hauls on the Vienna express run, and kept them in service until larger planes became a necessity in 1935. The ships were quietly sold to the Republican Air Force, after the start of the Spanish Civil War in 1936.

However, it was the airlines crisscrossing Mexico that made fullest use of Lockheeds as passenger- and cargo-carriers. For two decades nearly forty of the strong, sleek ships would be a familiar sight on dusty flying fields from Nogales on the Sonora-Arizona border down to Chetumal in the Yucatán Peninsula.

Theodore T. Hull of Los Angeles brought the first Vegas into the country in 1929. Hull, a thirty-six-year-old banker with a private pilot's license, had got the idea of servicing the Republic with an airline while on a flying tour of Latin America. He reasoned that making the big jump of converting Mexican transportation from slow rail and even slower muleback to airplanes would be an excellent business proposition.

In the lush days of early 1929 there were enough financial backers in the United States who agreed with him. He formed Corporación Aeronáutica de Transportes, S. A., picked up a couple of used Ryan Broughams, and then paid $18,500 apiece for some of the first Wasp-powered Lockheed Vegas ever put directly to work on a passenger airline.

C.A.T.—as the company was always called—began operations on March 9, 1929, flying the 638-mile transcontinental route from Matamoros, Tamaulipas, on the Gulf of Mexico, to Mazatlán, Sinaloa, on the Pacific.

Hull didn't economize on aircraft and he didn't economize on talent, either. He wanted experienced men who could start and run a sizable air network right from scratch. The majority of C.A.T.'s original personnel were North Americans: ex-Army Major Bernard A. Law of St. Louis, a onetime flying associate of Colonel Lindbergh's, was manager of operations; Paul Braniff working with Law supervising operations; Lloyd Anderson, the chief pilot, who held Mexican license No. 10 (Hull himself had No. 30); and, among the two dozen other Yankee pilots, "Little Jack" O'Brien, formerly of Roscoe Turner's Nevada Airlines. From New Zealand came Lowell Yerex, ex-RAF.

Soon more pilots and employees came down from the States to join the outfit. Harold Bromley, his plans for a Pacific flight set back by the crack-up of his second *City of Tacoma,* took a job with the Hull system. He ferried a new Vega down to the Mexican company in the autumn of 1929; with him was another newcomer, a young mechanic-pilot named Gordon S. Barry. Also temporarily out of work and thus glad to be flying Vegas south of the border was a stocky flyer from Oklahoma who got Mexican license No. 96 in the name of Wiley Post. Neither the authorities of the Republic nor C.A.T. officials saw anything wrong in hiring a one-eyed airline pilot.

On August 11, 1929, Theodore Hull and a Mexican newspaper reporter stowed themselves in with the mailbags to pioneer another and even longer route: from México, Distrito Federál, the capital city, to Ciudad Juárez, Chihuahua. Lloyd Anderson and Jack O'Brien took turns in the cockpit of a new Vega for the 1,104-mile inaugural flight.

With Torreón, Coahuila, as their central base, C.A.T. ships were soon flying daily trips in four directions across the country, and covered a branch from Chihuahua up to the bordertown of Nogales as well. Pratt & Whitney had to send a resident service representative to arid Torreón airport to keep all the Wasp engines of the line's Lockheeds humming.

It wasn't all easy flying. At Guadalupe, Nuevo León, Harold Bromley added to his reputation for bad luck by flipping over a new ship. At Mazatlán, on the Pacific Coast, C.A.T. pilot Julian Wagy had another Vega badly damaged in a collision with a military plane coming in to land. In October 1929 still another Lockheed was demolished in a fatal crash against a hill near Monterrey, Nuevo León. A month later a brand-new Vega—one only four days out of the factory—met a similar fate: Flying north from the Federal District, pilot John A. Carmichael and three passengers, including the Governor of

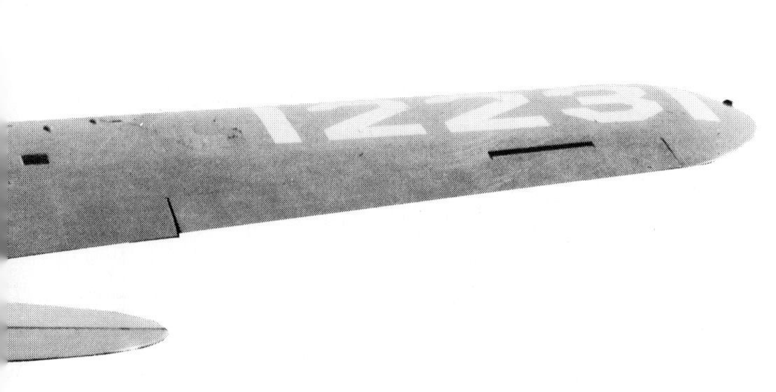

Smooth lines make a sale to Swissair: view at factory shows first ship with interim U.S. registration on wing.

Theodore T. Hull (left), founder of C.A.T. in 1929, and (right) Lloyd Anderson, chief pilot for the pioneer line.

Aguascalientes, were killed when their plane hit a mountain in the overcast.

Hull's system attracted business and expanded its routes despite minor and major accidents. In 1930 it carried 2,283 passengers; the first half of the next year saw nearly double that number. The Vegas all operated their first flights with U.S.A. registration, but were gradually licensed by the Mexican civil aviation authority.

Perhaps the C.A.T. line might have developed into a major carrier had it not been for the North American stock market crash of 1929, and the subsequent drying-up of capital from the north. The Mexican line had also had competition from the burgeoning Pan American Airways system, whose subsidiaries were blanketing the country and establishing parallel routes.

Tragedy dealt the telling blow to C.A.T. on November 25, 1931. Ferrying a new Bellanca monoplane from Wilmington, Delaware, to the company's base in the Republic, Theodore Hull had trouble over Sunbury, Pennsylvania. The ship, its engine inexplicably wide open, dived straight into the shallow Susquehanna River. Dreams of expanding the Hull system died with the founder.

Bernard Law kept the line in operation out of Torreón for a few more months, then closed down, bankrupt, in 1932. Two of the line's flyable Vegas went to Paul Mantz back in California. Another went at auction to satisfy a judgment in favor of a disgruntled mechanic who claimed to have been fired without cause. Law stayed long enough to liquidate C.A.T. and then went into the mining business. By 1933 the only vestige of the once prosperous airline was one old Vega body, a few Lockheed wings that needed recovering, five used Wasp engines, and $500 worth of assorted Lockheed parts—struts, landing gear, diaphragms.

The "old Vega Body" was destined to fly again. Law sold it to a Chicago charter operator who mated it with a used Vega wing from Detroit, and flew the result for four years. The Lockheed that went on the block was sold for less than $4,700 (pesos), a good reason for such a bargain being that it had no instruments and no seats. It was bought and put briefly in service by a tiny line on the Yucatán Peninsula: Cía. de Transportes Aéreos, plying

One of Mexico's earliest airliners (certificate no. 14), this Vega opened Hull's México, D.F.–Texas mail route.

Walter Varney (far right) and Frank Rose stand by as movie actress Jane Wyatt christens L.A.O. flagship.

between Mérida on the north coast and Payo Obispo, now Chetumal.

Early in 1934 Walter Varney got an offer to run an airline slanting down the length of the Republic of Mexico, together with the fat mail-carrying contract which his California operation lacked. There was express, too, and the opportunity to snatch work from under the nose of the Mexican affiliate of Pan American Airways.

Four of Varney's Orion fleet that flew Mexican routes for Líneas Aéreas Occidentales, S.A., in 1934 and 1935.

Varney switched to Mexican registration under the name of Líneas Aéreas Occidentales, S. A., moving his headquarters south from Alameda, California, to operate the line out of Grand Central Air Terminal in Burbank. Franklin Rose was again president, with a son of the ex-president of the Republic, General Plutarco Elías Calles, as second in charge.

The five remaining Varney Speed Lines Orions flew from Los Angeles to México, D.F., three days a week, plus another run clear down to Tapachula on the Chiapas-Guatemala border. Along with the airmail there were always passengers, express, freight, and, more often than not, a good-sized gold shipment to go winging high above the heads of frustrated bandidos.

Since the winds of Latin-American politics are subject to sudden change, the departure of Varney's L.A.O. from the Mexican scene was precipitate. One day L.A.O. was in operation: The next day found Pan Am's Aerovías Centrales flying the Los Angeles–Tapachula run.

With the sudden cancellation of Varney's contract, his pilots had to fly four Orions out of Mexico in a hurry to avoid attachment by a zealous oil company. The *Winter Wind* got off and away with just ten minutes to spare; but the *Coast Wind* was caught, to be sold eventually to international agents for use in the Spanish Civil War.

Aerovías Centrales used three of their own Lockheed Orions over routes similar to those flown by the ousted white-and-red Varney ships. Pan American and its subsidiary alternated in operating out of Brownsville, Texas, with U.S.A. registration, or from across the Rio Grande out of Matamoros, Tamaulipas, with Mexican papers. These particular Pan Am Orions had an unfortunate history, all three being demolished in accidents within two years.

Down in the southernmost state of the Republic, a

young flyer named Francisco Sarabia set up a brand-new line to continue the former L.A.O. service from the nation's capital to Tapachula. He based it in Tuxtla Gutiérrez and called it Transportes Aéreos de Chiapas, S.A.

Sarabia relied on California airplane broker Charley Babb for the equipment that would make his TACSA operation "Mexico's largest independent airline." Babb bought and resold to him several good used Lockheed Vegas, including *The Blue Streak*, the Executive model once owned by William Gibbs McAdoo, and *Miss Streamline* of the General Tire & Rubber Company.

Ferrying one of his Vegas south in December 1938, the boyish Sarabia set a new speed record of 6 hours and 34 minutes for the 1,650-mile Los Angeles–México, D.F., flight. This set him to planning other long-distance attempts. He bought the Gee Bee racing plane *Q.E.D.*, renamed the tricky speedster *Conquistador del Cielo*, and made a record flight nonstop from the Mexican capital to Washington, D.C. As he took off June 7, 1939, from Bolling Field for the return flight, Sarabia was killed when his Gee Bee crashed in the Potomac River.

Back in Tuxtla, Señora de Sarabia tried to keep TACSA in operation, but renamed the company Cía. Aeronáutica Francisco Sarabia, S. A., in her husband's memory. Effego Cabrera, Sarabia's chauffeur, married the widow and helped continue the airline.

CAFSSA mechanics and maintenance men thought nothing of completely overhauling a Lockheed right out on an open, windswept airport, rigging primitive block and tackle to hoist engines and wings, and ignoring the lack of shade and protection a hangar would have given. In 1940 the line needed an airplane: Sarabia crews quickly put together a composite Vega, using the wing of one damaged ship and the fuselage of another.

It could be rightly said that, as a result of the skill and prowess with which Mexican woodworkers patched up damaged Lockheeds, any restored Vega in the Republic by the 1940s was likely to be "an amalgamation of parts and pieces flying in formation." Using planes of this nature, and other ships leased, the Cabreras kept their Sarabia line going until 1942. Then, with the stringencies of war and litigation, they lost their routes to the bigger, Pan American–subsidized Cía. Mexicana de Aviación.

Even before the Sarabia system went out of business,

Francisco Sarabia, who built TACSA with four used Vegas.

Keeping Sarabia ships on the flight line is up to skilled crew, here making on-the-spot repairs to a cracked-up Vega; result (below) *has fuselage of red plane, wing of white one—and dual registration.*

Barry's pilots don't get second guesses on this one-way strip, whacked out of the mountains at Tayoltita.

Making an airline (left to right)*: Gordon S. Barry, Judith Barry, Capt. Marcial Huerta Jones, and, refueling on the wing, Capt. Abraham Carasco.*

however, it was eclipsed by still another country-wide operation. After C.A.T. folded in 1932 mechanic-pilot Gordon S. Barry drifted over to Mazatlán, where he was hired to fly the planes of the San Luis Mining Company. San Luis, a California concern, built an airstrip "not much bigger than the deck of an aircraft carrier" at Tayoltita, Durango, and used planes to carry out the gold and silver from their mines in the Sierra Madres.

Barry became adept at herding the company Orion up a narrow canyon, in and out of the one-way Tayoltita field. With the brown hillsides thrusting up violently on all sides, it took an expert to drop a Lockheed onto the short airstrip with a cargo of mail and mining supplies, or to get it off with a payload of gold. You got in and out, or else: there was no chance to haul up the landing gear and go around again.

In 1936 Gordon Barry formed his own airline. He called it Líneas Aéreas Mineras, S.A., with the idea of catering exclusively to the needs of Mexican mining firms. Gordon's partner in the venture was Miguel A. Zuniga of México, D.F. No stranger to Lockheeds, Zuniga had been the company's representative in the Republic back in the palmy days when Fred Keeler and Allan Loughead headed the Burbank factory, and both he and Barry were sold on the Vega's capabilities for transport in the rough country they intended to serve.

Based at Mazatlán, the new mining airline began operation with the San Luis company's old Orion. Then, like Sarabia, Barry and Zuniga became one of Charley Babb's best customers for good used Vegas. All told, LAMSA flew eleven of them, the largest Vega fleet ever owned and flown by any airline outside the United States.

To GORDON S. BARRY and JUDITH, his lovely wife with my greatest admiration for their struggle for LAMSA in Mexico's skies, and their unforgetable LOCKHEED VEGAS.

Gordon Barry married pretty Judith Martinez of Mazatlán, and gradually his line expanded its business and began to carry passengers, mail, and express in addition to mining supplies and precious metals. LAMSA territory included most of the old C.A.T. routes, plus a new one down the length of the Republic to Salina Cruz, Oaxaca, and Suchiate, Chiapas.

Unlike Theodore Hull, who had first brought him south of the border, Barry made a practice of hiring and training Mexican personnel. Through the years some twenty-seven Mexican pilots put time on Vegas, flying for LAMSA. By 1942 the veteran Lockheeds were carrying over 5,000 passengers a year, and hundreds of Mexicans who had never seen a train considered air travel commonplace.

World War II and the lack of replacement equipment forced changes in Barry's LAMSA. In a state of national emergency, the Mexican federal government called in United Air Lines from the United States to finance and operate the 1,500-mile, border-to-border airline which Gordon and Judith Barry had worked so hard to build.

United changed the name to Líneas Aéreas Mexicanas, S.A., and continued flying the routes with larger, twin-engine planes. Still, as long as the faithful Vegas were flyable, the new LAMSA kept them airborne. The last of the old Barry fleet, and the last Lockheed in foreign airline service, was finally dismantled and scrapped in 1949.

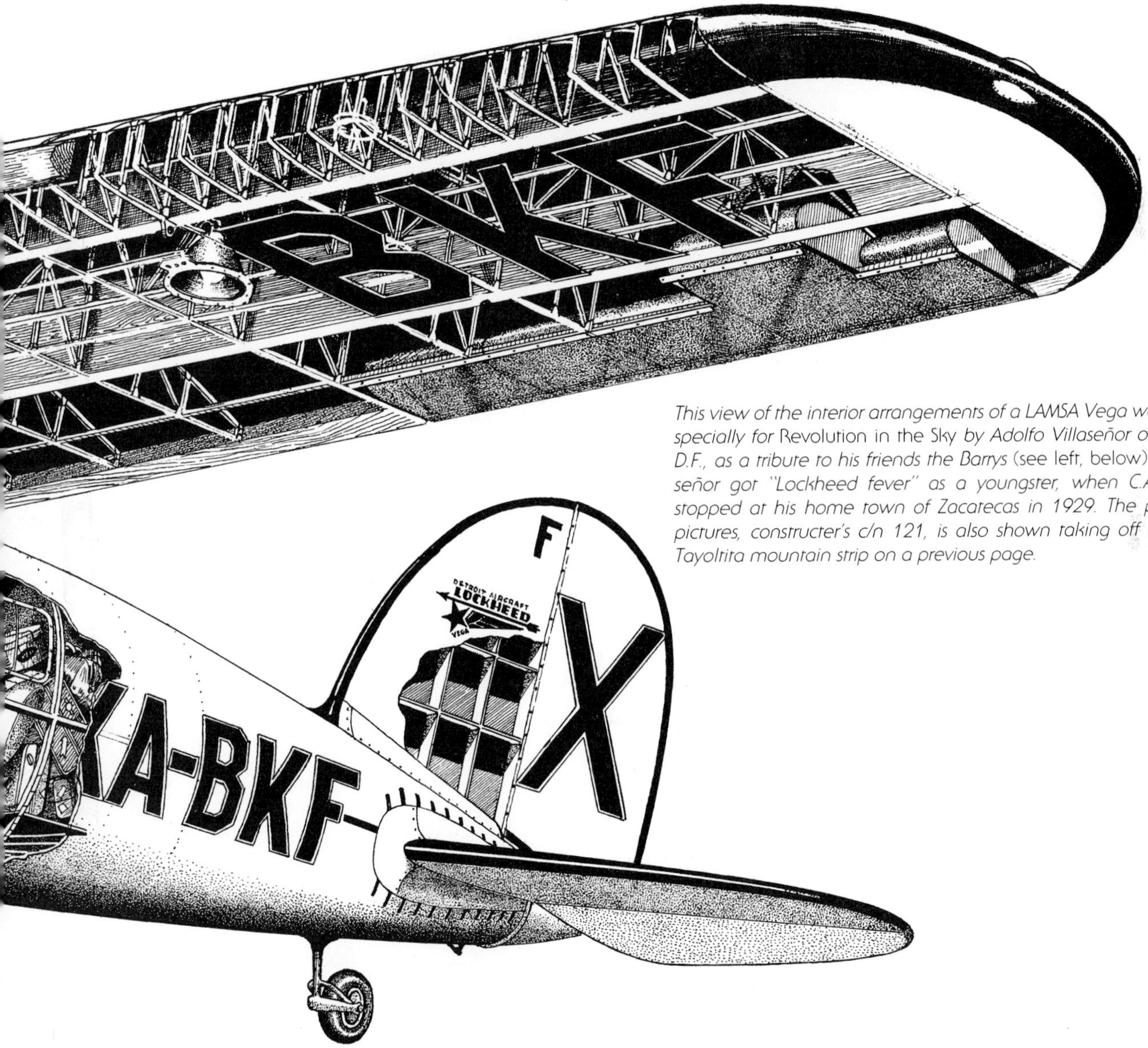

This view of the interior arrangements of a LAMSA Vega was drawn specially for Revolution in the Sky *by Adolfo Villaseñor of México, D.F., as a tribute to his friends the Barrys* (see left, below). *Sr. Villaseñor got "Lockheed fever" as a youngster, when C.A.T. ships stopped at his home town of Zacatecas in 1929. The plane he pictures, constructer's c/n 121, is also shown taking off from the Tayoltita mountain strip on a previous page.*

14

SINEWS OF WAR

For the three years following the appearance of the first Lockheed Vegas in 1927, military flyers had admired the fleet ships, and fought to get a chance for a ferry flight during their leaves. These planes had speed and range, something sorely needed in the United States Army Air Corps of that day. In a between-the-wars era, with serious talk of total disarmament, the Air Corps consisted of a small group of loyal officers and men, getting by with little rank and less pay, but well aware of the dangers that might arise if America neglected adequate air power.

Army squadrons were composed of stubby, maneuverable little Curtiss and Boeing pursuit and attack planes, big lumbering Keystone bombers, and Douglas observation ships. There were no transport squadrons, only a handful of Fords and Fokkers for carrying cargo and occasional personnel, and all attached as an afterthought to various flying fields and headquarters posts.

The idea of speeding commanding officers to various distant military units in a matter of hours appealed to the Air Corps. They were well aware of what the civilian record-breakers were doing, and conceived a speed plane of their own—a "command transport."

With niggardly appropriations from Congress to be eked out, General James E. Fechet, Chief of the Corps, cautiously ordered tests to begin in 1930. The Army borrowed planes at first, making trials with a Consolidated Fleetster, two Lockheed Vegas, two Lockheed Altairs, and a couple of Northrop Alphas. They were in the YC

Test pilot Marshall Headle indicates how new landing gear will pull up flush with wing surface of experiment plane.

series of Air Corps model designations: "Y" for "experimental," and "C" for "cargo and transport."

Jumping at this first chance to spread their wings and enfold the military market, Detroit Aircraft and Lockheed engineers put together a Duralumin Vega with Hi-Speed landing gear. They gave special attention to streamlining details, and installed an experimental "doughnut" tail wheel set nearly flush with the fuselage. On the nose was hung a Pratt & Whitney Wasp power plant, hopped up by supercharging to nearly 600 hp. The resulting Army Air Corps Lockheed, designated the Y1C-17, was one whale of a speed package. Her top was a healthy 221 mph, and she was faster than any plane, fighters included, that the Army could put in the air.

Testing the shiny new beauty fell to Captain Ira C. Eaker, a career officer from Texas. Chunky and intense, Captain Eaker had handled the stick of just about everything the Army had managed to juggle into the sky. The year before, along with Major Carl Spaatz and Lieutenants Halverson and Quesada, he'd been chief pilot of the *Question Mark*, the Air Corps's Fokker, which established a world's refueling endurance record of 150 hours aloft.

Seeking to find just how fast and how far the special Lockheed would travel, Eaker made ready to assault the west-to-east nonstop transcontinental record set by Captain Frank Hawks in The Texas Company's Air Express. Preparations to squeeze out every iota of speed included even such small items as removing the door handle and streamlining the hinges. Special tanks filled the 4-windowed cabin and were topped off with 486 gallons of Ethyl gasoline. In the cool morning hours of March 10, 1931, Eaker and the Vega were ready to go.

Lights of the Long Beach Field glistened on the silvery fuselage and rocking yellow wing as the captain twice tried to coax the heavily laden speed ship into the air. It was dead calm. Squashed under the 3-ton weight, the tires and doughnut tail wheel set the ship to swerving dangerously. Eaker had their pressure boosted to 85 pounds. At the last minute Sergeant Roy Hooe, his mechanic and also a veteran of the *Question Mark*'s flight, clambered up to the cockpit and tucked a small hatchet in among the captain's belongings. Eaker grinned.

Just then a little breeze sprang up and the Vega was trundled into position for a third try. Lifting a load of a thousand pounds more than her own weight, she was off the runway under Ira Eaker's steady hand, and airborne in 4,000 feet. Hooe and the tiny crowd saw the ship climb steadily until her lights disappeared in the darkness.

The Speed Vega streaked through the night across the continent, averaging about 240 mph. Captain Eaker was amazed and very pleased: flying at 16,000 feet into the dawn he'd arrive over New York far ahead of the old cross-country record. Before nine o'clock he was across the Mississippi and over the hill country of southern Illinois

Hi-Speed wire-braced landing gear reduces drag, helped make Y1C-17 the Army's fastest ship in its day.

—but he had exhausted the gasoline in his fuselage tanks and was switched to wing tanks. Then he noticed the gas-pressure needle drop to zero. The Wasp engine began to spit and die. On the reserve tank the same thing happened; and this time the engine wouldn't restart. Vainly working the wobble pump, the captain switched from tank to tank. It was no good. The plane was in a gentle slide, and Eaker turned her south toward the Ohio River.

In the sudden quiet behind the motionless propeller, the Army flyer slid open the little side window and peered ahead in the whistling airstream. He was considering a bail-out when he saw that he could just stretch his glide to a meadow on the other side of the Ohio. Jockeying quietly in over some tall trees, he touched down at about 75 mph. The ship rolled across the field, tore through a fence without a tremor, and turned over in the plowed wet ground beyond. Eaker came to rest standing on his head in a welter of broken glass and oozing mud. He could smell dripping gasoline and then battery acid. Struggling to get out of his seat belt and parachute harness, it took him twenty minutes to get upright, crawl back over the gas tanks, and chop his way out of the sealed door. Sergeant Hooe's hatchet turned out to be a godsend.

Later investigation disclosed that specially installed, rigid gaslines had leaked and admitted air to shut off the flow. The battered and wrinkled Y1C-17 was salvaged and taken to Wright Field, but never repaired. The Air Corps reported that their Vega's 1,740-mile trip was accomplished in 7 hours and 20 minutes. Despite the unfortunate ending, the significance was very evident: no loaded airplane had ever flown so far, so fast.

Having forcefully shown how useful a command transport plane could be to the Army, Ira Eaker went back to Burbank for another Lockheed. Thirty-five and a bachelor, flying was the thing he lived for.

Specially streamlined, this single-place Speed Vega impressed the Army even though it clocked only 33 flying hours.

This time the plane had still another innovation. Lockheed engineers—the team of Jimmy Gerschler, Dick Palmer, Dick Von Hake—had worked out some ideas for a fully retractable landing gear. This wasn't a drawing-up of the wheels into a protruding bubble, like those of the much-publicized Boeing Monomail, but involved completely enclosing them in the surface of a slick, clean lower wing.

The new gear was first tried in September 1930, using a rebuilt Sirius demonstrator. The ship was mounted high on horses in the shop to undergo test after test. The original gear was entirely mechanical, with a system of cables and pulleys cranked by hand. In the hot tin hangar a rigger in the forward cockpit cranked and sweated, while down below Von Hake and his men carefully watched again and again as the big Airwheels tucked themselves into the wing. Finally it was approved for flight, and tested by Marshall "Babe" Headle.

Colonel Lindbergh was interested in having this gear installed on his Sirius, but ended up with alterations to accommodate floats in preparation for his North Pacific survey flight of 1931. The plane with retractable landing gear was carefully wrung out all during the winter, and tested by several top flyers. The company gave it a new "star" name to match its other models, calling it the Altair.

Vance Breese, the famous California aircraft designer and test pilot, was connected with Detroit-Lockheed during this period, and flew the Altair often. There was talk of his herding it around the world with John Henry Mears instead of the second Vega that the theater man had ordered. Breese and Mears sent the ship rocketing across valley and mountains to set a new Oakland-Burbank record of 92 minutes in March 1931.

Soon afterward the Army and Captain Eaker took over the Altair for some more long-distance testing. Firman Gray of Lockheed's final assembly occupied the rear cockpit on Eaker's first hop in the low-wing speedster. Letting down at San Diego, Gray thought about the retractable landing gear—which Eaker hadn't. There was no communication between cockpits, so Firman slid down in his seat, stretched out a long leg and kicked the captain in the seat of the pants. Frantic pointing, sign language, and the mouthed word "gear" got the Army flyer to wind down the wheels.

Still confident of a cross-continent speed record to prove the worth of the Air Corps's Lockheeds, Captain Eaker tried again. The Altair was not as souped up, or specially streamlined, as the Speed Vega had been, but retractable landing gear gave the low-winged job a good 30 more miles per hour than its predecessor, the Sirius.

Taking off from Burbank on April 11, Eaker had hopes of reaching Long Island in 11½ hours. He recorded time by smoking—"one cigar, one hour"—and occasionally munched on an apple. At a twelve-minute refueling stop in Wichita, he was a minute and a fraction ahead of the Hawks record. Things looked good and he settled down to enjoy his cigars.

Again bad luck dogged the captain's efforts. Over Newark, Ohio, the clutch on his supercharger began to slip and the plane lost power. There was nothing for it but to turn back and finish the flight at Port Columbus. Eaker was disappointed but his tribute to the Altair was: "I've never flown a more comfortable and more satisfactory plane." On his recommendation, the Army Air Corps took formal title to the ship and designated it the Y1C-25. Once again "no plane ever flew so far, so fast": flight time was 9 hours and 40 minutes.

A sister ship of the first Altair—this one remodeled from a DL-2, or metal, Sirius—was also procured by the Army in 1931. With its blue fuselage and yellow wing polished to high luster, it was assigned as the personal command plane of F. Trubee Davison, Assistant Secretary of War. As executive assistant to the Chief of Air Corps, General James E. Fechet, Captain Eaker flew both Lockheeds out of Washington's Bolling Field.

The Duralumin Altair (designated the Y1C-23) had an improved retractable landing gear, operated by a hydraulic oil pump. It was used to fly General Fechet and Secretary Davision about the nation on Air Corps matters. Eaker flew the secretary to the air maneuvers of 1931, and the general on inspection tours, including a trip down to France Field in the Canal Zone.

But for distance and speed flights the wooden Altair (Y1C-25) remained Ira Eaker's favorite. She was still in civilian colors and license when he entered her in the National Air Races at Cleveland in the late summer of 1931. The captain himself wore a simple business suit instead of his usual leather jacket, jodhpurs, and boots. Outdistanced by Jimmy Doolittle in a fast Laird biplane, and Harold Johnson and Beeler Blevins in their new Orions, Eaker brought the Altair cross-country to fourth place in the first Bendix Trophy Race.

This was not enough for the captain, and he tried the unusual. With a defiant pirate's skull-and-crossbones emblazoned on her tail, Eaker entered the Altair in the closed-course, 50-mile Thompson Trophy Race. This was the first and only time a Lockheed ever competed in the Thompson. Pitted against the small, specially built racers —Gee Bees, Lairds, a Wedell-Williams, and Benny Howard's tiny *Pete*—Eaker put the big Altair flashing around the pylons with the best of them.

After completing the Thompson race in fifth place, Ira Eaker gave the crowd an extra thrill. He found that the cables had jumped the pulleys of his landing gear, and the wheels just wouldn't wind down. Circling Cleveland for forty-five minutes to use up his gas, the Air Corps pilot finally set the Y1C-25 down on her belly, sliding along in a cloud of dust and splinters.

It wasn't the first time he'd done it. On the way to Panama in the other Altair he'd made a wheels-up landing in Mexico, with General Fechet aboard. There was little damage that time outside of a bent propeller.

Later in the year it happened again. After ferrying Secretary Davison to North Beach, New York, Lieutenant Elwood Quesada found that the hydraulic gear of the Y1C-23 refused to lower all the way. The secretary, due for a party with friends, considered bailing out; then, after an animated consultation with the pilot, it was decided to risk a wheels-up landing. If Eaker could do it, they could, too. Pete Quesada, though he had only two hours' flight time on Altairs, carefully circled Mitchel Field and hopefully pumped the gear again. It still stuck halfway. Then he fishtailed the 23 down to just above the ground and let her drop. She slid to a screeching halt in less than fifty feet, and the unruffled Davison hopped out to keep his dinner date.

Between Ira Eaker and Pete Quesada, the two Lockheed Altairs were belly-landed at least five times with comparatively little damage. What had seemed a dangerous thing eventually became commonplace with the exigencies of World War II.

The wooden Y1C-25, kept at Wright Field in Dayton for evaluation, was stripped in September 1932 and burned to test the efficiency of bottled carbon dioxide as a fire extinguisher. Secretary Davison's Duralumin Y1C-23 was given tests in the full-scale wind tunnel set up by the National Advisory Committee for Aeronautics at Langley Field, Virginia, in 1932. Experiments showed variable results in takeoff characteristics using 8-foot-3-inch, 9-foot, and 3-bladed propellers. Mounted in the huge drafty hangar at the tunnel's open maw, the Lockheed resembled a pretty blue-and-yellow bug about to be swallowed by a hungry carp.

With the change in Administration and Davison's departure, the Altair bore the Capitol dome insignia of Bolling Field. Gradually it was relegated to workaday chores, and flown by noncoms. The last single-engine Lockheed to serve in the Army Air Corps, it received the obscure designation Detroit T-23, and in 1942 was reported scrapped at Pennsylvania's Middletown Air Base.

Also built by Detroit Aircraft for the Army was a standard Duralumin Vega, designated the Y1C-12. This was tested and evaluated by the Wright Field pilots in 1930–31, and is supposed to have been equipped with a special metal wing developed by the matériel division of the Air Corps. As strictly a cargo carrier for Army use this

Debut of a new Lockheed star: no longer a "special Sirius," final version is named Altair, becomes Army's Y1C-25.

Only Sirius DL-2 model built. Converted to Altair and sold to USAAC.

Army Air Corps's second Altair has metal fuselage, is used to transport top brass as the Y1C-23.

particular Vega did not inspire much enthusiasm in its pilots. They reported it "almost impossible" to enter, and, for comfort, "just fair." It took off too slowly, landed too fast, and was said to have a tendency to spin at low speed if the controls were handled abruptly.

The Y1C-12 was considered an ugly duckling among the Air Corps's eagles and was attached to a number of squadrons as a transport and courier plane. After twice surviving minor crack-ups while assigned to the 36th Pursuit Group, at Langley Field, it was scrapped in 1935.

With success as a speedy transport in both high- and low-wing versions, Lockheed planes were naturally prominent in the thoughts of Air Corps planners. But it was a notable break with tradition when Washington and Dayton agreed to try out an experimental low-wing *fighter* airplane.

Robert J. Woods, an engineer for the Detroit Aircraft Corporation, mocked up a design for Army inspection in March 1931. Based mostly on Altair experience, it had a metal-skinned fuselage and tail surfaces, enclosed back-to-back cockpits for pilot and gunner, and was to be powered by a huge 600-hp Curtiss Conqueror V-1570C liquid-cooled engine. All this was mounted on a regular wooden Lockheed wing, with mechanical retractable landing gear. Detroit-Lockheed was delighted with their fighter's prospects, and felt that the project might just prove a way out of their financial doldrums. Called the XP-900, the prototype was assembled as a joint effort of both Detroit and Burbank, and delivered to the Air Corps on September 29, 1931.

Y1C-23 undergoes tests in giant wind tunnel at Langley Field, Virginia, in 1932.

Y1C-12, assigned to cargo duties with 36th Pursuit Squadron at Langley Field. Flew 999 hours for USAAC.

Woods and the others who contributed design and workmanship did a superb job with the XP-900. It was the very first monoplane fighter ever bought by the United States military, as well as the first with retractable landing gear. The trim ship was armed with a .30-caliber and a .50-caliber machine gun synchronized to fire through the 3-bladed propeller, plus another .30-caliber weapon for the gunner in the rear cockpit. Powerful, maneuverable, lethal, it was far ahead of its time—a vision of the fighters that would later fill the skies in World War II.

The Army evaluation pilots found that the XP-900 could climb 1,820 feet per minute and breeze along at 214 mph. This was over 40 miles an hour faster than the Berliner-Joyce P-16s for which it was under consideration as a replacement. The advent of a monoplane fighter was an eye-opener for designers of military equipment all over the world.

On acquisition, the Air Corps designated the new pursuit plane as the YP-24. They had it for testing at Dayton for just twenty days, and flew it only twenty hours.

In the cool, bright morning of October 19, 1931, the YP-24 was flown off from Wright Field for one of a series of routine checks. At the controls was Lieutenant Harrison G. Crocker, a veteran Army flyer and test pilot for the Evaluation Unit. He'd mastered the intricacies of all types of military planes, and already had a couple of hours' flight time on this one.

Crocker, dressed in a heavy flying suit and moccasins, put the ship through her paces and took her up to 22,000 feet to try her climbing ability. For a time he lazily circled

The plane that almost saved the day: XP-900, 2-place pursuit ship built at Detroit for the Army in 1931.

XP-900 predicts shape of future military aircraft as it makes test run over Detroit before delivery to Army.

Dayton. Then, deciding to land, the Lieutenant pushed the control lever for the landing gear over to RELEASE and began to wind the wheels down.

Snap!

The tubular shaft broke off at the bolthole just above the universal joint that connected it to the crank. With the trouble right there in the cockpit beside him, Crocker could do nothing. Turning the shaft by hand was impossible, and from this position he couldn't see the wheels.

The test pilot circled Wright Field and the ground crews saw his predicament. One wheel was stuck partly down, the other dangled loosely. A training plane was quickly dispatched to fly alongside the YP-24, with the words WHEELS HALF DOWN chalked on its side where Crocker couldn't fail to see the warning.

Crocker nodded and then began to throw his ship into violent maneuvers. He spun, looped, dived, and snap-rolled the airplane. The wheels didn't go down, but one vigorous gyration managed to slap them up into the wing, and the test pilot locked them there.

Now it was time to try a belly-landing. Captain Eaker had done it twice already, and Lieutenant Crocker was game to try. Granted, the ship was new and unproved, and the Curtiss in-line engine considerably bulkier than the Wasps which powered the Altairs. But Crocker was confident in his ability to put the ship down, and to him the risk appeared less than ditching his plane and falling to earth under a piece of silk.

Coming in for a try, the test pilot got a wave-off. General H. Conger Pratt, Chief of the Matériel Division, had arrived on the scene and made a quick decision. Another

Crash at Dayton gives YP-24 (former XP-900) a total of 20 flying hours, but Army Air Corps ordered five more.

ship was sent up, this time with the chalked command: GENERAL SAYS JUMP.

Sadly the Lieutenant turned toward the long reservation at Fairfield Air Depot, loath to leave the snappy fighter, but now under orders. He leveled off at low speed, stood up in the cockpit, and cut the switch. Bundled up and dragging the seat chute, he clambered over the side just as the plane fell off in a spin, slowly whirling toward the earth. With a protruding propeller below and a stabilizer above, this was no time to jump. Clinging to the padding, Crocker paused, then reached back in to level the ship off only 500 feet above the ground. The crew, which had raced up to the jump site, stood petrified as the pilot calmly climbed back in the cockpit, started the engine, and zoomed the ship back up to 4,000 feet.

Crocker's second attempt to leave went well. His chute boomed open, and he slowly drifted down to suffer no more damage than "a couple of banged-up fingers."

The pilotless YP-24 made two wide circles of the air depot, slowly losing altitude. Once it headed straight for the crowd that had gathered and, as they scattered for their lives, capriciously veered away. Traveling at high speed, it struck the field on one wing tip, bounded into the air in a dust cloud, and crashed to a stop a hundred feet farther on. The accident investigation team found only a hole where the big Curtiss engine had buried itself. Few pieces of the wing remained that were bigger than a shingle. Amazingly, the cockpit which Crocker had vacated was virtually intact, its clock still ticking away in the sudden silence.

In the fall sunshine the bright broken metal of the snapped gear shaft shone up accusingly, a reminder of man's often misplaced faith in machines. Harrison Crocker wasn't one to think of these things. He was back at his desk, hard at work, inside the hour.

Even though the prototype was gone, the fighter design developed by Bob Woods was worth some more of the same. The Army placed orders with Detroit Aircraft for five Y1P-24's at $27,600 each, and then topped it with another for five attack versions of the pursuit ship, to be designated YA-9s.

Had Detroit-Lockheed been able to fill these contracts, the joint firm might have been in the military airplane business then and there, and for good. However, right at this time Detroit folded with a crash as resounding as that of the XP-900. Lockheed was dragged along with the holding company into receivership. Worst of all, there was no money to build pursuit and attack planes, and the Air Corps contracts were defaulted.

Out of this fiasco Lockheed at least salvaged the memory of an airplane-that-might-have-been, and the knowledge that the design lived on to make a decided contribution to national defense. Bob Woods went from defunct Detroit Aircraft to the Consolidated company in Buffalo, to redesign the YP-24 as the almost identical YP-25. Despite the loss of two prototypes in fatal crashes during tests, the Air Corps accepted the planes and from them came the Consolidated P-30, ordered in quantity in 1935. Woods's revolutionary concept of a low-wing fighter became something that all the major aircraft companies of the world were to emulate. Years later, the Lockheed company was to build more of its own fighters —the P-38 of World War II, the Korean conflict's jet P-80, and the F-104, bulwark of a more modern worldwide defense. The half-forgotten little Detroit-Lockheed XP-900 on which hopes were pinned and dashed in 1931, was the first of them all.

With all the activity going on in the Army, it was not like the Navy to be hesitant in acquiring a command

XRO-1 embodies two firsts for the U.S. Navy, has a Cyclone engine for flying past the Army.

Tactful Mister Turner sheds his uniform to deliver the Navy's new Altair command transport to Anacostia.

transport of its own. Assistant Secretary of the Navy for Aeronautics was young David S. Ingalls. Largely at his instigation, a new metal Altair was purchased from Detroit-Lockheed in October 1931. The Navy went its rival service one better, and hung a 625-hp Wright Cyclone power plant on the nose.

Secretary Ingalls wanted to see naval aviation give some consideration to a plane with retractable landing gear, and the Lockheed was the first U.S. Navy aircraft to be so equipped. It was also the first low-wing monoplane in naval service, with the exception of imported Junkers float planes and a racer.

The Altair was tested by Marshall Headle before being flown East for delivery by none other than Roscoe Turner. Instead of his pale-blue uniform with its Sam Browne belt, the irrepressible Roscoe handled the ferry flight dressed in a dark business suit, derby hat, spats, and gloves.

The ship was designated the XRO-1, and was kept and maintained at the Anacostia Naval Air Station. Vance Breese demonstrated it for Washington aviation and military editors at 240 mph. Colonel Lindbergh, after being shown how to draw up the landing gear, is reported to have coaxed it four miles faster than that.

The ship was taken up on cautious early flights by Lieutenant R. B. Pirie; then as many naval pilots as possible were urged to become familiar with it and make recommendations. Secretary Ingalls flew it a good deal himself on various trips about the nation, and the Altair was considered his personal command plane. Another of Anacostia's chief test pilots also put a good many hours on the blue-and-white XRO-1. He was Lieutenant A.P. "Putt" Storrs, famed for his acrobatic flying with the Three Seahawks.

The Army and Navy command transports and the YP-24 fighter were developed and used by a country at peace. It remained for Spain, torn by civil war from 1936 to 1939, to give Lockheed aircraft their baptism of fire.

The part played by American airplanes in the Spanish conflict is little known, but more than a hundred of them were used by both sides. Late in 1936, the Spanish Republic began negotiations for secondhand airplanes, seeking air power of all types to combat the Italian squadrons and the German Condor Legion that were being used against them by the insurgent forces of General Francisco Franco.

Soviet Russia sent both men and airplanes to the Spanish Republic and was adequately reimbursed with Spanish gold. Hot-and-cold support for the Loyalist cause also came from France and Mexico. The United States endeavored to maintain a policy of nonintervention, but ran into complications in the enforcement of an embargo on war material, including aircraft of all types.

Willing to pay top prices, the Spanish embassies in Washington and Mexico City set about procuring used transport planes. Purchasing commissions and independent buyers were sent from Spain, and even the Communist International network was empowered to make purchases. In the confusion, the various agencies found themselves bidding against each other and created a seller's market.

The profits to be gained in such traffic were considerable, and it was natural that a few men cynically ignored the first, toothless "moral embargo" imposed by President Franklin D. Roosevelt. Until Congress could pass a real embargo act that covered Spain, they rushed about the country, acquiring old airplanes.

It was a cloak-and-dagger business, with changing middlemen, false-front "import-export companies" and fast-switching "citizens of unknown nationality." The

State Department frowned on the deals, but could do little to halt shipments when a bonafide export license had been applied for legally, and issued.

The Spanish Republicans knew the speed and cargo-carrying capacities of Lockheeds, and asked for them specifically. It was up to U.S. aircraft brokers to scrounge around and find a supply to fill the demand. The answer to "What happened to all the Lockheed Orions?" is a simple one: of the total of thirty-five built, fourteen were sold and delivered to the Spanish Republic. A Sirius and a Vega brought to sixteen the Lockheeds to see service with the Loyalists.

Rudolf Wolf, Inc., ostensibly a Wall Street dealer in jute and burlap, sent Orions to Europe on the Dutch freighter *Waalhaven*. Among their exports were two that once flew for Varney, an ex–Northwest Airways job, and the planes formerly owned by Dr. John R. Brinkley and Laura Ingalls. (A sixth, an ex-TWA cargo ship, force-landed in Ohio while being ferried to New York for shipment.)

Accompanied by two American aircraft mechanics, Wolf's shipment was consigned to a dealer in the Netherlands, but was off-loaded at Le Havre, where the planes were assembled. Flown to Le Bourget, Villacoublay, and Toussus-le-Noble airfields, they were tested and approved by French pilots of the *Centre de Essais des Avions Nouveaux* (CEPANA) before delivery to Spain.

The French Air Ministry had acquired Michel Détroyat's Orion, bought as an entry in the MacRobertson Race of 1934. By order of Pierre Cot, the French Air Minister and a supporter of the Spanish Republic, this plane was flown to Madrid in July 1936 by Edouard Corniglion-Molinier. His passengers were the famous French writer André Malraux and his wife, making a preliminary trip to Spain prior to Malraux's involvement in the establishment of an "international" squadron of hastily acquired French bombing aircraft. The new Spanish ambassador, Alvaro de Albornez, was flown back to Paris.

The French Orion was shortly put at the disposal of the Spanish Government. For a few days it shuttled back and forth between the two countries, carrying government officials and news correspondents. Then a forced landing in the province of Teruel, Spain, ended its usefulness. Spanish mechanics reportedly *sawed* off the wings!

Swissair's two bright-red Orions were acquired in France and sent on direct to Spain. Still bearing their Swiss registration letters they were often flown by Joseph Rosmarin, a veteran transport pilot from Brooklyn. Rosmarin, one of the war's first American volunteers, flew in Spain for over a year. He piloted the Orions as courier planes, transporting Republican military staff and government personnel between Alicante and the various battlefronts. In one fifteen-day period he flew more than a hundred hours. Occasionally Joe and the ex-airliners were pressed into service carrying badly needed munitions to the fight-

Thirteen more fast Orions like F. C. Hall's Sheridan *went to the Spanish Republican Air Force as warplanes.*

One of two Orions sold by airline through France.

Swissair's first "Rote Orion."

Phillips's Orion bought by Spanish agents.

Dr. Brinkley's Cyclone-powered Orion escaped to Algeria in March 1939, the only Orion to survive the conflict.

American pilot Joe Rosmarin flew Orions on transport missions in the Spanish Civil War.

ing lines. Attacked by Nationalist fighters, he wrote off one "Red Orion" in a successful wheels-up landing with a load of Spanish V.I.P.'s.

The embattled Spanish Loyalists counted upon aid from Mexico. Among the procurers of aircraft were General Robert Fierro, Fritz Beiler, a German-Mexican, and Carlos Panini, who was about to start his own airline. General Fierro sent both his own personal planes, the Sirius *Anahuac*, with which he'd made his famous New York to Mexico City flight in 1930, and his Vega, a veteran of C.A.T. airline days. Spanish Republican ships, dodging Nationalist cruisers and Italian submarines, slipped out of Vera Cruz across the perilous Atlantic with these planes, plus six more Orions that had once flown for the airlines and for Oklahoma and Texas oil operators.

The white *Anahuac*, assigned to the Basque front, and the black Orion *Auto-da-Fé* are both reported as "crashed in Spain." Other Lockheeds were doubtless destroyed on the ground by wave after wave of raiding Nationalist Fiats, Heinkels, Dorniers, and Savoia-Marchettis.

Another American volunteer pilot, Edwin Lyons, recalled flying the Vega on cargo runs between Quintanar de la Zarga and Madrid. The high-powered Orion *Doctor Brinkley III* was reportedly shot down, while still carrying the doctor's name and her U.S. registration numbers. The news services got hold of the story that Brinkley and his airplane had both perished in the fighting. The doctor himself happened to be incommunicado on his yacht off Nova Scotia that summer and it took considerable explaining to convince his friends and patients that he was hale and hearty and far from Spain.

Despite the story, the Brinkley Orion appears to have been the only Lockheed of this series to survive the Spanish Civil War. When hostilities came to an end more than fifty planes were flown out of Republican Spain. Among them was this sole Lockheed Orion, flown to Oran in French Algeria on March 30, 1939. It was eventually turned over to the victorious Nationalists, and its ultimate fate is unrecorded.

A footnote to the participation of Lockheeds in the Spanish Civil War was provided by a Czechoslovakian airplane, the trimotored Avia 51. This aircraft was developed by Robert Nebesar, who had worked as an aerodynamics engineer for Detroit Aircraft and then returned to his native Prague. Cigar-shaped and streamlined with cowls and pants, the metal plane clearly showed the influence of the designer's days in the Motor City.

Just three of Nebesar's 7-place trimotors were built in 1933 by the Czechoslovak Aircraft Works. They were supposedly sold to Estonia, but in actuality shipped to Spain. In the course of delivery, the tramp steamer transporting the three airplanes reportedly was sunk without a trace.

The appearance of the Lockheed Orion, and especially its performance on the European routes of Swissair, contributed to the design of other transport aircraft, all of which were soon to be put to military use.

The British designers A. H. Tiltman and N. S. Norway (the latter the famous novelist, "Nevil Shute") acknowledged that a photograph of the Orion influenced their decision to build a low-winged cantilever monoplane with retractable landing gear. The result was seen in the Airspeed AS.5 Courier, and the Airspeed Envoy, which evolved into the ubiquitous Oxford trainer used by the Royal Air Force.

The German airline, Deutsche Lufthansa, wanted a faster small transport to match Swissair's speedy Orion. For them the Heinkel-Flugzeugwerke Company designed the Heinkel He 70, unofficially dubbed "Der Blitz." Still another Orion-like low-winger produced in Germany was the Junkers Ju 60 and Ju 160 which followed. These six-passenger transports were operated by Lufthansa between 1933 and 1939.

Finally, in 1932, the Kharkov Aviation Institute team of designers in the Ukraine produced the KhA1-1, a Russian six-seater, low-wing, monocoque-fuselaged transport with a marked resemblance to the Orion. A number were reportedly intended for the Moscow-Tiflis express services of the Russian airline Aeroflot, and some were utilized for pre–World War II military transport in the U.S.S.R.

Though the Spanish war took the cream, by 1941 there were still some single-engine Lockheeds in good condition—good enough to be conscripted into service in World War II.

Don Marshall, Lockheed Aircraft representative at Dallas, sold his Vega, the last one built, to the Army Engineers' Los Angeles District. It was given an Army serial number and designated a UC-101.

Similarly, the third-from-last Orion, the former *Early Bird* owned by the *Detroit News* was acquired in 1942 by the War Department; in Army drab, it was called a UC-85. Nicknamed *Scuttlebutt,* this ship was flown during the war out of March Field, California. Its usual pilot was Colonel A. Paul Mantz, who was certainly no stranger to Lockheeds of the type.

Two other Vegas, an old Wedell-Williams Air Service transport, and a former Phillips Petroleum ship, were sold to the Army Engineers operating out of San Francisco. The latter plane was destroyed in a hangar fire at Van Nuys, California. The former was reported only as in service "outside the continental limits of the United States." Its actual use in the war effort is unknown. Clarence Chamberlin's Altair *Miss Stratosphere* also went to the

Designer Robert Nebesar based Czech trimotor on his experiences with Lockheed DL-1s.

Drafted in WW II is USAAF's Orion UC-85, former peacetime news-gatherer Early Bird.

Army Engineers. Used for some early antiradar testing, it was written off in a California accident.

As thousands of aircraft poured from the factories, there was soon no real use for "draftees" such as the Vega UC-101 and the Orion UC-85. They were put up for sale even before the war ended. Don Marshall of Lockheed bought back his Vega and then sold it again at a good profit through broker Charlie Babb. The surplus Orion went to Danny Fowlie of Van Nuys, California.

One more Vega can be classed as a World War II participant. It was Glen Kidston's old London-to-Capetown record-breaker of 1931. After cracking up in the MacRobertson Race this metal job was sold to parties in Australia. Five years later, at the outbreak of the war, the Vega was impressed into the Royal Australian Air Force. As an RAAF A42-1 it performed various chores at the military airfields "down under." The ship still had its old Wasp engine, which finally became unserviceable in 1944. The Aussies endeavored to install other engines and were going to try another Wasp from a smashed Sikorsky amphibian when the war ended and there was no need.

As the wrecker's torch cut up the Vega in October 1945, there was no thought that here was the ship that had once been the fastest airplane on two continents.

15

THEY ALL FLEW LOCKHEEDS

Airplanes designed for the exclusive use of large corporations had their origin only a little over fifty years ago. During the twenties, the well-known Fokker and Ford Trimotors were occasionally refinished by individual owners as "flying offices." But it remained for Lockheed to put a business airplane into standard production. This was the specially equipped Vega Executive.

The prototype Executive model came out of Burbank in time for exhibit at the Detroit Aircraft Show of April 1929. Standard equipment in this businessman's airplane included a folding desk and a brand-new typewriter, convertible seating, curtained windows, and a lavatory. Since pre-Depression executives were expected to mix business with pleasure, "a big compartment for golf clubs and luggage" was provided.

With its smooth fuselage to pass the airflow the Vega Executive was advertised as "reducing noise and vibration to a degree that dictation, typing, or taking a nap may now be included in the flying program of progressive businessmen and women who would make the most of hours spent in air travel."

Lockheed's first Executive was soon sold to the Independent Oil & Gas Company of Tulsa, Oklahoma, and was used by the firm's vice president, Gillette Hill, for business trips and sales promotion. The white-and-blue Vega gathered good publicity as the official plane for the International Air Derby run from Mexico City to Kansas City in 1930. And in devising an emblem for Independent's Tailwind Aviation Gas, the Lockheed was com-

First Executive Vega begins by carrying oilmen. Still flies today.

bined with the company's "big I" trademark.

Before long, Independent was taken over by the Phillips Petroleum Corporation of Bartlesville, Oklahoma, and they traded the first Executive job for a newer Vega in a deal with Parks Air College of East St. Louis, Illinois.

Phillips Petroleum owned and flew three Vegas and two Orions over a period of nine years. Aviation-minded Frank Phillips, founder of the company, was the generous sponsor of such famed flyers as Art Goebel, Bennie Griffin, and Wiley Post. Will D. (Billy) Parker, the popular, longtime manager of Phillips's aviation department, flew the Lockheeds all over the country in sales work, paced the National Air Races derbies, and set up a few intercity records of his own. Promoting Phillips 77 Aviation Gasoline for individual and airline use throughout the Mid- and Southwest, Parker's company bought the very last Lockheed Orion ever built. And later they acquired the final Vega to come off the assembly line in Burbank. Billy Parker, who flew the ships for nearly a decade, probably had thousands of hours on both types.

Over in Ponca City was the Marland Oil Company, another Oklahoma oil producer and competitor of Phillips's. To check pipelines and deliver executives to distant cities in a hurry, Marland bought a Lockheed Vega early in 1929. Ray Shrader, later in charge of operations for Braniff Airlines, got his first experience with Vegas as Marland's pilot. The company was soon merged with Continental Oil Company, and the triangular Conoco trademark replaced that of Marland Oil on the ship's wings. After four years the original Vega was traded in on a new one equipped with Goodyear Airwheels and the NACA cowl. The second Conoco Lockheed had an extra-long existence as an executive plane: Continental pilots flew the red-white-and-green plane until 1944.

Mention has already been made of Roscoe Turner, his lion cub Gilmore, and their work in publicizing California's Gilmore Oil Company. On July 16, 1930—three weeks after making a new cross-continent record—man, lion, and Air Express set a new mark for the three-nation flight from Vancouver, British Columbia, nonstop to Agua Caliente, Baja California, Mexico, of 9 hours, 14 minutes and 30 seconds.

Even when not breaking records, the two made a stellar publicity team. At the best hotels they simply signed the register "Roscoe and Gilmore," and were universally accepted. Unfortunately the lion grew fast, and soon his 500-pound bulk was more payload than Roscoe could afford to carry.

After 25,000 miles of flying, Gilmore had to be grounded, and was put on exhibit in a special enclosure on the grounds of the United Air Terminal in Burbank. Among the crowds that flocked about his cage, the lion could always sense the presence of either Turner or his longtime mechanic, Don Young, and had a special type of growl to greet them. But the uncanny thing was that, among the hundreds of planes that put down and took off from the terminal, Gilmore *always* came alert with recognition on the arrival or departure of the Lockheed in which he'd flown so many miles. Since it was the only Air Express flying in the area, perhaps he recognized it with a special lion's sixth sense, or by some peculiar swish of the parasol wing inaudible to human ears.

Eventually, title to the sturdy Air Express went to Colonel Roscoe Turner himself, and when not flying racers he used it for personal transportation for eight years. Through an arrangement with the Macmillan Petroleum Corporation of Long Beach, California, he flew the ship as *Roscoe Turner's Macmillan Ring-Free Express* and publicized their products as he had those of Gilmore Oil. Roscoe had quite an affection for the ship and referred to it as "my baby." Finally, after eleven years of rough service, the plane was declared unairworthy, and Don Young reluctantly dismantled and scrapped it.

And Gilmore?

Since the lion had so long been his companion and friend, Roscoe Turner put Gilmore in a Los Angeles private zoo, and paid for his upkeep for over twenty-five years. When the famous lion died in 1957, his pilot arranged for a taxidermist's services and flew Gilmore east to a permanent resting place in the Turner Trophy Room at his Indianapolis home.

"He's not one of the trophies," explained Roscoe. "The trophies belong to him as much as they do to me."

After Roscoe's wings were folded in 1970, Gilmore was sent to Washington to grace the racing exhibit at the National Air and Space Museum.

The first Lockheed Vega to be sold to a major oil corporation went to a subsidiary of The Texas Company in the summer of 1928. Bert E. Hull, president of the Texas Pipe Line Company, used the plane to survey routes and completed jobs from the air. Painted red, with white trim, Hull's *Texaco 2* was piloted all over the Southwest on pipeline business. At the controls of the Whirlwind-powered ship were company pilots Frank Hawks, Bert Pidcoke, or Matt Nieminen. Hawks soon became famous on a national scale, flying the oil firm's Lockheed Air Express *Texaco 5* on its transcontinental record-breaking trips.

President Hull recalled his pilots handling the early Vegas "as carefully as if flying an empty eggshell"; and that wings and fuselages were occasionally punctured by Texas hailstones. In checking a pipeline installation far out on the plains, it was customary to buzz the adjacent landing area until the crew below drove off the grazing herds of cattle or sheep. In 1931, using a Vega and makeshift landing fields of this nature, Texas Company pilot Hal P. Henning conducted officials on a 5,000-mile

---

The Executive model Vega included a portable typewriter and a concealed lavatory that was accessible when a passenger seat was folded down.

Motor installation for a Wright Whirlwind engine (left) *and a Pratt & Whitney Wasp* (right).

tour of oil-field properties in Oklahoma and Texas.

In addition to two Vegas operated by the pipeline subsidiary, and Frank Hawks's short-lived but well-remembered Air Express, The Texas Company also flew a Sirius. This was *Texaco 16,* a twin-cockpit job brightly painted red and white, which was used for publicity at air shows and for fast transport in 1932–33 by aviation department manager J. D. "Duke" Jernigan.

A second major oil company to buy and fly the wooden Lockheeds was Standard Oil of New Jersey. Manager of their newly formed aviation department was Edwin E. Aldrin, who went to Burbank in September 1928 to take delivery of the second Pratt & Whitney Wasp-engined Vega to be produced. The red-and-white ship was used to test various blends and aviation gasolines and oils produced by Standard. In the spring of '29, Major Aldrin shipped the Vega to Europe. Accompanied by his wife, Marion, and a mechanic, he took a 6,000-mile business trip to France, Italy, Germany, Austria, Switzerland, Czechoslovakia, England, and The Netherlands. Since this was the first Lockheed ever seen on the continent, it attracted crowds each time the Aldrins set down at an airdrome. And even with a leisurely trip, it was a foregone conclusion that the ship would set a few new European intercity speed records.

Later in the year, this first Standard Oil Vega was traded in on a newer model equipped with oversize

Standard Oil of New Jersey's Vega, piloted by Maj. Edwin E. Aldrin (right), *toured the U.S. and gave Europeans their first sight of a Lockheed.*

wheel pants, and the NACA cowl. The original Wasp engine went into the new ship and before long had hauled the successive Lockheeds some 65,000 miles. This plane, called *No. 1*, and an identical sister ship, *No. 6*, flew for the Stanavo Specification Board, a subsidiary formed by the Standard companies of New Jersey, Indiana, and California to coordinate nationally the promotion and sale of Stanavo Aviation Gasoline and Oils. Since Stanavo's trademark was a symbolic eagle-airplane, the two Vegas were given impressive paint jobs in the form of giant American eagles whose broad wings stretched along the full cantilever of the Lockheeds and whose outsize claws reached down the wheel fairings.

Informally dubbed the Flying Trademarks or the Stanavo Eagles, the colorful ships were based at Newark Airport, and flew everywhere and often. At one time Major Aldrin held an unofficial transcontinental record with *No. 1*. On a business trip—with stops at Albuquerque, Tulsa, and Dayton—his flying time for the whole junket was only 15 hours and 40 minutes.

Both Major Robert E. Ellis and Lieutenant Will W. White were associated with Stanavo as assistants to Aldrin. Ellis flew one eagle-Vega from Miami to Newark in 8 hours in 1930, and White was copilot on the record-breaking flight the other ship made to Buenos Aires the same year.

The *No. 1* eventually had the colors of its eagle paint job reversed when converted into Jimmie Mattern's second *Century of Progress*. Stanavo Vega *No. 6* also appeared in both white-eagle and red-eagle versions before sale in 1936 to Joe Costa as the *Crystal City*.

Though backed by a long-established international combine, Shell Petroleum products were still new to many Americans in the early 1930s. In 1929 ex-Army flyer John A. Macready was hired by Shell Oil of San Francisco to organize an aviation department. The personable major, three times winner of the Mackay Trophy and onetime holder of world's distance, duration, and altitude records, had piloted the Army's T-2 on the first transcontinental nonstop flight in 1923.

Standard, Richfield, and other California oil companies were very much in the aviation business and Shell had been criticized for dragging its feet. Major Macready changed all this. At first he simply built goodwill for Shell Oil and publicized the name. Many executives and prospective customers were taken in Shell planes for their first pleasure trips aloft. Exhibitions, record-breaking hops, and flying just a cut above pure barnstorming put the red-and-yellow scallop emblem very much in the public eye.

Gradually, Macready and his pilots contacted airport owners and officials, and set up a chain of outlets for Shell aviation products. They taught other company sales personnel that this untapped market was worthy of future development—which called for many hours and many miles of day in, day out flying. Prominent among the aircraft flown by the aggressive and popular major were a pair of Lockheed Vegas. Decked out in the familiar Shell colors, one was stationed at Alameda, California, across the bay from company headquarters, and the other in Seattle. Over a fourteen-year period (1930–44) Shell owned and flew a Lockheed fleet that included four Vegas and a Sirius.

John Macready promotes a new image, more sales for Shell.

One of Shell Petroleum's top assets: Jimmy Doolittle.

The Sirius was a very early experimental model, built at the same time as the prototype for Colonel Charles A. Lindbergh in late 1929. Lindbergh and Macready exchanged ideas on their new ships and the colonel flew the Shell job on tests as well as his own. Macready recalls the Sirius as "a good airplane." He flew it on a 3,500-mile tour of the Pacific Northwest and Canada and also raced the low-winger over a mile course at Alameda for an unofficial speed record of 206 mph.

After only a few months' operation Macready had the fast ship at an air show in Tracy, California. Seeking to give the crowd a thrill, he put the Sirius in a power dive, with the idea of zooming up again just over the heads of the spectators. On the way down, the plane developed a terrific wing flutter. The major, shaken about as badly as the Lockheed, managed to land safely. Walking away white-faced, he put in a call to Burbank and told the company to "come and get it." Apparently, though it had been flown full out on the time trials, this particular Sirius could not withstand the strain of a power dive. Returned to the factory, it was never flown again.

What Shell Oil was doing for aviation on the West Coast, the Shell Petroleum Corporation of St. Louis proposed to accomplish in the Midwest. On the recommendation of Macready and other astute officials who knew men, this company hired another well-known Army aviator: James H. Doolittle.

Major Jimmy Doolittle hailed from California. For years he was an irrepressible daredevil, and those who read of his exploits in test-flying and racing airplanes in the twenties were apt to forget that he had also earned a doctorate in aeronautical engineering at M.I.T. Jimmy could not only fly like a demon, but knew the technical side of airplanes and their engines. He was the first man to perform an outside loop in an airplane, and the first to make a completely blind flight—feats he planned ahead as carefully as if for one of his air races.

Shell Petroleum purchased a $25,000 Lockheed for Doolittle, a sleek panted and cowled Vega with special Executive interior. Jimmy was to use it to promote the company out of St. Louis, as Major Macready was already doing for the other Shell organization on the West Coast.

Doolittle expected to leave Mitchel Field on Long Island with his wife and two boys on February 27, 1930. He realized that the Vega was overloaded with household baggage when the cockpit door behind him came unlatched and he nearly tumbled into the cabin. The ship shed its landing gear and dug into the frozen sod on its belly. Nobody was hurt, but the major's first day as a civilian oil company employee was not exactly auspicious.

Shipped back to Burbank and rebuilt, the Vega served both Doolittle and James G. Haizlip, another ex-Army and airline pilot who joined Shell at the same time. Soft-spoken, handsome Jimmy Haizlip shared honors with Jimmy Doolittle in meteoric trips across the country with racing planes, and in winning trophies at the National Air Races. One of his accomplishments was to fly the Shell Vega to victory in the Transport Race at the 1930 NAR in Chicago. For several years both Jimmys could be found either flying a Lockheed out of St. Louis on oil company business, or setting records with a series of fast, specially built racing planes sponsored by Shell. It all helped sell aviation—and petroleum products.

Short and chunky Jimmy Doolittle got hold of another Lockheed in 1932. This was the experimental Altair with wooden wing and metal fuselage that had been flown briefly as a mail plane by Transcontinental & Western Air. Lockheed was barely keeping in existence as a company at the time, but managed to convert the ship to an Orion. This was accomplished in the deserted factory by chief engineer Dick Von Hake and his assistant, Jimmy Gerschler. Working without pay, Miss Nina Wyatt typed the stress analysis and paperwork on the plane, and became Mrs. Gerschler as a result of the association. The trio's combined efforts produced the only metal Orion ever to take the air.

Called *Shellightning*, the Orion was beautifully painted with scalloped wings and big Shell emblems on the nose and tail. Jimmy Doolittle made hundreds of trips in this Lockheed, and the ship was very much in evidence at air shows, airport dedications, and business conclaves across the territory of all three Shell companies in the United States. The presence of the famed racing pilot was enough to insure good attendance at any air event.

Perhaps the most unusual use made of the *Shellightning* was a special flight in the summer of 1932. This was the George Washington Bicentennial Airplane Flight to commemorate the 157th anniversary of the founding of the U.S. Postal Service. The plan was to fly in one day over all the American towns visited by George Washington in his entire lifetime. Mailbags would be dropped at thrity significant historical spots.

Jimmy Doolittle took up the idea with enthusiasm and enlisted the aid of Alpheus F. Maple, editor of Shell's New York house organ, to go along and drop mailbags. As a crowning touch, they also took Miss Anne Madison Washington, great-great-grandniece of the first president, in the plane as passenger.

Jimmy got the Orion off from Kittery, Maine (Washington's visit farthest north), in the early dawn of July 25, 1932. The route took him over Boston, Providence, New Haven, New York, and all the tiny places made famous by the Father of his Country. It was a problem in both navigation and landmark identification for Jimmy to pick out places like Monmouth Courthouse, New Jersey; Valley Forge, Pennsylvania; Wakefield, Viginia; and Sunbury, North Carolina.

Al Maple, as a peacetime bombardier, next sent bags plummeting down to watchers at Winchester, Virginia;

Doolittle and his famed Shellightning, *only metal Orion ever built, furnish thrills at conventions and make a 2,600-mile flight in one day to carry commemorative U.S. mail in George Washington's footsteps.*

Fort Necessity, Pennsylvania; and Point Pleasant, West Virginia. Turning north the speeding Lockheed cut across western New York from Fort LeBoeuf (Waterford, Pennsylvania) to Fort Stanwix (Rome, New York), and then among the Adirondack foothills to Crown Point and Ticonderoga.

Miss Washington "enjoyed every bit" of the trip. But it was a weary Jimmy Doolittle who, flying low and following the railroad tracks and Hudson River, finally headed down the last stretch to New York. In the summer twilight, Maple let out the last mailbag, which landed almost at the feet of the postmaster standing on the parade ground at West Point. George Washington would never have believed that Jimmy Doolittle covered all the places in the span of a single day, from dawn to dusk. The entire 2,600-mile flight took *Shellightning* just 15 hours and 40 minutes.

Manufacturers of rubber products also had a good field in the aviation industry, both for advertising and development of new products. Mention has already been made of the B. F. Goodrich Company's Lockheed Vega *Miss Silvertown,* and the racing, cross-country, and speed-trial work done with her by company pilot Lee Shoenhair. In addition to transporting executives, the ship was used in experiments with various airplane tires, brakes, and wheels, during which the white speedster went by the more prosaic designation of *Test Plane No. 3.*

One of the greatest contributions to safe flying—the first De-icer—was tested initially by Goodrich in 1931. The pulsating rubber overshoes were designed to be at-

Miss Silvertown *is fitted for rubber "overshoes" to combat wing ice-up. Goodrich Company's speed queen made first complete test of De-icers on any aircraft in 1931, innovation was standard transport equipment thereafter.*

tached to the leading edges of both the wing and tail surfaces of an airplane, and inflated by compressed air to break off ice accumulations—thus making it possible for the airstream to carry the ice away. After extensive tests in a refrigerated wind tunnel at Akron, and exploratory application on a mail plane, Goodrich completely equipped their Lockheed with the De-icers.

Billy Brock first flew the rubber-shod *Miss Silvertown* above the Ohio landscape and found no noticeable difference in the ship's stability. Then test pilot Charlie Meyers circled the white Vega high into the wintry clouds, deliberately picked up a good thick layer of ice, and successfully eliminated it. Further tests by Jimmy Doolittle on Shell Petroleum's Vega and the Orion *Shellightning* proved the worth of De-icers. The next year Goodrich's inflatable rubber boots were adopted as standard equipment on scheduled transport planes and military aircraft.

Another Akron firm, the General Tire & Rubber Company, had already had experience with one Lockheed. They briefly owned the Hornet-powered Air Express which Henry J. Brown flew to beat out Goodrich's *Miss Silvertown* in the 1929 transcontinental nonstop race. In 1934 General got another Lockheed, the former Shell Petroleum Vega which had been flown by Doolittle and Haizlip. General's pilot was Ray W. Brown, an Army-trained flyer who came with the ship from Shell. Used for executive transport primarily, General's plane was named *Miss Streamline*.

The rubber company's wooden Vega was succeeded in 1937 by one with a Duralumin fuselage, *Miss Streamline 2nd*. This ship had been an airliner in the Southwest, and was flown for a time with an eagle paint job by Stanavo, whose pilots declared that it "flew cockeyed." Ray Brown didn't seem to have any trouble jockeying the shiny metal Vega, and it carried the officials of General Tire on business and pleasure jaunts until 1941.

Ray Brown and Miss Streamline 2nd *fly for General Tire.*

Other businesses made use of the speed and eye-appeal of Lockheeds. The Prest-O-Lite Storage Battery Corporation of Indianapolis had a white Vega, *Prest-O-Lite II*, which was in the charge of company pilot Dick Knox. Elmer O. Beardsley and Walter F. Piper of Chicago used a red-and-gold Vega in their business of manufacturing foundry machinery. The partners were pilots who flew not only for pleasure but also for getting a part to a customer in a hurry. When the first Beardsley & Piper Lockheed was accidentally destroyed by fire, this unusual pair of flying executives immediately bought another. And proceeded to pilot the ship some 60,000 miles a year for a decade.

Out of Detroit, Captain Russell Young flew a beautiful black-and-yellow Vega Executive for McAleer's Polish. The *Miss McAleer* advertised the product on its wing, and red cans of McAleer's were painted on the fuselage. Naturally this was one airplane that could always be counted on to be kept shined to a brilliant luster, and its dazzling appearance did much to sell the product. C. H. McAleer, head of the company, developed an even glossier polish, which was claimed to add from 2 to 5 miles per hour to the speed of the Vega.

Miss McAleer was completely radio equipped, including a set for passengers and a broadcasting loudspeaker. This voice from the sky could be heard for over a mile, telling the countryside below the merits of McAleer's Polish.

One Vega used in business was built under unusual circumstances. Richard Von Hake, the Lockheed chief engineer who personally assembled Jimmy Doolittle's Orion, was laid off during the company's reorganization days of 1932–33. He bought a metal Vega fuselage from the defunct Detroit Aircraft Corporation's receivers for $2,000 and had it shipped to California. Von Hake himself assembled the DL Vega with a stock wooden wing, and readied it for sale through the virtually assetless Lockheed company.

The ship went from Burbank to John Morrell & Co., a well-known meat packing firm, and was flown out of Ottumwa, Iowa. Piloted by Cliff P. Kysor, and known as *Morrell's Pride II*, the two-tone green Vega was primarily used to bring customers into Morrell's plants at Ottumwa and Sioux Falls, South Dakota. The *Pride*, after a subsequent career as an airliner in the Southwest and Alaska, is still in existence, the only remaining Vega with a Detroit-built Duralumin fuselage.

In the 1930s Parks Air College of East St. Louis, Illinois, was one of the nation's best and most popular schools of flying instruction. Oliver L. Parks, a top auto salesman,

First known flying ambulance is this Aerial Transport Vega, the Invalid Coach, *fitted out in January 1929.*

founded the school in 1927, and trained thousands of aircraft and engine mechanics as well as pilots. Like Lockheed, the air college was affiliated for a time with the Detroit Aircraft Corporation combine, and obtained Vegas for student instruction. Parks's candidates for rating as transport pilots all had to put in twelve hours' solo time buckled in one of the school's Lockheeds, of which the college owned three over the years. Often the wooden ships from Burbank were repaired or completely rebuilt by maintenance students in the shops at East St. Louis. Other Lockheeds were put to similar uses in flight- and ground-training schools throughout the nation.

Lawrence B. Talbot's California Aerial Transport put the nation's first commercial air ambulance into operation in 1930. A Lockheed Vega painted white with big red crosses on each side, it contained a suspended, form-fitting bed, rigged to remain level during flight. Equipment included a first-aid cabinet, stretchers, hot pads, blankets, sheets, and pillows. There was room to seat an attendant doctor and nurse at the bedside.

Larry Talbot's *Invalid Coach* was kept on call in the transport company's hangar at Los Angeles Municipal Airport. Later on, Joe Lewis and Viola Neil operated a similar Vega as the Aerial Hospital Service out of Union Air Terminal in Burbank; and in 1938 Lauretta M. Schimmoler endeavored to found an Aerial Nurse Corps, utilizing a chartered Vega from United Air Services at the same field.

Typical of the charter flyers who made good use of Lockheed looks, speed, and reliability was R. E. Morrison. Red was a University of Kansas graduate and former teacher of history and math. He was coaching high school athletics in Santa Cruz, California, when he caught the "Lindbergh fever" in 1927 and learned to fly. He was good enough to hold down a job as personal pilot for an exacting taskmaster: publisher William Randolph Hearst.

Early in 1931 Morrison acquired a damaged Lockheed Vega for $5,000, and had it put in shape at the factory. He knocked around with the ship for a while, flying out of Mills Field in San Francisco, and then set out to find a less crowded base of operations.

In the spring of 1932, Red's wanderings took him to the grass and sod field that passed for the Municipal Airport at Helena, Montana. A lone spectator, Jake Fritz, greeted the pilot on his arrival, and introduced him to the county commissioner in charge of the field. Then and there were laid the foundations of Morrison Flying Service. And it was a sample of Red's persuasive enthusiasm that Jake Fritz became his first flight student.

Scratching out a livelihood in a strange town was no picnic for the red-headed barnstormer. He stumped the state, selling all the sightseeing hops he could promote for his Vega, and gave advance instruction in it to budding transport pilots. There was no place Red wouldn't go for a charter, provided the air was flyable and the ground landable. With his Whirlwind-powered Lockheed, he might turn up at Wolf Point, Montana, with a rancher with cattle for sale, or at Los Angeles Metropolitan Airport with a tired businessman and party, set for a Hollywood fling. It was said that "by a combination of ebullience, fearlessness, and unfailing energy, Red Morrison sold the people of Helena—and Montana—on aviation as a service."

Red lost his beloved and well-cared-for Vega in the spring of 1935, after five years of daily flights. Making a

Red Morrison, whose Vega flew every day for five years.

forced landing high in the mountains of southwest Montana, the ship's landing gear let go. It wasn't feasible to remove the plane from such a remote area: Morrison walked out and simply left it there. Though Red died in a 1942 bomber crash, the Morrison Flying Service, which he started with his faithful Vega, was continued by his widow, operating a charter service out of Helena Municipal Airport.

Best known for his movie stunting and air racing, A. Paul Mantz started a charter business in 1933. An Alameda, California, boy, Mantz got his training from the Army, and for a spell operated a flying school at Palo Alto. In 1931 he breezed into Union Air Terminal at Burbank with a little J5-powered Stearman. He had only a few acquaintances, so he had to start on the flightline with the rest of the helmet-and-goggles boys, ballyhooing for hop customers and an occasional student. Despite the Depression, Mantz prospered, while other ambitious pilots found themselves without financial lift under their wings and had to settle back into humdrum lives. Paul's secret was service as good or better than commercial airlines could offer. His motto of Anywhere—Anytime meant something, and before long the Mantz-operated United Air Services, Ltd., had five planes going on charter, forest patrol, student training, or exhibitions.

For speed in transporting the movie moguls and stars of Hollywood anywhere in the Western Hemisphere, Paul acquired two Lockheed Vegas and kept them ready to fly at the ring of a phone. Mexico was a frequent destination, or the gambling halls of Nevada. On one flight to Las Vegas a party from the flicker colony was in full swing as Mantz headed his Vega across the Mojave Desert. Seated up in the office, Paul felt and heard "a terrific explosion" in the cabin behind him. There was a moment's dead silence. Then giggles began, and more laughter told him it was only the popping cork of an extra-powerful bottle of champagne.

The stocky boss of United Air Services gradually added flying *in* the movies to his list of services, and it became the work for which he was chiefly noted. Camera mounts were devised to fit anywhere on any type of plane, and mock-up aircraft interiors were supplied to the studios to use for close-up scenes. If Paul Mantz foresaw a need for some special equipment, he'd either buy or build it.

In the course of this work Mantz probably owned, controlled, or had the use of a greater number of Lockheeds than any pilot of the times. Over a thirty-year period he had at least seven Vegas in his stable, plus a Sirius and an Orion.

Mantz used his Vegas for flying sequences in such motion pictures as *Wings in the Dark*, with Cary Grant and Myrna Loy, and *The Bride Came C.O.D.*, with Bette Davis and Jimmy Cagney. In 1938 he cracked up a Vega with the markings of Barrancas Airways on location at St. George, Utah. Though Paul stepped out unhurt, the ship was a washout and all the scenes of *Only Angels Have Wings* in which it appeared had to be shot all over again. With lethal-looking "bombs" under the wings, the Mantz Sirius appeared in movies as a dive bomber. And in the tradition of Hollywood make-believe, the Orion, with British markings, passed for a shot-up fighter, crash-landed on the tarmac.

For the great aviation epic *Men with Wings*, Mantz mustered his full force of camera planes and vintage aircraft, and spared no expense to strive for true authenticity. In the script, Fred MacMurray, preparing to fly to Paris, overshoots Roosevelt Field and lands in the cold Atlantic. Searchers Ray Milland and Andy Devine find him perched disconsolately on the wing of his nearly submerged Vega *Miss Patricia*. Just after the hero's rescue the plane dramatically and realistically sinks. So skillfully were the air and process-screen shots of this sequence made that most moviegoers firmly believed that the trim white Lockheed had actually been sacrificed in making the movie.

With excellent foresight that movies and television would always need typical airplanes representative of the passage of time and the pageant of aviation history, Mantz procured and preserved dozens of old airplanes. Some were stored and others kept in flying condition. From an aeronautical boneyard of planes, parts, and pieces, he could either produce an original or build a replica authentic enough to pass inspection by movie buffs and aviation historians.

With a partner, Frank G. Tallman, Mantz set up Tallmantz Aviation, Inc., at the Orange County Airport in Santa Ana, California. In the stable of their "Movieland of the Air" were two Lockheeds.

Parts of Only Angels Have Wings *had to be re-shot after Paul Mantz* (right) *clobbered his "Barrancas Airways" Vega.*

Film stars Fred MacMurray and Andy Devine on location for Men With Wings *with one of Mantz's vintage Vegas.*

For a decade the Tallmantz Vega, built in 1929, was the oldest Lockheed still flying. As *The Viking,* she carried Donald MacMillan's Arctic photo party of 1931 and also spent many years as the *Elizabeth Lind,* operating on floats out of Seattle. Mantz and Tallman bought her in 1956 and, in anticipation of a proposed motion picture on Amelia Earhart, had the Vega painted red and gold and relicensed with Amelia's old number. The film was never shot, but the plane did appear in *The Carpetbaggers.* Next, Continental Airlines leased the ship for the company's thirtieth anniversary. In 1964 the paint trim was changed to the red and white of Varney Air Transport, Continental's immediate ancestor, and the Vega was sent on a national publicity tour. No longer flying, and still in VAT livery, this Vega is now on exhibit at the Ford Museum in Dearborn, Michigan.

The other Tallmantz Lockheed was the only Orion still in existence. Originally built as an Altair in 1931, the ship went from TWA to conversion as the *Shellightning* made famous by Jimmy Doolittle. Paul Mantz himself flew it in the Bendix Races of 1938 and 1939, and bought it back from later owners in 1955. After both Mantz and Tallman were killed in airplane accidents, their company's assets were dispersed. The Orion eventually went to Swissair. It was repainted in the original brilliant red-and-white scheme of their first wooden Orion of 1932, and the airline presented the restored metal version to the Swiss Air Transport Museum in Lucerne, where it hangs today.

The *Detroit News* was the first newspaper to adapt an airplane to the needs of a modern metropolitan daily. Aeronautics editor of the *News* was young James V. Piersol, who reasoned that the paper should have a plane

Frank G. Tallman (on wing) and A. Paul Mantz operated a collector's paradise with foresight—and profit.

of its own. The ship should be able to carry 500 pounds of newspapers in a comfortable closed cabin, and should have an unobstructed full cantilever wing to expedite aerial photography. Speed was the prime requisite, and it was not strange that Piersol's choice was a Lockheed Vega. The publishers thought long and hard about approving the purchase, but once it was made they were never sorry.

Bought in the summer of 1929, the *Detroit News* Vega was equipped with landing lights and night-flying aids, and stocked with blankets, rations, and other emergency equipment. Special aerial cameras were mounted for shooting air views from the open door. The cabin could be blacked out for use as a darkroom, and there was a typewriter and desk for use of flying reporters. In addition, provisions were made for quick conversions of the Lockheed from wheels to either floats or skis. With an initial outlay of $27,709.50 the *News* had a plane-of-all-work, ready to fly to the Arctic or the tropics at short notice.

Frank Byerly was chosen as pilot, to be supplemented by Jimmy Piersol. The cameraman was William Kuenzal, who had made the first aerial photograph of Detroit from a Burgess hydroplane back in 1912. The Vega itself was painted a special shade known as Detroit News Red and cream lettering proclaimed the name of her owners.

During the first year of operation The *News* Lockheed flew nearly 46,000 miles on work that included coverage of news stories, aerial photography, and the distribution of newspapers. On wheels, skis, and pontoons the ship made 388 flights over thirty-one states and provinces. Among the diverse assignments given the plane were the reporting and photographing of forest fires in northern Michigan, finding and interviewing a missing witness 300 miles from the scene of a crime, delivering papers to businessmen on a cruise of the Great Lakes, and bringing back special photos of the Detroit Tigers opening spring training in Florida.

The publishers estimated that the Vega cost just 62 cents a mile to operate, including the pay of pilot and cameraman, and that in its travels some three million people must have seen the plane close enough to read *Detroit News* on its wings and fuselage. Piersol's flying crew made excellent use of the Vega for five years. Then they traded her back to Lockheed for a brand-new Orion, which would prove even more useful at newsgathering. Named *Early Bird*, it was one of the last Orions to come out of Lockheed's assembly hangar.

The *Detroit News*'s radio station WWJ was by now an

Detroit News's *Vega covers headline events on wheels, skis, and floats, made nearly 400 special flights for stories.*

Early Bird's *camera pod can aim at news for the Detroit daily, while on-board reporter radios his story to the newsroom.*

integral part of the newspaper and would play an important part in the design features of the new plane. Again it was aviation editor Jimmy Piersol who chose the Lockheed, and went out to Burbank to supervise personally the construction of this one. Though the popular trend in 1934 was toward metal construction, it was thought that the wooden monocoque design was still the best to minimize camera vibration and the background noises encountered in broadcasting.

Piersol and Lockheed engineers contrived to install a complete broadcasting station in the cabin of the new Orion, with a special FCC license for either voice or code. They arranged openings for cameras in the bottom of the fuselage at both sides and at the rear. In addition, in a pod mounted flush in the left wing was a special aerial camera, controlled by the pilot and aimed by pointing the plane at the subject. Like the newspaper's old Vega, there was still ample room for flying reporters and their desks.

Piersol usually piloted the *Early Bird* himself, and for years the red-and-cream ship was a familiar sight over Detroit, with its bulbous camera eye winking to record the news and sports events of the day while WWJ radio reporters gave on-the-spot descriptions.

Lockheeds were universally coveted, but the original price tag of $20,000 to $25,000 for a new ship made it hard for an individual to go out and buy one outright. Still there were a number of men and women of means who could both afford the plane and a personal pilot to fly it.

Oil operators of Texas and Oklahoma who had struck it rich were excellent customers for the early Vegas, and hired ex-barnstormers to pilot them across the great distances of the Southwest. Tulsa's Lockheed dealer was Erle P. Halliburton, an airline operator and the wealthy patentee of a process for cementing oil wells. He sold a number of Vegas to his friends—and every plane being used for speedy business transportation was likely to produce a well-heeled customer for another.

F. C. Hall, the Oklahoma City oil-lease broker, owned three successive Lockheed Vegas, all named for his daughter, Winnie Mae. He paid his pilot Wiley Post $250 a month; good wages for the times. Later on, he had an Orion, and still later, a twin-engine Electra.

Other Vegas were owned by John J. Moran of the Moran Drilling Company, Wichita Falls, Texas; by William H. Dunning's Sequoia Oil Company of Fort Worth, and by the Julian Oil and Royalties Company and the Kessler Oil & Gas Company, both of Oklahoma City. G. W. Mennis of Fort Worth's Texas Worth Tool Company died in his Vega in an accident in 1930 near Alvord, Texas.

Jobe Pundt of the American Liberty Oil Company of Dallas flew a speedy Sirius. Later there were Orions crisscrossing the skies above Tulsa, flying for the Barnsdall Oil Company and John Mabee's Mabee Consolidated Corporation. L. E. "Red" Gray flew many of the Southwest oilmen, and another popular pilot was Frank Hover.

Plane that inaugurated airborne politicking is Raymond Robins (top); *Continental Oil's Vega* (second) *finally went to Alaska; Ruth Nichols raced Asa Candler's Orion* (third); *Phillips's Vega* (bottom) *later worked in movies.*

The oil operators did not have a monopoly on the privately owned Lockheeds. Asa Candler, Jr., son of the founder of the Coca-Cola firm, owned three of them. When his first Vega was burned in a hangar fire at Atlanta, he quickly bought another. Then he acquired one of the earliest Orions—the ship his pilot, Beeler Blevins, flew in the 1931 Bendix Race to Cleveland. Morgan Belmont of the Wall Street firm of August Belmont & Company had an early Executive Vega, which was piloted by Ernest L. Benway.

New York's Guggenheim family, well known for their support of all manner of aeronautical activities, owned a Lockheed Air Express, and later a Vega. The parasol-wing job was always kept in immaculate condition, and was piloted by young Russell W. Thaw. In 1932 the ship was purchased by the prominent Protestant minister Dr. Daniel A. Poling. Chicago social reformer Raymond Robins, Poling's associate in the Allied Forces for Prohibition movement, had recently disappeared—a victim of amnesia, as it turned out. Meanwhile, Poling had had his white-red-and-blue Lockheed christened *Raymond Robins* in honor of his missing friend.

With Russ Thaw as pilot, Poling made a truly whirlwind political tour, stumping thirty-one states in behalf of President Hoover and the cause of Prohibition during the final weeks of the '32 campaign. Though the contest ended with defeat for the Republican candidate, this pioneer trek demonstrated the value of flying as a vote-gathering technique of the future.

Smiling Russ Thaw went back to piloting the Guggenheims, after his journeys with Poling. Their next plane, a Lockheed Vega, had been completely rebuilt at the factory. Incorporating the latest aeronautical improvements as they came on the market, the Guggenheim Vega was one of the first certified airplanes—that is, receiving an Approved Type Certificate from the U. S. Department of Commerce—to be equipped with the hydraulically operated Hamilton two-pitch propeller. Its takeoff performance was phenomenal, and Russ frequently got the Lockheed off the ground in less than five seconds.

During a South American junket, Thaw, while flying Mrs. Edmond A. Guggenheim, had a tangle with some stumps on a field in Surinam. The Vega was shipped back to California for repair, and its next owner first saw the ship in pieces on the floor of the factory in Burbank. He was Herbert G. Fales, an official of the International Nickel Company in New York.

Fales personally flew the white, blue-trimmed Lockheed for both business and pleasure. With its five tanks holding 232 gallons, the ship had a range of 1,200 miles, enabling the Nickel executive to cover every part of the United States, and go into Canada and Mexico, with a minimum of refueling stops. Fales put 750 hours on the plane during six years' ownership, and recalled the Vega as "a very fine airplane."

A similar Vega named *Ariel* was the property of Miss Margery Durant, daughter of auto manufacturer W. C. Durant. Miss Durant hired Charles La Jotte of Santa Monica, California, to pilot her on travels over three continents.

The *Ariel* seemed to have an affinity for boundary fences. Twice it tangled with them, once at Roosevelt Field and again at the airport in Santa Barbara, California. Miss Durant sailed for Europe with the white Lockheed in April 1931. With La Jotte as pilot and Everett Smith as traveling mechanic, she made a successful 7,000-mile air tour of England, France, Italy, North Africa, and the Near East.

Miss Durant liked to fly and she liked to cook. About the time that Charley La Jotte's seat was beginning to feel hard and his eyes weary from scanning the endless sands of Egypt, she might hand him up a plate of cinnamon toast and a steaming cup of coffee, prepared on a little Sterno stove. During these open-flame sessions, mechanic Smith worried about gas fumes from the fuel tanks directly overhead, and would stand by with a fire extinguisher at the ready. Miss Durant never learned to fly the *Ariel,* but it served the much-traveled lady for three years before it was sold to an airline.

Another aviation enthusiast—though not a pilot—was William Gibbs McAdoo. Well established as an industrialist, McAdoo had been Woodrow Wilson's Secretary of the Treasury, boss of the railways during World War I, and a leading candidate for the Democratic nomination for the Presidency. In 1929, as a corporation lawyer with offices in both Los Angeles and Washington, the sixty-five-year-old McAdoo purchased a Lockheed Vega for his personal transportation. He remarked wryly that it was "faster to go to Washington by plane than by way of the Electoral College."

Equipped with desk, typewriter, and chemical toilet, McAdoo's Vega was one of the special Executive models, and was named *The Blue Streak*. His pilot was Army-trained Harry Ashe, a safe and sane flyer who in three years transported the lawyer-politician over 140,000 miles. In October 1930 the *Streak* carried Ashe, McAdoo, and a secretary from coast to coast in 16 hours and 11 minutes—an unofficial record.

Another prominent, but more controversial, Lockheed owner was Dr. John R. Brinkley of Milford, Kansas, and later of Del Rio, Texas. Brinkley, a dapper and goateed North Carolinian, was fabuloulsy well off as a result of his much publicized "special operation" involving the transplanting of goat glands to produce rejuvenation. He was both denounced as a charlatan and hailed as a medical wizard.

The owner of yachts, diamonds, Cadillacs, and the world's most powerful radio station, Brinkley was a natural prospect for a personal airplane to transport him between ports of his medical empire. Carl Squier, Lock-

Pilot Russell Thaw (top, left) *and Dr. Poling on their whirlwind tour in 1932, and* (below) *Dr. Brinkley poses with vigor galore while George MacDonald beams from the office.*

Margery Durant and Ariel *are greeted by British officers at Cairo in 1931, and* (below) *Howard Hughes, manufacturer-pilot noted for being camera-shy, visits with airplane broker Charles H. Babb* (right) *in Glendale, California.*

heed's general manager and top salesman, journeyed to Milford in a rented car, hoping to sell the doctor on an Orion. Brinkley not only ordered, but took such a liking to Carl that he offered him a free operation if he ever needed it. In the meantime he insisted on sending the bemused Californian back to his hotel in Kansas City in a limousine, with a driver to follow behind with the rental. The check Squier received was like nothing the man from Lockheed had ever seen before or since: it had DR. JOHN R. BRINKLEY in huge letters from corner to corner.

When the new white-and-black Orion was finished, the name was prominent on the fuselage. Brinkley, flamboyant for a purpose, was out for all the publicity mileage he could run up, and the official name for the ship was, as might be expected, *Doctor Brinkley III*.

The Kansas medico hired George A. MacDonald to fly the Orion, and prudently registered the ship in the pilot's name in order to avoid any unpleasantness should the plane be involved in law-suits. MacDonald shuttled the doctor between Milford and Del Rio, and to anywhere else in the country that he had a mind to go.

The *Doctor Brinkley III* had a 645-hp Wright Cyclone engine on the nose, and for a period was probably the fastest privately owned cabin monoplane in the air. To balance the weight of the big Wright, MacDonald had to stash a couple of 100-pound sacks of sand in the tail.

Brinkley had enemies, and on one occasion his Orion was cleverly sabotaged in such a manner that the landing-gear lock would break when the plane touched down. It happened: the wheels folded, the plane bellied in and slid to a grinding halt. As the dust settled, Mac ducked his head and turned to tell the doctor and three other portly gentlemen to "get out quick."

But the narrow oval cabin was completely empty, the folding seats upright as though they had never been occupied. The amazed pilot then discovered that his passengers were all gathered about the cowl, waiting for *him* to get out.

After three years of intensive flying *Doctor Brinkley III* was traded in on one of the new twin-engine Lockheed Electras. The Orion subsequently served the Spanish Loyalists as a high-powered transport for military and political personnel during the bloody Civil War of 1936–39.

In addition to the business executives who used airplanes for speedy transportation, there was a small and select group of men and women who simply and unabashedly flew for fun. They were "sports flyers," a term that has gradually gone out of style and use, but which aptly described a person to whom flying was as much a sport as motor boating or polo, and who usually had the money to indulge in it.

A number of this group liked the looks of Colonel Lindbergh's new low-winged Sirius, and wanted ones of their own. Young Stafford L. "Casey" Lambert of the St. Louis pharmaceutical family was very much in the market, so

Despite crash of demonstrator (top), Casey Lambert bought a new Sirius.

Identification plate carried by Continental Oil's Vega throughout nine ownerships until the ship was damaged beyond repair in 1954; the "194" is Lockheed factory's serial number. Plate was stolen by the Reverend Father Boardman C. Reed.

Detroit-Lockheed sent test pilot Herb Fahy to Missouri with a brand-new demonstrator. On April 12, 1930, Herb took Lambert up and taught him a bit of how to handle the streamlined, tandem-cockpit ship. Later in the day Casey's friend Herbert Condie showed up and naturally wanted a ride, too. Fahy was generous with the company ship.

"Go ahead, Casey, you take him. You can fly it just as good as I can," said Herb.

Lambert and Condie took the Sirius up, circling over St. Louis. Putting her through her paces, they were in a shallow dive at around only 190 mph when the ailerons began to flap and the wings began to flutter. Casey and his friend watched numbly as both ailerons vanished and parts of the wings detached themselves in the airstream. There was nothing to do but nose the ship up under full power and take to the silk. Lockheed lost a demonstrator, one of the very few to be destroyed by structural failure.

Unfazed by the accident, and his sudden initiation into the Caterpillar Club, Casey Lambert still liked the Sirius and quickly agreed to buy another, provided the engineers installed counter-balanced ailerons. He flew it for over two years without any trouble, but was of the personal opinion that it was "the most dangerous" aircraft to come out of Burbank.

The mixed reception of the Sirius didn't bother other prospective buyers. H. Walter Blumenthal ordered one shortly after Lambert got his. In July 1930 freelance test pilot Jimmy Collins delivered the Sirius to its New York buyer—with an unsuccessful try at bettering the transcontinental record thrown in.

The Blumenthal Sirius was a beautiful ship, painted red with white teardrop trim. It was a special model called a Sport Cabin Sirius, and had both the tandem cockpits to the rear, and a small four-windowed cabin ahead. A novice pilot, Blumenthal actually took flying lessons in this Lockheed, considered by most to be a pretty hot ship.

Blumenthal kept the Sport Sirius for two years before disposing of it to another sports flyer: Bernarr Macfadden. Though the publisher finally soloed and flew small planes, he left the flying of his various Lockheeds to hired pilots, and normally only traveled with them as a passenger. It is significant that all three of the Lockheeds in which Macfadden flew personally were open-cockpit jobs. The technicalities of the aircraft didn't interest him particularly. What got him was the joy of being up there, master of his ship, with the control stick in his fist and his head in the slipstream.

Another New Yorker who shared this passion was Reginald L. "Pete" Brooks. A mainstay of the exclusive Aviation Country Club on Long Island, Pete bought and flew the Lockheed Air Express that went to the Guggenheims and then to Dr. Daniel Poling.

There were women sports flyers, too. Amelia Earhart, Ruth Nichols, and Laura Ingalls were all originally in this class before graduating to more than amateur status. Also prominent for a time was Mrs. Joan Fay Shankle of Boston, the first licensed woman pilot in Massachusetts. In 1930 Mrs. Shankle bought the fourth Lockheed Sirius built, and it didn't bother her a bit that its registration number was 13W. She and her husband, Army Air Corps Captain Clarence E. "Chris" Shankle, flew the plane on cross-country journeys, and Joan participated with it in the 1931 National Air Races at Cleveland.

The Shankle Sirius was usually hangared at a private airstrip that served the couple's ranch near Tubac, Arizona. There was even an aircraft and engine mechanic hired from Lockheed living there to keep the ship flying. Occasionally Joan and Chris pressed the low-wing speedster into such lowly chores as carrying grain and feed to the ranch. Once while in flight some loose bales of hay were sucked completely out of a loose baggage compartment door, and were scattered all over the Arizona landscape while the Shankles flew blind. With the introduction of retractable landing gear, Mrs. Shankle had the Sirius converted to an Altair, and the Wasp engine was supercharged for peak performance. After faithfully serving the lady for frequent trips from the Southwest to New England, the plane was eventually acquired by Colonel Clarence Chamberlin and named *Miss Stratosphere.*

As the Lockheed company began production of its all-metal, twin-engine Electra model, the manufacture of the wooden planes was gradually curtailed. In 1934 San Francisco's W.P. "Frank" Fuller of the Fuller Paint Company family, purchased the very last Vega to be built. Soon there were second-hand planes coming on the market, and those who flew for pleasure could scout the aircraft brokerage firms in search of a good used Lockheed, often one that had had a part in making aviation history.

Charles H. Babb of the Grand Central Air Terminal in Glendale, California, sold dozens of used Lockheeds in the thirties and into the forties. His customers were air-

Last Vega was built in 1934, went to W. P. Fuller, next to USAAF as their UC-101, then to Charles Babb for resale.

lines, foreign buyers, executives and sports flyers. Charley Babb probably held title to more Lockheeds in his lifetime than any other man. There was seldom a month but what the list of Babb's Bargains contained one or more Vegas, with an occasional Sirius, Air Express, or an Orion for sale. Depression prices for used Vegas ranged from $9,500 for a Wasp-engine job with pants and cowl, to $2,250 for a workhorse older model with a Wright Whirlwind engine. Orions went for from $17,500 down to $10,000, depending on equipment and condition.

Broker Babb not only sold whole airplanes, but dealt in component parts as well. His shops rebuilt and refurbished the planes as they came in, and readied them for sale. Stored in Charley Babb's hangar was the wing of the *Blue Flash,* the Explorer which Roy Ammel had piled up in Panama after his record flight from New York in 1930. The Explorer's wing was nearly 6 feet longer than those of the standard Lockheed Sirius, Altair, and Orion. Babb also had a fuselage of one of Transcontinental & Western Air's Orions. It seemed a perfectly natural thing to mate the two into a complete airplane.

The California aircraft broker found a surprising customer for his bastard Orion-Explorer. Wiley Post, with his *Winnie Mae* highly modified for her stratosphere flights, needed another, reasonably priced ship for his personal transport. He bought the hybrid plane in February 1935.

When Wiley's friend and fellow-Oklahoman Will Rogers suggested a leisurely trip around the world in reverse of the famous Post speed trips, the flyer jumped at the chance. He was weary and discouraged over the apparent failure of his stratosphere flying, and needed a vaca-

Converted from Sirius, this Altair was flown by transatlantic flyer Clarence Chamberlin. Name reads: MISS STRATOSPHERE—SHE'S THE TOPS.

tion. With the *Winnie Mae* stored in Bartlesville, Oklahoma, the famed pair decided to take the newer Orion. There would be no records this time—just a pleasure trip up through Alaska, Siberia, Russia, and perhaps home by way of Iceland and Greenland. Post was far from a rich man, and Rogers volunteered to pay the expenses.

Will Rogers—cowboy, humorist, actor, well-loved public figure—had been called "America's No. 1 air passenger," and it was probably true. Will loved flying, made friends with all his pilots, boosted aviation every chance he got. No stranger to Lockheeds, by 1935 he had flown over 500,000 miles in both scheduled and unscheduled planes, and never took a train if he could help it. Among his goals was gradually to become the "world's airplane reporter": batting out his daily newspaper column, giving the Rogers slant on things from wherever the news was happening.

Will and Wiley made ready for their trip. They took the Orion on a shakedown flight to Oklahoma, using the fixed landing gear which came with the ship. This gear was eliminated in favor of pontoons, for much of the Arctic and trans-Siberian route that was to be traveled would be over water. A big pair of Edo floats was fitted on the red-painted plane at Seattle, and the vacationists prepared to leave for Juneau and the Far North.

There had been some fears expressed about the safety of the hybrid Orion. She had a big 550-hp Wasp engine and a 3-bladed propeller on her nose. Lockheed engineers had refused to have anything to do with the makeup of the plane to begin with, and of course did not approve of giving the half-breed the additional weights of floats. Even Wiley Post himself must have known that the ship was dangerously nose-heavy. But he was one of the world's most skillful pilots, and probably felt he had the ability to handle her.

Post and Rogers left the States early in August. Jaunty Will had explicit faith in his pilot. "Old Wiley will have to duck his head when we pass that Arctic circle," he wrote. "We're off for somewhere in a Red Bus. . . ."

"Somewhere" was a broad tidal river, flowing into the Arctic Ocean fifteen miles south of Barrow, Alaska. On August 15, 1935, Post and Rogers left Fairbanks, bound for the jumping-off point that in other years had welcomed Wilkins, Eielson, and the Lindberghs.

Eskimo seal hunters near the native village of Walakpi saw the "big red bird" coming winging up from the south, very low. When it landed near their tents, a "man with a rag on sore eye" and a "big man with boots" climbed out and asked the direction of Barrow. Clair Oakpena, spokesman for the hunters, pointed north across the featureless terrain.

Post tinkered with the engine a few minutes while Rogers, as might be expected, "just gabbed" and exchanged grins with the Eskimos. Then the pair got back in the plane and taxied across the river to take off into the wind. Wiley Post rocked the Orion to get it up on step, and roared off the water in a steep climbing turn. The dripping floats flashed in the half-light of the Arctic summer night.

Only fifty feet up the engine stopped cold. Like a dish pushed from the edge of a table, the plane fell off, dragged a wing in the water and crashed on its back. The "man with a rag on sore eye" and the "big man with boots" did not answer when the seal hunters called loudly. Clair Oakpena ran most of the way to Barrow with the news, and an Army Signal Corps operator radioed it to a shocked and unbelieving world. The lives of one of America's finest flyers and of her best-loved humorist had come to an end in the shallow water beside the bleak Arctic tundra.

In Washington the Smithsonian Institution had long been interested in acquiring the famous *Winnie Mae* for

Joe Crosson waves to Rogers (on wing) *and Post as they get set to leave Fairbanks on their next-to-last takeoff. Wreck of the Orion-Explorer* (below): *shallow water at Walakpi, Alaska, shows why the flyers were killed instantly.*

its National Air Museum. When approached on the subject, Post would usually say that he couldn't afford to give the ship away, any more than he could his automobile. He needed it in his work. Even when awarded one of his numerous medals, a gold one, Wiley remarked:

"Say, I may have to hock this thing sometime to get gasoline."

Josh Lee, Congressman from Oklahoma, thought that something tangible should be given Post to show the appreciation of the nation, and introduced a bill to award him $25,000 as a sort of "national gift." By a quirk of fate this bill came up for consideration on the floor of Congress on the very day that news of the fatal crash in Alaska was received. By an alteration the money went to Mrs. Mae Post, and "by arrangement" she in turn presented the faithful *Winnie Mae* to the Smithsonian.

Paul Garber, curator of the Institution's Air Museum, was sent to Bartlesville for the *Winnie Mae*. He found her in a hangar with a black bow tied on the propeller. Garber decided not to risk flying the famous plane back to Washington, and packed and crated her in a freight car in which he rode himself.

Later the Smithsonian representative went looking for the original landing gear to put with the white-and-blue airplane. He had to let his boss know his wherabouts daily, and on return was called on the carpet:

"I want an explanation of these facetious telegrams you've been sending me!"

Garber was surprised. What had he sent that was facetious? The official tossed over a sample: AM IN DALLAS LOOKING FOR WINNIE MAE'S PANTS.

The *Winnie Mae*, still battered and grimy from Post's stratosphere flights and rough belly-landings, hung for over twenty years in the main building at the Smithsonian Institution. In recent years the ship has been completely restored and repainted, and is now a major exhibit of the National Air and Space Museum. Thousands of visitors each year learn the story of the *Winnie Mae*, or relive their air-minded youth at the sight of her—beautiful, yet somehow lonely: as if waiting for Wiley to put his deft touch on her controls and make her airborne once more.

Today, two Lockheed Vegas are still flying. Robert Taylor, long-time president of the Antique Airplane Association, finally got title to one in 1964. It was the DL-1B Special job which a laid-off Lockheed engineer assembled from a metal fuselage and stock wooden wing in 1933. Taylor and a partner, Jack Lowe, had the bent and rotted "remains" of this Vega trucked from California to Ottumwa, Iowa, the base from which it had first flown for the Morrell meat packing company thirty years before. After a four-year rebuild and restoration, beginning in 1965, the Vega was flown intermittently by Bob Taylor. On loan, with a red-paint job, it appeared in the 1976 TV special "Amelia Earhart." Taylor sold the ship late in 1983 to Tom A. Thomas of Frederick, Oklahoma. Colonel Thomas's Mid-America Air Group uses the Vega for exhibit and limited flights.

David D. Jameson of Oshkosh, Wisconsin, is the current owner of the other Vega still airworthy. A restorer and pilot of other antique aircraft; Wacos, Monocoupes, and a Ryan Brougham, Dave had a longtime burning desire to own and fly a Lockheed. He got his wish fulfilled early in 1963.

Jameson's Vega was built back in 1929, the original Executive model first owned by the Independent Oil & Gas Company of Tulsa, Oklahoma. After being flown for over a decade by Midwestern owners, the Lockheed went to Mexico as an airliner toward the end of World War II. It was damaged in minor accidents several times but was always repaired by competent Mexican woodworkers. Among other replacement parts, this first Executive Vega got most of a new fuselage, and the large tail from a later model.

Hycon Manufacturing Company of Pasadena, California, returned the plane to the United States in 1956. Hycon wanted the predominantly wooden airplane for geophysical exploration work, using their Varian Magnetometer. After the tests were complete the old Vega went to a buyer in Texas, who damaged the ship in landing.

At this point the giant General Electric Company stepped in. They wanted one of the rare wooden birds for a special purpose, and this was the only one available. In conjunction with the United States Air Force, G.E. was conducting extensive tests to evaluate equipment designed as countermeasures to radar. A wooden, high-performance airplane with shielded engine was just what they needed. They proceeded to make the Vega over to their requirements, using thousands of dollars to rebuild the Lockheed, whose interior was stripped to make room for the complicated USAF equipment. The antiradar tests ran from 1957 to 1961, and the results are still classified. Droning about in the high altitudes above Schenectady and Rome, New York, as well as Dayton, Ohio, General Electric's vintage Vega fulfilled purposes which its designers and original builders back in Burbank never dreamed of.

Missions complete, the Lockheed, painted a drab nonmetallic white, was put up for sale. Dave Jameson bought the thirty-four-year-old airplane on the last day of 1962 after months of negotiation.

Dave's path as owner and pilot of the onetime first Vega Executive was not an easy one. When gingerly testing the ship at Schenectady, before ferrying her to Wisconsin, Jameson found the brakes weak and crunched his prize into a snowbank alongside the runway. The Lockheed had to be shipped to Oshkosh on a truck.

With landing gear, wing tip, and a main bulkhead to

Dave Jameson's Winnie Mae, *the last airworthy wooden Lockheed Vega. It's the same airplane pictured on page 159.*

be replaced, Jameson worked slowly and carefully, with the assistance of especially qualified older-aircraft mechanics Preston Snyder and Hugh Ziebell. A complete overhaul was accomplished, and it was decided to give the ship a paint job and trim to match Wiley Post's *Winnie Mae* as she appeared at the height of her fame. Dave even acquired the original registration number: 105W.

The result, after six years of rebuilding, was the beautiful "new" *Winnie Mae*. Dave Jameson toured the country with her, eliciting starry eyes at every stop. At antique aircraft fly-ins, whenever a judging contest was held, the Vega was named Grand Champion. Now insured for $500,000, Dave's blue-and-white dazzler is currently on loan as an exhibit in the Experimental Aircraft Association's museum at Oshkosh.

When these two remaining examples are gone from the skies, the log books of the revolutionary early Lockheed aircraft will be closed forever.

SELECTED BIBLIOGRAPHY

Aeronautical Chamber of Commerce of America, Inc., *Aircraft Year Book*. New York, 1926–1934.

Balchen, Bernt, *Come North With Me*. New York, 1958.

Bennett, D.C.T., *Pathfinder*. London, 1958.

Cathcart-Jones, Owen, *Aviation Memoirs*. London, 1934.

Civil Aeronautics Board, *Handbook of Airline Statistics*. Washington, 1961.

Clarke, Basil, *Atlantic Adventure*. London, 1958.

Collins, Jimmy, *Test Pilot*. Garden City, 1935.

Collinson, Clifford, and Capt. F. McDermott, *Through Atlantic Clouds*. London, 1934.

Corrigan, Douglas, *That's My Story*. New York, 1938.

Davies, R.E.G., *A History of the World's Airlines*. London, 1964.

———, *Airlines of the United States Since 1914*. London, 1972.

———, *Airlines of Latin America Since 1919*. Washington, 1984.

Day, Beth, *Glacier Pilot*. New York, 1957.

De La Croix, Robert, *They Flew the Atlantic*. Paris, 1958.

Earhart, Amelia, *The Fun of It*. New York, 1932.

———, *Last Flight*. New York, 1937.

Ellis, F. H. and E. M., *Atlantic Air Conquest*. London, 1963.

Emme, Eugene M., *Aeronautics & Astronautics*. Washington, 1961.

Field, John C. W., *Bridging the Pacific*. Sutton Coldfield, England, 1951.

Forden, Lesley, *Glory Gamblers*. Alameda, Calif., 1986.

Fraser, Chelsea, *Heroes of the Air*. New York, 1940.

French, Joseph Lewis, editor, *Conquerors of the Sky*. Springfield, Mass., 1932.

Garber, Paul E., *The National Aeronautical Collections*. Washington, 1956.

Grierson, John, *Sir Hubert Wilkins*. London, 1960.

Hawks, Frank, *Speed*. New York, 1931.

———, *Once To Every Pilot*. New York, 1936.

Heinmuller, John P.V., *Man's Fight To Fly*. New York, 1945.

Hoagland, Roland W., editor, *The Blue Book of Aviation*. Los Angeles, 1932.

Hoare, Robert J., *Wings Over the Atlantic*. London, 1956.

Jablonski, Edward, *Atlantic Fever*. New York, 1972.

Juergens, Philip L., *Of Men and Stars*. Burbank, Calif., Lockheed Aircraft Corporation, 1957–1958.

Juptner, Joseph P., *U.S. Civil Aircraft, Vols. 1–9*. Los Angeles, 1962–81.

Kingsford-Smith, Sir Charles, *My Flying Life*. London, 1937.

Larkins, William T., *U.S. Navy Aircraft 1921–1941 and U.S. Marine Corps Aircraft 1914–1959*. New York, 1988.

Lindbergh, Anne Morrow, *Hour of Gold, Hour of Lead*. New York, 1973.

———, *North to the Orient*. New York, 1935.

———, *Listen! The Wind*. New York, 1938.

Lougheed, Victor, *Vehicles of the Air*. Chicago, 1909.

Mattern, Jimmie, *Cloud Country*. Chicago, 1936.

Myles, Eugenie Louise, *Airborne From Edmonton*. Toronto, 1959.

Nichols, Ruth, *Wings for Life*. Philadelphia, 1957.

Parsons, Bill, *The Challenge of the Atlantic*. St. Johns, Nfld., 1983.

Post, Wiley, and Harold Gatty, *Around the World in Eight Days*. New York, 1931.

Potter, Jean, *The Flying North*. New York, 1947.

Reichers, Louis T., *The Flying Years*. New York, 1956.

Reynolds, Quentin, *The Amazing Mr. Doolittle*. New York, 1953.

Roseberry, C. R., *The Challenging Skies*. New York, 1966.

Satterfield, Archie, and Lloyd Jarman, *Alaska Bush Pilots in the Float Country*. Seattle, 1969.

Smith, Henry Ladd, *Airways*. New York, 1942.

Taylor, P. G., *Pacific Flight*. London, 1935.

———, *The Sky Beyond*. Boston, 1963.

Thaden, Louise, *High, Wide and Frightened*. New York, 1938.

Underwood, John, *Madcaps, Millionaires and "Mose."* Glendale, Calif., 1984.

Wilkins, Capt. George H., *Flying the Arctic*. New York, 1928.

Also Consulted

AAHS Journal
Aero Digest
Air Classics
Air Progress
Air Travel News
Airway Age
American Airman
American Modeler
Antique Airplane News
Antique Airplanes
Armchair Aviator
Aviation
Aviation Quarterly
Aviation Week
Esso Air World
Flight
Flying
Historical Aviation Album
Lockheed Star
Los Angeles Times
Model Airplane News
New York Daily News
New York Herald Tribune
New York Times
Pacific Flyer
Popular Aviation
Quadrant Aerographic
San Francisco Chronicle
Sport Aviation
Sportsman Pilot
The Aeroplane
U.S. Air Services
Western Flying
Wings/Airpower
Wingspan

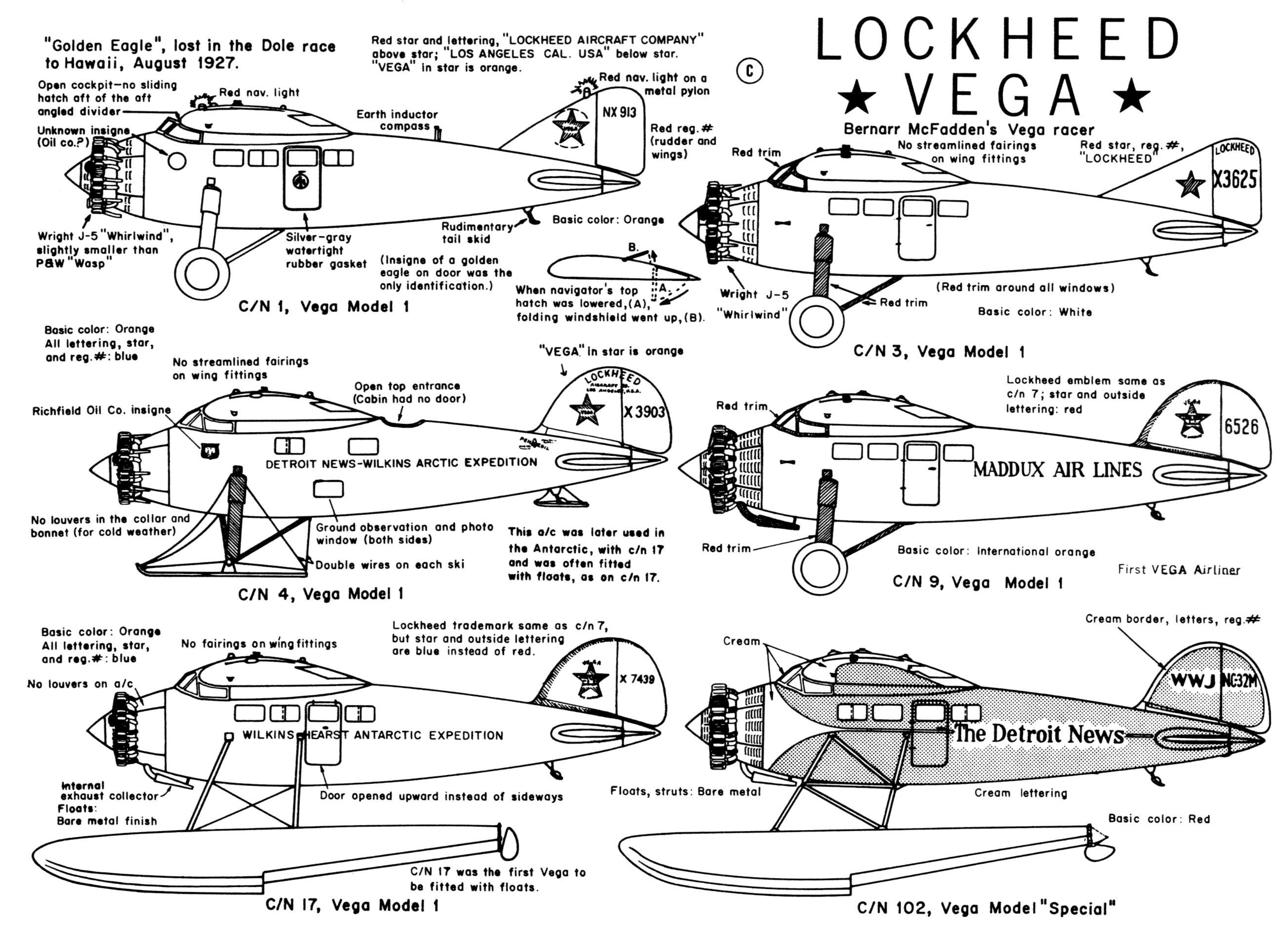
LOCKHEED
★ VEGA ★
©
"Golden Eagle", lost in the Dole race to Hawaii, August 1927.
Red star and lettering, "LOCKHEED AIRCRAFT COMPANY" above star; "LOS ANGELES CAL. USA" below star. "VEGA" in star is orange.
Open cockpit—no sliding hatch aft of the aft angled divider
Red nav. light
Red nav. light on a metal pylon
Unknown insigne (Oil co.?)
Earth inductor compass
NX 913
Red reg. # (rudder and wings)
Wright J-5 "Whirlwind", slightly smaller than P&W "Wasp"
Silver-gray watertight rubber gasket
Rudimentary tail skid
Basic color: Orange
(Insigne of a golden eagle on door was the only identification.)
B.
A.
When navigator's top hatch was lowered,(A), folding windshield went up,(B).
C/N 1, Vega Model 1
Bernarr McFadden's Vega racer
Red trim
No streamlined fairings on wing fittings
Red star, reg. #, "LOCKHEED"
LOCKHEED
X3625
Wright J-5 "Whirlwind"
Red trim
(Red trim around all windows)
Basic color: White
C/N 3, Vega Model 1
Basic color: Orange
All lettering, star, and reg. #: blue
No streamlined fairings on wing fittings
"VEGA" in star is orange
Open top entrance (Cabin had no door)
Richfield Oil Co. insigne
LOCKHEED
X 3903
DETROIT NEWS-WILKINS ARCTIC EXPEDITION
No louvers in the collar and bonnet (for cold weather)
Ground observation and photo window (both sides)
Double wires on each ski
This a/c was later used in the Antarctic, with c/n 17 and was often fitted with floats, as on c/n 17.
C/N 4, Vega Model 1
Red trim
Lockheed emblem same as c/n 7; star and outside lettering: red
6526
MADDUX AIR LINES
Red trim
Basic color: International orange
First VEGA Airliner
C/N 9, Vega Model 1
Basic color: Orange
All lettering, star, and reg. #: blue
No fairings on wing fittings
Lockheed trademark same as c/n 7, but star and outside lettering are blue instead of red.
No louvers on a/c
X 7439
WILKINS-HEARST ANTARCTIC EXPEDITION
Internal exhaust collector
Floats: Bare metal finish
Door opened upward instead of sideways
C/N 17 was the first Vega to be fitted with floats.
C/N 17, Vega Model 1
Cream border, letters, reg. #
Cream
WWJ NC32M
The Detroit News
Floats, struts: Bare metal
Cream lettering
Basic color: Red
C/N 102, Vega Model "Special"

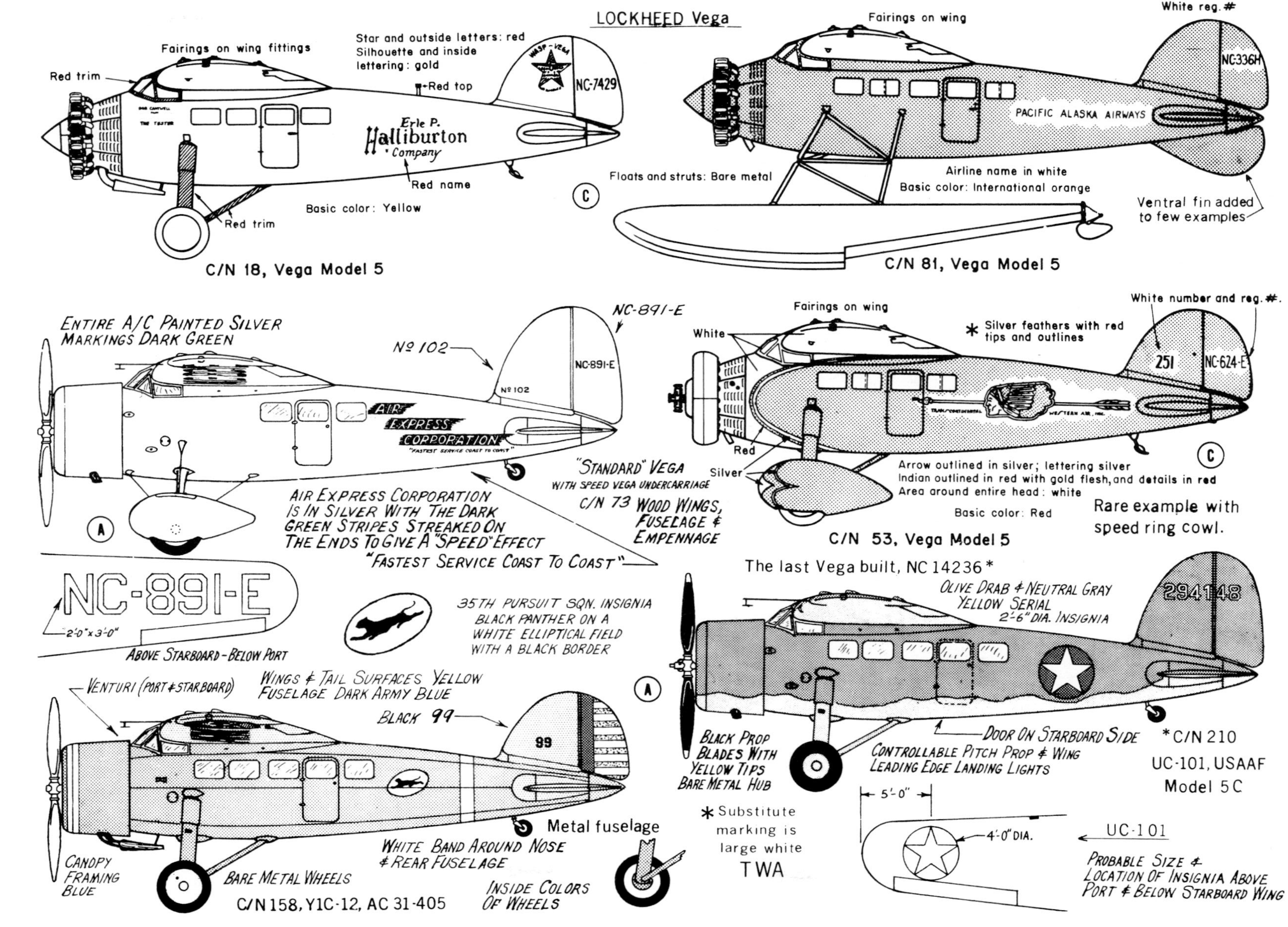
LOCKHEED Vega
Fairings on wing fittings
Red trim
Star and outside letters: red
Silhouette and inside lettering: gold
Red top
NC-7429
Erle P. Halliburton Company
Red name
Basic color: Yellow
Red trim
C/N 18, Vega Model 5
Fairings on wing
White reg. #
NC336H
PACIFIC ALASKA AIRWAYS
Floats and struts: Bare metal
Airline name in white
Basic color: International orange
Ventral fin added to few examples
C/N 81, Vega Model 5
ENTIRE A/C PAINTED SILVER
MARKINGS DARK GREEN
Nº 102
NC-891-E
AIR EXPRESS CORPORATION
"STANDARD" VEGA
WITH SPEED VEGA UNDERCARRIAGE
C/N 73 WOOD WINGS, FUSELAGE & EMPENNAGE
AIR EXPRESS CORPORATION IS IN SILVER WITH THE DARK GREEN STRIPES STREAKED ON THE ENDS TO GIVE A "SPEED" EFFECT
"FASTEST SERVICE COAST TO COAST"
NC-891-E
2'-0" x 3'-0"
ABOVE STARBOARD - BELOW PORT
Fairings on wing
White
White number and reg. #.
* Silver feathers with red tips and outlines
251
NC-624-E
Red
Silver
Arrow outlined in silver; lettering silver
Indian outlined in red with gold flesh, and details in red
Area around entire head: white
Basic color: Red
Rare example with speed ring cowl.
C/N 53, Vega Model 5
The last Vega built, NC 14236 *
OLIVE DRAB & NEUTRAL GRAY
YELLOW SERIAL
2'-6" DIA. INSIGNIA
294148
35TH PURSUIT SQN. INSIGNIA
BLACK PANTHER ON A WHITE ELLIPTICAL FIELD WITH A BLACK BORDER
VENTURI (PORT & STARBOARD)
WINGS & TAIL SURFACES YELLOW
FUSELAGE DARK ARMY BLUE
BLACK 99
99
Metal fuselage
WHITE BAND AROUND NOSE & REAR FUSELAGE
CANOPY FRAMING BLUE
BARE METAL WHEELS
INSIDE COLORS OF WHEELS
C/N 158, Y1C-12, AC 31-405
BLACK PROP BLADES WITH YELLOW TIPS
BARE METAL HUB
DOOR ON STARBOARD SIDE
CONTROLLABLE PITCH PROP & WING LEADING EDGE LANDING LIGHTS
*C/N 210
UC-101, USAAF
Model 5C
* Substitute marking is large white TWA
5'-0"
4'-0" DIA.
UC-101
PROBABLE SIZE & LOCATION OF INSIGNIA ABOVE PORT & BELOW STARBOARD WING

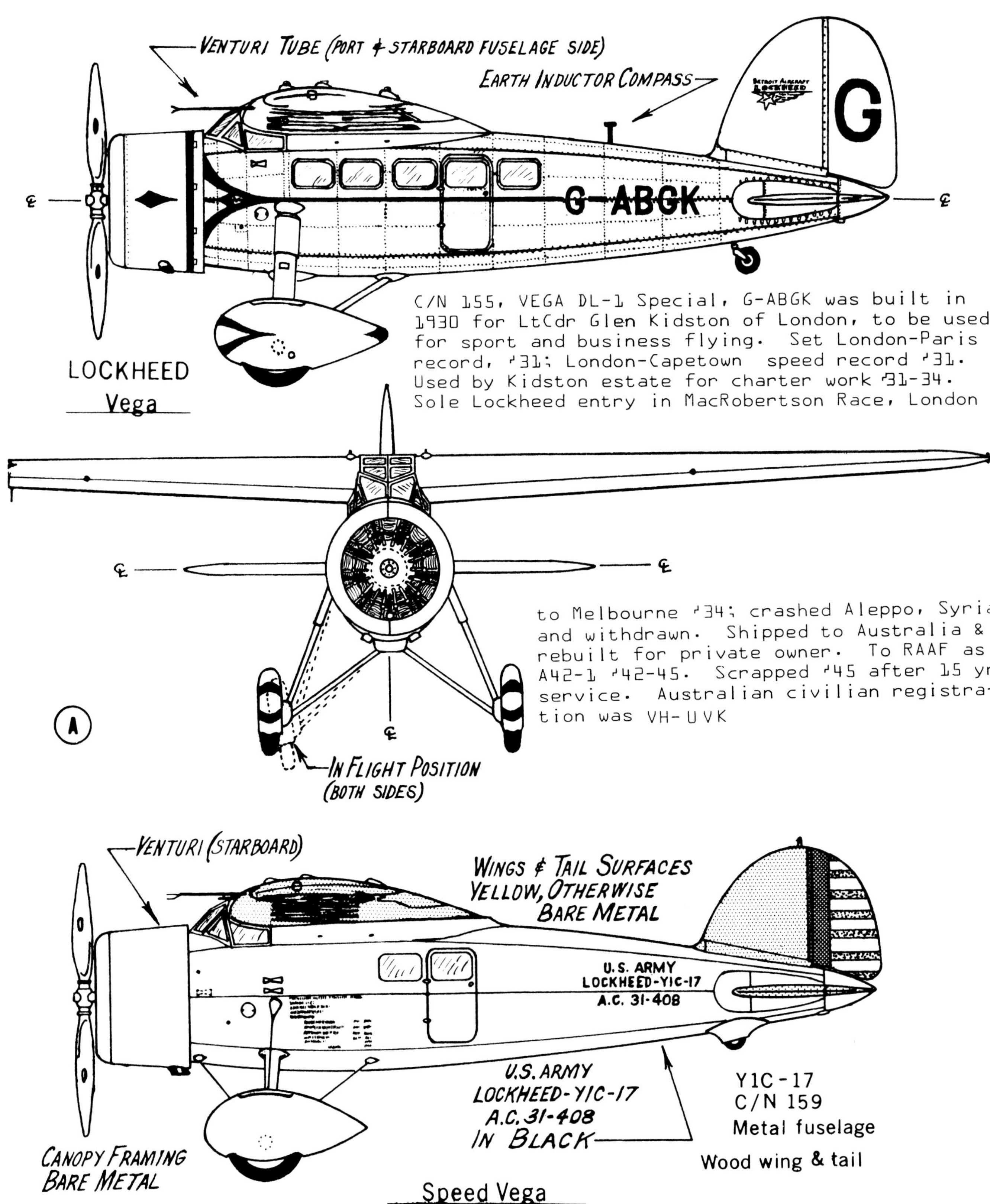

FASTEST USAAC AIRCRAFT OF IT'S TIME (221mph), "NO LOADED AIRPLANE EVER FLEW SO FAR, SO FAST"; L.A.-TOLU, KY., 1740 mi, 7hr 20min* 10 MAR 31. PILOT-IRA C. EAKER, CAPT., A.C.
*AV 240 mph, 16,000 ft. — LOCKHEED DL-1B SPECIAL, 600 hp Sup WASP.

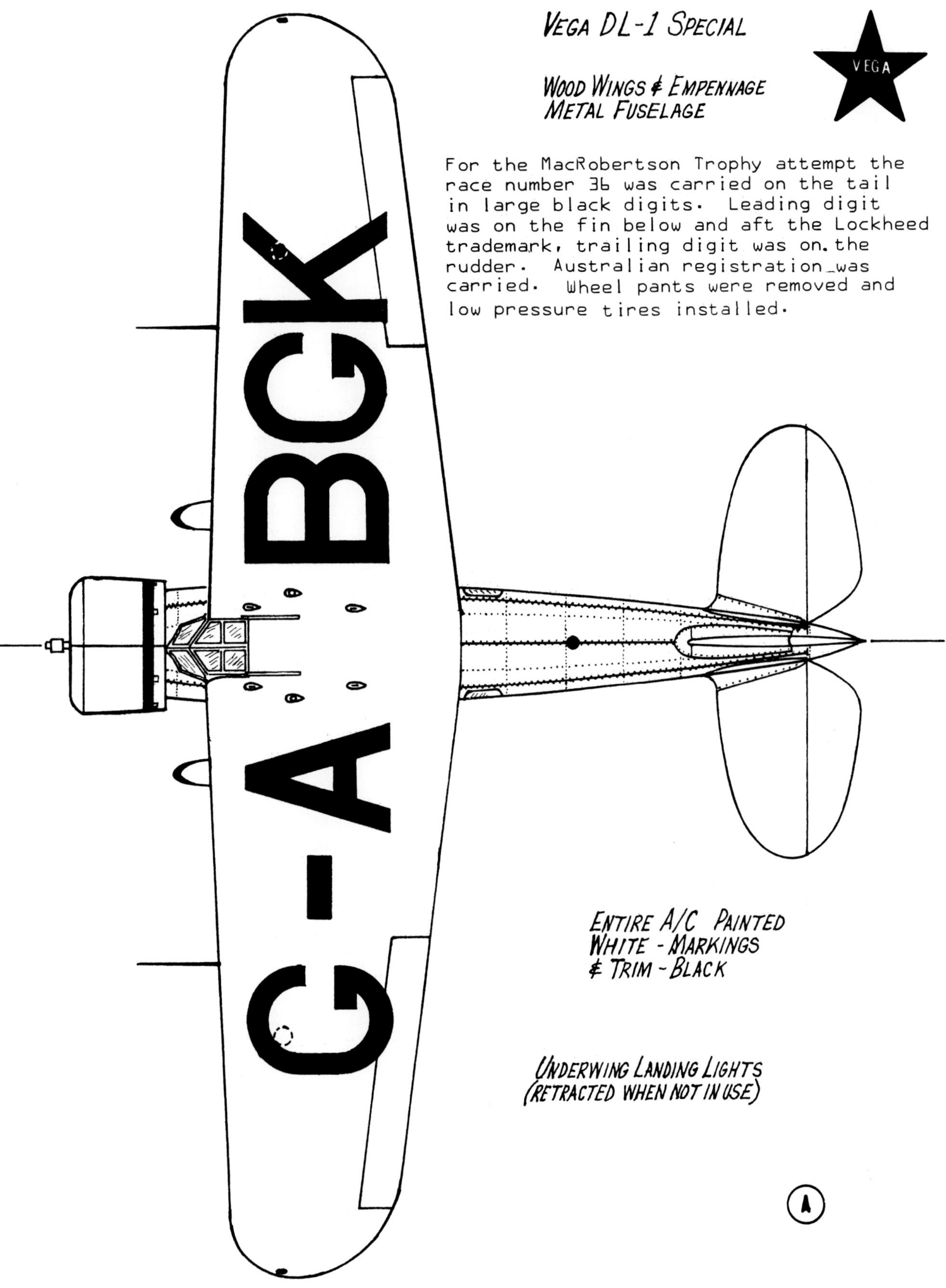
VEGA DL-1 SPECIAL
VEGA
WOOD WINGS & EMPENNAGE
METAL FUSELAGE
For the MacRobertson Trophy attempt the race number 36 was carried on the tail in large black digits. Leading digit was on the fin below and aft the Lockheed trademark, trailing digit was on the rudder. Australian registration was carried. Wheel pants were removed and low pressure tires installed.
G-ABGK
ENTIRE A/C PAINTED WHITE - MARKINGS & TRIM - BLACK
UNDERWING LANDING LIGHTS (RETRACTED WHEN NOT IN USE)
A

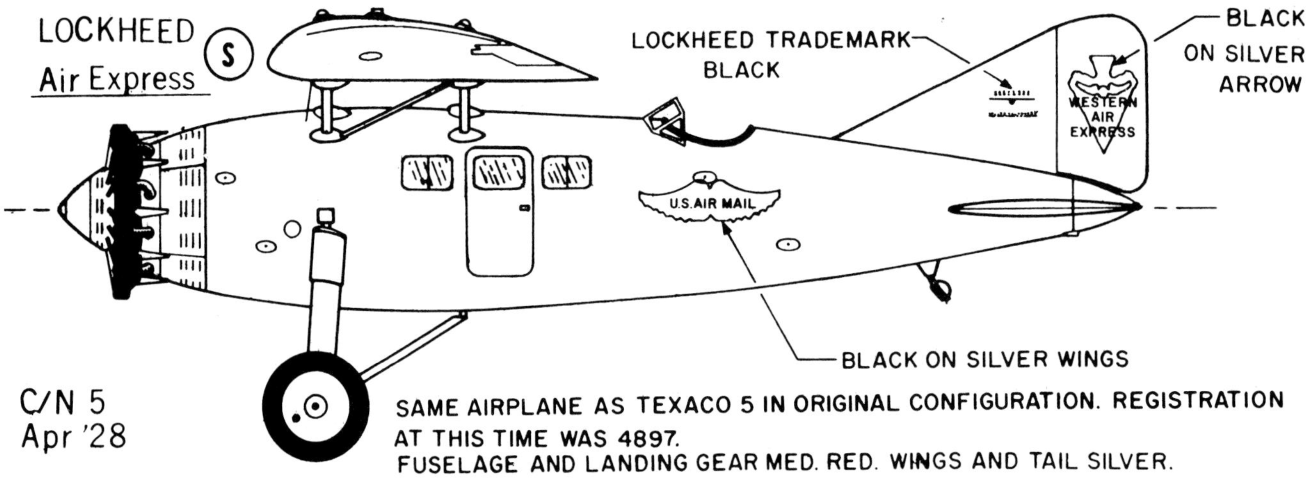

SAME AIRPLANE AS TEXACO 5 IN ORIGINAL CONFIGURATION. REGISTRATION AT THIS TIME WAS 4897.
FUSELAGE AND LANDING GEAR MED. RED. WINGS AND TAIL SILVER.

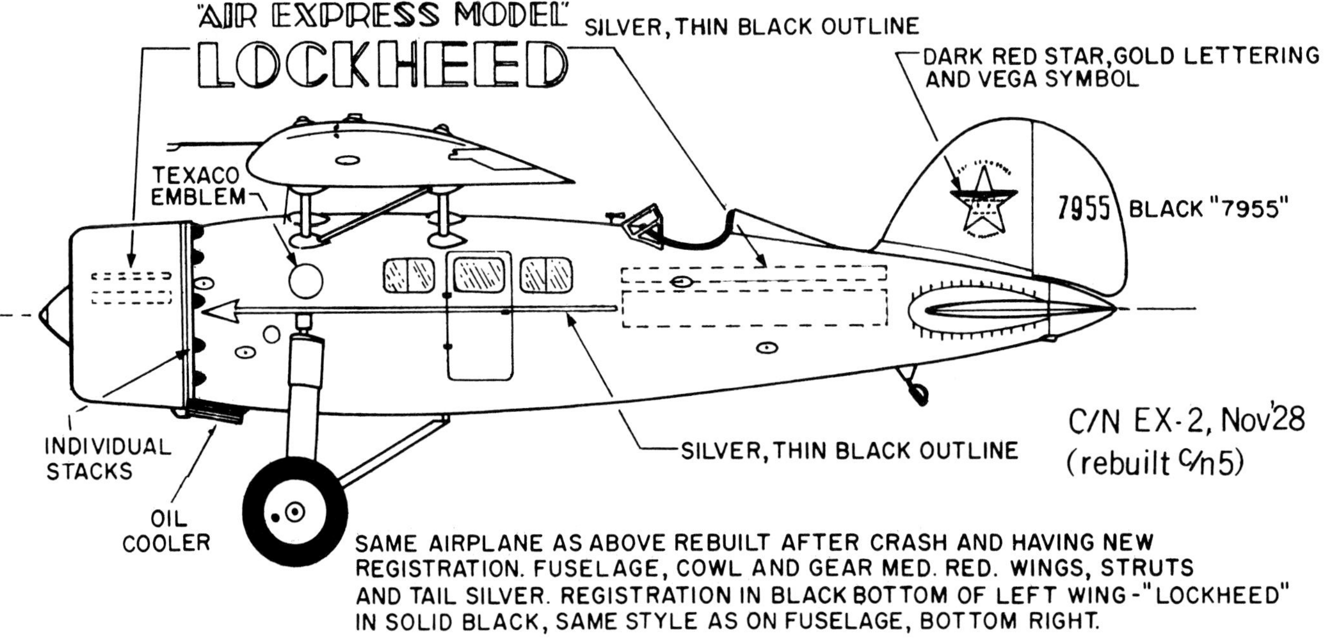

SAME AIRPLANE AS ABOVE REBUILT AFTER CRASH AND HAVING NEW REGISTRATION. FUSELAGE, COWL AND GEAR MED. RED. WINGS, STRUTS AND TAIL SILVER. REGISTRATION IN BLACK BOTTOM OF LEFT WING - "LOCKHEED" IN SOLID BLACK, SAME STYLE AS ON FUSELAGE, BOTTOM RIGHT.

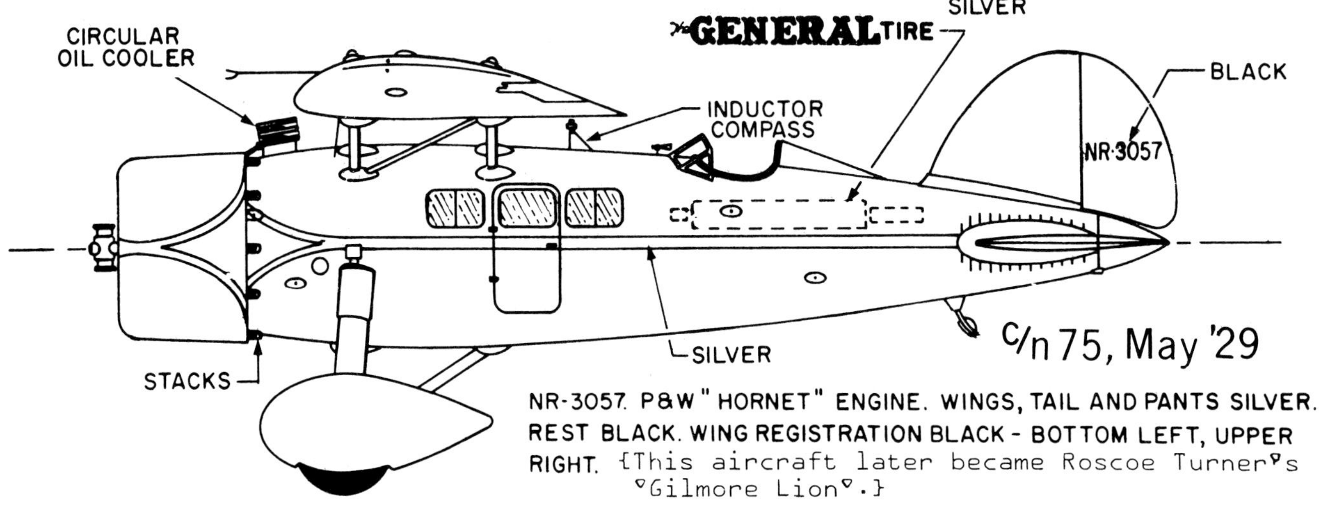

NR-3057. P&W "HORNET" ENGINE. WINGS, TAIL AND PANTS SILVER. REST BLACK. WING REGISTRATION BLACK - BOTTOM LEFT, UPPER RIGHT. {This aircraft later became Roscoe Turner's "Gilmore Lion".}

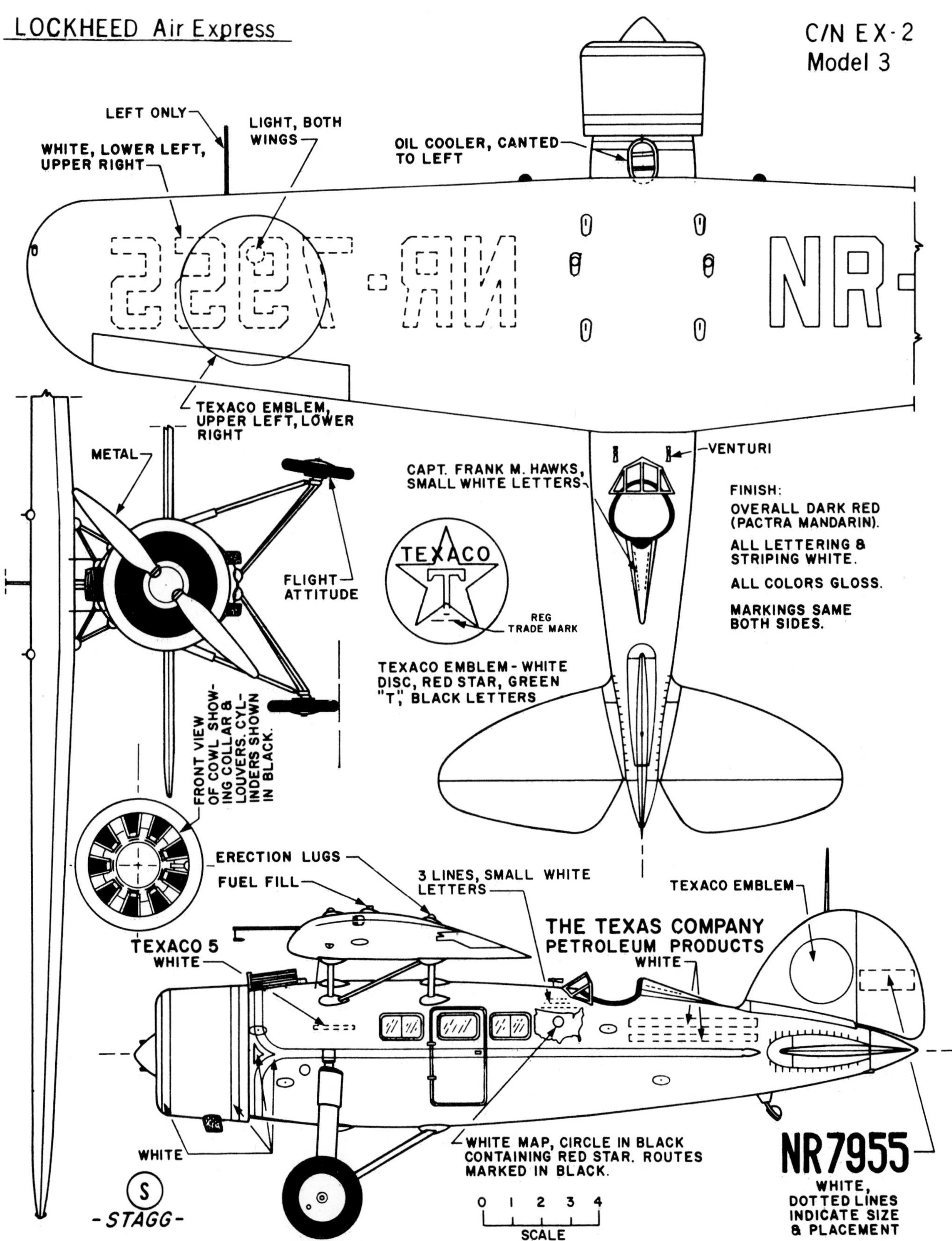

{In it's relatively short life Texaco 5 had each style of exhaust system used with the Wasp engine.}

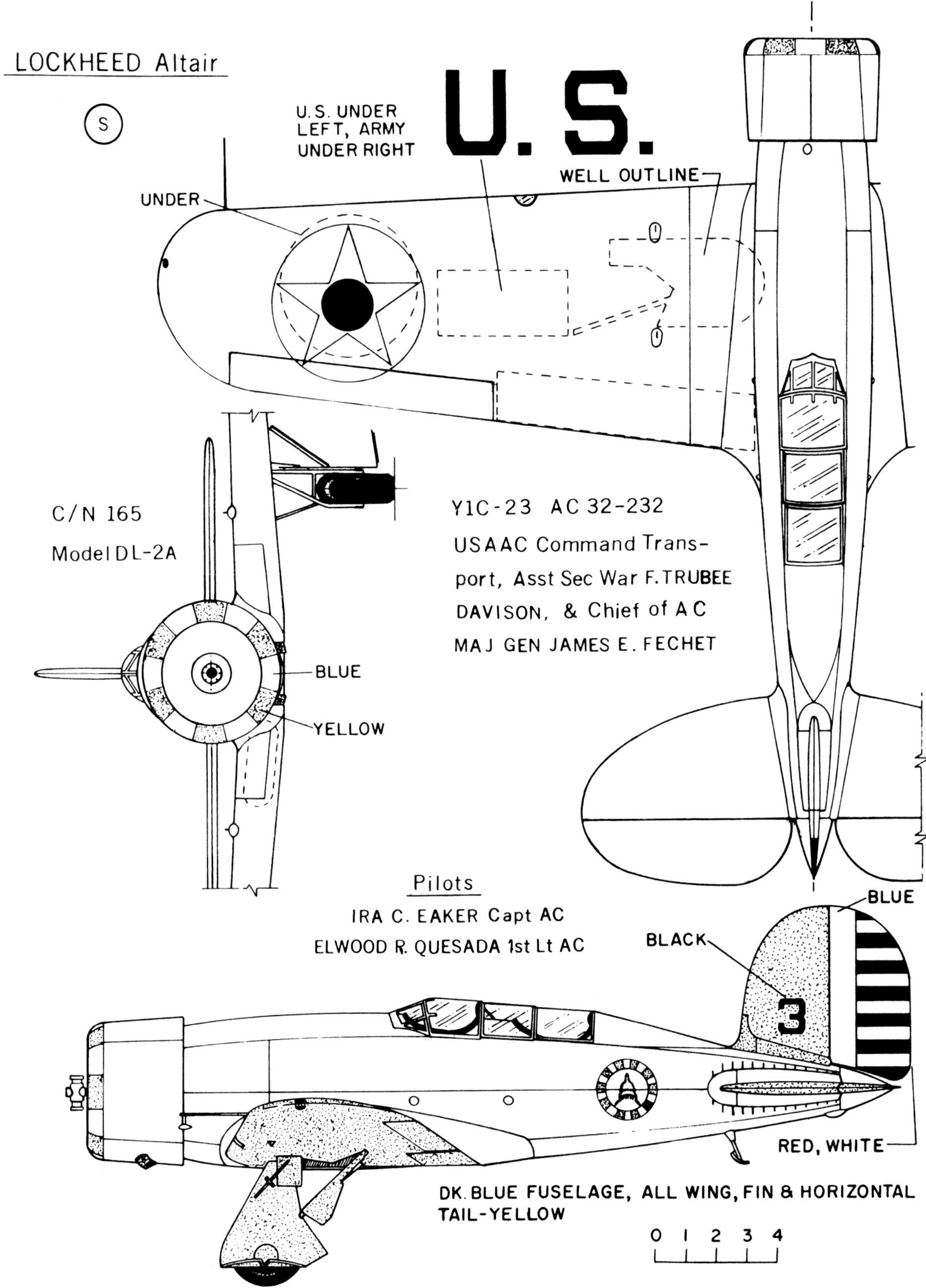
LOCKHEED Altair
S
U.S. UNDER
LEFT, ARMY
UNDER RIGHT
U.S.
WELL OUTLINE
UNDER
C/N 165
Model DL-2A
Y1C-23 AC 32-232
USAAC Command Transport, Asst Sec War F.TRUBEE DAVISON, & Chief of AC MAJ GEN JAMES E. FECHET
BLUE
YELLOW
Pilots
IRA C. EAKER Capt AC
ELWOOD R. QUESADA 1st Lt AC
BLUE
BLACK
3
RED, WHITE
DK. BLUE FUSELAGE, ALL WING, FIN & HORIZONTAL TAIL-YELLOW
0 1 2 3 4

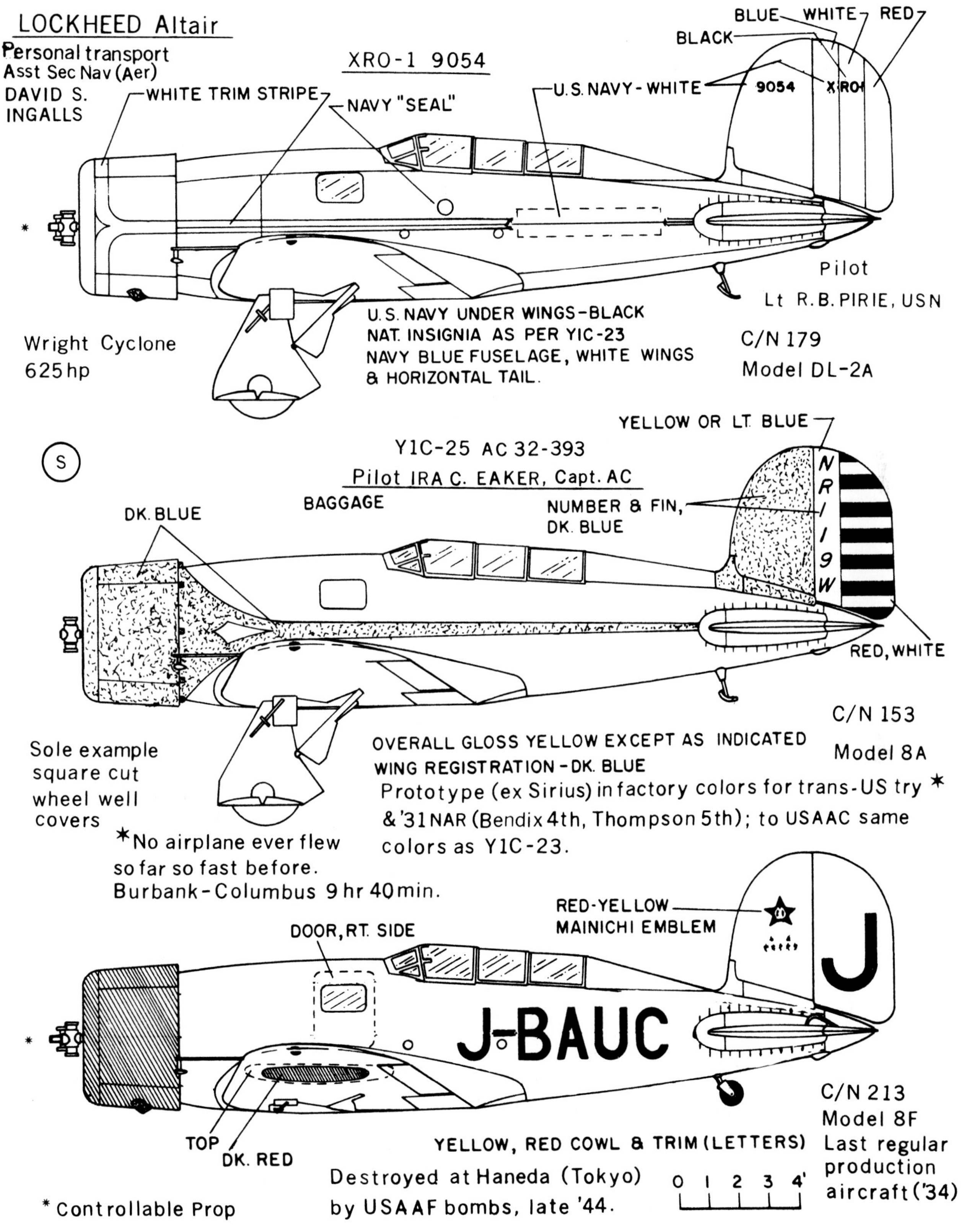
LOCKHEED Altair
Personal transport
Asst Sec Nav (Aer)
DAVID S. INGALLS
XRO-1 9054
WHITE TRIM STRIPE
NAVY "SEAL"
U.S. NAVY - WHITE
BLUE
WHITE
RED
BLACK
9054
XRO1
Pilot
Lt R.B. PIRIE, USN
U.S. NAVY UNDER WINGS-BLACK
NAT. INSIGNIA AS PER Y1C-23
NAVY BLUE FUSELAGE, WHITE WINGS
& HORIZONTAL TAIL.
Wright Cyclone
625hp
C/N 179
Model DL-2A
YELLOW OR LT. BLUE
Y1C-25 AC 32-393
Pilot IRA C. EAKER, Capt. AC
BAGGAGE
DK. BLUE
NUMBER & FIN, DK. BLUE
NR119W
RED, WHITE
C/N 153
Model 8A
Sole example square cut wheel well covers
OVERALL GLOSS YELLOW EXCEPT AS INDICATED
WING REGISTRATION - DK. BLUE
Prototype (ex Sirius) in factory colors for trans-US try * & '31 NAR (Bendix 4th, Thompson 5th); to USAAC same colors as Y1C-23.
*No airplane ever flew so far so fast before. Burbank-Columbus 9 hr 40 min.
RED-YELLOW MAINICHI EMBLEM
DOOR, RT. SIDE
J
J-BAUC
C/N 213
Model 8F
Last regular production aircraft ('34)
TOP
DK. RED
YELLOW, RED COWL & TRIM (LETTERS)
Destroyed at Haneda (Tokyo) by USAAF bombs, late '44.
0 1 2 3 4'
* Controllable Prop

LOCKHEED Sirius

{Earth inductor compass removed. Replaced by more modern navaids.}

Final configuration, Lindbergh Sirius. The long chord cowling covers a 710 HP Cyclone; Hamilton controllable pitch propeller. Stored in Smithsonian Collection.

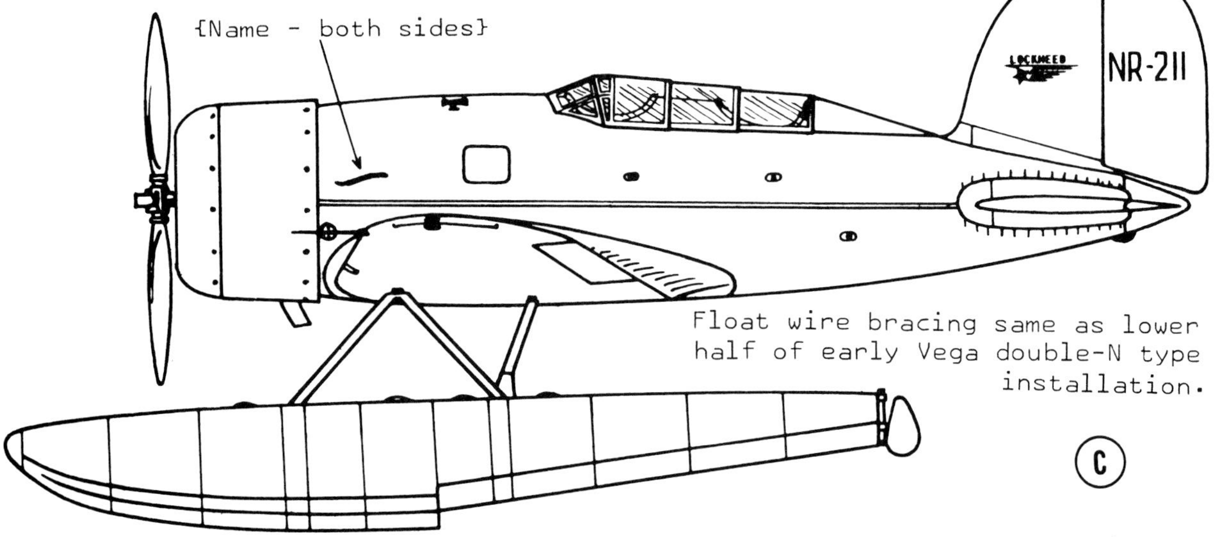

{Name - both sides}

LOCKHEED

NR-211

Float wire bracing same as lower half of early Vega double-N type installation.

C

Fuselage is gloss black, with gold stripe. Wings and tail brilliant red-orange similar to a non-glowing dayglo. Name, "TINGMISSARTOQ", painted in irregular letters on both sides, probably white. Floats and struts anodized metal. Registration gloss black.

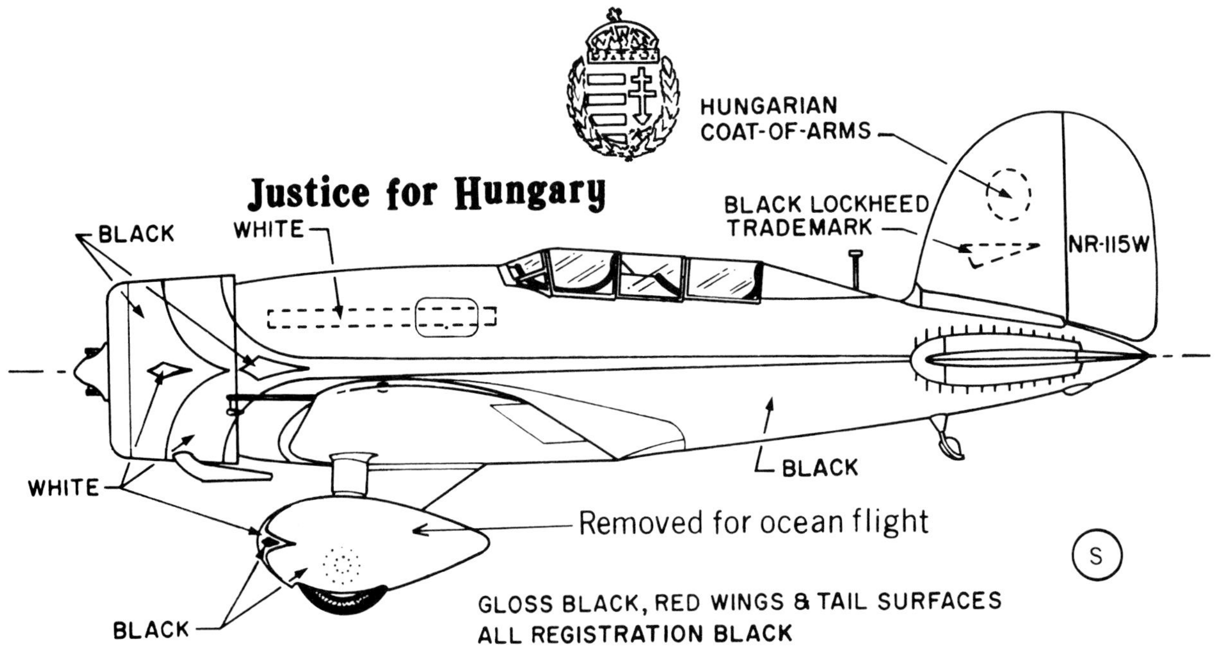

C/N 166 SIRIUS 8A, NR-115-W, built for trans-Atlantic flight New York to Hungary. Accomplished via Harbour Grace, NF in July '31. Pilots were Alexander Magyar and George Endres. Crashed, burned at Rome, Italy, May '32.

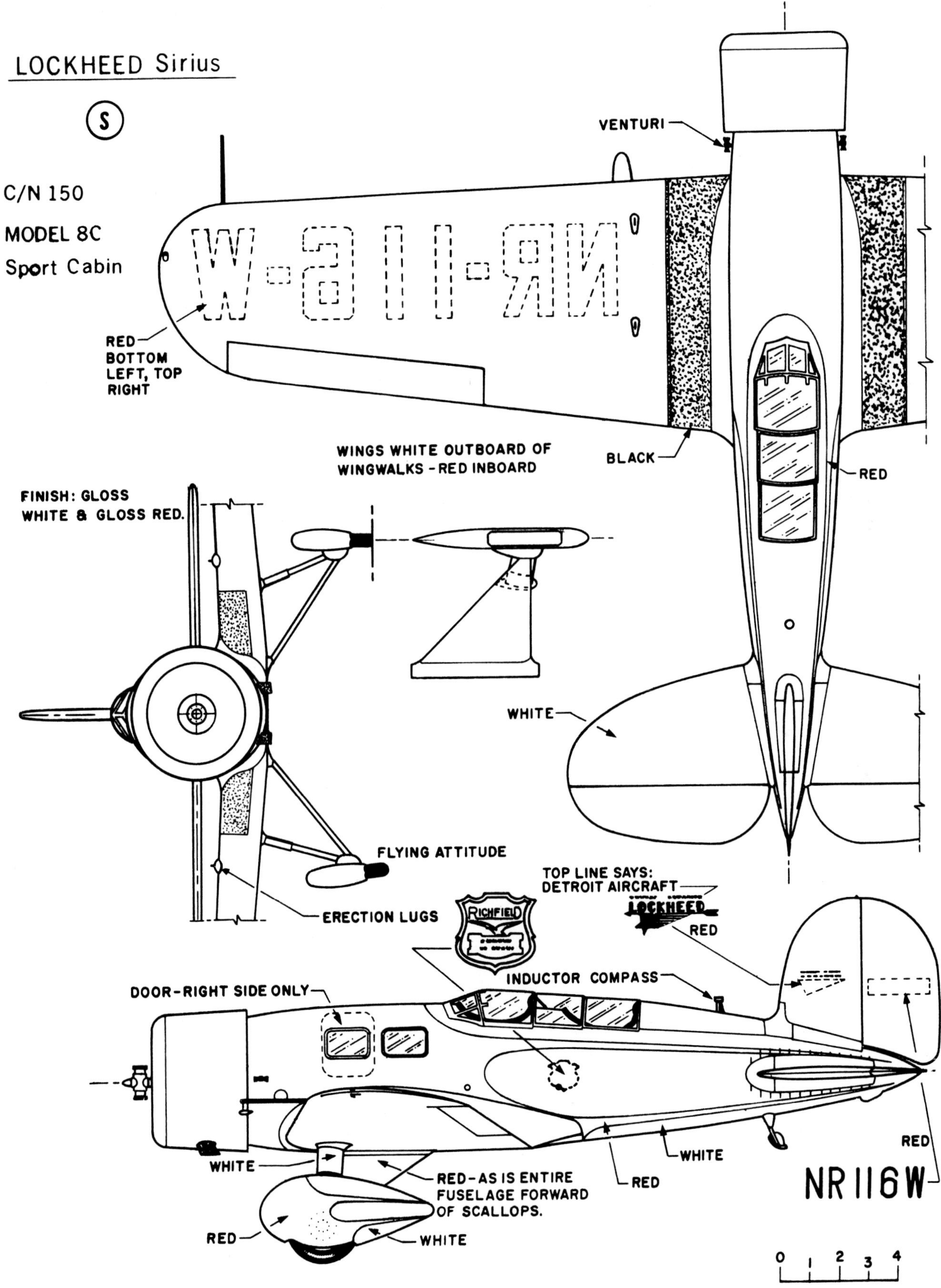
LOCKHEED Sirius
S
C/N 150
MODEL 8C
Sport Cabin
VENTURI
RED BOTTOM LEFT, TOP RIGHT
WINGS WHITE OUTBOARD OF WINGWALKS - RED INBOARD
BLACK
RED
FINISH: GLOSS WHITE & GLOSS RED.
WHITE
FLYING ATTITUDE
ERECTION LUGS
TOP LINE SAYS: DETROIT AIRCRAFT
LOCKHEED
RED
RICHFIELD
INDUCTOR COMPASS
DOOR-RIGHT SIDE ONLY
WHITE
RED-AS IS ENTIRE FUSELAGE FORWARD OF SCALLOPS.
RED
WHITE
WHITE
RED
RED
NR116W
0 1 2 3 4

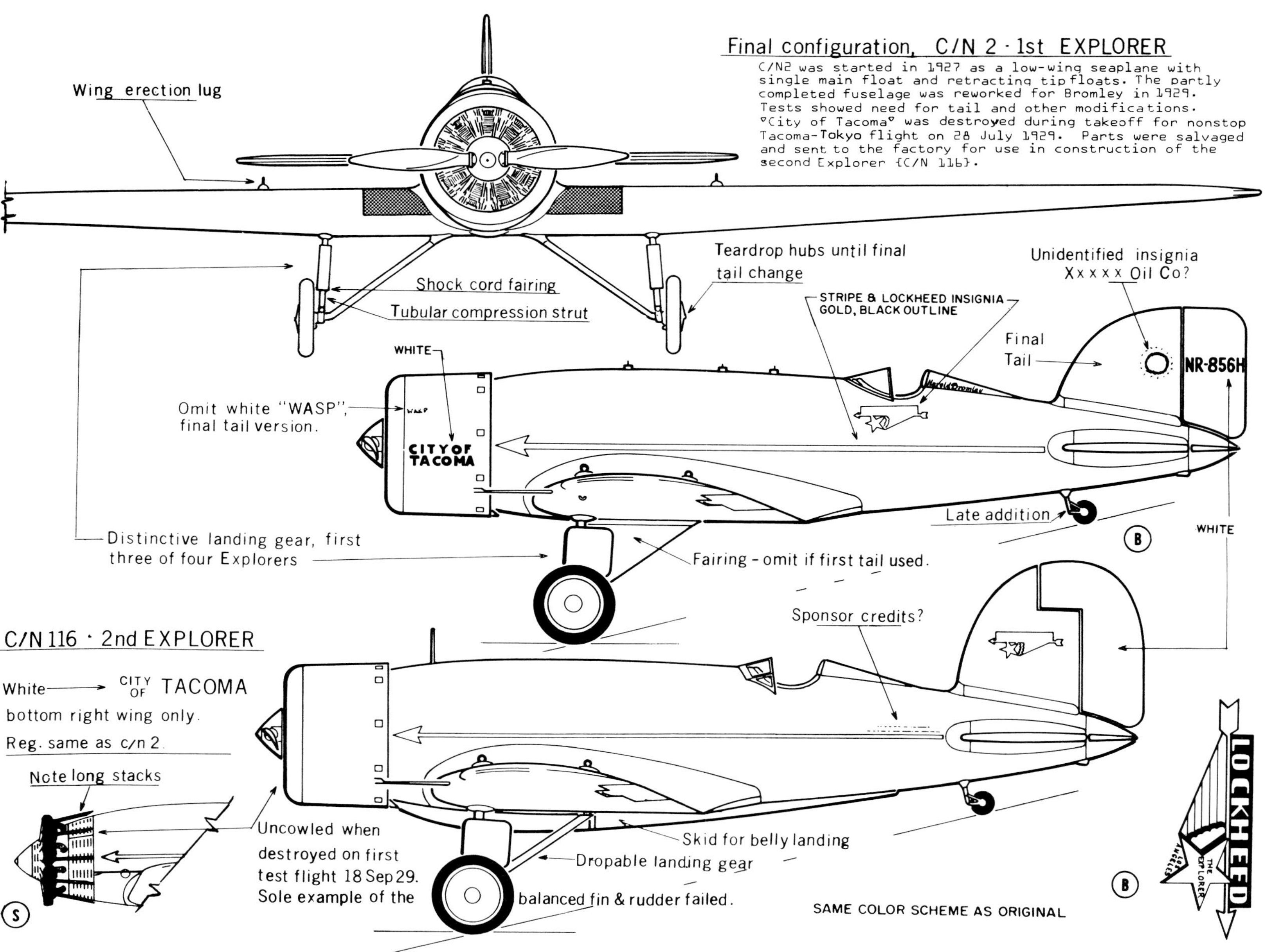
Final configuration, C/N 2 · 1st EXPLORER
C/N2 was started in 1927 as a low-wing seaplane with single main float and retracting tip floats. The partly completed fuselage was reworked for Bromley in 1929. Tests showed need for tail and other modifications. "City of Tacoma" was destroyed during takeoff for nonstop Tacoma-Tokyo flight on 28 July 1929. Parts were salvaged and sent to the factory for use in construction of the second Explorer (C/N 116).
Wing erection lug
Shock cord fairing
Tubular compression strut
Teardrop hubs until final tail change
Unidentified insignia Xxxxx Oil Co?
STRIPE & LOCKHEED INSIGNIA GOLD, BLACK OUTLINE
Final Tail
NR-856H
WHITE
Omit white "WASP", final tail version.
WASP
CITY OF TACOMA
Late addition
WHITE
B
Distinctive landing gear, first three of four Explorers
Fairing - omit if first tail used.
Sponsor credits?
C/N 116 · 2nd EXPLORER
White → CITY OF TACOMA bottom right wing only.
Reg. same as c/n 2.
Note long stacks
Uncowled when destroyed on first test flight 18 Sep 29. Sole example of the balanced fin & rudder failed.
Skid for belly landing
Dropable landing gear
S
B
SAME COLOR SCHEME AS ORIGINAL
LOCKHEED
THE EXPLORER
LOS ANGELES

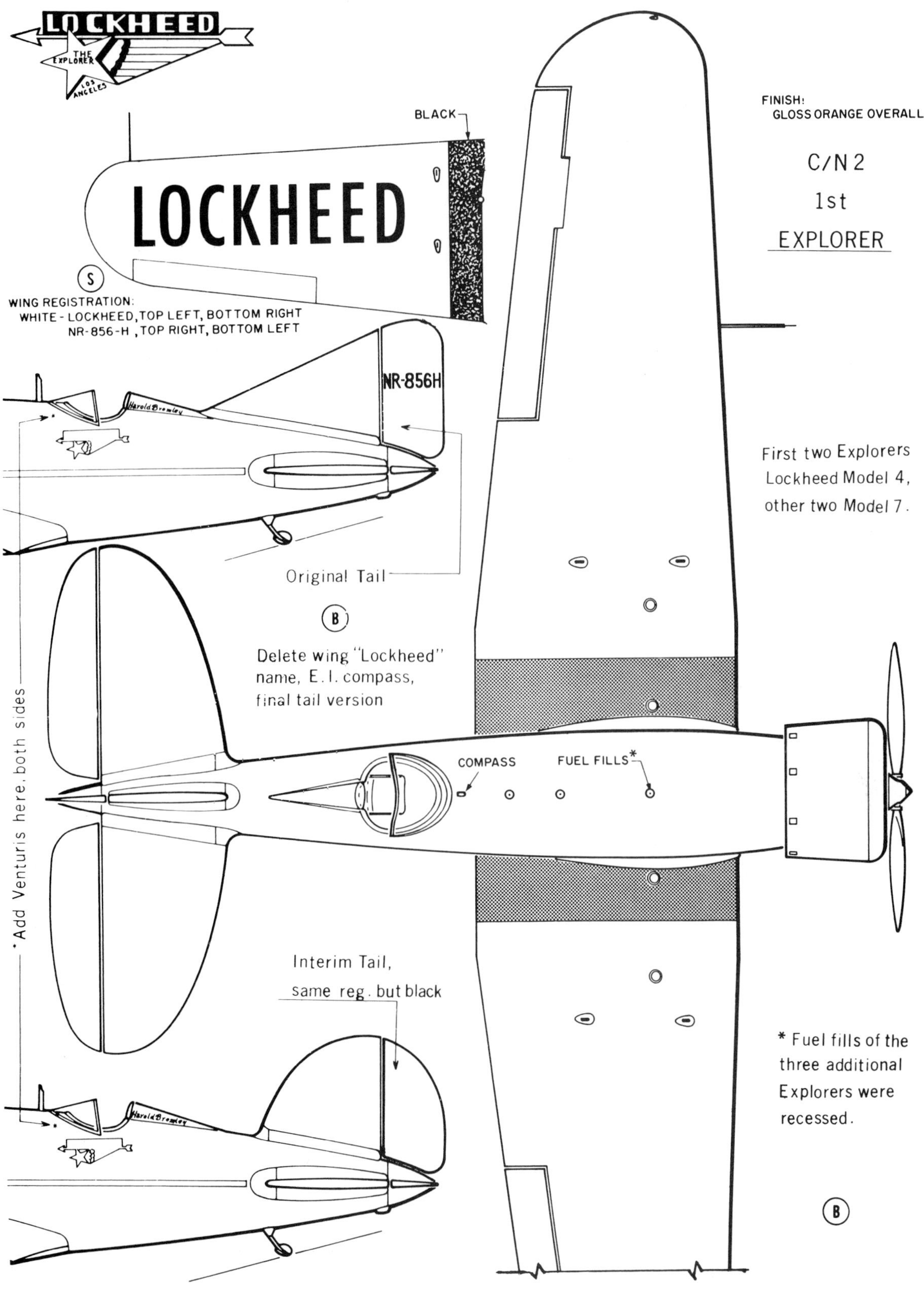
LOCKHEED
THE EXPLORER
LOS ANGELES
BLACK
LOCKHEED
S
WING REGISTRATION:
WHITE - LOCKHEED, TOP LEFT, BOTTOM RIGHT
NR-856-H , TOP RIGHT, BOTTOM LEFT
NR-856H
Original Tail
B
Delete wing "Lockheed" name, E. I. compass, final tail version
* Add Venturis here, both sides
COMPASS
FUEL FILLS*
Interim Tail, same reg. but black
FINISH:
GLOSS ORANGE OVERALL
C/N 2
1st
EXPLORER
First two Explorers Lockheed Model 4, other two Model 7.
* Fuel fills of the three additional Explorers were recessed.
B

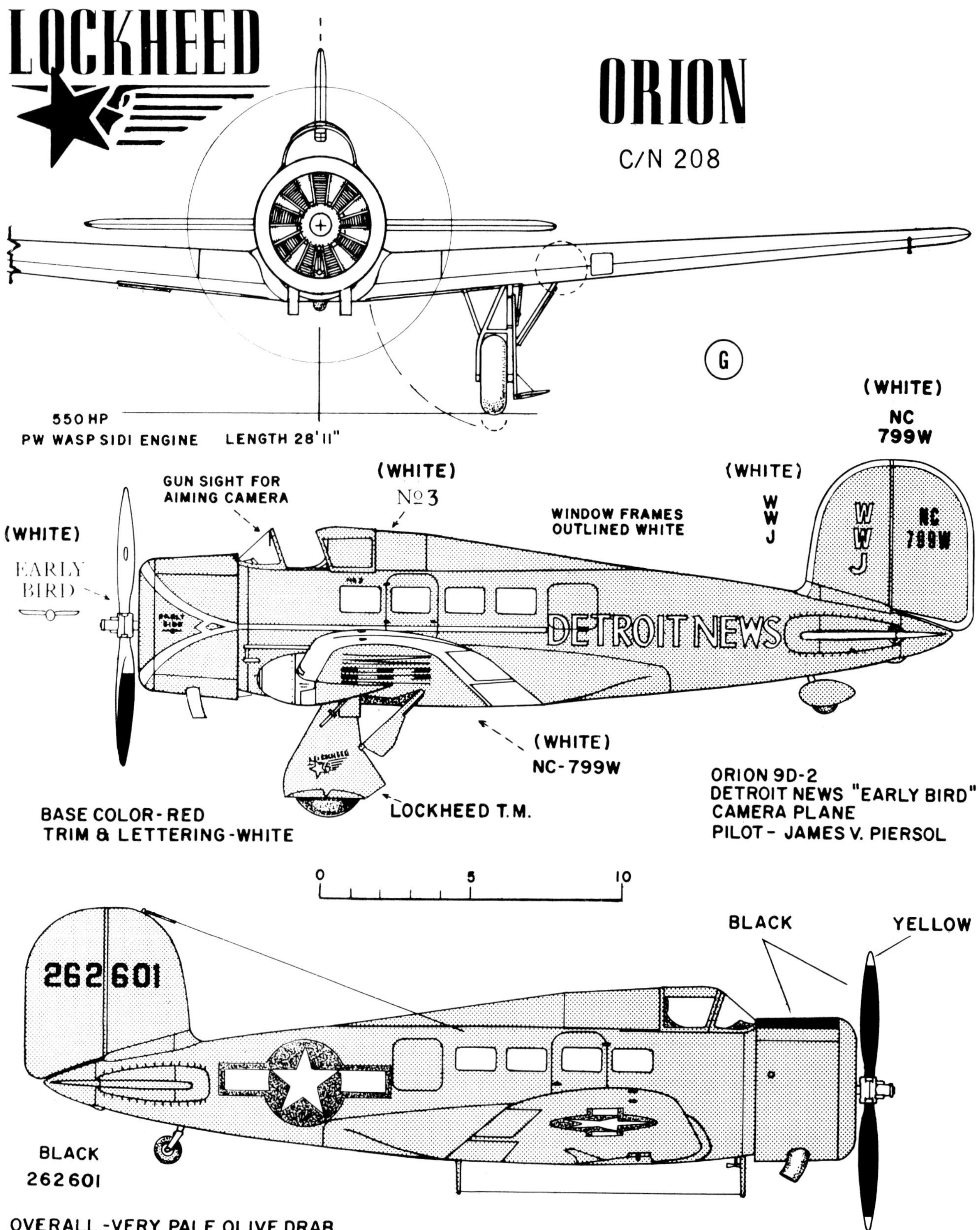

OVERALL-VERY PALE OLIVE DRAB
NATIONAL INSIGNIA-4 POSITIONS, DARK BLUE & WHITE

THIS PLANE NICKNAMED "SCUTTLEBUT", HOWEVER, THERE IS NO EVIDENCE OF NAME BEING PAINTED ON.

USAAF UC-85 (Ex Detroit News "Early Bird")
PILOT-COL. PAUL MANTZ
MARCH FIELD, CAL. 1942-44

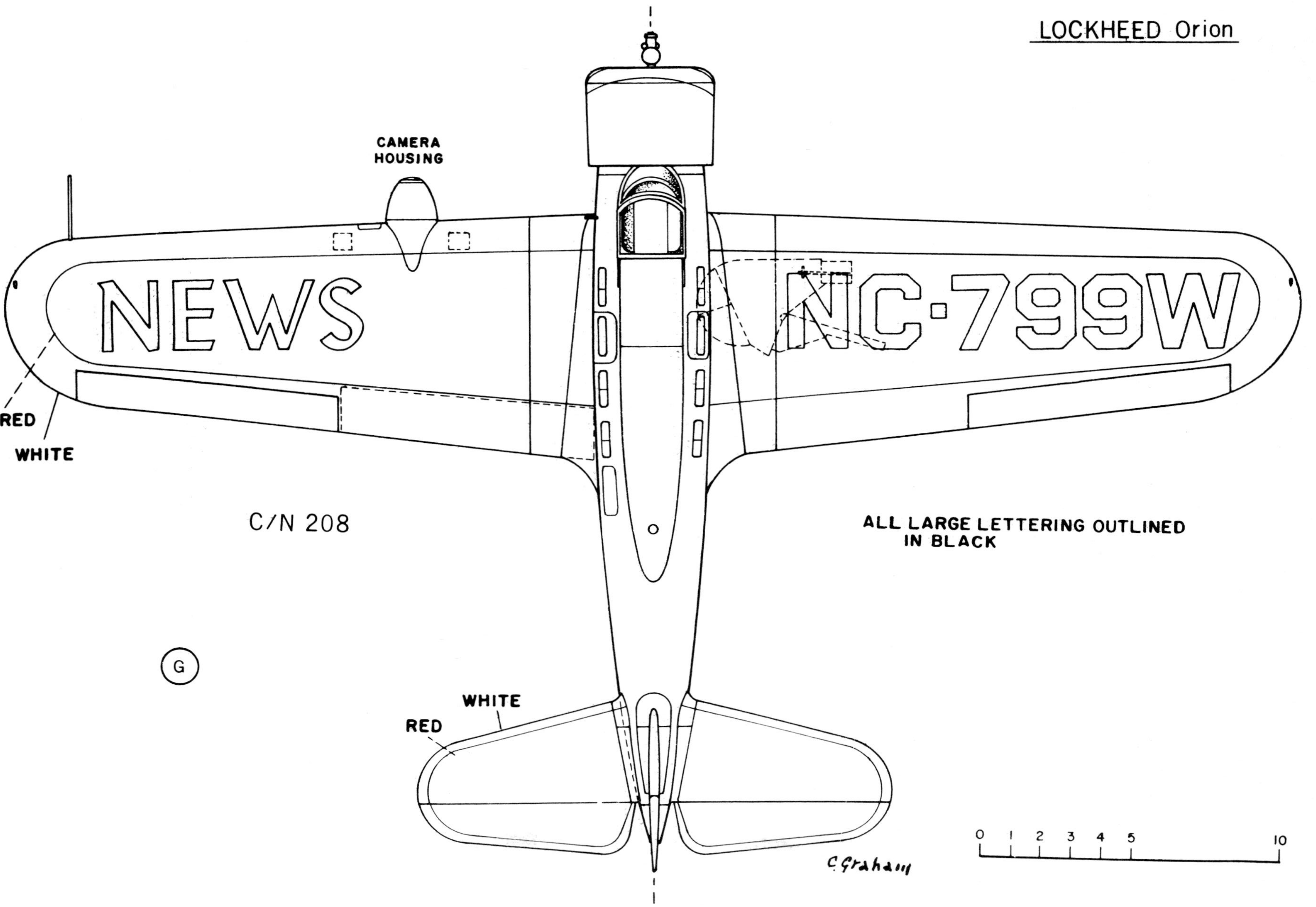

LOCKHEED Orion
CAMERA HOUSING
NEWS
NC-799W
RED
WHITE
C/N 208
ALL LARGE LETTERING OUTLINED IN BLACK
G
WHITE
RED
0 1 2 3 4 5 10
C. Graham

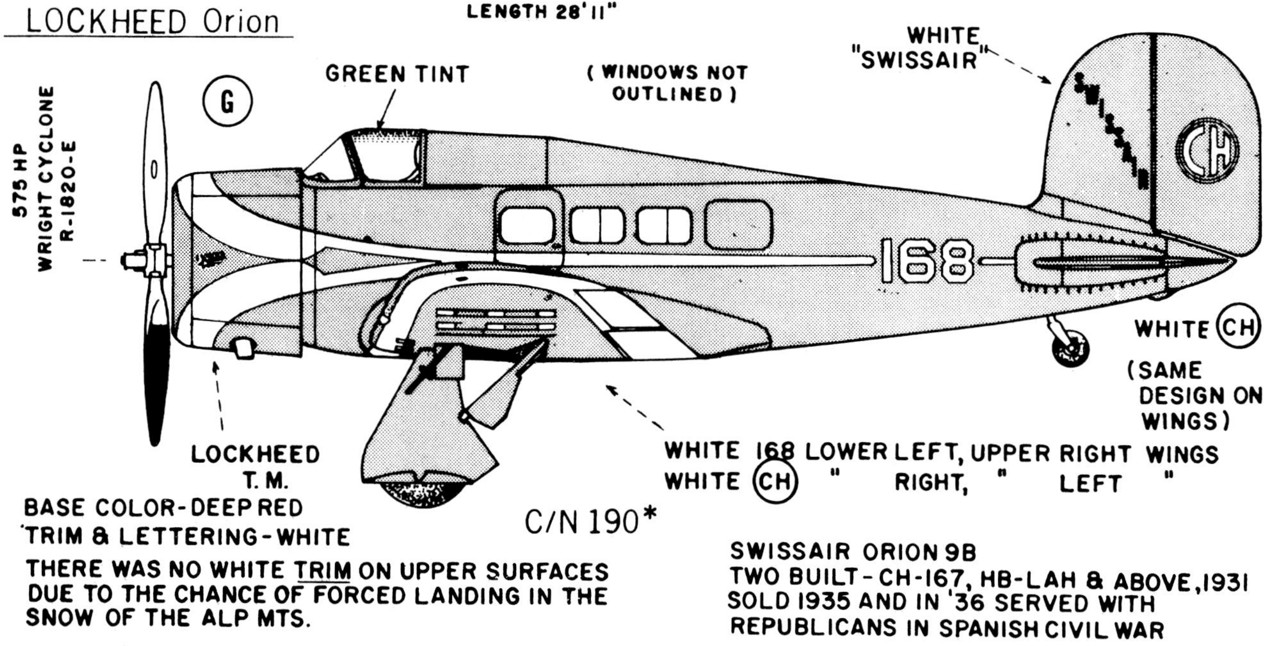

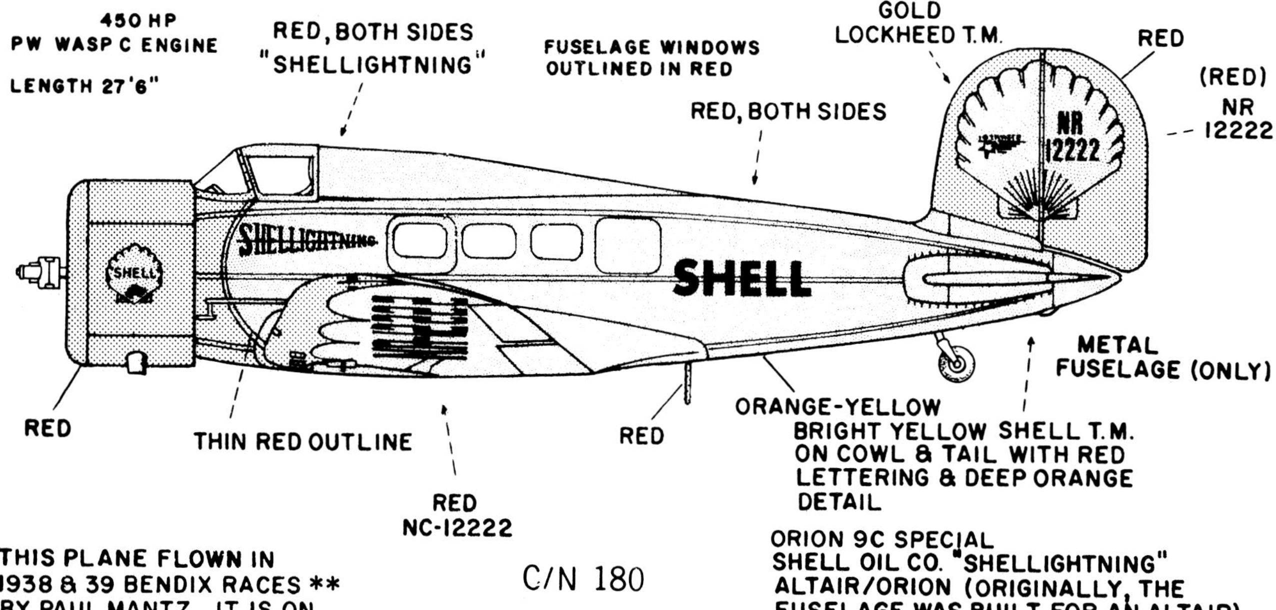

**650hp WRIGHT CYCLONE, BUMPED COWLING.

REFERENCES:

Journal of the American Aviation Historical Society, Vol 1 No 1, Spring 1956, "A Survey of Lockheed Orion History", Chalmers A. Johnson.

Air Classics, Summer 64, Issue 2 - Photo of Tallmantz Orion in spurious American Airways markings. This is NC-12222, the former "Shellightning", later raced by Paul Mantz. The sole metal fuselage Orion, it is changed from normal appearance by racing fairings, various landing gear parts missing, wrong cowling, etc.

Air Progress, Aug-Sep 63, "Sixty Best Commercial Airplanes", Peter M. Bowers.

*HB-LAJ (& H) WERE FIRST U.S. AIRLINERS SOLD IN EUROPE, SET MANY RECORDS, INSPIRED He-70, ETC. TO SPAIN (REP AF) '36.

(Above) *The Swiss Air Transport Museum restored and painted c/n 180 to look just like c/n 189 did when Swissair flew it.*

(Below) *A closer look at the Hungarian coat of arms on the tail of* Justice for Hungary *(see scale drawing on page 190).*

BUILDING THE LOCKHEEDS

Since this book is about individual airplanes and their achievements at the hands of the men and women who flew them, a certain amount of data concerning their builders, designers, and manufacturing processes was presented in only general terms in the main body of their story. Such information is presented in capsule form below so that the simultaneous making of aviation history by Lockheed airplanes may be better understood and appreciated.

THE MANUFACTURERS

The Lockheed company went through a number of corporate changes in its half century of growth from producer of a single home-built airplane to today's industrial giant. They are:

1912–13: Alco Hydro-Aeroplane Company of San Francisco, formed to finance the building of the Loughead brothers' first creation, the Model G. Principal investor was Max Mamlock, head of the Alco Cab Company.

1916–21: Loughead Aircraft Manufacturing Company of Santa Barbara, Calif. Burton R. Rodman, president; Allan H. Loughead, vice president; Malcolm Loughead, secretary-treasurer; Anthony Stadlman, factory superintendent; John K. Northrop, engineer. This company built the F-1 Flying Boat, two Curtiss HS2Ls for the U.S. Navy, and the S-1 Sport Biplane. It was liquidated in 1921.

1926–29: Lockheed Aircraft Company of Los Angeles (a Nevada corporation formed 12/13/26). Fred E. Keeler, president; Allan H. Loughead, vice president and general manager; Ben S. Hunter, executive vice president; W. Kenneth Jay, secretary-treasurer; John K. Northrop, chief engineer; Anthony Stadlman, factory superintendent.

Built prototype Vega and four others in small factory in Hollywood, then moved 3/28 to Burbank, Calif. Brought out the Air Express (1928) and Explorer (1929). Jay and Northrop left company in 6/28, succeeded by Whitley C. Collins and Gerard F. Vultee. Approximately 77 airplanes completed or under construction by this management up to 7/29. Complete change of officers at that time except for chief engineer Vultee.

1929–31: Lockheed Aircraft Corporation, Burbank, Calif., a Division of **Detroit Aircraft Corporation,** Detroit (commonly called "Detroit-Lockheed"). Edward S. Evans, president; Carl B. Fritsche, vice president; James Work, general manager. After negotiations beginning in April, the Detroit combine, both a holding and manufacturing concern, acquired 87 percent of the assets of Lockheed in July 1929.

Detroit (DAC) set up Lockheed Aircraft Corp. (LAC) as a division. Carl B. Squier was appointed general manager, and sent to Burbank, succeeding the former officers. Approximately 90 airplanes built under this management, including 11 with Duralumin fuselages assembled in Detroit. Brought out the Sirius (1929). Chief engineer Vultee succeeded by Richard A. Von Hake early 1930. Brought out the Altair (1930) and the Orion (1931). From the Detroit shops came the XP-900 (Army YP-24) (1931). Both DAC and its LAC Division went into receivership 10/31. Detroit Aircraft Corp.'s assets were subsequently liquidated.

First Detroit-built metal Vega was flown by both Lindbergh and Earhart, leased and finally sold to Transcontinental & Western Air.

1931–32: Title Insurance & Trust Company of Los Angeles, Receivers for Lockheed Aircraft Corporation, Burbank. Carl B. Squier continued as general manager during receivership, which lasted from 10/27/31 to 6/16/32. Small skeleton crew built four airplanes during this period. The company's assets were purchased 6/32 for $40,000 through the efforts of investment broker Robert E. Gross. Capital for the purchase was supplied by Walter T. Varney, Mr. and Mrs. Cyril Chappellet, Jacqueline S. Walker, and Thomas Fortune Ryan III.

Since 1932: Lockheed Aircraft Corporation of Burbank, Calif. (a California corporation formed 6/21/32). Lloyd C. Stearman, president and general manager; Carl B. Squier, vice president and sales manager; Robert E. Gross, treasurer; Cyril Chappellet, secretary; Richard A. Von Hake, chief engineer; Hall L. Hibbard, assistant chief engineer. The new company concentrated on repair jobs and conversions of existing Lockheed aircraft, while planning and building a new transport, the Electra. Walter T. Varney soon sold out his interest to engage in new airline ventures, and Thomas F. Ryan took similar action later. In 1933 Hall Hibbard became vice president and chief engineer; Courtlandt S. Gross joined the firm as assistant treasurer; and from Michigan came Clarence L. Johnson as a flight test engineer. The new Electra was test-flown on 2/23/34, and after its introduction all efforts were placed on production of all-metal, twin-engined aircraft. Twenty-three of the "old" single-engine Lockheeds were built between 1932 and 1937 by the new management, completing the series. Lloyd Stearman resigned as president 12/34, to be succeeded by Robert E. Gross, who was to head the company for over a quarter of a century. Gross died in 1961.

The Electra series of the 1930s established a worldwide reputation for Lockheed as a manufacturer of airliners. An order from abroad in 1938 brought about warplane configuration of the then-current type, the Lodestar. As "Hudsons," 3,000 bombers went winging from Burbank to Britain to face the Nazi onslaughts during WW II. With entry of the United States into the war, some 16,000 more military aircraft poured from Lockheed plants, among them the P-38s, the highly maneuverable Lightning fighters that served on all fronts.

From the Gross-directed Lockheed Aircraft Corp. next came the P-80 Shooting Star, the first jet aircraft to be made operational with the Air Force, and forerunner of an improving series of over 8,000 that served through the Korean War with distinction. For the Navy, the company produced over 1,000 patrol bombers and antisubmarine warfare planes, ranging from the P-2 Neptune to the new P-3A, which bears a proud old Lockheed name: Orion.

In the postwar commercial field, luxurious four-engined Lockheed Constellations set new standards and schedules on the world's airlines, to be followed by the prop-jet Electra transport, and the Jetstar for executive flying.

Today Lockheed has diversified its interests and grown in a number of directions. The company's C-130 Hercules family of troop-cargo transports can carry unbelievable loads to far places. Lockheed's 1500-mph F-104 Starfighter was the bulwark of Western Defense, and its components were produced in seven nations. Equally famed are the U-2 high altitude and reconnaissance aircraft. Lockheed divisions build the Polaris fleet ballistic missile for the Navy, the Agena space vehicle, rocket escape systems for Mercury and Apollo, and rocket motors for the Army's Mauler. Other branches are engaged in shipbuilding and heavy construction, development of the Aerogyro rigid rotary-wing aircraft, and the carrying out of important scientific research programs in space travel, communications, and oceanography.

THE ENGINEERS

Many men contributed to the design and construction of the early Lockheed airplanes. Among them were:

Allan Haines Loughead (Lockheed). Born Niles, Calif., 1/20/89. A self-taught mechanic and engineer. With brother Malcolm designed a 3-place tractor seaplane, built it, and flew it from San Francisco harbor 6/15/13. The brothers established the Loughead Aircraft Manufacturing Co. (*q.v.*) and built the F-1 Flying Boat, 2 Curtiss seaplanes, and the S-1 Sport Biplane. With Malcolm, John K. Northrop, and Anthony Stadlman, Allan devised the Lockheed process for making monocoque fuselages. With Northrop and others founded the Lockheed Aircraft Co. (*q.v.*). Contributed much to design and construction of the original Vega and, as general manager, supervised company affairs 1927–29. Withdrew from the company in 7/29 on purchase by Detroit Aircraft Corp. interests.

As president of Loughead Brothers Aircraft Corp., Ltd., of Glendale, Calif. (1930–34), Allan designed the 5-place Olympic (or Alcor) Duo-Four, a high-wing monoplane with twin Menasco C4 125-hp engines, mounted side by side on the nose. In 1934 he finally changed his name to Lockheed. A new company, Alcor Aircraft Corp. of San Francisco (1937–39), saw Lockheed building the Alcor C-6-1 Jr. Transport, a low-wing 8-place job with engines mounted similarly to those of the Duo-Four. Only one of each of these experimental airplanes were built. During WW II, he was associated with firms in Grand Rapids, Mich., that manufactured aircraft parts, and later engaged in Southern California real estate. Semiretired, he lived in Tucson, Ariz., until his death in 1969.

John Knudsen Northrop. Born, Newark, N.J., 11/10/95. Familiarly called "Jack." Son of a contractor in Santa Barbara, Calif.; worked as garage mechanic and architectural draftsman; engineering training largely self-taught. Worked with Loughead brothers and designed wings of their F-1 Flying Boat (1916–17). With Allan and Malcolm Loughead and Anthony Stadlman, devised the Lockheed process of forming monocoque fuselages, and developed the S-1 Sport Biplane.

With Douglas Aircraft (1923–26), and then with Lockheed Aircraft Co. (*q.v.*) as chief engineer. Designed and built the first Lockheed Vegas, the Air Express, and began work on low-wing model, originally planned as a seaplane. Resigned from Lockheed 6/28.

With ex-Lockheed treasurer W. Kenneth Jay formed Avion Corp. of Glendale, Calif., later the Northrop Aircraft Corp. division of United Aircraft & Transport Corp., and still later the Northrop Corp., a subsidiary of Douglas Aircraft Co., Inglewood, Calif. (1929–37). Chief engineer for these companies, during which time he developed a series of low-wing, all-metal transport aircraft, the Northrop Alpha-Delta series, which somewhat resembled, and were in airline competition with, the Lockheed Orion. Cofounder (1939), president and director of engineering of present-day Northrop Aircraft, Inc. Retired (1952) to engage in consulting work from his home in Santa Barbara, Calif., until his death in 1981.

Anthony Stadlman. Born Kourim, Czechoslovakia, 1/12/86. Educated in Prague; an early designer, builder and pilot of aircraft. Associated with small early aircraft firms in Illinois and Michigan (1911–18), experiments with seaplanes in Wisconsin. Became plant superintendent for Loughead Aircraft Manufacturing Co. (*q.v.*). With Allan and Malcolm Loughead and John K. Northrop, devised the Lockheed process of forming monocoque fuselages. Superintendent of construction for Lockheed Aircraft Co. (*q.v.*). Later an aeronautical engineer and consultant in San Francisco, where he died at 96.

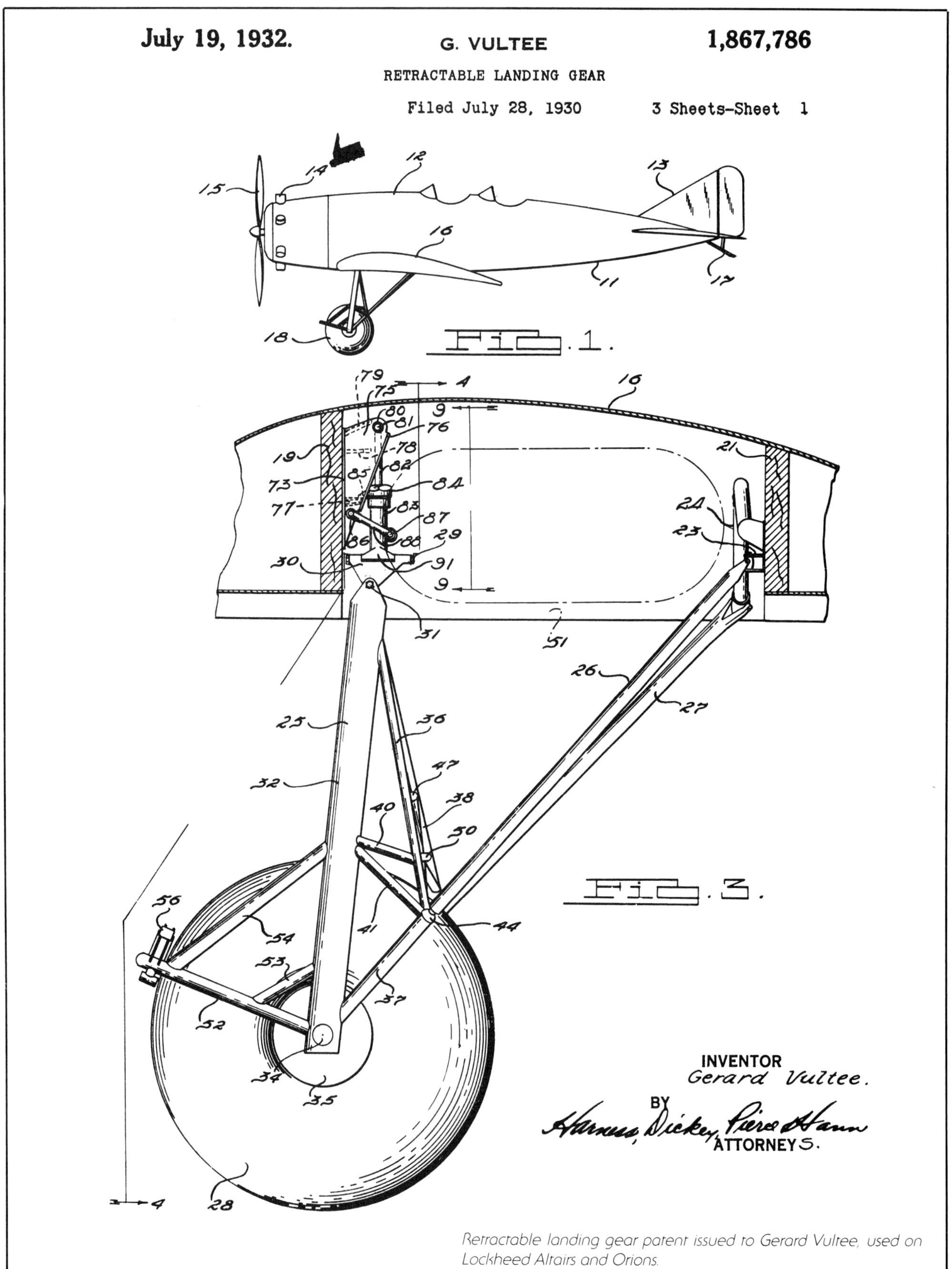

Retractable landing gear patent issued to Gerard Vultee, used on Lockheed Altairs and Orions.

Gerard F. Vultee. Born in California in 1900. Nicknamed and usually called "Jerry," his name often appears as "Gerald." Attended California Institute of Technology (1921–23), where he studied some of the first courses offered in aeronautical engineering. Worked for Douglas Aircraft (1926) and came to Lockheed in 1928 as assistant to John K. Northrop. First job there was to check Northrop's stress analysis of the Vega and Air Express. Became chief engineer of Lockheed on Northrop's departure 6/28. Directed the application of the low-drag NACA engine cowling in its first commercial use; on the original (rebuilt) Air Express (1928–29). Developed low-wing design begun by Northrop to produce the Explorer and the Sirius, the latter along specifications laid out for requirements of Col. Charles A. Lindbergh.

Left Lockheed early 1930 to supervise drafting and engineering courses at Curtiss-Wright Technical Institute in Los Angeles, and briefly served as chief engineer for Emsco Aircraft Corp. of Downey, Calif. Vultee's design for a 10-passenger single-engine transport accepted and built by Airplane Development Corp. of Glendale, Calif. (1932), with which Vultee became associated. Firm later called the Vultee Aircraft Division of Aviation Manufacturing Corp., building attack bombers and trainers. Vultee, who finally learned to fly, was killed with his wife, Sylvia, in a private plane accident near Sedona, Ariz., 1/29/38. Company continued as Vultee Aircraft Corp., and is now recognizable as the "V" in the Convair Division of General Dynamics Corp.

Carl B. Squier (left, rear) *and Richard A. Von Hake.*

Richard A. Von Hake. Came to Lockheed Aircraft in 1929 as a draftsman and assistant to Jerry Vultee. A rare combination of pilot, engineer, and business manager, Von Hake worked on the Explorer and Sirius with Vultee, and became chief engineer of the company early in 1930 when Vultee resigned. He was kept at work during Depression-ridden "Detroit Aircraft days" at Lockheed, and worked on the development of fully retractable landing gear in converting the Sirius to the Altair. Also responsible for the Orion, plus many repair and modification jobs.

During a lay-off period in 1933, while the newly reorganized company got going, Von Hake bought the components and assembled a metal Vega on his own, using a small crew. Rehired by the new Lockheed management (*q.v.*), he was factory superintendent 1933–*c.*40.

The work of both Vultee and Von Hake was supplemented by project engineers **James Gerschler** and **Richard W. Palmer.**

Jimmy Gerschler, who came to Lockheed as a draftsman in 1928, was closely associated with all the early developments in Burbank. He analyzed and approved many standard Lockheed models, and contributed special modifications such as the design of the dropable landing gear for Wiley Post's *Winnie Mae.*

Dick Palmer was a Vultee associate who worked out the mechanics of the Lockheed fully retractable landing gear, and later that which operated hydraulically. After leaving the company, he designed a record-breaking racer for Howard Hughes, and trainers and warplanes as chief engineer of Vultee Aircraft Corp.

Working independently in Detroit was **Robert J. Woods,** who engineered the Detroit-Lockheed XP-900 fighter for Army evaluation. Woods was later a project engineer for Consolidated Aircraft, and became chief engineer of Bell Aircraft Corp., Buffalo, N.Y.

With Lockheed's new owners in 1932 came **Lloyd C. Stearman** (1898–1975), already a famous name in aviation. As president and general manager of the reorganized company he planned a design for a single-engine, 10-passenger, all-metal transport, but it was shelved in favor of the twin-engined Electra. Stearman's capable assistant, **Hall L. Hibbard,** succeeded Von Hake as chief engineer of Lockheed in 1933.

Also connected with the engineering and many modifications of the final Vegas and Orions to come off the production line were **George H. Prudden,** famed for his design work on early all-metal aircraft, and **Clarence L. "Kelly" Johnson,** who first flew with Wiley Post and Kingsford-Smith in 1933 as a young flight-test engineer.

THE PROCESS

Lockheed's wooden monocoque fuselage construction was of particular importance as a practical demonstration that a stressed-skin structure allows the same interior height and breadth of fuselage at a 35 percent saving of the cross-sectional area, while reducing drag and saving much weight and material. The ideal streamlined shape of the wooden Lockheed set a fashion for this general-purpose type of plane, and both inspired and influenced a worldwide development in the design of later, larger, all-metal tranports.

The monocoque (French for "single shell") fuselage as first devised consisted of a perfectly uniform tube of plywood: stiff, strong, fish-shaped in contour, with transverse diaphragms or

Single-shell fuselage in the making: note cover for monocoque mold and (left) *half-shell drying.*

bulkheads spaced at intervals to hold the plywood skin rigidly in place. Building up three-plys of such a structure on a form with each thin piece individually glued and tacked in place was an expensive and laborious process, and the result was often warped and unstuck in spots before completion. Only a very few early aircraft were constructed in this manner.

The Lockheed process was devised in 1918 for building the fuselage of the little S-1 Sport Biplane at Santa Barbara, Calif. It was the joint development of ideas and practical application put forward by Malcolm Loughead, Allan Loughead, John K. Northrop, and Anthony Stadlman. The four men received exclusive patent rights for its use.

The inventors first made a wooden pattern in the dimensions of one half a fuselage, suspended it with the curved surface downward in a long box, and filled the spaces between with a good grade of reinforced concrete. The resulting mold resembled a long bathtub of tapering depth. Over the concrete mold was hung a wooden cover, to the underside of which was attached a long, inflatable-rubber bag matched to the depression in the mold.

Only the best-sliced, vertical-grain spruce veneer was used in making Lockheed fuselages, the three thicknesses of the completed skin totaling between 5/32" and 3/16" in all. The inner and outer layers, about 1/24" thick, ran longitudinally from nose to tail, while the center ply was 1/16" spruce with the grain at right angles to the other two layers. The gore-shaped longitudinal strips tapered from approximately 1" wide at the ends to 6" at the center. They were first stacked in bundles of thirty and cut to the required shape. Next they were mocked up on a fuselage framework with a few tacks, and jointed with strips of paper tape in their proper relation; then they were stacked like folding screens until time for use.

The middle layer of short plywood strips running in the other direction was also laid up over the wooden form, with its stub ends attached all the way around to a 2 × 3 band of laminated spruce called the "transfer ring."

When a fuselage was to be made, everybody in the shop was called in and armed with a brush and a pot of casein glue. The outer layer of plywood stripping was placed in the mold, and the inner surface liberally sloshed with glue. At the same time the middle layer was coated on the outside, and picked up as a unit by means of the transfer ring to be placed inside the first. The second layer was in turn coated, and then the last layer placed inside the other two. Next, the cover was lowered and bolted down by means of "I" beams and bolts set in the concrete, and air pressure applied to the inflatable rubber bag. Expanded, it nearly filled the space between the cover and the plywood shells.

With ample manpower, this procedure took only about twenty minutes from the first vigorous application of glue until the whole shell was under pressure at 15 to 20 pounds per square inch, or 150 tons over the whole half-fuselage. The shell remained under this uniform pressure in the concrete mold for twenty-four hours (later reduced to eight), and was then placed on a drying rack for removal of any excess moisture. All the wooden Lockheeds were manufactured using 10-to-30-ton concrete molds of this type, and the process was employed successively at the plants in Santa Barbara, Hollywood, and Burbank.

The skelton framework to which the fuselage half-shells were joined consisted of elliptical, laminated spruce rings, ranging from 3" square at the bulkheads where wing and landing gear would be attached, to only ¾" square, back near the tail. The Lockheed labor force would again be called in for the

Fuselage framework being readied for application of finished half-shells.

Fitting plywood halves to fuselage rib cages.

Wing skeleton.

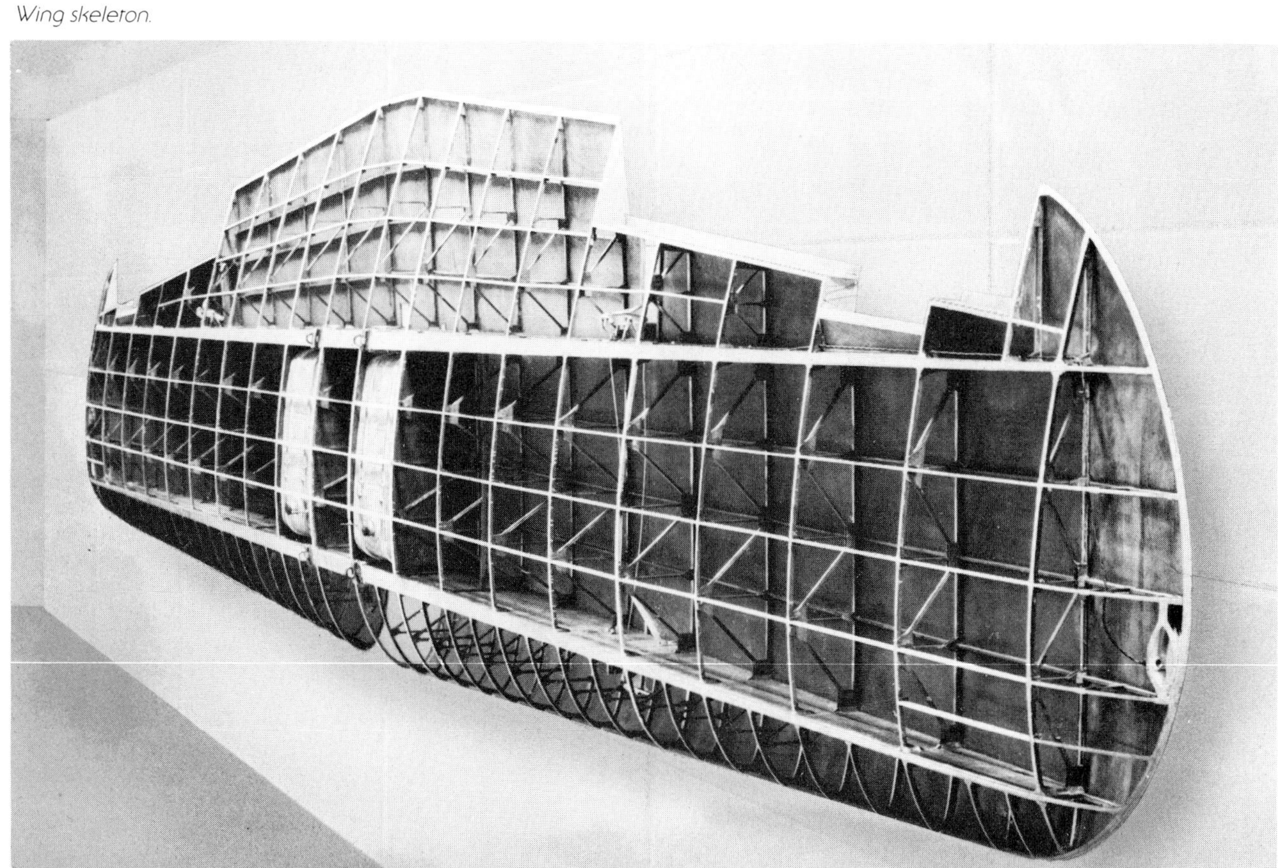

Solid, one-piece spars and wooden wings take shape.

Final assembly line, with engine about to go on an Orion.

tacking session—using barbed, cement-coated brass nails—to assemble the fuselages.

Cutting out windows from the finished fuselage was a simple procedure, and the piece removed for the door opening was made into the door itself. The outer surface of the shell structure was carefully sealed, sanded completely smooth, and treated with two coats of sand surfacer before being painted with final coats of shiny lacquer.

Two dozen of the earliest Lockheeds were finished with only the bare wood surface for a base. Then it was decided to apply a fabric covering over all, and heavy sheets of unbleached muslin were stretched out and evenly bonded to the wooden fuselage's oval surface. These were lacquered to an even higher gloss, and provided a stronger and smoother exterior.

Several complete half-shells were always kept in stock at the factory, even long after production of wooden airplanes had come to an end. They could be used for both major and minor repairs to a damaged fuselage. For a small hole, the repairman simply removed the plywood section between bulkheads, and carefully spliced in a new section.

The original Burbank factory was fronted by an office in an old ranch house, with room for the engineers' drafting tables in its former kitchen. The plant itself covered only 23,000 feet of floor space, with mill and glue rooms, an assembly section, a metal fittings department, machine shop, sheet metal department, and small lumber sheds. Wings were first installed on the field behind the factory. Later, two hangars were erected to serve for final assembly, painting, and storage.

The thick, but graceful, cantilever wings were constructed with long spars and covered with sheets of thin spruce plywood veneer. Their reinforced ribs used a modified stiffening truss based loosely on the Pratt patent design. It usually took ten of the factory's ace "wood butchers" a week to assemble a wing from precut stock parts.

The metal-fittings department fashioned items like Lockheed landing gears and tail skids, and the welded steel tubing for the motor mounts that extended forward from the last bulkhead at the nose of the airplanes.

A mutt named "Contact" was a longtime factory mascot.

SUPPLEMENT A

INDIVIDUAL HISTORIES OF ALL SINGLE-ENGINE LOCKHEEDS

C/n 1–214

Note: There are 217 accountable c/ns—1–214, plus the special c/ns EX-2 and 619, and the XP-900 with no c/n.

KEY

Registered owners are in capitals-and-small-capitals. Obvious middlemen, dealers, short-term operators, etc., where not important, have been omitted. Formal names given planes are in italics (as *Winnie Mae*, etc.).

C/n = Serial number given by manufacturer (from the British "constructor's number," used internationally).

Type = Designation given by manufacturer (as Vega, Orion, etc.).

Model = Number, or number-and-letter symbol, assigned by the manufacturer to a modification of a given type (as Altair 8D, etc.).
DL = Metal fuselage (from "Detroit-Lockheed," which as used in *Model* designation indicates combination of a Duralumin fuselage made by Detroit Aircraft Corp. with a wing made by Lockheed Aircraft Corp., Burbank, Calif., a Division of Detroit Aircraft Corp.).

Reg = Registration (*i.e.,* license) number assigned aircraft by the U.S. Bureau of Commerce (later Civil Aeronautics Authority), or by the corresponding agency of another government. U.S. prefixes:
None = very early usage, or Temporary
NC or C = Commercial
NR or R = Restricted
NX or X = Experimental
N = since 1948

Mfg = Date given by manufacturer as to: when aircraft was completed; or date of delivery; or date of first flight; or approximation of any of these.

Eng = Type and serial number of original engine installed. Manufacturers abbreviated as:
WW = Wright Whirlwind
P&W = Pratt & Whitney
WC = Wright Cyclone

ATC = Approved Type Certificate with number, awarded after testing by the U.S. Department of Commerce. Special jobs were covered by ATC Memos.

Other abbreviations:

Acc = Accident
CAA = Civil Aeronautics Authority; its predecessor, the Bureau of Air Commerce; or its successor, the Federal Aviation Agency.
DAC = Detroit Aircraft Corp., Detroit (1929–31)
LAC = Lockheed Aircraft Corp., Burbank, Calif.
L/g = Landing gear
NAR = National Air Races
P = Place (as 5P, meaning a 5-place ship)
Ptd = Distinctive color(s), etc.
T/o = Takeoff

C/n 1

Type Vega
Model 1
Reg X 2788, NX 913 (Also X 1013, 2779 & 2804—not applied)
Mfg 2/1 to 6/15/27
Eng WW J5 #7550
ATC None

First Lockheed Vega. Built in Hollywood. First application for experimental license 5/9/27. First test flight by Edward Bellande 7/4/27. Sold to George Hearst, San Francisco (1927), as an entry in the Dole Race from Oakland to Hawaii. Ptd orange, red trim; named *Golden Eagle.* Took off Oakland 8/16/27, with John W. Frost, pilot, and Gordon Scott, navigator. Missing, no trace found. (*Note:* LAC made regular application 5/24/27 for "4-passenger Vega Mfg's #50." Built in Hollywood "about May 1, 1927, for tests and demonstrations." Temp. Lic. #2779 issued 6/1/27, but was changed to #2804 6/2/27. In the confusion of early licensing procedures, *five* different registration numbers were apparently assigned to Lockheed Vega c/n 1.)

C/n 2

Type Explorer
Model 4
Reg NR 856H
Mfg 6/18/29
Eng P&W Wasp #1555
ATC none

Started 1927 with fuselage for low-wing job; planned 1928 as a single-float, retractable outrigger-pontoon seaplane for possible use by Sir Hubert Wilkins. Completed as low-wing monoplane with wheels for A. Harold Bromley, Tacoma (1929), to be used Tacoma-Tokyo flight; ptd orange; named *City of Tacoma.* Badly damaged t/o acc Tacoma 7/28/29. Salvageable portions returned to LAC, rebuilt using old reg, new c/n 116 (*q.v.*).

C/n 3

Type Vega
Model 1
Reg 3625, X 3625
Mfg 12/1/27
Eng WW J5CA #7634
ATC none

First Lockheed demonstrator; flown by LAC test pilots 1927–28. Ferried by R. C. Moffat to N.Y.C. for use of first Eastern distributor for LAC, Air Associates, Inc., Roosevelt Field, N.Y. Sold to Bernarr Macfadden, N.Y.C. (1928–29), cost $19,400. Used by reporter Zoe Beckley flight N.Y.C.–Mexico City 8/28 to interview Pres. Plutarco Calles; nonstop L.A.–N.Y.C. attempt 3/29. Wrecked t/o Belle, Mo., 3/29/29.

C/n 4

Type Vega
Model 1
Reg X 3903, R-48 (Argentina)
Mfg 1/9/28
Eng WW J5CAB #8160
ATC none

Bought by Capt. George H. Wilkins, San Francisco (1928–30) for 1928 *Detroit News*–Wilkins Arctic Expedition. Special hatch behind wing, windows in fuselage bottom; ptd orange, blue trim. Flown by Lt. Carl Ben Eielson and Capt. Wilkins from Barrow, Alaska, to Green Harbor, Spitzbergen 4/15–20/28. First trans-Arctic airplane flight; first plane to fly over Antarctica (11/16/28). Stored outdoors at Deception I. (South Shetland Is.) between Wilkins-Hearst expeditions of 1928–29 and 1929–30. Given to ARGENTINE REPUBLIC (1930–*c.* 1948); cracked up before planned exhibition tour. Left to rot away at Morón Airport, Buenos Aires.

C/n 5

Type Air Express
Model 3
Reg 4897
Mfg 4/12/28
Eng P&W Wasp #272
ATC none

First Air Express; second Lockheed completed with P & W Wasp; first LAC product flown by Col. Charles A. Lindbergh (6/28). Sold WESTERN AIR EXPRESS, INC., Los Angeles (1928); badly damaged WAE maiden trip in landing Las Vegas 6/6/28, but no injuries. Returned to LAC; on rebuild given new reg (7955), special c/n EX–2 (*q.v.*).

C/n 6

Type Vega
Model 1
Reg NC 4097
Mfg 2/28
Eng WW J5A #8272
ATC none

Sold through distributor Air Associates, Inc., of N.Y.C. to ERLE P. HALLIBURTON, Duncan, Okla. (1928), who took on LAC agency himself. Flown in '28 Ford Reliability Air Tour, pilot Robert Cantwell. Sold NORTHERN AIRLINES, INC. (N.D.) (later INTERNATIONAL AIRWAYS, INC., Minot, N.D.) (1928–31); DAKOTA AIR SERVICE, Ryder, N.D. (1931–32); IOWA AIRWAYS CORP., Fort Dodge (1932–33); WILLIAM A. COOKE, Blue Ash, Ohio (1933–34). PAUL F. JONES & JENNINGS B. MCJUNKIN, Youngstown, Ohio (1934); washed out Youngstown, Ohio 6/24/34.

C/n 7

Type Vega
Model 5
Reg X 4769
Mfg 3/15/28
Eng P&W Wasp #690
ATC none

First Wasp-powered Lockheed. Sold to HARRY J. TUCKER, Santa Monica, Calif. (1928); ptd white, red and blue trim; named *Yankee Doodle*. Piloted by Lee Shoenhair, Arthur Goebel, and Charles Collyer with owner Tucker on record-breaking flights, races. Made first nonstop flight L.A.–N.Y.C. 8/19–20/28; first airplane to fly nonstop in both directions; first to fly nonstop coast-to-coast with a passenger. Demolished acc near Palace Station, Ariz., 11/3/28. Collyer, Tucker killed.

C/n 8

Type Vega
Model 1
Reg 5885
Mfg 6/29/28
Eng WW J5A #8420
ATC none

Test-flown by Art Goebel. Sold to AIR ASSOCIATES, INC., Roosevelt Field, N.Y. (1928–29); used as demonstrator. Washed out Garden City, N.Y., 5/19/29; minor injuries to pilot, five passengers.

C/n 9

Type Vega
Model 1
Reg NC 6526, XA–BHG (Mexico)
Mfg 7/6/28
Eng WW J5C #8554
ATC none

Early airliner with MADDUX AIR LINES, INC., Los Angeles (1928–29). Acc San Diego 6/22/29, Clarence Wood pilot; fuselage replaced by LAC with c/n 42 (fuselage only), WW J5 #9269 installed. CURTISS-WRIGHT FLYING SERVICE, Los Angeles (1929–31); acc Fallon, Nev., 5/12/31. Purchased "as is" by CARL B. SQUIER, Burbank, Calif. (gen. mgr. LAC for DAC) (1931–32); converted to Model 5C under ATC 384 with P&W Wasp C #2851. PHILIP H. PHILBIN, AIR EXPRESS CORP., N.Y.C. (1932–33); modified to 2P or 553-lb cargo ship with Hi-Speed 1/g. Acc Columbus, Ohio. *c.* 12/32; repaired in Detroit. CAPITOL AIRLINES, INC. (later CAPITOL SPEED LINES, INC.), Sacramento and San Bruno, Calif. (1933–34); restored to Model 5C. VARNEY SPEED LINES, INC., Burbank; VARNEY SPEED LINES, SOUTHWEST DIVISION, El Paso (1934–35). Operated briefly by LINEAS AEREAS OCCIDENTALES, S.A., Burbank (1934), with Mexican reg. VAT, INC., El Paso (1935–37); new fuselage, P&W Wasp #4522 installed 11/36. Turned on back acc El Paso 5/15/37; no injuries. Not repaired.

C/n 10

Type Vega
Model 1
Reg NC 6911
Mfg 8/19/28
Eng WW J5A #8949
ATC 49

Demonstrator for AIR ASSOCIATES, INC., Roosevelt Field, N.Y. (1928–29). Owned briefly by AMELIA EARHART, N.Y.C. (1929); turned in for c/n 36 (NC 31E). Dismantled by LAC.

C/n 11

Type Vega
Model 1
Reg NC 7044
Mfg 7/31/28
Eng WW J5 #8952
ATC 49

Airliner MADDUX AIR LINES, INC., Los Angeles (1928–30); ptd orange; cost $13,500. During routine check at LAC engine broke off almost entirely just ahead of cockpit; replaced overnight with duplicate orange fuselage. CURTISS-WRIGHT FLYING SERVICE, INC., Inglewood, Calif. (1930–31); H. T. BOOKER, Stockton, Calif. (1931–34); LOREN L. MILES, Los Angeles (1934–35). GRAND CENTRAL CHARTER SERVICE, Glendale, Calif. (1935–45); with WW J5 #D9071; named *Miss Patricia*, later *Miss Patsy*; used in movie *Men with Wings*. LEO YODER, Los Angeles (1945–46); SUMNER N. CASE, Kansas City (1947–49). FLETCHER C. HANDLEY, Kingfisher, Okla. (1949–52), with P&W R-985 AN-1; used to fly whiskey into dry Midwestern states. Scrapped 1952.

C/n 12

Type Vega
Model 1
Reg 7162, C 7162, NC 7162
Mfg 8/30/28
Eng WW J5C #9013
ATC 49

Sold to TEXAS PIPE LINE CO., Houston (1928–30), cost $14,750; ptd red, white trim; named *Texaco 2*. Used by head of company Burt E. Hull for business trips; piloted by Frank Hawks, Bert Pidcoke, Matt Nieminen, etc. Transferred to THE TEXAS CO., N.Y.C. (1930–31). Overhauled by DAC 3/31. THOMAS R. NAVIN, Chicago (1931–32); purchased less motor, equipped with speed ring half-cowl. Washed out Chicago 2/5/32.

C/n 12B

Type Vega
Model 1
Reg NC 7425
Mfg 8/31/28
Eng WW J5A #9033
ATC 49

Given c/n 12B instead of c/n 13 "for obvious reasons." Sold to Northern California LAC distributor CHADBOURNE AIRCRAFT SALES CO., San Francisco (1928–29), cost $12,537. Used as demonstrator; acc Del Paso, Calif., 5/6/29, pilot H. McM. Lemcke. Repaired 1930. RALPH E. MORRISON, San Francisco (1930–31), Helena, Mont. (1932–35); used for charter. With Morrison made forced landing in mountains near Fishtrap, Mont., 4/21/35. Damaged, abandoned at site.

C/n 14

Type Vega
Model 1
Reg NC 7426, NR 7426
Mfg 9/19/28
Eng WW J5AB #9106
ATC 49

Airliner for UNIVERSAL AIR LINES, INC., Chicago (1928–31); cost $14,750; transferred to AMERICAN AIRWAYS, INC., Robertson, Mo. (1931). VANCE BREESE & BURKE D. ADAMS, Detroit (1931). CHAMBERLIN FLYING SERVICE, INC., Jersey City (later Jackson Heights, N.Y.) (1931–36?); purchased less engine, equipped with borrowed Packard Diesel R-980 engine; converted to 7P, with navigation hatch in wing, under CAA Memo 2–427 of 11/9/32; named *Miss Teaneck* (unofficially called The Flying Furnace). Established still-existing world altitude record for diesel-powered aircraft (19,928 feet), Ruth Nichols pilot 2/14/32. A. PAUL MANTZ, Burbank, Calif. (1936); FRED O. YEAGER FETTERMAN, Brooklyn, N.Y. (1936–37). Washed out Roosevelt Field, N.Y., 5/15/37 ("Aircraft unlicensed and flying in violation."—CAA).

C/n 15

Type Vega
Model 1
Reg NC 7427
Mfg 10/19/28
Eng WW J5A #9139
ATC 49

Sold to SANTA MARIA AIRLINES, INC., & HANCOCK FOUNDATION COLLEGE OF AERONAUTICS, Santa Maria, Calif. (1928–29) for short-line charter service, instruction. GRANT B. SCHLEY, Santa Barbara, Calif. (1930–31); J. S. WAKEFIELD, San Diego (1931); WILSON AERO CORP., Burbank, Calif. (1931–32). THOMAS SLINGSBY, VALLEY AIRLINES, Sacramento (1932–33), with WW J5 #8255. N. B. RICH & R. W. KENYON, Boston (1933–34); CHARLES B. WHITEHEAD FLYING SERVICE, N.Y.C. (1934); WACO SALES OF NEW YORK, Roosevelt Field, N.Y. (1934–35); EAST CAROLINA AIRLINES, INC., Wilmington, N.C. (1935–36). JOE LEWIS, Burbank (1936–37); used as ambulance for Aerial Hospital Service. Destroyed acc Santa Maria 5/26/37.

C/n 16

Type Vega
Model 1
Reg NC 7428
Mfg 9/29/28
Eng WW J5 #9189
ATC 49

Sold to CONTINENTAL AIR EXPRESS, INC., Los Angeles (1928–30); used on Los Angeles–San Francisco line. Repossessed by PACIFIC FINANCE CORP., Los Angeles (1930). MARGARET BROMLEY (Mrs. A. Harold), Glendale, Calif. (1931); DR. V. S. TISDAL, Elk City, Okla. (1931–33); MRS. CLARA A. BRADWAY, Oklahoma City (1933–34). BRANIFF AIRWAYS, INC., Oklahoma City (1934–35), who converted to airliner, equipped with speed ring half-cowl. A. PAUL MANTZ, UNITED AIR SERVICES, Burbank, Calif. (1935–36); with WW J5 #B9189. Washed out Nogales, Son., Mexico, 2/17/36.

C/n 17

Type Vega
Model 1
Reg X 7439
Mfg 9/1/28
Eng WW J5A #9048
ATC 49

Sold to CAPT. SIR GEORGE HUBERT WILKINS, N.Y.C. (1928–30) for use in Antarctica by Wilkins-Hearst expeditions of 1928–29 and 1929–30. First Vega to be flown off water, test pilot Joe Crosson, San Pedro, Calif., 9/28. Sold to ARGENTINE REPUBLIC, Buenos Aires (1930–?). Reported crashed and burned "somewhere in the pampas" early 1930s.

C/n 18

Type Vega
Model 5
Reg X 7429, NC 7429, NR 7429
Mfg 8/27/28
Eng P&W Wasp B #826
ATC none

Personal plane of ERLE P. HALLIBURTON, Duncan, Okla., and Los Angeles (1928–31); ptd yellow, named *The Tester.* Flown by Robert W. Cantwell to win Class C transcontinental air derby and Free-for-All in 1928 NAR, racing number 22. Fitted with NACA cowl; won Civilian Cabin Ship Race, 1929 NAR. Also used as standby airliner for Southwest Air Fast Express, Tulsa (1929–30). R. L. ROBBINS, Fort Worth (1931–32); navigation hatch cut in fuselage to rear of wing, WW J5 installed. Named *Fort Worth,* used on Seattle-Tokyo nonstop refueling attempts 7/8–9/31 and 8/2–3/31 (reinstalled original Wasp *c.* 7/15/31). W. N. GREGORY JR., Augusta, Ark. (1932–33), with Wasp C #2869. Demolished acc Valmeyer, Ill., 4/18/33. Pilot Gregory, four passengers killed.

C/n 19

Type Vega
Model (unassigned)
Reg X 7430
Mfg 9/4/28
Eng P&W Hornet #223
ATC none

Bought as entry in transcontinental nonstop race to 1928 NAR at Los Angeles by LT. COL. WILLIAM THAW, Pittsburgh (1928), cost $30,000. Ptd purple and gold; racing number 33; pilot John P. Morris, Pittsburgh. On eve of race sold to MACFADDEN PUBLICATIONS, INC., N.Y.C., for $35,000; named *True Story.* Demolished acc near Decatur, Ind., 9/13/28 during race. Thaw, Morris injured.

C/n 20

Type Vega
Model 5
Reg X 7440, NC 7440
Mfg 9/19/28
Eng P&W Wasp CB #853
ATC none

Sold to STANDARD OIL DEVELOPMENT CO., N.Y.C. (division of Standard Oil of New Jersey) (1928–29). Flown by Maj. E. E. Aldrin of the company, taken on European tour in 1929: first Lockheed airplane to fly in Europe. Traded in at LAC on new Vega (c/n 118), and original Wasp engine put in latter. Reg canceled and ship dismantled by LAC *c.* 12/29.

C/n 21

Type Vega
Model 5
Reg X 7441
Mfg 12/24/28
Eng P&W Wasp CB #928
ATC 93

Sold to Lockheed distributor SCHLEE-BROCK AIRCRAFT CORP., Detroit (1928–29); used as demonstrator. Washed out Chicago 7/25/29. Wing and engine salvaged.

C/n 22

Type Vega
Model 5
Reg NC 7952
Mfg 12/4/28
Eng P&W Wasp CB #941
ATC 93

Used by LAC in East as demonstrator (1928–29), sold to AMELIA EARHART, N.Y.C. (1930–33). Damaged acc Norfolk, Va., 9/25/30. Repaired by DAC 8–9/31, fuselage replaced by that of Vega c/n 68 (*q.v.*), and made a Vega 5B. New Wasp #3812 installed 1932; ptd deep red, gold trim. Used by Miss Earhart for first woman's transatlantic solo flight 5/20–21/32. First woman's solo transcontinental nonstop flight, Los Angeles–Newark, 8/32. Sold for permanent exhibition to FRANKLIN INSTITUTE, Philadelphia (1933–66) with Wasp #888. NATIONAL AIR AND SPACE MUSEUM, Smithsonian Institution, Washington, D.C. (1966—). On prominent display.

C/n 23

Type Vega
Model 5
Reg NC 7953, XA-BFU (Mexico)
Mfg 12/28
Eng P&W Wasp CB #956
ATC 93

Airliner for UNIVERSAL AIR LINES, INC., Chicago (1929–31). Transferred to AMERICAN AIRWAYS, INC., Robertson, Mo. (1931); LAC (1931). BRANIFF AIRWAYS, INC., Oklahoma City (1931–37); converted to Vega 5C with larger fin and rudder. Cracked up St. Louis 1937. Repaired and sold by AERO BROKERAGE CO., Los Angeles, to GORDON S. BARRY, El Paso; flown on Barry's LINEAS AEREAS MINERAS, S.A. (LAMSA), Mazatlán, Sin., Mexico (1937–1944); LINEAS AEREAS MEXICANAS, S.A. (also LAMSA), México, D.F. (1944–46). CAPT. CARLOS CERVANTES PEREZ, Ensenada, B.C., Mexico (1946). Thought to have been dismantled, parts incorporated with three other ex-LAMSA Vegas to make Cervantes's three flyable ships.

C/n 24

Type Vega
Model 5
Reg NC 7954, NR 7954
Mfg 8/12/28
Eng P&W Wasp #920
ATC none

Purchased by F. C. HALL, Chickasha, Okla. (1928–29), for $20,240, with special paint and lettering. The first *Winnie Mae*, named for Hall's daughter, and flown by his pilot Wiley Post. Sold back to LAC (1929). NEVADA AIRLINES, INC., Los Angeles (1929–30); named *Sirius* and flown by Capt. Roscoe Turner in '29 NAR and on cross-country flights. One of first Vegas to be fitted with both NACA cowl and wheel pants. COL. ARTHUR C. GOEBEL, Los Angeles (1930–36); modified to 1P for '30 NAR, racing number 62; NR reg; reconverted to NC in 1934. LAURA INGALLS, Great Neck, N.Y. (1936–41); equipped with Wasp SC1 #1533 in '41. Washed out Albuquerque 8/11/41. Miss Ingalls unhurt.

C/n 25

Type Vega
Model 5
Reg NC 194E
Mfg 12/28
Eng P&W Wasp CB #971
ATC 93

Owned by distributor SCHLEE-BROCK AIRCRAFT CORP., Detroit (1929–30); equipped with floats, flown on their Arrowhead International Airlines of Duluth. G. W. MENNIS, TEXAS WORTH TOOL CO., Fort Worth (1930); demolished acc Alvord, Texas, 4/27/30. Pilot James H. Kelly, Mennis, another passenger killed.

C/n 26

Type Vega
Model 5
Reg NC 195E
Mfg 12/11/28
Eng P&W Wasp CB #989
ATC 93

First flown by NEVADA AIRLINES, INC., Los Angeles (1929–30). Repossessed; sold to BRANIFF AIRWAYS, INC., Oklahoma City (1930–33); converted to Vega 5C with larger fin and rudder. Destroyed acc St. Louis 4/22/33.

C/n 27

Type Vega
Model 5
Reg 196E
Mfg 12/11/28
Eng P&W Wasp CB #1058
ATC 93

One of two brand-new Vegas (c/n 27, c/n 39) destroyed by fire which swept tents of Los Angeles Auto Show 3/5/29. Recorded in name of RULE & SONS INSURANCE CORP., Los Angeles, who paid the claims.

C/n 28

Type Vega
Model 1
Reg NC 7805, X 7805, NR 7805
Mfg 12/11/28
Eng WW J5C #9214
ATC 49

Demonstrated and sold on the spot to CROMWELL-HUNT AERO SERVICE, San Angelo, Texas (1928–29). Damaged acc Clarksville, Tenn., 3/4/29; repaired by LAC with c/n 45 (fuselage only). CROMWELL AIR LINES, San Angelo (1929–30); R. O. DULANEY JR., Fort Worth (1930–31); back to LAC (1931–32). C. C. SPANGENBERGER, Dallas (1932–33); equipped with 240-hp Guiberson Diesel engine; ptd red and black; reg then NR. A. Harold Bromley made various cross-country flights with ship, including one nonstop N.Y.–L.A. hop in preparation for a Pacific flight attempt. CARDIFF & PEACOCK, LTD., Bakersfield, Calif. (1933); converted back to WW J5 engine. Washed out Dos Palos, Calif., 7/11/33.

C/n 24: Nevada airliner (previously the first Winnie Mae*) ends up (literally) expounding pacifism ("No A.E.F.") with Laura Ingalls in New Mexico.*

C/n 29

Type Vega
Model 1
Reg NC 7894
Mfg 11/10/28
Eng WW J5C #9235
ATC 49

Sold to LAC distributor Schlee-Brock Aircraft Corp., Detroit (1928–29); based at Duluth; flown on their subsidiary Arrowhead International Airlines. M&S Co., Antigo, Wis. (1929–30). Washed out St. Paul 4/30/30.

C/n 30

Type Vega
Model 1
Reg 7895, CF-AAL (Canada), AN-ABP (Nicaragua)
Mfg late 1928
Eng WW J5A #9243
ATC 49

Sold to Commercial Airways, Ltd., Edmonton, Alta., Canada (1929–31). Ptd orange, flown by Capt. W. R. May on early airmail routes of northern Canada; operated on wheels, skis, floats. Returned to LAC for installation WW J6 (300-hp) engine, also 9" nose shortening 1930. Transferred to Canadian Airways, Ltd., Winnipeg (1931–36). Canadian Pacific Airlines, Vancouver (1936–44); International Current Aviation Enterprises, N.Y.C. (1944); Jack Baker & Cia. Inter-Americana de Aviacion, Managua, Nicaragua (1944–45); Jimmy Angel, Managua (1945); Tropical Air transporte, Managua (1946–?). Sold or taken by Angel outside Nicaragua in 1946. Final disposition unknown.

C/n 31

Type Vega
Model 1
Reg NC 7896
Mfg 10/28
Eng WW J5C #9244
ATC 49

Sold through LAC distributor Schlee-Brock Aircraft Corp., Detroit, to Wolverine Flying Service, Ltd., Lansing, Mich. (1929–30). Washed out Lansing 2/10/30.

C/n 32

Type Vega
Model 1
Reg NC 7973, NR 7973
Mfg 12/28
Eng WW #9250
ATC 49

Operated as demonstrator by Schlee-Brock Aircraft Corp., Detroit (1929–30). Gentry Shelton, St. Louis (1930–31) used ship on his Shelton-Jefferson Airways as an airliner. Accs St. Louis 7/1/30 and 6/21/31; repaired by Parks Air College, East St. Louis, Ill. Reg NR and sold to Ruth Stewart, St. Louis (1931–32); Mrs. Stewart and Mrs. Debbie Stanford planned a N.Y.C.–Buenos Aires flight. Demolished acc near Newville, Pa., 1/5/32. Mrs. Stewart and Mrs. Stanford killed.

C/n 33

Type Vega
Model 1
Reg NC 32E
Mfg 1/29
Eng WW #9285
ATC 49

Sold to California Aerial Transport, Los Angeles (1929–32); ptd white with red cross, named *Invalid Coach,* used as an ambulance. Frank Oldfield, Los Angeles (1932–33); United Air Services, Burbank, Calif. (1933–34). Crashed San Bernadino, Calif., 7/9/34. Pilot George E. Hague and two passengers killed, one injured.

C/n 34

Type Vega
Model 1
Reg C 33E, R 33E, N-41, LN-ABD (Norway)
Mfg 10/28
Eng WW J5C #9293
ATC 49

Commercial and restricted licenses to LAC. 400-gal gas capacity. For "Polar Exploration." Sold to Schlee-Brock Aircraft Corp., Detroit (1929); Bryde & Dahl, Sandefjord, Norway (1929–37), for use in whale hunting and exploration in the Antarctic. Mounted on pontoons, flown by Comdr. Hjalmar Riiser-Larsen and Lt. Finn Lutzow-Holm in Antarctica 1929–30. Used for whale hunts in Greenland waters 1931. Named: *Qarrtsiluni* ("soul of the whale"). Norsk Luftfoto A/S (1937–38). Fitted with skis and flown as photo plane in Norway. Scrapped 1938 and engine used to power a propellor-driven sledge in Norwegian mountains.

C/n 35

Type Vega
Model 1
Reg NC 34E, X 34E
Mfg 1/29
Eng WW #9302
ATC 49

LAC demonstrator (1929). Flown by test pilot Herb Fahy for 36-hour-56-min endurance record 5/28–29/29 Burbank, Calif. Washed out Flint, Mich., 8/4/29.

C/n 36

Type Vega
Model 1
Reg NC 31E
Mfg 1/29
Eng WW #B9314
ATC 49

LAC demonstrator (1929). Acquired by Amelia Earhart, N.Y.C. (1929–30), in exchange for c/n 10 (*q.v.*). Flown to third place women's L.A.–Cleveland race 1929 ("powder-puff derby"). Turned in for c/n 22. Parks Air College, East St. Louis, Ill. (1930–37); used by school for instruction and charter; engine equipped with speed ring half-cowl; ptd red, cream. Acc East St. Louis 3/8/34. St. Louis Flying Service, St. Louis (1937); Mountain Flying Service, Denver (1937). Disposition unknown.

C/n 37

Type Vega
Model 1
Reg NC 35E
Mfg 2/29
Eng WW #9319
ATC 49

LAC demonstrator (1929–30). Parks Air College, East St. Louis, Ill. (1930–31); used for instruction. Back to LAC as demonstrator (1931); Thomas R. Navin, Navin Air Transport, Chicago (1931). Washed out near Lansing, Kan., 9/22/31. Pilot Andrew Kelson, passenger killed.

C/n 38

Type Vega
Model 1
Reg NC 197E
Mfg 2/29
Eng WW #9321
ATC 49

LAC demonstrator (1929–30). Airliner for Wedell-Williams Air Service, Inc., Patterson, La. (1930–36). After acc Orange, Texas, 10/12/30, converted to Vega 5 under ATC 93, and P&W Wasp #71 installed. North American Aviation, Inc., N.Y.C. (1936–37); Charles H. Babb, Glendale, Calif. (1937–41); converted to 2D under ATC Memo 2-377 and P&W Wasp, Jr., #13 installed. Marshall Searle, Searle Aero Industries, Inc., Beverly Hills, Calif. (1941–43). War Dept., U.S. Engineer's Office, San Francisco (1943–?) ("Ship gov't property in operation outside the continental limits of the U.S."—CAA). Final disposition unknown.

C/n 39

Type Vega
Model 1
Reg 198E
Mfg early 1929
Eng WW J5B #9322
ATC 49

One of two brand-new Vegas (c/n 27, c/n 39) destroyed by fire which swept tents of the Los Angeles Auto Show 3/5/29. Recorded in name of Rule & Sons

C/n 40: George Westinghouse's Elizabeth Lind *went to Tallmantz Aviation, was painted and reregistered for an Amelia Earhart movie, and was loaned for Continental Airlines' thirtieth anniversary. It is now in the Ford Museum at Dearborn, Michigan.*

INSURANCE CORP., Los Angeles, who paid the claims.

C/n 40

Type Vega
Model 1
Reg NC 199E, NR 199E, N 965Y
Mfg 1/20/29
Eng WW J5A #9347
ATC 49

Sold to MONTANA DEVELOPMENT & AIR TRANSPORT CO., Kalispell (1930). Fitted with floats and taken on air survey and photo expedition to Labrador and Greenland by MACMILLAN ARCTIC EXPLORATION CO., Los Angeles (1931), under Comdr. Donald B. MacMillan with pilot Charles Rocheville. Named *The Viking;* fitted as Vega 2D, with P&W Wasp, Jr., #7, under ATC Memo 2–377 of 8/21/31, NR reg. PAUL S. GRADE, Los Angeles (1932); MACE NAYLOR, Beverly Hills (1933); GEORGE T. WESTINGHOUSE, Bainbridge, Wash., and Tucson, Ariz. (1935–54). Prd gray-blue, named *Elizabeth Lind.* Flown on both floats and wheels. LANA R. KURTZER, Seattle (1955); A. PAUL MANTZ, Santa Ana, Calif. (1956–61); TALLMANTZ AVIATION, INC., Santa Ana (1961–66). Re-reg. 1962 with old Amelia Earhart number N965Y (of c/n 171, q.v.), prd red and gold. Leased 1964 to Continental Airlines for publicity tour. Prd white, red trim, in Varney Air Transport (VAT) livery. FORD MUSEUM, Dearborn, Mich. (1966—). On prominent display.

C/n 41

Type Vega
Model 1
Reg NC 200E, N 161N
Mfg 1928
Eng WW J5A #8526
ATC 49

Sold to ALASKA-WASHINGTON AIRWAYS, Seattle (1929–30); prd orange; named *Taku.* NORTHWEST AIR SERVICE, INC., Seattle (1930); flown by John Blum to win Seattle-Chicago race of 1930 NAR. W. H. MUIRHEAD, FLOYD A. HART & W. H. FLUHRER, Medford, Ore. (1930–33); replacement fuselage only of c/n 44 installed. STANLEY G. FULLER, Milford, Iowa (1934–41); VIC EDE, Des Moines (1946); equipped with speed ring half-cowl, and small pants. LES MAULDIN, Brownsville, Texas (1946–61); hangared to 1960, restored 1960–61, with rebuilt WW J5. Washed out 5/19/61 near Brownsville on way to exhibition at Harlingen AFB. No injuries.

C/n 42

Type Vega
Model —
Reg 201E (canceled)
Mfg 1929
Eng —
ATC —

Fuselage only, used as replacement on Vega of Maddux Air Lines (c/n 9) after acc San Diego 6/22/29. Reg canceled.

C/n 43

Type Vega
Model —
Reg —
Mfg 1929
Eng —
ATC —

Fuselage only, used as replacement on Cromwell-Hunt Air Service Vega (c/n 28) after acc Clarksville, Tenn., 3/4/29.

C/n 44

Type Vega
Model —
Reg —
Mfg 1929
Eng —
ATC —

Fuselage only, used as replacement on Vega (c/n 41) during ownership of F. A. Hart and W. H. Fluhrer, Medford. Ore.

C/n 45

Type Vega
Model —
Reg —
Mfg 1929
Eng —
ATC —

Fuselage only, used as replacement on Maddux Air Lines Vega (c/n 11). Work done overnight by LAC crew.

C/n 46

Type Vega
Model —
Reg —
Mfg 1929
Eng —
ATC —

Fuselage only, assigned to William Brock of SCHLEE-BROCK AIRCRAFT CORP., DETROIT. Use unknown.

C/n 47

Type Vega
Model —
Reg —
Mfg 1929
Eng —
ATC —

Fuselage only, sold to THE TEXAS CO., Pipeline Division, Houston. Probably used as replacement on their *Texaco 2* (c/n 12).

C/n 48

Type Vega
Model 5
Reg NC 432E
Mfg 2/29
Eng P&W Wasp #1073
ATC 93

Sold to ALASKA-WASHINGTON AIRWAYS, Seattle (1929–30); ptd orange; named *Juneau.* With pilot Anscel Eckmann, navigator Robert E. Ellis, and mechanic Jack Halloran made first nonstop Stateside–Alaska flight (Seattle–Juneau) 4/15/29. Equipped with floats, and later a radio transmitter. Ship "returned to LAC" sometime in late '29 or '30. (*See* c/n 113, Reg. #102N.)

C/n 49

Type Vega
Model 5
Reg NC 433E
Mfg 2/29
Eng P&W Wasp #1096
ATC 93

Sold to NEVADA AIRLINES, INC., Los Angeles (1929–30). Repossessed by LAC. BRANIFF AIRWAYS, INC., Oklahoma City (1930–31); converted to Vega 5C with larger fin and rudder 11/30 under ATC 384; ptd red, white trim. Destroyed acc Kewanee, Ill., 12/5/31. Two passengers killed, pilot and three passengers injured.

C/n 50

Type Vega
Model 5
Reg NC 434E, XA-BFT (Mexico)
Mfg 2/29
Eng P&W Wasp #2098
ATC 93

Sold to NEVADA AIRLINES, INC., Los Angeles, used as airliner (1929–30). Repossessed by LAC. BRANIFF AIRWAYS, INC., Oklahoma City (1930–37); converted to Vega 5C under ATC 384. GORDON S. BARRY, El Paso (1937), and Barry's LINEAS AEREAS MINERAS, S.A. (LAMSA), Mazatlán, Sin., Mexico (1937–44). Flown with passengers, mail and express; ptd light blue. LINEAS AEREAS MEXICANAS, S.A. (also LAMSA), México, D.F. (1944–45); acc Monclova, Coah., 2/22/45; no injuries. Parts used to repair line's other Vegas.

C/n 51

Type Vega
Model 5
Reg NC 435E
Mfg 2/29
Eng P&W Wasp #1169
ATC 93

Sold to ERLE P. HALLIBURTON, Tulsa, flown by his SOUTHWEST AIR FAST EXPRESS (1929–30). TEXAS PIPE LINE CO., Houston (1930). Demolished acc Houston 11/22/30. Pilot Bert Pidcoke killed.

C/n 52

Type Vega
Model 5
Reg NC 513E
Mfg 3/29
Eng P&W Wasp #1137
ATC 93

Sold through LAC distributor SCHLEE-BROCK AIRCRAFT CORP. of Detroit to subdistributor OHIO LOCKHEED SALES CORP. (later called MIDDLE STATES AIRLINES), Akron (1929). Airliner on Cleveland-Pittsburgh route. Demolished acc Pittsburgh 8/12/29. Pilot H. E. Smith killed.

C/n 53

Type Vega
Model 5
Reg NC 624E
Mfg early 1929
Eng P&W Wasp #1186
ATC 93

Sold to ERLE P. HALLIBURTON, Tulsa, and flown by his SOUTHWEST AIR FAST EXPRESS (1929–30). Transferred to new S.A.F.E., INC., Dallas (1930). TRANSCONTINENTAL & WESTERN AIR, INC., N.Y.C. (1931–33). Their #251; reconditioned and new wing installed 7/31. HANFORD'S TRI-STATE AIRLINES, Sioux City, Iowa (later HANFORD AIRLINES, INC., Kansas City) (1935–37). Destroyed in hangar fire, Sioux City 1/20/37.

C/n 54

Type Vega
Model 5
Reg NC 657E
Mfg 4/29
Eng P&W Wasp #1427
ATC 93

Sold to ALASKA-WASHINGTON AIRWAYS, Seattle (1929–32); flown on floats; ptd orange, named *Ketchikan,* later *Wrangell.* Converted to Vega 5B under ATC 227 by LAC 6/30. ALASKA SOUTHERN AIRWAYS, INC., Seattle (1932); SHELL AVIATION CO., LTD., San Francisco (1932–33). Washed out Seattle 4/27/33.

C/n 55

Type Vega
Model 5
Reg NC 658E
Mfg 12/28
Eng P&W Wasp #1389
ATC 93

Sold to ERLE P. HALLIBURTON, Tulsa, and flown by SOUTHWEST AIR FAST EXPRESS (1929–30). Minor acc Sweetwater, Texas, 3/18/30; repaired by LAC. Transferred to new SOUTHWEST AIR FAST EXPRESS, Dallas (1930–31). GEORGE A. THORNE, N.Y.C. (1931–32); rebuilt 1931 as Vega 5C under ATC Memo 2–385 of 9/22/31. Foreign flight by pilot Robert S. Fogg and sale to Katherine Christie, Toronto, planned, but not made. Minor acc Saranac Inn, N.Y., 7/15/32. Edo E4545 floats installed 1932. SKYLOFT, INC., N.Y.C. (1933); ptd red. Demolished acc near Leipsic, Del., 8/19/33. Pilot Harold E. McMahon killed.

C/n 56

Type Vega
Model 2/5
Reg NC 606
Mfg 3/29
Eng WW J6 #10167
ATC 140/252

Sold to Ohio Lockheed Sales Corp., Akron (1929); Schlee-Brock Aircraft Corp., Detroit (1929). Converted 1931 by Detroit Aircraft Corp., to Vega 5 with P&W Wasp #1472. Chicago-Detroit Airways, Chicago (1931). Crashed Chicago 9/14/31. Pilot Al Malvick killed.

Cn/57

Type Vega
Model 2
Reg NC 574E
Mfg 1929
Eng WW J6 #10186
ATC 140

Sold through distributor Schlee-Brock Aircraft Corp., Detroit (1929), and flown on their Arrowhead International Airways out of Duluth (1929–30). C. J. Conner & Dr. A. C. Chesher, New Hobbs, N.M. (1930–?), with WW #10390. Damaged accs Littlefield, Texas, 3/1/30 and Seminole, Texas, 12/10/30. Parts stored at Santa Barbara, Calif. (1934), but apparently never repaired.

C/n 58

Type Vega
Model 2
Reg NC 623E, XA-BKG (Mexico)
Mfg 1929
Eng WW J6 #10212
ATC 140

Sold through distributor Schlee-Brock Aircraft Corp. Detroit (1929), to Williams Iron Works, Tonkawa, Okla. (1929-30). John J. Moran, Moran Drilling Co., Wichita Falls, Texas (1930); Embree H. Hunt, Temple, Texas (1930–34). Converted to Vega 5, ATC 93, P&W Wasp #2256 installed. Lloyd Earl, Fort Worth (1935–37). Charles H. Babb, Glendale, Calif. (1938); converted to 2D, with Wasp, Jr., #71. Transportes Aereos De Chiapas, S.A. (TACSA), Tuxtla, Chiapas, Mexico (1939); name changed to Cia. Aeronautica Francisco Sarabia, S.A. (CAFSSA) (1939–40). Damaged acc Ixtepec, Oaxaca, 3/13/40. Wing placed and flown for time on fuselage of Vega c/n 59 *(q.v.)*. Further rebuild as original uncertain.

C/n 59

Type Vega
Model 5
Reg NC 2874, XA-BHB, XA-BAW (Mexico)
Mfg 4/29
Eng P&W Wasp #1679
ATC 49/93/227

Originally with WW J6 #10343, but Wasp installed by LAC. Sold to Corp. Aeronautica de Transportes, S.A., Torreón, Coah., Mexico (1929–32). Cost: $18,500. Prtd red, ivory trim. Wasp #1652 installed. Held in default of payment by Huesteca Petroleum Co., Torreón (1932–33); A Paul Mantz, United Air Services, Ltd., Burbank, Calif. (1933) with Wasp #1678. Sydney Flying Service, Inc., Tulsa (1933–34); Leigh Taliaferro, Ponca City, Okla. (1934). L. H. Wentz, Ponca City (1934–35). Rebuilt. John E. Grimmett, Ponca City and Midland, Texas (1935–36) with Wasp #1517. Transportes Aereos de Chiapas, S.A. (TACSA), Tuxtla, Chiapas, Mexico (1936–39) with Wasp #1652. N/C to: Cia Aeronautica Francisco Sarabia, S.A. (1939–42). Flew in 1940 with wing of c/n 58 *(q.v.)*. Washed out México, D.F., 11/26/42. No injuries.

C/n 60

Type Vega
Model 2/5
Reg NC 2875, XA–DEC (Mexico)
Mfg 4/29
Eng WW J6 # 10366
ATC 49/140/93/384

Sold to Schlee-Brock Aircraft Corp., Detroit (1929); Canadian-American Airlines, Inc., Ltd., Minneapolis (1929); E.S. Shank, Shank Flying Service, Morgan and Robbinsdale, Minn. (1929–31); Hanford's Tri-State Airlines, Inc., Sioux City, Iowa (1931–36). Wing from c/n 53 installed in 1934. Converted to Vega 5 with P&W Wasp #2238, then #2237 in 1935. Acc: Pembina, N.D. 8/9/34. Repairs and spare Vega wing "Ser. #72" and Wasp #2054 installed. Hanford Airlines, Inc., Kansas City, Mo. (1936–38) with Wasp #4765 and radio equipment. Mid-Continent Airlines, Inc., Kansas City, Mo. (1938–40); R. L. Brown and D. S. Zimmerley, Kansas City, Mo. (1938–40); R. L. Brown and D. S. Zimmerley, Kansas City, Mo. (1940–41) with Wasp #4818. Fred Elmer Secor, Los Angeles (1941–42) as camera plane. Charles H. Babb, Glendale, Calif. (1942–43); Lineas Aereas Mineras, S.A., México, D.F. (1943–46); Capt. Carlos Cervantes Perez, Ensenada, B.C., Mexico (1946–?). Last reported damaged and derelict on beach near Ensenada in late 1940s.

C/n 61

Type Vega
Model 5B
Reg NC 2845, XA-BHJ (Mexico)
Mfg 5/29
Eng P&W Wasp #1747
ATC 227

Sold to Corp. Aeronautica de Transportes, S.A., Torreón, Coah., Mexico (1929–32). Prtd red, ivory trim; airliner for C.A.T. After liquidation of assets in 1933, sold as "one old airplane body." Frank Michelson, Detroit (1934–36). Rebuilt at Detroit with used wing and Wasp C1 #829. Michael Hanratty, Chicago (1936–38). Washed out Chicago 1/8/38.

C/n 62

Type Vega
Model 2/5/5B
Reg NC 2846, XB-BHA (Mexico)
Mfg 5/29
Eng WW J6 #10343
ATC 140/93/227

Engine changed 7/29 to P&W Wasp #1678. Sold to Schlee-Brock Aircraft Corp., Detroit (1929); Nevada Airlines, Inc., Los Angeles (1929); C.A.T. Lines, El Paso, Texas (1929). Transferred to Corp. Aeronautica de Transportes, S.A., Torreón, Coah., Mexico. (1929–33) Mexican Cert. #14. Made inaugural México, D.F.–El Paso flight with mail 8/17/29. Prtd red, ivory trim. Listed in C.A.T. bankruptcy, but disposition unknown.

C/n 63

Type Vega
Model 5
Reg NC 625E, NR 625E
Mfg 4/25/29
Eng P&W Wasp #1347
ATC 93

Sold to Marland Production Co., Ponca City, Okla., which became Continental Oil Co. (1929–33). Converted by LAC to Vega 5C under ATC 384 in 2/33. Marron Price Guggenheim, Roslyn, N.Y. (1933–34). Flown by Russell W. Thaw. Reg NR for South American Flight. Damaged acc Paramaribo, Surinam, 3/25/34. Sold through LAC to Herbert G. Fales, West Newton, Mass., later N.Y.C. (1934–40). P&W Wasp S3D1 #4820 installed; prtd white, blue trim. Used by Fales for business and pleasure trips with International Nickel Co. While in hands of Paul Mantz for sale in West, caught fire and destroyed, Hermosillo, Son., Mexico, 5/30/40.

C/n 64

Type Vega
Model 2
Reg NC 857E
Mfg 5/29
Eng WW J6 #10390
ATC 140

Sold to Schlee-Brock Aircraft Corp., Detroit (1929–30), as airliner on their subsidiary Canadian-American Airlines, out of Minneapolis. By sheriff's sale to M&S Co., Antigo, Wis. (1930). Michael M. Rubner, Rubner Flying Service, Chicago (1930–31). Destroyed acc Toledo 5/11/31. Pilot Rubner and passenger killed, another hurt.

C/n 65

Type Air Express
Model 3
Reg NC 514E, P-BDAH (Brazil)
Mfg 3/14/29
Eng P&W Wasp C #1141
ATC 102

Sold to New York, Rio, and Buenos Aires Line, N.Y.C. (1930), on floats, for service in Brazil and Argentina. Named *Maraca.* NYRBA acquired by Pan American Airways, Inc, N.Y.C., who reported airplane stored in Buenos Aires 1/31. Disposition unknown.

C/n 66

Type Vega
Model 5B
Reg NC 858E, AN-ABL (Nicaragua)
Mfg 1929
Eng P&W Wasp #2036
ATC 227

Original owners and operators unknown. Vandemark Flying Service, Lockport, N.Y. (1932–33); Columbia Airways, Bloomsburg, Pa. (1935–36); Standard Aerial Surveys, Newark (1937–41); Harold E. Curran, Syracuse (1944). Jimmy Angel & Jack Baker, Managua, Nicaragua (1944–45). Destroyed acc Boaco, Nicaragua, 2/19/45.

C/n 67

Type Vega
Model 5/5B
Reg C 859E, R 859E
Mfg 5/29
Eng WW J6 #10509
ATC 140/93

C License to LAC. Engine replaced 6/29 with P&W Wasp #1747. Sold to Associated Aviators, Inc., Wausau, Wis. (1929). R. Lic. for racing as 1 PCLM, 150 gal gas tanks in cabin. Entered in 1929 NAR nonstop Los Angeles–Cleveland race. Forced landing at Willard, N.M. Returned for installation of new P&W Wasp #2037. Crashed in storm north of Needles, Calif., 9/2/29. Pilot John P. Wood killed, mechanic Ward Miller parachuted safely.

C/n 68

Type Vega
Model 5B
Reg NC 868E
Mfg 5/29
Eng P&W Wasp #2035
ATC 227

Demonstrator for LAC (1929–31), particularly in eastern U.S. Damaged minor accs Newark 2/20/30 and Washington, D.C., 9/24/30. Repaired, but DAC decided it was "worn out." Fuselage incorporated into Amelia Earhart's Vega (c/n 22) in 1931. Still exists as part of that airplane. Exhibited at National Air and Space Museum, Washington, D.C.

C/n 69

Type Vega
Model 5
Reg NC 869E, NR 869E
Mfg 1929
Eng P&W Wasp #1677
ATC 93

Sold through Schlee-Brock Aircraft Corp., Detroit (1929) to Cromwell Air Lines, San Angelo, Texas (1930); James J. Mattern flew for Cromwell. James J. Mattern (Jimmie Mattern Fast Flying Service), Fort Worth (1931–32). Rebuilt and fitted for round-the-world flight; ptd red and blue, white trim; named *Century of Progress.* New cockpit made aft of wing to become only dual-controlled Vega so equipped. Flown by Mattern and Bennett Griffin N.Y.C.–Harbour Grace–Berlin 7/5–6/32. Crashed Borisov, U.S.S.R., 7/6/32; pilots unhurt. Some portions salvaged, returned to U.S. and incorporated into c/n 118 *(q.v.),* which got c/n 69's old registration.

C/n 70

Type Vega
Model 5
Reg NC 870E
Mfg 1929
Eng P&W Wasp #1790
ATC 93

Assigned to distributor-airline Middle States Airlines, Inc., Akron (1929). Demolished during delivery flight near Clovis, N.M. 8/11/29. Pilot Orville Stephens, three passengers killed.

C/n 71

Type Vega
Model 5/5B
Reg C 871E, XA-BHL (Mexico)
Mfg 5/29
Eng WW J6 #10518
ATC 140/93

C License to LAC Engine replaced 7/29 with P&W Wasp #1737. Planned for sale, on floats to Old Gold, Adelaide, Australia (with c/n 83, *q.v.*). Export Cert. #E-234 issued 10/31/29, but canceled due to Australian import restrictions. Sold to Schlee-Brock Aircraft Corp., Detroit (1929); Corp. Aeronautica de Transportes, S.A., Torreón, Coah., Mexico (1929–32). Ptd red, ivory trim. New Wasp #1926 installed. Unlisted in liquidation of C.A.T. assets in 1932. Disposition unknown.

C/n 72

Type Vega Executive
Model 5A/5C
Reg NC 898E, XA-DOK, XB-MAA (Mexico), N 174D, N 105D, NC 105W
Mfg Spring, 1929
Eng P&W Wasp #1616
ATC 93/384

Sold through LAC Distributor Erle P. Halliburton, Tulsa, to Independent Oil & Gas Company, Tulsa (1929–30). First Vega fitted out as an Executive model—with table, typewriter, chemical toilet, etc. Ptd white, blue trim. Independent acquired by Phillips Petroleum Corp., Bartlesville, Okla. (1931); Parks Air College, East St. Louis, Ill. (1931); Robert E. McGlynn and Maurice V. Foley, East St. Louis, Ill. (1931–32). Rebuilt as Vega 5C. John Wyeth, Wyeth Hardware & Mfg. Co., St. Joseph, Mo. (1932–38), with P&W Wasp #1711. Flown by pilot H.C. Brasfield. Iowa Aerial Surveys, Des Moines (1939–40) with P&W SC1 #221 and alterations as a photo plane. Register & Tribune Employees Credit Union, Des Moines (1940–42). Charles H. Babb, New York, N.Y. (1942–44). Cia. Red Area Mexicana, S.A. (RAMSA), México, D.F. (1944–49), with Wasp H #21944 (RAMSA owned/operated by Gordon and Judith Barry). Luis Stuck, México, D.F. (1949–55). Hycon Manufacturing Co., Pasadena, Calif. (1955–57), with P&W R-1340 AN1 #121016. Elwell K. Nold, Houston (1957). Major overhaul. General Electric Co., Schenectady, N.Y. (1957–62). Restricted operation in antiradar testing. David D. Jameson, Oshkosh, Wis. (1963–) Restored as replica of *Winnie Mae* of 1933. Still flying 1988.

C/n 73

Type Vega
Model 5/5C
Reg NC 891E
Mfg 5/29
Eng P&W Wasp #1449
ATC 93/384

Sold to Schlee-Brock Aircraft Corp., Detroit (1929); Ohio Lockheed Sales Corp., Akron (1929); Middle States Air Lines, Inc., Akron (1929–31). Acc Rydal, Ga. 1/10/30. Returned to LAC and new fuselage installed as Vega 5C. Lockheed Aircraft Corp. Burbank, Calif. (1931); Midland Air Express, Inc., Kansas City, Kan., with Wasp #682. Default in payment, LAC/DAC in receivership (1932); Philip H. Philbin, Jr., New York (1932); Air Express Corp., New York (1932–33). Their #102. Modified by ex-DAC employees to cargo carrier, with Hi-Speed l/g. Ptd silver, green trim. Capitol Air Lines (Later Capitol Speed Lines, Inc.), Sacramento (1933–34). Varney Speed Lines, Burbank and later El Paso (1934–35); Varney Air Transport, Inc., El Paso (1935). Crashed Rattlesnake Butte, near Walsenburg, Colo., 5/1/35. Pilot John J. Montijo killed.

C/n 74

Type Vega
Model 5B
Reg NC 892E
Mfg 5/29
Eng P&W Wasp #1472
ATC 227

C/n 72: 1 airplane, 6 guises.

Sold to Schlee-Brock Aircraft Corp., Detroit (1929). Operated out of Duluth, Minn., on floats. Was to have been sold to subsidiary Arrowhead International Airways, Ltd., Port Arthur, Ont., Canada, under Export #E-232, but export canceled. Demolished in accident, Hamilton, Ont., 5/14/30. Pilot Don H. Walker.

C/n 75

Type Air Express
Model 3
Reg NX 3057, NR 3057, NC 3057
Mfg 5/13/29
Eng P&W Wasp #1389
ATC 102

Demonstrator for LAC. Engine replaced with Wasp #1449, P&W Hornet #247 and Hornet #491. Unsuccessful transcontinental record flight by Herb Fahy, 1929. First Lockheed use of wheel pants. Prd black, silver trim. Sold to General Tire & Rubber Co., Akron (1929–30). Named *The General Tire.* Flown by Henry J. Brown to first place, NAR Los Angeles–

Cleveland nonstop race 1929. GILMORE OIL CO., LTD., Los Angeles (1930–32). Flown by Col. Roscoe Turner to east–west transcontinental record 5/30, and in NAR and other events. Ptd cream, red trim, with special compartment for "Gilmore," a lion cub mascot. Named *The Gilmore Lion*. Wasp engine installed 11/30. COL. ROSCOE TURNER, Los Angeles (1932–38). Flown in advertising MacMillan Motor Oil as *Roscoe Turner's Ring-Free Express*. Acc near Cleveland, Ohio, 3/11/35. Repaired. Dismantled; fuselage burned 1940; wing sold to A. Paul Mantz.

C/n 76

Type Air Express (later Vega)
Model 3
Reg NC 306H
Mfg 5/29
Eng P&W Wasp #1525
ATC 102

Sold to T.A.T. FLYING SERVICE (TEXAS AIR TRANSPORT), Fort Worth (1929–30); damaged, Big Spring, Texas, 9/12/29. Repaired using fuselage only of c/n 93 (temporary reg 523K, unapplied). Transferred SOUTHERN AIR TRANSPORT FLYING SERVICE, Fort Worth (1930–31). AMERICAN AIRWAYS, INC., N.Y.C. (1931–32); PETER R. BEASLEY, RECEIVER, DAC, Detroit (1932–33). Converted by ex-DAC employees to Vega 5C under ATC 384. RAPID AIR LINES CORP., Omaha (1933–34), with Wasp C #1506; named *Aksarben Comet*. HANFORD AIRLINES, INC., Sioux City, Iowa (1934–37); damaged Albany, Minn., 10/17/34; restoration intended; stored. Destroyed in hangar fire Sioux City 1/20/37.

C/n 77

Type Air Express
Model 3
Reg NC 307H
Mfg 5/22/29
Eng P&W Wasp #1617
ATC 102

Sold to NEW YORK, RIO & BUENOS AIRES LINE (NYRBA), N.Y.C. (1930); in service in Argentina. Named *Marajo*. NYRBA acquired by PAN AMERICAN AIRWAYS, INC., N.Y.C. (1930–32). Sold less engine to GEORGE & KATHERINE DAUFKIRCH, N.Y.C. and North Beach, N.Y. (1932–33); BERNARR MACFADDEN, N.Y.C. (1933–34); AIR ENGINEERS, INC., N.Y.C. (1934–36); E.S. EWAN, N.Y.C. and Fort Lauderdale, Fla. (1936–38). Given by Capt. Ewan, less engine, to LINDSAY-HOPKINS VOCATIONAL SCHOOL, MIAMI (1938–4?); used for training in shopwork. Scrapped during WWII.

C/n 78

Type Vega
Model 5
Reg NC 9424
Mfg 5/29
Eng P&W Wasp #1554
ATC 93/169

Sold to UNITED STATES AIR TRANSPORT, INC., Washington, D.C. (1929); WASHINGTON–NEW YORK AIR LINE, Washington (1929); WASHINGTON FLYING SERVICE, Washington (1929–30); PAN AMERICAN GRACE AIRWAYS, N.Y.C. (1930–35). Ptd Green, silver trim. Flown on Chilean airmail routes. Washed out Lima, Peru, 5/8/35.

C/n 79

Type Vega Executive
Model 5A (special)
Reg NC 308H, NR 308H, X 308H
Mfg 5/29
Eng P&W Wasp #1517
ATC 93

Sold to B. F. GOODRICH CO., Akron (1929–31). Operated as advertising, executive and experimental plane. Ptd white, blue trim; named *Miss Silvertown*, also *Test Plane No. 2* and *Test Plane No. 3*. Pilot Leland F. Schoenhair set world speed records, tried for transcontinental records, participated in 1929, 1930 NAR events. Damaged Dubois, Pa., 6/23/29; rebuilt at LAC with c/n 95 (replacement fuselage only) 1929. Used in Goodrich Rubber's De-icer experiments 1931. Washed out Vineland, Ont., 5/16/31.

C/n 80

Type Vega Executive
Model 5A
Reg NC 309H, XA-BAM (Mexico)
Mfg 6/29
Eng P&W Wasp #1518
ATC 93

Sold to WILLIAM GIBBS MCADOO, Los Angeles (1929–35), for personal transport; pilot Harry Ashe; ptd blue, named *The Blue Streak*. Converted for extra equipment under ATC Memo 2–284 of 10/10/30. TRANSPORTES AEREOS DE CHIAPAS, S.A. (later CIA. AERONAUTICA FRANCISCO SARABIA, S.A.), Tuxtla, Chiapas, and México, D.F. (1935–40), with Wasp #1814; ptd red, ivory trim and wings. Briefly fitted with wing from XA-BKG (c/n 58) after acc Tapachula, Chiapas, 4/18/38. Final disposition *c.* 1940 uncertain.

C/n 81

Type Vega
Model 5
Reg NC 336H, RX-14 (Panama)
Mfg 6/28/29
Eng P&W Wasp #1543
ATC 93

C/n 76: Air Express flew on Texas air routes. Converted to a Vega, it became Rapid Air Lines' Aksarben Comet.

Demonstrator for LAC (1929–30); flown 1929 Ford Air Tour by Wiley Post. Sold to ALASKA-WASHINGTON AIRWAYS, INC., Seattle (1930–32); operated on floats; ptd orange. Acc Mercer I., Wash., 9/12/30; repaired at LAC with new fuselage, elevators. Named *Petersburg.* NICK BEZ, Seattle (1932–34), with Wasp #1427. ALASKA SOUTHERN AIRWAYS, INC., Seattle (1934). PACIFIC ALASKA AIRWAYS, INC. (subsidiary of PAN AMERICAN AIRWAYS, INC.) N.Y.C. and Fairbanks (1934–36), with Wasp B #814. P.F. HOTCHKISS, Fort Worth (1936), with Wasp #1470. E. L. TAYLOR, JR., Tyler, Texas (1936–37); MARCOS A. GELABERT, Panama City (1937–?). Disposition unknown.

C/n 82

Type Vega
Model 5
Reg NC 397H
Mfg 7/29
Eng P&W Wasp #1603
ATC 93

Original reg 504K unapplied. Sold as airliner to U.S. AIR TRANSPORT (WASHINGTON-NEW YORK AIR LINE), Washington, D.C. (1929). Damaged on delivery flight, East St. Louis, Ill., 7/15/29. WASHINGTON FLYING SERVICE, Washington, D.C. (1929–30). Converted to 6P under ATC 169. PAN AMERICAN-GRACE AIRWAYS, INC., N.Y.C. (1930–33?); ptd silver, green trim; flown in Chile as U.S. Mail carrier. Damaged Santiago 1/10/31; repaired by Curtiss-Wright Export Co. at Santiago 1932. Reported scrapped, 1933.

C/n 83

Type Vega
Model 2A
Reg NC 505K
Mfg 8/29
Eng WW J6 #A-10726
ATC 252

Originally to have had P&W Wasp #1617, but Wright installed. Built on order (with c/n 71 C871E, *q.v.*) for OLD GOLD, Adelaide, Australia. Aircraft were to have been exported through Canada, due to Australian ban on nonempire imports. Export Cert. #E-233 issued, but canceled due to Canadian noncompliance. LAC letter of 9/24/30 states ship "dismantled."

C/n 84

Type Vega
Model 5
Reg NC 392H
Mfg 8/29
Eng P&W Wasp #1652
ATC 93

Sold to CORP. AERONAUTICA DE TRANSPORTES, S.A. (C.A.T.), Torreón, Coah., Mexico (1929–?). Disposition unknown. Reported crashed in airline service.

C/n 85

Type Vega
Model 5
Reg R 393H
Mfg 7/29
Eng P&W Wasp #1653
ATC 93

New plane with temporary reg R 393H issued to LAC. Prepared for General Tire & Rubber Co. of Akron. Crashed during delivery flight near Randsburg, Calif., 8/4/29. Pilot Virgil Cline killed.

C/n 86

Type Vega
Model —
Reg —
Mfg mid-1929
Eng —
ATC —

Reported as only "fuselage with chassis" supplied to SCHLEE-BROCK AIRCRAFT CORP., Detroit. Application and use unknown.

C/n 87

Type Vega
Model 5
Reg NC 394H
Mfg 6/29
Eng P&W Wasp #1615
ATC 93

Sold to DR. WALTER M. CROSS (later MID-CONTINENT AIR TRANSPORT, and CROSS AIRWAYS, INC.), Kansas City (1929–30); price $19,450. Fitted w/pants and cowl. Crashed Aransas Pass, Texas, 7/10/30. Pilot Gene Gabbert and four passengers killed.

C/n 88

Type Vega Executive
Model 5A
Reg NC 395H, (XA–BHM Mexico?)
Mfg 8/29
Eng P&W Wasp #1815
ATC 93

Sold to AUGUST BELMONT & CO., N.Y.C. (1929–30), Ernest Benway, pilot; lent to Col. and Mrs. Lindbergh for trip to Miami. Back to DAC, Detroit (1930). CORP. AERONAUTICA DE TRANSPORTES, S.A. (C.A.T.), Torreón, Coah., Mexico (1930–?); ptd red, ivory trim; used as airliner. No record of disposition.

C/n 89

Type Vega Executive
Model 5A
Reg NC 396H
Mfg 8/29
Eng P&W Wasp #1792
ATC 93

Demonstrator for LAC, Burbank, Calif. (1929); damaged Yuma 8/19/29; no injuries; repaired by LAC. G. RAY BOGGS, Los Angeles (1929–30); repossessed by LAC (1930). Damaged Seattle 3/22/30; no injuries. Plane scrapped.

C/n 90

Type Vega
Model 5B
Reg NC 504K
Mfg 8/29
Eng P&W Wasp #1900
ATC 227

Sold to CORP. AERONAUTICA DE TRANSPORTES, S.A. (C.A.T.), Torreón, Coah., Mexico (1929–30); ptd ivory, with red arrow. Damaged near Monterrey, Nuevo León, 5/27/30; no injuries. Wreckage burned.

C/n 91

Type Air Express
Model 3
Reg 521K (canceled)
Mfg 7/29
Eng —
ATC 102

Fuselage only, sold to THE TEXAS CO., N.Y.C. (1929), as replacement on their *Texaco 5* (c/n EX–2, *q.v.*).

C/n 92

Type Air Express
Model 3
Reg NC 522K
Mfg 8/27/29
Eng P&W Wasp #2256
ATC 102

Sold to REGINALD L. BROOKS, N.Y.C. (1930–32), used for sports flying. EDMOND GUGGENHEIM, N.Y.C., & MARRON PRICE GUGGENHEIM, Roslyn, N.Y. (1932). DR. DANIEL A. POLING, N.Y.C. (1932–34); ptd white, red-and-blue trim; named *Raymond Robins.* Russell W. Thaw was pilot for both Guggenheims and Poling. SWIFLIGHT AIRCRAFT CORP., Jersey City (1934). Crashed near Palmetto, Ga., 4/27/34. Pilot Hugh Herndon and mechanic Ed Sherman parachuted.

C/n 93

Type Air Express
Model 3
Reg 523K (canceled)
Mfg 8/27/29
Eng —
ATC 102

Fuselage only, sold to TEXAS AIR TRANSPORT, Fort Worth (1929), as replacement on their Air Express c/n 76.

C/n 94

Type Vega
Model 5
Reg NC 974H
Mfg 8/29
Eng P&W Wasp #1748
ATC 93

Sold to ALASKA-WASHINGTON AIRWAYS, INC., Seattle (1929–32); flown as airliner on Edo floats; named *Sitka.* ALASKA SOUTHERN AIRWAYS, INC., Seattle (1933–34); named *Baranof.* Destroyed acc Pinta Bay, Chichagof I., Alaska, 10/10/34.

C/n 95

Type Vega
Model 5
Reg 892E (canceled)
Mfg mid-1929
Eng —
ATC 93

Fuselage only, sold to B. F. GOODRICH CO., Akron (1929), as replacement for their Vega c/n 79.

C/n 96

Type Vega Executive
Model 5A
Reg NC 975H, TI-62 (Costa Rica), XA-FAL and XB-KAQ (Mexico)
Mfg 7/29
Eng P&W Wasp #1791
ATC 93

Sold to W.H. DUNNING, JR., Fort Worth (1929–30); W.T. PONDER, Dallas (1930–31). BRANIFF AIRWAYS, INC., Oklahoma City (1931–34); converted to Vega 5C under ATC 384; damaged Graham, Okla., 11/23/34; repaired by Braniff. TRANSPORTES AEREOS CENTROS AMERICANOS DE COSTA RICA, San José (?–1945); charter service and special trips; ptd red. COMUNICACIONES AEREOS DE VERACRUZ, S.A., Villahermosa, Tab., Mexico (1945–47), with Wasp #1834. CAVSA acquired by AEROVIAS LATINOS-AMERICANOS, S.A., Jalapa, Veracruz (1947–48), with Wasp C #4065. RAMIRO GARZA, México, D.F. (1948); ALFONSO BRITO, México, D.F. (1949). Crashed Cutzamala de Pinzón, Gro., 4/29/49. Pilot José Caleti and one passenger killed.

C/n 97

Type Vega
Model 5
Reg NC 46M
Mfg late 1929
Eng P&W Wasp #1901
ATC 93

Airliner for CORP. AERONAUTICA DE TRANSPORTES, S.A. (C.A.T.), Torreón, Coah., Mexico (1929). In service just four days: on second trip crashed Cerro del Carbón Mountain north of México, D.F., 11/4/29. Pilot John A. Carmichael and three passengers, including Governor of Aguascalientes, killed.

C/n 98

Type Vega
Model 5
Reg NC 31M
Mfg 7/29
Eng P&W Wasp C #1816
ATC 93

Sold to BEARDSLEY & PIPER, Chicago (1929–30), for use in their foundry machinery business. Accidentally burned Chicago 6/25/30. Replaced by c/n 125.

C/n 99

Type Vega
Model 5
Reg NC 47M
Mfg 9/9/29
Eng P&W Wasp #1925
ATC 93

Sold to JULIAN OIL CO., Oklahoma City (1930). Rebuilt 5/31 as 5C, ATC 384, as 7P for MIDLAND AIR EXPRESS, Kansas City (1931–32). Damaged Cheyenne 9/1/31; overhauled by DAC 10/32. PHILIP H. PHILBIN, AIR EXPRESS CORP., N.Y.C. (1932–33). Damaged Livingston Manor, N.Y., 12/9/32; rebuilt at Detroit with wing of c/n 107 *(q.v.)*; modified to cargo carrier with Hi-Speed l/g; ptd silver, green trim. ALASKA AIR EXPRESS, INC., Seattle (1933–34); operated on floats. By marshal's sale to NORTHWEST AIR SERVICE, Seattle (1934–36). Rebuilt (Vega 5C) 3/36. WILBUR IRVING, IRVING AIRWAYS, Juneau (1936); ALASKA AIR TRANSPORT, INC., Juneau (1936–42), named *Nugget;* ALASKA COASTAL AIRLINES, Juneau (1942–58), ptd dark blue, yellow trim. Crashed near Tenakee, Alaska, 1/15/58. Pilot Fred B. Sheldon killed, two passengers injured.

C/n 100

Type Vega
Model 5B
Reg NC 48M, XA–BHK (Mexico)
Mfg 10/29
Eng P&W Wasp C #1926
ATC 227

Sold as airliner to CORP. AERONAUTICA DE TRANSPORTES, S.A. (C.A.T.), Torreón, Coah., Mexico (1929–32). Mortgaged to Huasteca Petroleum Co. of Torreón (1932). A. PAUL MANTZ, UNITED AIR SERVICES, LTD., Burbank, Calif. (1933–38). Rebuilt by LAC 1934. Converted from Vega 5B to 5C, 1935, with Wasp #1815. Accs. Pomona, Calif., 2/2/36; Las Vegas 5/30/36; Brawley, Calif., 7/21/38. Wasp H #882 installed 1938. Cracked up during filming of *Only Angels Have Wings* near St. George, Utah, 12/13/38. Dismantled and scrapped.

C/n 101

Type Vega
Model 5B (modified)
Reg NC 49M
Mfg 10/29
Eng P&W Wasp #2097
ATC 227

Sold to ASA CANDLER, JR., Atlanta (1930–31); baggage compartment sealed off under ATC Memo 2–274, 9/29/30. To DAC as demonstrator (1931–32). HANFORD'S TRI-STATE AIRLINES, INC. (later HANFORD AIRLINES, INC.), Sioux City, Iowa (1932–38). Accs Minneapolis 9/7/34 and Ellendale, N.D., 8/1/37. Repaired. CHARLES H. BABB, Glendale, Calif. (1938–41). ALASKA AIR TRANSPORT, INC., Juneau (1941–42), as Vega 5C with Wasp #4528. ALASKA COASTAL AIRLINES, Juneau (1942–52). Destroyed by fire Sitka 11/14/52.

C/n 102

Type Vega
Model Special/5C
Reg NC 32M, NC 19958, XA-DAI (Mexico)
Mfg 7/29
Eng P&W Wasp C #1824
ATC Memo 2-256 of 8/13/30/ 384

Built for EVENING NEWS ASSOCIATION, Detroit (1929–34); used as news-gathering-and-photo plane, with special equipment. Ptd red, white trim, named *Detroit News;* operated on wheels, skis, and floats. PITTSBURGH AIRWAYS and CENTRAL AIRLINES, INC., Pittsburgh (1934–35); BRANIFF AIRWAYS, INC., Oklahoma City (1935). Braniff #9. Converted to Vega 5C under ATC 384 8/35. PHILIP WHITMARSH, Los Angeles (1935–42). Named *Wings Over Africa* and used in movie work. Applied for export to the Philippines, but canceled and issued Reg #NC 19958 c. 8/35. Sold by broker Charles H. Babb to LINEAS AEREAS MINERAS, S.A., Mazatlán, Sin., Mexico (1942–43), with Wasp SC1 #1540. Price: $6,750. Wasp #4844 installed and Wasp #3161 in 6/43. Washed out, burned Parral, Chih., Mexico, 6/23/43.

C/n 103

Type Vega
Model 5B
Reg NC 534M, XA-BHI, and XB-AAD (Mexico)
Mfg late 1929
Eng Wasp C #2005
ATC 227

Sold to CORP. AERONAUTICA DE TRANSPORTES, S.A. (C.A.T.), Torreón, Coah., Mexico (1929–32); ptd red, ivory trim; cost $18,500. Mortgaged and sold 1932. Brief service on CIA. DE TRANSPORTES AEREOS, Mérida, Yucatán (1933). COL. ROBERTO FIERRO, México, D.F. (1934–36), with Wasp C #1737. Sold to agents of SPANISH REPUBLICAN AIR FORCE (1937–?). Reported based at Quintanar de la Zarga during Spanish Civil War; used to fly supplies and personnel to Madrid. Lost prior to 8/22/37.

C/n 104

Type Vega
Model —
Reg 535M (canceled)

C/n 102: Radio reporter's plane for the Detroit News *next flew passengers on Central and Braniff routes, appeared in movies with two different licenses, and ended up as an airliner in Mexico.*

Mfg c. 10/29
Eng P&W Wasp #2006
ATC (?)

Apparently partially assembled. LAC requested cancellation of reg 1/4/30, and reported plane "used for replacement on a repair job."

C/n 105

Type Vega
Model 5B
Reg NC 536M
Mfg 10/29
Eng P&W Wasp #2007
ATC 227

Sold to Asa Candler, Jr., Atlanta (1929–30); destroyed hanger fire 3/4/30.

C/n 106

Type Vega
Model 5B
Reg NC 537M
Mfg 5/30
Eng P&W Wasp #2006
ATC 227

Sold to Wedell-Williams Air Service, Inc., New Orleans (1930–31); used as airliner. Washed out Marshall, Texas, 1/7/31.

C/n 107

Type Vega Executive
Model 5A
Reg NC 538M
Mfg 11/29
Eng P&W Wasp #1927
ATC 93

Demonstrator for DAC (1929–31), and for personal transport of DAC president Edward S. Evans. Wasp #2851 installed. Used by Amelia Earhart to set NAA women's speed trial record 11/29. Acc 7/8/31 Port Columbus, Ohio; rebuilt as Vega 5C by LAC 1931. Converted to 7P under ATC 384, with larger tail and Airwheels. Washed out Greencastle, Ind., 10/14/31. Wing used to rebuild c/n 99 *(q.v.)*.

C/n 108

Type Vega Executive
Model 5A
Reg NC 539M, NR 539M, XA–BFP (Mexico)
Mfg 1/30
Eng P&W Wasp SCI #2254
ATC 93

Sold to Shell Petroleum Corp., St. Louis (1930–34). Acc Mitchel Field, N.Y., 2/16/30; rebuilt by LAC. Flown by James H. Doolittle and James G. Haizlip on various cross-country and racing missions. Converted to Vega 5C under ATC 384, 2/13/34. General Tire & Rubber Co., Akron (1934–37). Named *Miss Streamline*; flown by Roy W. Brown; Wasp #2246 installed 1936. Transportes Aereos de Chiapas, S.A. (later Cia. Aeronautica Francisco Sarabia, S.A.), Tuxtla, Chiapas, Mexico (1937–41). Washed out Mérida, Yucatán, 3/41. No injuries.

C/n 109

Type Vega
Model 5B
Reg NC 540M, XA–BLZ (Mexico)
Mfg 8/29
Eng P&W Wasp C # 2699
ATC 227

Sold to Wedell-Williams Air Service, Inc., New Orleans (1929–34); flown on their airline routes. Converted to Vega 5C under ATC 384 on 2/13/34. Charles H. Babb, Glendale, Calif. (1937–41). Miguel A. Zuniga, México, D.F. (1941–42), with Wasp SCI #2440. Leased as an airliner, flying for Líneas Aéreas Mineras, S.A. (LAMSA), Mazatlán, Sin., in which Zuniga had an interest. Wasp replacements 1941–42: #1679, #1340, #2440, #2005. Acc Parral, Chihuahua, 11/16/42; no injuries. Dismantled at LAMSA shops in Torreón. Parts used on other Vegas of line.

C/n 110

Type Vega
Model —
Reg 541M (canceled)
Mfg early 1930
Eng —
ATC —

LAC wrote CAA 6/3/30: "Plane ¾ completed. Uncertain as to immediate completion." Reg canceled and incomplete plane doubtless used as replacement, a repair or new job.

C/n 111

Type Vega
Model —
Reg 100N (temporary)
Mfg 11/29
Eng P&W Wasp #2006
ATC —

Uncompleted. LAC wrote CAA 9/24/30 to effect that NC 100N had been dismantled and would not be flown. Requested cancellation of temporary registration.

C/n 112

Type Vega
Model 5B
Reg NR 500V
Mfg early 1930
Eng P&W Wasp C
ATC 227

Sold to John Henry Mears, N.Y.C. (1930), for round-the-world flight. Special radio and equipment; ptd red and silver; named *City of New York*. Pilot Henry J. Brown. Flight begun; crashed Harbour Grace, Newfoundland, 8/3/30. Brown and Mears unhurt.

C/n 113

Type Vega
Model 5
Reg NC 102N
Mfg 3/30
Eng P&W Wasp #1073 (?)
ATC 93

Apparently this airplane was originally c/n 48 NC 432E *(q.v.)* of Alaska-Washington Airways, which had been returned to LAC for rebuild. Given new fuselage to which Reg #102N had been assigned, and completed with A-W markings and named *Juneau*. Damaged in acc, Inglewood, Calif., 3/26/30. Not delivered and license canceled.

C/n 114

Type Vega
Model 5
Reg 103N (canceled)
Mfg 9/29
Eng —
ATC 93

Fuselage only; partially completed, converted to 7P Vega under ATC 227, and given c/n 126 *(q.v.)*.

C/n 115

Type Vega
Model —
Reg 104N (canceled)
Mfg 9/29
Eng —
ATC —

Fuselage only. LAC writes CAA 7/2/30: "Cancel registration as this is a shell only, not even partially complete and in storage."

C/n 116

Type Explorer
Model 4
Reg NR 856H
Mfg 9/29
Eng P&W Wasp #1555
ATC none

Built for A. Harold Bromley's projected Tacoma to Tokyo flight, using portions of wrecked Explorer c/n 2 *(q.v.)*. Same reg as original and also named *City of Tacoma*. Equipped with belly skid and provision made for dropable l/g. Had an experimental counterbalanced vertical rudder. Washed out Burbank, Calif., 9/18/29, on first test when rudder tore off in flight. Test pilot Herb Fahy injured. Later a third Explorer built for Bromley, c/n 147 *(q.v.)*.

C/n 117

Type Vega
Model 5B
Reg NC 105N, NR 105N
Mfg late 1929
Eng P&W Wasp C #2038
ATC 227

C/n 117: Stanavo Eagle *becomes Costa's* Crystal City.

Sold to STANDARD OIL DEVELOPMENT CO., N.Y.C. (1929–35). Used for testing and evaluation of aviation fuels, oils, and lubricants, and for advertising by affiliated Standard Oil of New Jersey and the Stavano Specification Board. Flown by Maj. Edwin E. Aldrin, Robert Ellis, Will W. White, and other Stavano pilots. Originally prd red, white trim; later with full-length simulated eagle paint job, white on red, and still later red on white. Named *No. 6*, and unofficially called the Stanavo Eagle, and The Flying Trademark. JOSEPH COSTA, Corning, N.Y. (1936–37). Prd white, named *Crystal City*; prepared for South American flight with possible South Atlantic hop to Portugal. Washed out Conceição do Serro, Minas Gerais, Brazil, 1/15/37. Costa unhurt.

C/n 118

Type Vega
Model 5B
Reg NC 106N, NR 869E
Mfg late 1929
Eng —
ATC 227

Sold to STANDARD OIL DEVELOPMENT CO., N.Y.C. (1929–33). Standard Oil's Vega c/n 20 traded in to LAC and its engine, P&W Wasp CB #853, installed in this ship. Flown by Stanavo pilots to set several intercity speed records. Originally prd white, red lettering; then with eagle outline, and later with full-length simulated eagle paint job, red on white. Named *No. 1*, and also called Stanavo Eagle and The Flying Trademark, like its sister ship c/n 117. Used 1930 by Foreign Advertising & Service Bureau of New York, with pilots Will W. White and Clement McMullen for goodwill flight N.Y.C.–Buenos Aires 2/14–19/30. Set speed records every leg of 51-hour-36-min flight. JIMMIE MATTERN, INC., Chicago, Ill. (1933). Landing gear, stabilizer, gas tanks of c/n 69 *(q.v.)* installed. Registration changed to that of c/n 69, NR 869E, but full-length eagle paint job retained, red on blue and white. Named *Century of Progress.* Wasp C #1677 installed. Mattern made first N.Y.C.-Norway nonstop flight 6/3–4/33. Went on in round-the-world solo flight attempt; cracked up 80 miles west of Anadyr, Siberia, 6/33. Mattern unhurt. Plane abandoned.

C/n 119

Type Vega
Model 5B
Reg NC 102W
Mfg 3/30
Eng P&W Wasp #1427
ATC 227

Sold to ALASKA-WASHINGTON AIRWAYS, INC., Seattle (1930); airline operation on floats. Caught fire and burned after forced landing Kingston, Wash., 8/4/30. No injuries.

C/n 120

Type Vega
Model 5B
Reg NC 103W
Mfg 3/4/30
Eng P&W Wasp #1555
ATC 227

Sold to ALASKA-WASHINGTON AIRWAYS, INC., Seattle (1930); airline operation on floats. Lost out of Prince Rupert, B.C., 10/28/30, w/pilot Robert Renehan, 2 others.

C/n 121

Type Vega
Model 5B
Reg NC 104W, XA-BKF, XA-FAF (Mexico)
Mfg 4/30
Eng P&W Wasp C #2896
ATC 227

Sold to WEDELL-WILLIAMS AIR SERVICE, INC., Patterson, La. (1930–36). Converted to Vega 5C under ATC 384 on 3/20/35; rear cabin metal-lined. NORTH AMERICAN AVIATION, INC., N.Y.C. (1936). CHARLES H. BABB, Glendale, Calif. (1938), with Wasp SD #4351X. LINEAS AEREAS MINERAS, S.A. (LAMSA), Mazatlán, Sin., Mexico (1939–44); cost $7,500; prd dark green, ivory trim. Damaged in hurricane which collapsed hanger roof Mazatlán 10/43; rebuilt in LAMSA shops at Torreón. LINEAS AEREAS MEXICANAS, S.A. (also LAMSA), México, D.F. (1944–46). CAPT. CARLOS CERVANTES PEREZ, Ensenada, B.C., Mexico (1946–47); PEDRO MARRIQUE FILATTI, México, D.F. (1947–?). Rented to Servicio Aéreo Panini for service between México, D.F., and Tlapa, Gro. Final disposition unknown.

C/n 122

Type Vega
Model 5B/5C
Reg NC 105W, NR 105W
Mfg 6/30
Eng P&W Wasp S 3088
ATC 227/384

Sold to F. C. HALL, Oklahoma City (1930–32). Prd white, blue trim. Named *Winnie Mae* (Later *The Winnie Mae of Oklahoma).* Flown by Hall's personal pilot, Wiley Post. Won Los Angeles–Chicago nonstop race of 1930 NAR. Record flight around the world with Post and Harold Gatty, 6/23–7/1/31. WILEY POST, Oklahoma City (1932). W. M. FAIN, Oklahoma City (1932–33); FAIN & POST DRILLING CO., Oklahoma City (1933–35). Acc Chickasha, Okla. 4/22/33. Repaired. Flown by Post on record solo flight around the world 7/15–22/33. Badly damaged in acc Quincy, Ill. 9/21/33. Rebuilt by Braniff at Oklahoma City. Used by Post in high-altitude flight experiments, 1934–35. Equipped with dropable l/g and belly skid. WILEY POST, Oklahoma City (1935). Purchased by Act of Congress 1935 and on prominent display at NATIONAL AIR AND SPACE MUSEUM, Washington, D.C.

C/n 123

Type Vega
Model 5B
Reg NC 106W
Mfg 4/30
Eng P&W Wasp C #2898
ATC 227

Sold to JULIAN OIL & ROYALTIES CO., Oklahoma City (1930–31). Named *The Cherokee*, piloted by L. E. Gray: W. M. NEWTON, Oklahoma City (1931). BRANIFF AIRWAYS, INC., Oklahoma City (1931–34); in service on airline routes. Crashed near Columbia, Mo., 12/8/34. Pilot Lewis Bowen killed.

C/n 124

Type Vega
Model 5B
Reg NC 107W, XA-BFR (Mexico)
Mfg 4/30
Eng P&W Wasp #3160
ATC 227

Sold to W. T. PONDER, Dallas (1931–32). BOWEN AIR LINES, Fort Worth (1932–36); converted to Vega 5C under ATC 384 as of 4/22/35. LINEAS AEREAS MINERAS, S.A., Mazatlán, Sin., Mexico (1937–38), with Wasp C #2909; cost $5000; ptd red, ivory wings. Flown on LAMSA airline routes. Crashed México, D.F., 5/5/38. Pilot Miguel Angel Padilla killed, five passengers injured.

C/n 125

Type Vega
Model 5B
Reg NC 152W, XA-DAH (Mexico)
Mfg early 1930
Eng P&W Wasp C #3161
ATC 227

Sold to BEARDSLEY & PIPER, Chicago (1930–42); used by partners of engineering firm as executive transport; ptd red, gold trim. LINEAS AEREAS MINERAS, S.A. (LAMSA), Mazatlán, Sin., Mexico (1942–44); ptd brown, with white arrow; flown on airline routes. Cracked up San Luis Potosí 5/11/44. No injuries. Parts used to maintain other Vegas for successor airline (after 1944) Líneas Aéreas Mexicanas, S.A. (also LAMSA), México, D.F.

C/n 126

Type Vega
Model 5B
Reg NC 160W
Mfg 7/29/30
Eng P&W Wasp #3164
ATC 227

Sold to TEMPLE BOWEN, BOWEN AIR LINES, Fort Worth (1930). Destroyed by tornado three days after factory completion date at Houston 8/1/30.

C/n 127

Type Vega
Model 5B
Reg NC 161W, XA–DAM (Mexico)
Mfg 7/30
Eng P&W Wasp C #3167
ATC 227

Sold to BOWEN AIR LINES, Fort Worth (1930–36); flown on Bowen routes, converted to Vega 5C under ATC 384 as of 4/22/35. CHEMICAL PROCESS CO., Breckenridge, Texas (1937–?). CHARLES H. BABB, Glendale, Calif. (1942), with Wasp SCI #5012. LINEAS AEREAS MINERAS, S.A. (LAMSA), Mazatlán, Sin., Mexico (1943–44); LINEAS AEREAS MEXICANAS, S.A. (also LAMSA), México, D.F. (1944–49). Dismantled *c.* 6/49.

C/n 128

Type Vega
Model 5B
Reg NC 162W
Mfg 7/30
Eng P&W Wasp #3200
ATC 227

Sold to WILLIAM H. DUNNING, SEQUOIA OIL CO., Fort Worth, and Beverly Hills (1930–32). Windows blocked out and bore name of "Air Express & Trading Co." (1930). A. WESTON KIMBALL, KIMBALL FLYING SERVICE, Sacramento (1932–33); J. B. MILLER, Los Angeles (1933). SHELL AVIATION CO., LTD., San Francisco (1933); named *Shell Oil No. 6.* Plane "practically washed out" acc near Pasco, Wash., 11/11/33; pilot William G. Fletcher killed. Rebuilt with new fuselage, etc., for CHARLES H. BABB, Burbank, Calif. (1934). H. C. LIPPIATT, Burbank (1935). HANS MIROW, MIROW AIR SERVICE, Nome (1935–42). Accs Nome 4/28/36, Nome 4/8/38, Anchorage 4/16/40; repaired and rebuilt in Seattle each time. ALASKA STAR AIRLINES, Anchorage (1942–44); ALASKA AIRLINES, INC., Anchorage (1944). Crashed and burned South Fork of Kuskokwin River 8/2/44. Pilot, four passengers escaped.

C/n 129

Type Vega
Model 5B
Reg NC 176W
Mfg 9/30
Eng P&W Wasp #3164
ATC 227

Sold to BOWEN AIR LINES, Fort Worth (1930–35); airliner on Bowen routes. Accs Houston, 12/11/30, and Jewett, Texas, 1/22/31; repaired. VARNEY AIR TRANSPORT, El Paso (1935–36). Crashed Rattlesnake Butte, near Walsenburg, Colo., 9/28/36. Pilot C. H. Chidlaw and two passengers killed.

C/n 130

Type Air Express
Model Special
Reg NR 974Y, NC 974Y
Mfg 5/31
Eng P&W Wasp #3899
ATC none

Originally ordered by Louis Wasmer, Spokane, Wash., and begun in mid-1930 with reg 177W (unapplied). Order canceled; ship not completed until 1931. Sold to ATLANTIC EXHIBITION CO., INC., N.Y.C. (1931–32), for transatlantic flight to be attempted by Laura Ingalls; flight not made. O. J. WHITNEY, INC., Jackson Heights, N.Y. (1932–33). LAURA INGALLS, Garden City, N.Y. (1933–36); converted to Air Express 3 under ATC 102 as of 5/1/33, with Wasp #1670. Flown by Miss Ingalls around South America, 2/28–4/25/34, for which she received Harmon Trophy. CHARLES H. BABB, Glendale Calif. (1936). CHOJIN & TAKAMOTO MASAKATSU, Alameda, Calif. (1936–40) (these brothers planned, but never made, a nonstop flight to Japan). RICHARD W. SNELL, Berkeley, Calif. (1940–41); PACIFIC AIRMOTIVE CORP., Oakland, Calif. (1941–42). Staked out during WW II near Reno; destroyed *c.* 1942 by windstorm.

C/n 131

Type Air Express
Model 3
Reg 182W (canceled)
Mfg mid-1930
Eng —
ATC 102

Ordered by Sam Wilson, Spokane, Wash., who placed the order through Vance Breece, then a salesman–test pilot for LAC and DAC. Apparently never completed.

C/n 132

Type Vega Executive
Model 5A
Reg NC 904Y
Mfg mid-1930
Eng P&W Wasp #3195
ATC 93

Sold to MCALEER MANUFACTURING CO. Detroit (1930–34); ptd black, yellow trim, named *Miss McAleer;* used for advertising and executive transport by industrial polish firm. Acc Flint, Mich., 6/24/31; repaired by DAC. Flown by Capt. Russell A. Young. CENTRAL AIRLINES, INC., Pittsburgh (1934); converted to airline service for their routes. Crashed near Everett, Pa., 9/12/34, on charter flight with tear gas from Pittsburgh to Providence, R.I. Pilot (CA operations mgr. Theodore Taney) killed when chute failed.

C/n 133

Type Vega
Model 5B
Reg NC 905Y, XA–DEB (Mexico)
Mfg 9/30
Eng P&W Wasp C #3201
ATC 227

Sold to Kessler Oil & Gas Co., Oklahoma City (1930), pilot Ted Hurlbut. Ben H. Wofford, Tulsa (1931). F. C. Hall, Oklahoma City (1931–32); ptd white, blue trim; named *Winnie Mae of Oklahoma City, Okla.*—the third and last of Hall's Vegas of similar name. Pilot for first three owners also Frank Hover. Hal Roach Studios, Culver City (1932–33); Hanford's Tri-State Airlines, Inc. (later Hanford Airlines, Inc.), Sioux City, Iowa, and Kansas City (1933–38). Flown on Midwest routes. Name changed to Mid-Continent Airlines, Kansas City (1938–41). Charles H. Babb, Glendale, Calif. (1942). Lineas Aereas Mineras, S.A. Mazatlán, Sin., Mexico (1943–44); cost $7,500; ptd red, white trim. Acc Durango 4/1/43; repaired in LAMSA shops at Torreón. Lineas Aereas Mexicanas, S.A. (also LAMSA), México, D.F. (1944–45?); damaged acc Tayoltita, Dur., *c.* 1945. Disassembled and parts sold (*see* c/n 60).

C/n 134

Type Vega
Model 5B
Reg NC 926Y, NR 926Y
Mfg 1930
Eng P&W Wasp #2100
ATC 227

Sold to Shell Oil Co., San Francisco (1930–35). Ptd orange-yellow, red trim; named *No. 4;* flown by Shell aviation mgr. Maj. John Macready and others. Lt. Felix Waitkus, American-Lithuanian Trans-Atlantic Flight Assn., Chicago (1935); ptd white, gold trim; named *Lituanica II.* Attempted nonstop flight N.Y.C.-Kaunas, Lithuania. Cracked up near Ballinrode, Ireland, 9/22/35; Waitkus unhurt. Rebuilt in Lithuania. Lithuanian Air Corps, Kaunas (1936–?). Supposed to have later been taken to Moscow when government taken over by U.S.S.R. in 1940.

C/n 135

Type Vega
Model DL-1
Reg NC 497H
Mfg 2/27/30 (Detroit)
Eng P&W Wasp #2095
ATC none

First Vega assembled by DAC, using Duralumin fuselage built at Detroit and wooden wing shipped from LAC. Used as demonstrator by DAC (1930–31). Used by Amelia Earhart to set three NAA speed/load trials records for women 6/30. Acc Lenox, Tenn., 7/23/30, pilot Luke Christopher of NAA. Rebuilt and remodeled by DAC as Vega DL–1B under ATC 308, with wire-braced Hi-Speed l/g. Leased for use by New York & Western Airlines, Inc., Pittsburgh (1931), and Transcontinental & Western Air, Inc., Kansas City (1931–32). Sold to Transcontinental & Western Air, Inc., N.Y.C. (1932–34); flown on TWA airline routes; their #253. Cracked up St. James, Mo., 1/31/34. Not rebuilt.

C/n 136

Type Vega
Model DL-1B
Reg NC 483M
Mfg 2/27/30 (Detroit)
Eng P&W Wasp
ATC 308

Demonstrator for DAC (1930–31), received ATC during this period. Under lease to Pittsburgh Airways, Inc. (New York & Western Airlines, Inc.), Pittsburgh (1931). Sold to New York & Western Airlines, Inc., Pittsburgh (1931). Repossessed by DAC 1931. Transcontinental & Western Air, Inc., Kansas City (1932–34). Run into by another plane on ground, Oklahoma City 12/4/32; repaired by TWA at Kansas City. Varney Speed Lines, Inc., El Paso (1934–35); Vat, Inc., El Paso (1935–37). Washed out El Paso 4/27/37. No injuries.

C/n 137

Type Vega
Model DL-1B
Reg NC 288W
Mfg 6/30 (Detroit)
Eng P&W Wasp
ATC 308

Demonstrator for DAC (1930–31). Sold to New York & Western Airlines, Inc., Pittsburgh (1931); repossessed by DAC (1931). Transcontinental & Western Air, Inc., Kansas City (1932–33); Hanford's Tri-State Airlines, Inc., Sioux City, Iowa (1934–35). Varney Air Transport, El Paso (1935–37), succeeded by Continental Air Lines, Inc., Denver (1937–41). Jerome Martin, El Paso (1941–47). New Mexico Board of Education, Las Cruces, N.M. (1948–?); used for vocational education; dismantled, scrapped.

C/n 138

Type Vega
Model 5C
Reg NC 934Y
Mfg late 1930
Eng P&W Wasp #3463
ATC 384

Sold to Margery Durant, Old Westbury, L.I., N.Y. (1930–33), for personal transport, pilot Charles La Jotte; named *Ariel.* Accs Roosevelt Field, N.Y., 12/22/30, and Santa Barbara, Calif., 3/22/31; repaired. Flown 1931 on pleasure trip to points in Europe, Africa, the Near East. Robert L. Copsey, Mercer Air Service, Newark (later

C/n 135: Assembly of first Vega with Duralumin fuselage, at Detroit Aircraft Company's plant in Detroit.

C/n 136: Second DL-1 Vega with TWA. After being damaged by ground collision with another plane, its new tail had a mix-up in painted numbers.

Summit, N.J.) (1933–34). CENTRAL AIRLINES, INC., Pittsburgh (1934). Washed out Pittsburgh 6/1/34.

C/n 139

Type Vega
Model 5B
Reg NC 997N, XA–BIT (Mexico)
Mfg 3/31 (Patterson, La.)
Eng P&W Wasp
ATC 227

Parts shipped to Patterson, La., and assembled by WEDELL-WILLIAMS AIR SERVICE, INC., Patterson and New Orleans (1931–36); flown on airline routes. Converted to Vega 5C under ATC 384 as of 3/3/35. CHARLES H. BABB, Glendale, Calif. (1937). TRANSPORTES AEREAS DE CHIAPAS, S.A., México, D.F. (1937); used as TACSA airliner. Run into by truck, Minatitlán, Veracruz, 9/10/37; repaired. FRITZ BIELER, México, D.F. (1937–42). Bieler hired to fly for Cía. Aeronáutica Francisco Sarabia, S.A., (successor to TACSA) during an emergency, 1942. Because of owner's German citizenship, Vega impounded by Mexican government 1942; overhauled by Cía. Mexicana de Aviación shops, and used by Minister of Communications. COL. ROBERTO FIERRO, MÉXICO, D.F. (1944–45). CIA. TRANSPORTES AEREAS DE SONORA, S.A., Guaymas, Son. (1945–46). Declared unairworthy 1946. Presumed scrapped.

C/n 140

Type Sirius
Model 8 (later 8 Special as seaplane)
Reg NR 211
Mfg 10–11/29
Eng P&W Wasp #2099
ATC none (300)

Developed by LAC to specifications of Col. Charles Lindbergh. Begun as an Explorer (temporary reg 139N), not eligible for NR reg. Completed 11/29 as Sirius 8. Sold to CHARLES A. LINDBERGH, N.Y.C. (1930–34); ptd black, orange wings. Carefully tested by Lindbergh before record transcontinental flight 4/20/30. First Lockheed to be fitted with sliding cockpit canopies. WC 1820 #13461 installed 8/30. Converted to Sirius 8 Special as seaplane, early 1931. Flown on Lindbergh survey flights, Pan American Airways 7–10/31, and 7–12/33, covering North Pacific, North Atlantic, and South Atlantic routes. Damaged Hankow, China, 10/2/31; returned to U.S. and rebuilt by LAC. New WC engine and floats with fuel tanks installed; ptd black, red wings. Finally named *Tingmissartoq* 1933. Presented 1934 to AMERICAN MUSEUM OF NATURAL HISTORY, N.Y.C. On exhibit there, and at AIR FORCE MUSEUM, Wright-Patterson AFB, Ohio (1934–60). NATIONAL AIR MUSEUM SMITHSONIAN INSTITUTION, Washington, D.C. (1960—); on prominent exhibition.

C/n 141

Type Sirius
Model 8
Reg NC 349V
Mfg 2/10/30
Eng P&W Wasp C #2100
ATC 300

SHELL OIL CO. (later SHELL AVIATION CO, LTD.), San Francisco (1930). Ptd orange-yellow and red. Flown by Shell's aviation mgr. Maj. John A. Macready on unofficial speed trials and cross-country trips. Developed wing flutter at air show, Tracy, Calif., 10/30 and returned to LAC. Dismantled and scrapped 12/30.

C/n 142

Type Sirius
Model 8
Reg NR 12W
Mfg 3/13/30
Eng P&W Wasp C #2110
ATC 300

Built for use of Mexican flyer Roberto Fierro. Flown as demonstrator by LAC and DAC. Crashed Roscommon, Mich., 4/25/30. Pilot Herbert J. Fahy killed; passenger (Mrs. Claire Fahy) unhurt.

C/n 143

Type Sirius (later Altair 8D)
Model 8A
Reg NC 13W
Mfg 3/13/30
Eng P&W Wasp #2854
ATC 300

Sold to JOAN FAY SHANKLE (Mrs. Clarence E.), Boston; Ft. Sill, Okla., and Tubac, Ariz. (1930–36). Flown by both Capt. & Mrs. Shankle on cross-country trips and by Mrs. Shankle in 1930 NAR. Converted to Altair 8D under ATC Memo 2–423 of 10/8/32. Acquired and flown by Clarence Chamberlin, Jersey City, but registered to LOUISE ASHBY (CHAMBERLIN), Fort Fairfield, Maine, & East Orange, N.J. (1936–40). Chamberlin named ship *Miss Stratosphere,* planned new Atlantic flight but did not make it. Sold through broker CHARLES H. BABB, N.Y.C. (1940). Reported acquired by U.S. Army Engineer's Office for use outside the U.S. Said to have been cracked up by Army pilot during WW II in vicinity of Bakersfield, Calif.

C/n 144

Type Sirius
Model 8
Reg NC 14W
Mfg 3/13/30
Eng P&W Wasp C #2140
ATC 300

Demonstrator for LAC and DAC, pilot Herbert J. Fahy. Washed out St. Louis 4/12/30. Pilot Stafford L. (Casey) Lambert and passenger Herb Condie left via parachute when ailerons became detached in flight.

C/n 145

Type Sirius (later Altair)
Model 8A
Reg NC 15W, NR 15W
Mfg 3/13/30
Eng P&W Wasp C #2851
ATC 300

Experimental Sirius demonstrator for LAC (1930–31). Flight tests as regular Sirius 4/30, and with new type fin and rudder 7/30. Converted to Altair & reg NR on 5/29/31. Sold to JAMES GOODWIN HALL, N.Y.C. (1931). Ptd yellow and black; named *The Crusader,* for anti-Prohibition organization in which Hall was an officer. Used for intercity speed record flights and in 1931 NAR. Crashed Meiers Corner, Staten Island, N.Y., 9/29/31. Passenger Peter J. Brady and housewife on ground killed; Hall miraculously escaped unhurt.

C/n 146

Type Sirius
Model 8A
Reg NC 16W
Mfg 3/13/30
Eng P&W Wasp C #2110
ATC 300

Sold to STAFFORD L. LAMBERT, Sappington Mo. (1930–32), for sports flying. THE TEXAS CO., N.Y.C., (1932–33); ptd red and white; named *Texaco 16;* flown by J. D. Jernigan. WACO SALES OF NEW YORK, INC., Roosevelt Field, N.Y. (1933–34); DIVERSIFIED SHARES, INC., Cleveland (later Dubois, Wyo.) (1934–35). CUBAN NAVAL AIR FORCE, Havana (1935–45); ptd. with naval insignia; rear cockpit closed off; named *4 de Septiembre.* Flown by Lt. Antonio Menendez y Palaez from Havana to Brazil, and across the South Atlantic to Seville, Spain, 1–2/36. Reported destroyed in hangar fire Havana 1945.

C/n 147

Type Explorer
Model 7 (special)
Reg NR 100W
Mfg 3/30
Eng P&W Wasp C #2853
ATC None

Longer wing than contemporary Sirius models, and single cockpit; 900-gal gas capacity. Built for projected Tacoma-Tokyo flight by Harold Bromley, named *City of Tacoma;* third plane of this name (*see* c/n 2 and c/n 116). During tests by LAC, crashed Muroc Dry Lake, Calif., 5/24/30. LAC test pilot H. W. Catlin killed.

C/n 148

Type Explorer
Model 7 (special)
Reg NR 101W
Mfg 4/30
Eng P&W Wasp C #3172
ATC None

Originally built for projected Paris-N.Y.C. flight by Col. Arthur C. Goebel. Single cockpit; 800-gal gas capacity; ptd. blue and yellow; named *Yankee Doodle*. Goebel did not take delivery. Sold to PURE OIL CO., Chicago (1930). Used for advertising, and prepared for flight from N.Y.C. to Paris (or Rome) with pilot Roy W. Ammel; ptd blue, white lettering; named *Blue Flash*. Damaged in ground fire Gila Bend, Ariz., summer 1930; repaired at LAC. Ammel made first nonstop flight N.Y.C.–Canal Zone 11/9-10/30. Cracked up Ancon, C.Z., 11/21/30; Ammel injured. Wing salvaged and eventually incorporated in Orion c/n 195 *(q.v.)*.

C/n 149

Type Sirius
Model 8
Reg XB–ADA (Mexico)
Mfg 4/30
Eng P&W Wasp #2889
ATC 300

Sold to COL. ROBERTO FIERRO, MEXICAN ARMY AIR FORCE, México, D.F. (1930–36). For use in special long-distance and record attempts; ptd. white, sun red trim; named *Anahuac*. Fierro and mechanic-copilot Arnulfo Cortes made first nonstop flight N.Y.C.–México, D.F., 6/21/30. Used for various duties by Mexican Army Air Force, with their insignia. Eventually became Gen. Fierro's personal plane in recognition of his flight. Sold to Spanish agents 1936, rumored price $25,000. Flown by SPANISH REPUBLICAN AIR FORCE (1937–?) Reported lost on Basque front prior to 8/22/37.

C/n 150

Type Sirius
Model 8C
Reg NR 116W, NC 116W
Mfg 4/18/30
Eng P&W Wasp C #3087
ATC none

Special model called Sport Cabin Sirius with both tandem cockpits and two-place cabin. Sold to HUGO WALTER BLUMENTHAL, N.Y.C. (1930–32). Reg NC under ATC Memo 2–374 of 8/10/31. Ptd red and white; piloted by Jimmy Collins until Blumenthal learned to fly. BERNARR MACFADDEN, N.Y.C. (1932–33); KATHERINE DAUFKIRCH, East Elmont, N.Y. (1933); INTERSTATE AERONAUTICAL CORP., Cleveland (1933–35). Involved three accs, final one reported at Detroit 9/14/35. Apparently kept (but never repaired) by SKYWAYS, INC., Cleveland (1935–37) and SAMUEL R. SAGUE, Cleveland (1937).

C/n 151

Type Sirius
Model 8A
Reg NC 117W
Mfg 4/18/30
Eng P&W Wasp C #3103
ATC 300

Sold to AIR SERVICES, INC., Roosevelt Field, N.Y. (1930–32); ptd white, red trim. EDWARD H. CONERTON, Mineola, N.Y. (1932–33); JOHN ENGLISH, Schenectady (1933). Cracked up Raleigh, N.C., 1933. FRANK CORDOVA, Roosevelt Field (1933); ANTHONY STINIS, Floyd Bennett Field, N.Y. (1933–34). Repaired; Wasp #1921 installed 5/34. PARAMOUNT PRODUCTIONS, INC., Jersey City (1934–36). UNITED AIR SERVICES, LTD. (A. PAUL MANTZ), Burbank, Calif. (1936–40); modified as photo plane, witth swivel cockpit camera and wing cameras 9/37; Wasp SCI #1815 installed 7/38. Crashed after midair collision Downey, Calif., 5/9/40. Pilot Walter Quinton and two passengers killed.

C/n 152

Type Sirius (later Altair 8D)
Model 8A (later 8 Special)
Reg NR 118W, NC 118W, X 118W, VH-USB (Australia), G-ADUS (G.B.)
Mfg 7/21/30
Eng P&W Wasp #3104
ATC 300

Built for CAPT. GEORGE R. HUTCHINSON, Baltimore, Md. (1930–31), to be used on New York–Paris record flight attempt. Forward cockpit closed off, special tanks; named *Richmond, Virginia, U.S.A.* Cracked up Los Angeles 8/2/30; flight plans abandoned. Rebuilt by LAC. DOUGLAS FAIRBANKS & VICTOR FLEMING, Beverly Hills, Calif. (1931), for sports flying by the actor and director. VICTOR FLEMING, Culver City, Calif. (1932–34). Converted to Sirius 8 Special, reg under ATC Memo 2–400 of 2/4/32. Sold back to LAC in 1934 and converted to Altair 8D with Wasp SE #5222 installed, and new wing with 2° dihedral. SIR CHARLES KINGSFORD-SMITH, Longueville, N.S.W., Australia (1934–35); rebuilt to qualify for MacRobertson Race London-Melbourne, 10/34; ptd blue and silver, named *Anzac*. Shipped to Australia, renamed *Lady Southern Cross*; withdrawn from race. Flown by Kingsford-Smith and Capt. P. G. Taylor on first Australia-U.S. flight 10/21–11/4/34. Altered under ATC Memo 2–423 and engine modified to SC1 to conform to British airworthiness requirements. Plane shipped to England 1935. Attempted London-Melbourne flight 11/35, disappeared over Bay of Bengal 11/8/35 with Kingsford-Smith and Tommy Pethybridge. Wheel from ship found floating off Burma 6/1/37.

C/n 153

Type Sirius (later Altair), YIC-25 (U.S. Army)
Model 8A
Reg X 119W, NR 119W, A.C. 32–393
Mfg 4/18/30
Eng P&W Wasp C
ATC 300

Regular Sirius built by LAC. Approved 9/19/30 for experiments with retractable l/g: first Lockheed to be equipped with fully retractable l/g. Tests made by Vance Breese and Marshall Headle. Officially converted to Altair, with Wasp B, as of 3/7/31. Turned over to U.S. ARMY AIR CORPS, Bolling Field, Washington, D.C. (1931–32), for official testing by Corps. Flown by Capt. Ira C. Eaker on crosscountry flights, and in both the Bendix and Thompson races at 1931 NAR. Fitted with P&W R-1340-17 #920. Ptd blue and yellow, Army striping on tail, but civil reg retained. Officially acquired by US-AAC 11/31 and stationed at Wright Field, Ohio. Damaged in belly-landing, written off 6/32. Hulk destroyed in tests of bottled carbon dioxide fire extinguishers Wright Field 9/27/32. Total flying hours: 153.

C/n 154

Type Vega
Model DL-1B
Reg NC 8497
Mfg 1930 (Detroit)
Eng P&W Wasp
ATC 308

Demonstrator for DAC (1930–31). Leased to Braniff Airways, Inc., Oklahoma City (summer 1931). On return ferry flight to DAC, crashed Chicago 7/12/31. Pilot Chester R. Bailes and a passenger killed.

C/n 155

Type Vega
Model DL-1 Special
Reg G-ABGK (G.B.), VH-UVK (Australia), A42-1 (RAAF)
Mfg 10/30 (Detroit)
Eng P&W Wasp C1
ATC Memo 2–316 of 1/3/31

Sold to LT. COMDR. GLEN KIDSTON, London (1930–31); ptd white, black trim; to be used for sport and commercial flying. Set London-Paris intercity record 1931; also new London-Capetown speed record 3/31–4/6/31, with Kidston, pilot Owen Carthcart-Jones, a radio operator and a mechanic. Use of plane administered by a trust after Kidston's death (1931–34). H. C. MILLER, Perth, Australia (1934–?). Only Lockheed entry in the MacRobertson Race London-Melbourne 10/34; flown by James Woods and D. C. T. Bennett; named *Puck*. Cracked up Aleppo, Syria, 10/21/34; Woods and Bennett injured. Eventually shipped to Australia and rebuilt. ROYAL AUSTRALIAN AIR FORCE, Melbourne (1942–45); impressed into RAAF service as auxiliary plane. Scrapped 10/45.

C/n 156

Type Vega
Model DL-1
Reg NC 8495, 239M
Mfg 11/30 (Detroit)
Eng P&W Wasp #3537
ATC 308

Sold to BOWEN AIR LINES, Fort Worth (1930–32); THE TEXAS COMPANY, N.Y.C. (1932); STAFFORD L. LAMBERT, Brooklyn, N.Y., & Minocqua, Wis. (1932), with P&W Wasp #2909. STANDARD OIL CO. OF NEW JERSEY, N.Y.C., (1932–34). Equipped with Air Wheels, given Stanavo Eagle paint job. Flown by James Mattern, Toronto-N.Y.C. 7/30/33, making first international radio broadcast from an airplane, en route. CENTRAL AIRLINES, INC., Pittsburgh (1934); BRANIFF AIRWAYS, INC., Oklahoma City (1934–37). Braniff #10. GENERAL TIRE & RUBBER CO., Akron (1937–40). Re-reg. NC 239M; flown by Roy W. Brown. Named: *Miss Streamline II*. Tested with pneumatic engine suspension, using P&W Wasp S1D1 #5326. BEECH AIRCRAFT CO., Wichita (1940); HARRY A. HAMMILL, Austin, Texas (1940–41); CHARLES H. BABB, Glendale, Calif. (1941). Acc Dallas, Texas, 11/6/41. Both wings broken. Not repaired.

C/n 157

Type Vega
Model DL–1
Reg NC 8496, XA-DAY (Mexico)
Mfg 11/30 (Detroit)
Eng P&W Wasp
ATC 308

Sold to BOWEN AIR LINES, Fort Worth (1930–35); GLEN HARROUN, Fort Worth (1935); EDWIN W. RITCHEY, Fort Worth (1936–41); CHARLES H. BABB CO., Glendale, Calif. (1942). LINEAS AEREAS MINERAS, S.A. (LAMSA), Mazatlán, Sin., Mexico (1943–44), with Wasp C1 #3163. Prd light blue on bare Duralumin. LINEAS AEREAS MEXICANAS, S.A. (also LAMSA), México, D.F. (1944–46?). Cracked up Parral, Chihuahua, *c.* 1945–46. No injuries. Sent to LAMSA's Torreón shops, but not repaired.

C/n 158

Type Vega, YIC-12 (USAAC)
Model DL-1
Reg A.C. 31-405
Mfg late 1930 (Detroit)
Eng P&W Wasp R-1340-7
ATC —

Standard Detroit-Lockheed Vega DL model for Army command transport evaluation. Sold to U.S. ARMY AIR CORPS, Dayton (1931–35). Tested at Wright Field, Dayton, then assigned to Bolling Field, Washington, D.C. (1930–32) Assigned to 36th Pursuit Sq., 8th Pursuit Grp., Langley Field, Va. (1932–35), as "#99"; later with 59th Service Sq. as "#103." Scrapped at Langley Field as of 5/16/35. Total flying hours: 999.

C/n 159

Type Vega Y1C-17 (USAAC)
Model DL-1B Special
Reg A.C. 31-408
Mfg 12/30 (Detroit)
Eng P&W Wasp R-1340-17
ATC —

Single–P Speed Vega, with Hi-Speed, wire-braced l/g, doughnut-tail wheel, cabin gas tanks, etc. Duralumin fuselage left bare, yellow wing and army insignia. Sold for evaluation to U.S. ARMY AIR CORPS, Dayton (1930–31). Assigned Wright Field, Ohio; later to Bolling Field, Washington, D.C. Used for attempted transcontinental record flight by Capt. Ira C. Eaker 3/31. Fastest USAAC plane of its time: rated 221 mph. Cracked up in forced landing Tolu, Ky., 3/10/31; Eaker unhurt. Wreckage taken to Wright Field; scrapped 4/22/31. Total flying hours: 33.

C/n 160

Type Vega
Model 5C
Reg NC 972Y
Mfg 5/31
Eng P&W Wasp #3898
ATC 384

Wing had been sent to DAC, returned to LAC for manufacturing. Sold to PARKS AIR COLLEGE, East St. Louis, Ill. (1931); PHILLIPS PETROLEUM CO., Bartlesville, Okla. (1931–36). AERO TRANSPORT CORP. Glendale, Calif. (1936–40), used for charter and movie work. E. DUKE GARTNER, Palm Springs, Calif. (1940–41); HERBERT L. WHITE, CALIFORNIA AIRCRAFT CORP., Van Nuys, Calif. (1941–43). U.S. ENGINEER'S OFFICE, WAR DEPARTMENT, San Francisco (1943), to be operated outside U.S. Destroyed in hangar fire Van Nuys 10/10/43.

C/n 161

Type Vega
Model DL-1B Special
Reg NC 12288
Mfg 3/33
Eng P&W Wasp SC1
ATC Memo 2–448 of 5/29/33

Richard Von Hake, laid off as chief engineer of LAC, paid $2,000 to DAC receivers for a metal Vega fuselage, completed the plane from Lockheed parts in Burbank, and turned it over to LAC for sale. Sold to JOHN MORRELL & CO., Ottumwa, Iowa (1933–34); pilot Cliff Kysor, used for executive transport and advertising meat products; prd two shades of green, red insignia; named *Morrell's Pride II*. BRANIFF AIRWAYS, INC., Oklahoma City (1934–39); converted and used as airliner. LLOYD EARL, Fort Worth (1939–42). C. F. LYTLE, GREEN CONSTRUCTION CO., and TEXAS & NORTHERN AIRWAYS, Sioux City, Iowa (1943–44); cost $10,000; used for personnel transport in construction of Whitehorse Division, Alaska Military Highway. NORTHERN AIR SERVICE, Fairbanks (1944–48), with Federal skis. NORTHERN CONSOLIDATED AIRLINES, Anchorage (1948–52), used on air routes, with Northwest skis. RUSSELL RIVERS, Fairbanks (1952–62); MARVIN M. GREENLEE, Fairbanks and Compton, Calif. (1962–64); MINT AVIATION COMPANY, JACK LOWE & ROBERT L. TAYLOR, Ottumwa, Iowa (1964–68); ROBERT L. TAYLOR, Ottumwa, Iowa (1968–83); TOM A. THOMAS, MID-AMERICA AIR GROUP, Frederick, Okla. (1983—).

C/n 162

Never assigned, never built.

C/n 163

Never assigned, never built.

C/n 164

Never assigned, never built.

C/n 165

Type Sirius (later Altair DL–2A), Y1C–23 (USAAC)
Model DL-2
Reg X 8494, NR 8494, A.C. 32–232
Mfg 8/30 (Detroit)
Eng P&W Wasp C #2036
ATC 378

Built as Sirius for experiments with metal fuselage by DAC (1930–31). Converted to metal Altair DL–2A, with Wasp E, retractable l/g, and 186-gal gas capacity as of 4/27/31. Sold to U.S. ARMY AIR CORPS, Washington, D.C. (1931–42). Command transport for use of Asst. Secy. of War F. Trubee Davison, and Chief of Air Corps Gen. James E. Fechet; pilot usually Capt. Ira C. Eaker, also Lt. Elwood R. Quesada. Official conversion to Altair under ATC Memo 2–386 of 10/17/31. After tests at Wright Field, Ohio, assigned to Bolling Field, Washington, D.C. (1931–38); Chanute Field, Ill. (1938). Condemned for further flying 9/23/38. Scrapped 6/42. Total flying hours: 1,075.

C/n 166

Type Sirius
Model 8A
Reg NR 115W
Mfg 4/30
Eng P&W Wasp C #3163
ATC 300

A standard Sirius with extra fuel tanks, full capacity 633 gals. Sold to EMIL SALAY, TREAS., HUNGARIAN-AMERICAN OCEAN FLIGHT, Flint, Michigan (1930–31). Prd black and red, white trim; named *Justice for Hungary*. Flown by George Endres and Alexander Wilczek (Magyar) N.Y.C.–Harbour Grace–Bicske (Hungary) 7/15–16/31. Received $10,000 prize for flight. Plane retained by Endres. Hungarian reg (if any) unknown. Crashed and burned Rome 5/21/32. Endres and Capt. J. Pittay killed. Engine and portions of plane on exhibit in museum at Budapest.

C/n 167

Type Sirius
Model 8A
Reg NC 167W
Mfg 7/30
Eng P&W Wasp #3168
ATC 300

Sold to WEDELL-WILLIAMS AIR SERVICE, INC., Patterson. La. (1930–32); LUCILLE TRAUTWEIN BOTTENFIELD, Dripping Springs, Texas (1932); JOHN (JOBE) PUNDT, AMERICAN LIBERTY OIL CO., Dallas (1932); C. E. GATES, Houston (1932–33); HARRY B. BARNHART, Dallas (1933); GLEN HARROUN, BOWEN AIR LINES, Fort Worth (1933–35). Converted by LAC to Sirius 8C under ATC Memo 2–374 as of 3/13/35. Apparently leased as mail carrier to Delta Air Lines, Inc., Atlanta, Ga., for Dallas-Charleston route. Crashed at Birmingham, Ala., 12/24/35; pilot R. C. Reinhard injured.

C/n 168

Type Orion
Model 9
Reg X 960Y, NC 960Y
Mfg 2/31
Eng P&W Wasp C #3900
ATC none

The first Lockheed Orion, originally referred to as a "Sirius 6-passenger cabin plane" and an "Altair Model 9." Approved with ATC 421 of 5/6/31. Sold to BOWEN AIR LINES, INC., Fort Worth (1931–33). Acc Fort Worth 8/26/31; ferried to LAC and repaired. Cracked up Tulsa 6/2/33, pilot R. Stein Lee and two passengers injured, one passenger unhurt.

C/n 169

Type Orion
Model 9
Reg NC 964Y, XA-BEI (Mexico), NC 13977, XA-BAY (Mexico)
Mfg 4/31
Eng P&W Wasp #3901
ATC 421

Sold to BOWEN AIR LINES, INC., Fort Worth (1931–34). Gear-up landing Austin, repaired by 5/12/31. C. G. PETERSON, N.Y.C. (1934). AEROVIAS CENTRALES, S.A., México, D.F. (1934–35); cost $7,975, with Wasp #1812. Operated by ACSA (Pan American subsidiary) on Mexican routes. PAN AMERICAN AIRWAYS, INC., N.Y.C. (1935–36). Based at Brownsville, Texas, with new U.S. reg. Back to Mexico with Pan Am subsidiary CIA. MEXICANA DE AVIACION, S.A., México, D.F. (1936). Crashed Pico de Orizaba, Veracruz, 8/3/36. Pilot Joaquin Rivadeneyra Vasquez killed.

C/n 170

Type Vega
Model 5C
Reg NC 959Y
Mfg 2–3/31
Eng P&W Wasp # 3717
ATC 384

Sold to PREST-O-LITE STORAGE BATTERY SALES CORP., Indianapolis (1931–36); named *Prest-O-Lite II*; pilot Dick Knox. BLUE BIRD AIR SERVICE, INC., Chicago (1936); prd red. Crashed Napierville, Ill., 9/29/36 while engaged in photographing Burlington RR's "Zephyr." Pilot Oscar Hanold and three passengers killed.

C/n 171

Type Vega
Model Hi-Speed Special 5C
Reg NR 965Y, X 965Y, NC 965Y
Mfg 3–4/31
Eng P&W Wasp # 2849
ATC none

Originally built on order of John Henry Mears, N.Y.C., to replace wrecked c/n 112 (*q.v.*); prd red and silver; named *City of New York*. Similar to his c/n 112 Vega except for having Hi-Speed wirebraced l/g. Mears did not take delivery. Sold to ELINOR SMITH, Freeport, N.Y. (1931–32), for projected Atlantic flight; renamed *Mrs.?*; acc Garden City, N.Y., 8/22/31; conventional l/g installed. Ocean flight not made. Transferred to PATRICK H. SULLIVAN (husband of Elinor Smith), N.Y.C. (1932); WILLIAM W. HARTS, JR., N.Y.C. (1932). AMELIA EARHART, Rye, N.Y. (1933–36): flown Hawaii-Oakland, Calif, 1/11–12/35; Los Angeles–Mexico City 4/19–20/35; and Mexico City–Newark 5/9/35; also in various cross-country flights and NAR events. SETH S. TERRY, Reno, Nev., and Quincy, Calif. (1936–39); GLOVER EDWIN RUCKSTELL, Boulder City, Nev. (1939–42). Used for charter and sightseeing; named *Record Breaker*. CHARLES H. BABB CO., N.Y.C. (1942–43), with Wasp S1D1 #3812. FRANK M. MATTHEWS, Bethlehem, Pa. (1943). Destroyed on ground by fire, Memphis 8/26/43.

C/n 172

Type Orion
Model 9
Reg NC 975Y, XB-AHQ (Mexico)
Mfg 5/31
Eng P&W Wasp C # 4217
ATC 421

Sold to NEW YORK & WESTERN AIRLINES, INC., Pittsburgh (1931); prd white, red trim. Repossessed by DAC (1931). PHILIP H. PHILBIN, JR., AIR EXPRESS CORP., N.Y.C. (1932–33); prd silver, green trim; their #104. Modified as cargo carrier. Acc Seligman, Ariz., 1/25/33; repaired and bought by PACIFIC AIRMOTIVE CORP., Burbank, Calif. (1933). SAN LUIS MINING CO., San Francisco (1933–36); operated for hauling gold out of Tayoltita, Dur., and Mazatlán, Sin., Mexico; pilot Gordon S. Barry. LINEAS AEREAS MINERAS, S.A. (LAMSA), Mazatlán (1936–37). Reported sold to SPANISH REPUBLICAN GOVERNMENT (1937–?). Disposition unknown.

C/n 173

Type Orion
Model 9
Reg NC 984Y, XA-BEJ (Mexico)
Mfg 5/31
Eng P&W Wasp C #4226
ATC 421

Sold to NEW YORK & WESTERN AIRLINES, INC., Pittsburgh (1931); prd white, red trim. Repossessed by DAC (1931). PHILIP H. PHILBIN, JR., AIR EXPRESS CORP., N.Y.C. (1932–33); prd silver, green trim; their #105. Modified as cargo-only carrier. Damaged 1/33, repaired. PHILLIPS PETROLEUM CO., Bartlesville, Okla. (1933–34); converted to reduced 5-passenger carrier 12/33 under ATC memo 2–367. AEROVIAS CENTRALES, S.A., México, D.F. (1934); cost $13,500. Operated on Mexican routes by ACSA (Pan American subsidiary). Crashed Burbank, Calif., 6/23/34. Pilot C. L. Bucher killed.

C/n 174

Type Orion
Model 9
Reg NC 988Y, NR 998Y, XA-BEL (Mexico), NC 13976, XA-BDH (Mexico)
Mfg 6/29/31
Eng P&W Wasp C #4218
ATC 421

Sold to ASA G. CANDLER, JR., Atlanta (1931–33) as executive transport; with modifications flown in Bendix Race 1931 NAR by Beeler Blevins; also by Ruth Nichols. H. C. LIPPIATT, Los Angeles (1933–34). CURRIER'S TABLETS, INC., Hollywood (1934); 3–5P installed under ATC Memo 2–367. AEROVIAS CENTRALES, S.A., México, D.F.

(1934–35); flown by ACSA, Pan American subsidiary, on Mexican routes. PAN AMERICAN AIRWAYS, INC., N.Y.C. (1935–36); based at Brownsville, Texas, with new U.S. reg. Again to Mexico, this time for Pan Am subsidiary CIA. MEXICANA DE AVIACION, S.A., México, D.F. (1936). Crashed at Poblado Francisco Rueda, Veracruz, 10/6/36. Pilot Hueodoro Cardenas killed.

C/n 175

Type Orion
Model 9
Reg NC 991Y
Mfg 6/23/31
Eng P&W Wasp C #3628
ATC 421

Sold to CONTINENTAL AIRWAYS, INC., Chicago (1931–32), for service on their Chicago-Washington airline; prd blue. Destroyed in hangar fire Chicago 2/5/32.

C/n 176

Type Altair
Model Special
Reg NR 998Y
Mfg 7/31
Eng WC #17781
ATC none

Special ship for MACFADDEN PUBLICATIONS, INC., N.Y.C. (1931–32); cost $32,000, prd black, upper portions gold leaf, named *The Gold Eagle*. Used for personal transport by publisher Bernarr Macfadden, and special flights by his pilot, Louis T. Reichers. Flown in 1931 NAR, and made first Montreal-Havana nonstop record 4/32. Renamed *Miss Liberty*. Flown by Reichers on New York–Harbour Grace–Dublin–Paris flight attempt. Crash-landed in ocean 17 miles off Kinsale Harbour, Ireland, 5/13/32. Reichers rescued. Plane abandoned.

C/n 177

Type Orion
Model 9
Reg NR 12220, NC 12220
Mfg 8/31
Eng P&W Wasp # 3176
ATC 421

Sold to CONTINENTAL AIRWAYS, INC., Chicago (1931–32); prd blue. Flown in Bendix Race of 1931 NAR by Continental pilot Harold S. Johnson, then placed in airline service. Acc La Porte, Ind., 9/15/31; pilot and six passengers unhurt. Overhauled. Destroyed in hangar fire Chicago 2/5/32.

C/n 178

Type Orion
Model 9
Reg NC 12221
Mfg 9/31
Eng P&W Wasp C #4107
ATC 421

Sold to NEW YORK, PHILADELPHIA & WASHINGTON AIRWAY CORP. (LUDINGTON LINES), Washington D.C. (1931). Prd white, red trim; flown briefly on airline routes. Crashed Camden, N.J., 11/5/31. Pilot Floyd L. Cox and four passengers killed.

C/n 179

Type Altair, XRO–1 (USN)
Model DL–2A
Reg 9054 (Navy)
Mfg 9/31
Eng WC #17331
ATC —

Ordered by Asst. Secy. of Navy David S. Ingalls for evaluation and use as naval command transport. First naval airplane with fully retractable l/g. Flight tests and trials for LAC by Marshall Headle, delivery to Navy by Roscoe Turner. Sold to U.S. NAVY, Washington, D.C. (1931–38?); stationed at Anacostia Naval Air Station; flown and evaluated by Lt. R. B. Pirie, Secy. Ingalls, and many naval aviators. Stored 8/33. Weight limits restricted 7/38. Further use and disposition unknown.

C/n 180

Type Altair (later Orion 9C Special)
Model DL–2A
Reg X 12222, NR 12222, NC 12222
Mfg 9/31
Eng P&W Wasp E #1783
ATC Memo 2–386 of 10/17/31

Experimental ship built by LAC. Leased for trial to Transcontinental & Western Air, Inc., Kansas City (1931); flown as mail carrier on TWA routes; their #252. Acc Columbus, Ohio 10/10/31; returned to LAC. Converted to Orion 9C Special 6/32, under ATC Memo 2–416 of 7/11/32; pilot's cockpit changed and baggage compartment became cabin. Sold to SHELL AVIATION CORP. (SHELL PETROLEUM CORP.), St. Louis (1932–38). Prd yellow-orange and red; named *Shellightning*; piloted by Shell's aviation mgr. James H. Doolittle on cross-country and exhibition flights. Acc Evansville, Ind., 7/14/32; WC #815 installed 1936. Cracked up St. Louis 5/7/36; stored, rebuilt by Parks Air College, East St. Louis, Ill. A. PAUL MANTZ, Burbank, Calif (1938–43); prd red, white trim; flown in Bendix races 1938 and 1939 NAR, and used as movie photo plane. MATT REDMOND PECK, Gardena, Calif. (1943); BARNSDALL OIL CO., Tulsa (1943–48); H. J. KENLEY, GENERAL AERIAL SURVEYS, Tulsa, (1948–51); JOSEPH CARL EATON, La Mesa, Calif. (1951–53); HENRY S. ROLLER, La Jolla and San Diego, Calif. (1953–55). Back to A. PAUL MANTZ, Santa Ana, Calif. (1955–62); TALLMANTZ AVIATION, INC. (1962–66); ROSEN-NOVAK AUTO CORP., Omaha (1966–68); DAVID JOHNSON, Peterborough, N.H. (1968–76); SWISS AIR TRANSPORT MUSEUM, Lucerne, Switzerland (1976—). Restored in configuration and markings of c/n 189, Reg. #CH-167 *(q.v.)*. On prominent display.

C/n 181

Type Orion
Model 9
Reg NC 12223, XA-BHA, XA-BEU (Mexico)
Mfg 9/26/31
Eng P&W Wasp # 4110
ATC 421

Sold to VARNEY AIR SERVICE, LTD. (later VARNEY SPEED LINES, INC., Alameda, Calif. (1931–34). Prd white, red trim; named *West Wind*. Transferred to Varney's Mexican airline, LINEAS AEREAS OCCIDENTALES, S.A., Burbank, Calif. (1934–35), with Mexican reg. J. B. MESSICK, El Paso (1935–36); GLOVER E. RUCKSTELL, Grand Canyon, Ariz. (1936); FRITZ BIELER, México D. F. (1937); JUAN H. GARCIA ECHEVESTE ("citizen of unknown nationality") (1937). Exported to SPANISH REPUBLICAN AIR FORCE (1937–?). Involved in Spanish Civil War. No record of disposition.

C/n 182

Type Orion
Model 9
Reg NC 12224, XA–BHB (Mexico)
Mfg 9/31
Eng P&W Wasp #4317
ATC 421

Sold to VARNEY AIR SERVICE, LTD. (later VARNEY SPEED LINES, INC., Alameda, Calif (1931–34). Prd white, red trim; named *South Wind*. Acc Alameda, Calif., 3/11/33, repaired with new wing. Transferred to Varney's Mexican airline, LINEAS AEREAS OCCIDENTALES, S. A., Burbank, Calif. (1934); renamed *West Wind*. Shipped to Europe for possible participation in MacRobertson Race London-Melbourne 1934; Franklin Rose pilot. Demonstrated to King Carol of Romania at Bucharest and sold. ROMANIAN ARMY AIR FORCE (1934–35?). Reported crashed north of Bucharest *c.* 1935.

C/n 183

Type Orion
Model 9
Reg NC 12225, XA–BHC (Mexico), F-AQAS (France)
Mfg 9/31
Eng P&W Wasp C #4323
ATC 421

Sold to VARNEY AIR SERVICE, LTD. (later VARNEY SPEED LINES, INC.) Alameda, Calif. (1931–34). Prd white, red trim; named *North Wind*. Transferred to Varney's Mexican airline, *Lineas Aereas Occidentales*, S.A., Burbank, Calif. (1934–35), with Mexican reg. C. A. Collins, Palm Springs, Calif. (1935–36); Charles H. Babb, Glendale, Calif. (1936). Rudolf Wolf, Inc., N.Y.C. (1936). Shipped via The Netherlands and France to Spanish Repbulican Air Force (1937–?). Involved in Spanish Civil War. No further disposition.

C/n 184

Type Orion
Model 9
Reg NC 12226
Mfg 10/31
Eng P&W Wasp #4522
ATC 421

Sold to Varney Air Service, Ltd. (later Varney Speed Lines, Inc.), Alameda, Calif. (1931–34). Prd white, red trim; named *East Wind.* Acc Alameda 12/24/32; repaired. Crashed Hayward, Calif., 3/25/33. Pilot Noel B. Evans, two passengers, eleven people on ground killed.

C/n 185

Type Orion
Model 9
Reg NC 12227, XA-BHD (Mexico), F-AQAV (France)
Mfg 10/31
Eng P&W Wasp #4523
ATC 421

Sold to Varney Air Service, Ltd. (later Varney Speed Lines, Inc.) Alameda, Calif. (1931–34). Prd white, red trim, named *Winter Wind.* Transferred to Varney's Mexican airline, Lineas Aereas Occidentales, S. A., Burbank, Calif. (1934–35), with Mexican reg. C. A. Collins, Palm Springs, Calif. (1935–36); named *El Marelro.* Aero Transport Corp., Glendale, Calif. (1936). Charles H. Babb, Glendale, Calif. (1936). Rudolf Wolf, Inc., N.Y.C. (1936). Exported via The Netherlands and France (French reg F-AQAV applied?) to Spanish Republican Air Force (1937–?); involved in Spanish Civil War. No record of disposition.

C/n 186

Type Orion
Model 9
Reg NC 12228, XA-BHE (Mexico)
Mfg 10/31
Eng P&W Wasp C #4524
ATC 421

Sold to Varney Air Service, Ltd. (later Varney Speed Lines, Inc.), Alameda, Calif. (1931–34). Prd white, red trim; named *Spring Wind.* Transferred to Varney's Mexican airline, Lineas Aereas Occidentales, S.A., Burbank, Calif. (1934–35) with Mexican reg. Confiscated 6/21/35 by Cia. Mexicana de Petroleo "El Aguila," S.A. ($7,800 due). Sold by them to Abel Espinosa, México, D.F. (1935–36); pilot Charles Baughan. Fritz Bieler, México, D.F. (1936–37). Mark Wolf ("from Arizona") (1937), for export. Obviously went to Spanish Republican Air Force (1937–?). Involved in Spanish Civil War. No record of disposition.

C/n 187

Type Orion
Model 9A Special
Reg X 12229, NC 12229
Mfg 11/31
Eng P&W Wasp SC #1927
ATC Memo 2-397 of 1/16/32

Sold to Hal Roach Studios, Inc., Culver City, Calif. (1932); 3° wing dihedral, 6" longer fuselage nose, retractable tail wheel. Prd white, red trim; named *The Spirit of Fun;* pilot James B. Dickson. Roach and Dickson made South American circuit 1932; plane shipped to Shanghai, flew from China to South Africa 1932. Crashed Victoria Falls, Northern Rhodesia, 11/17/32. Dickson killed, passengers Arthur Loew and Joseph Rosthal injured.

C/n 188

Type Altair
Model 8E
Reg X 12230, J-BAMC (Japan)
Mfg 1/32
Eng P&W Wasp S1D1 #4620
ATC none

Designed for export, with tandem cockpits, and either cargo or passenger cabin. Sold through Okura Trading Co., agents, to Mainichi Shimbun *(Daily News),* Osaka, Japan (1932–37). Used for special flights, airmail transport, newsgathering. Pilot Seizan Okura and flight engineer Tokushi Fuse made first round-trip flight Tokyo-Manila 11/10–26/35. Crashed Osaka 4/12/37. Pilot Oka and passenger killed.

C/n 189

Type Orion
Model 9B
Reg X 12231, CH–167, HB–LAH (Switzerland)
Mfg 2/16/32
Eng WC #17794
ATC 462

C/n 187: Hal Roach Studios' Spirit of Fun *flew movie executives on four continents.*

Sold to Curtiss-Wright Export Corp. N.Y.C. (1932); Swiss Air Traffic Limited Company, Zurich (1932–36). First and fastest U.S. commercial air transport plane sold to foreign airline market. Flown on Zurich-Munich-Vienna express service under Swissair director Balz Zimmermann. Sold through French agents to Spanish Republican Government, Madrid (1936–37). Used as V.I.P. transport and courier during Spanish Civil War. Flown by American pilot Joseph Rosmarin. Suffered belly-landing and scrapped.

C/n 190

Type Orion
Model 9B
Reg X 12232, CH-168 and HB-LAJ (Switzerland)
Mfg 2/25/31
Eng WC #17791
ATC 462

Sold to Swissair (Swiss Air Transport Co., Ltd.), Zurich (1932–35). Flown on European airline routes, and on special airmail speed flights to Tunis 5/20/33, and Istanbul 6/28/34; Swissair director Walter Mittelholzer pilot. Sold through French agents to Spanish Republican Government (1936–37). Used as transport and liaison aircraft during Spanish Civil War. No record of disposition.

C/n 191

Type Vega
Model 5C
Reg NC 980Y
Mfg 5/32
Eng P&W Wasp #2898
ATC 384

Assembled by laid-off employees under Firman Gray, during period of LAC reorganization. Sold to Braniff Airways, Inc., Oklahoma City (1932–35), for airline service. Crashed East Fort Worth 11/9/35. Pilot William C. Maus killed.

C/n 192

Type Orion
Model 9 Special
Reg NC 12277
Mfg 12/6/32
Eng P&W Wasp
ATC none

Used a fuselage started for Air Express 3. Built as a cargo plane, no passenger seating. Converted to pass/cargo Orion 9E under ATC 508 5/33. Purchased by Transcontinental & Western Air, Inc., Kansas City (1933); their #256; ptd red and white. Crashed in Missouri River at Kansas City 7/28/33. Pilot E. J. Noe killed.

C/n 193

Type Orion
Model 9E
Reg NC 12278
Mfg 5/17/33
Eng P&W Wasp
ATC 508

Used a fuselage started for Air Express 3. Made into a special cargo/passenger Orion 9E under ATC 508. Sold to Transcontinental & Western Air, Inc., Kansas City and N.Y.C., (1933–35); their #257; ptd red and white. Fitted with Goodrich De-icers 10/33. Acc Albuquerque 1/15/34, pilot H. H. Holloway injured; repaired. Robert Blair, Los Angeles (1935–37); used for charter. Cracked up Jackson, Ohio, 12/8/36. Purchased by LAC with intent to rebuild. Scrapped 1938.

C/n 194

Type Vega
Model 5C Special
Reg NC 12282, NR 12282
Mfg 1/26/33
Eng P&W Wasp SC1 #4950
ATC none

Sold to Continental Oil Co., Ponca City, Okla. (later Denver) (1933–44). Ptd red, green trim; used for executive transport. Acc Denver 6/13/34; repaired. Reg NR for special CAA propeller test at LAC 9/41. Manning & Brown, Inc., Denver (1944–45); Most & Bacon Air Service, Alhambra, Calif. (1945); A. Erwin Hobart, Beverly Hills (1945–47); Alexander Banks, East Palo Alto, Calif. (1947); Wayne R. McQueen, Culver City, Calif. (1947–48); James Baker, Concord, Calif. (1948); L. H. Roberts and Jack Thomas, Antioch, Calif. (1948–49). Donald J. Murphy, Anchorage (1949–54); ptd black, yellow trim. Broken in two by heavy snows, scrapped Anchorage 3/54.

C/n 195

Type Orion (later Orion-Explorer)
Model 9E
Reg NC 12283, NR 12283
Mfg 5/33
Eng P&W Wasp
ATC 508

Sold to Transcontinental & Western Air, Inc., Kansas City (later N.Y.C.) (1933–35); their #258; ptd red and white. Charles H. Babb, Glendale, Calif. (1935). Installed Explorer wing from c/n 148 *(q.v.)*, plus fixed l/g. Wiley Post, Oklahoma City (1935); ptd red; P&W Wasp S3H1 #5778 installed, also 3-bladed propeller; used EDO 5300 floats and rudders, installed at Seattle. Flown on projected "leisurely" world trip by Post with actor/humorist Will Rogers. Crashed near Walakpi, Alaska 8/15/35. Post and Rogers killed. Engine salvaged. Wreckage burned. Site marked by memorial stone.

C/n 196

Type Orion
Model 9F
Reg NC 12284
Mfg 7/33
Eng WC R-1820-F21
ATC 512

Registered to George A. MacDonald, Milford, Kan., and Del Rio, Texas (1933–36); MacDonald was personal pilot for Dr. John R. Brinkley, the actual owner. Ptd white, black trim; named *Doctor Brinkley III.* Traded to LAC on new Electra. Charles H. Babb, Glendale, Calif. (1936) Rudolf Wolf, Inc., N.Y.C. (1936–37). Exported via The Netherlands and France to Spanish Republican Air Force (1937–39). Reportedly survived Spanish Civil War. No further Record.

C/n 197

Type Orion
Model 9D
Reg NC 12285
Mfg 7/33
Eng P&W Wasp S1D1
ATC 514

Sold to American Airways, Inc. (later American Airlines, Inc.), Chicago (1933–34); their #145; ptd blue and orange. Acc Cash, Texas, 12/6/33; repaired. Converted to cargo carrier (no passengers). Washed out Memphis 11/15/34.

C/n 198

Type Orion
Model 9D
Reg NC 12286
Mfg 7/33
Eng P&W Wasp S1D1
ATC 514

Sold to American Airways, Inc. (later American Airlines, Inc.), Chicago (1933–34), combination mail and passenger ship; their #146; ptd blue and orange. Crashed near Sunbright, Tenn., 12/22/34. Pilot Russell Riggs killed.

C/n 199

Type Orion
Model 9D
Reg NC 12287
Mfg 8/33
Eng P&W Wasp S1D1
ATC 514

Sold to American Airways, Inc. (later American Airlines, Inc.), Chicago (1933–35), combination mail & passenger plane; their #147; ptd blue and orange. Gear-up landing Bassetts, Texas, 12/3/33; repaired. Washed out Pittsburgh Landing, Tenn., 1/10/35. Pilot John W. Johannpeter escaped via parachute.

C/n 200

Type Orion
Model 9D
Reg NC 229Y
Mfg 8/33
Eng Wasp S1D1
ATC 514

Sold to American Airways, Inc., Chicago (1933); their #148; ptd blue and orange. Crashed after mid-air fire west of El Paso 11/21/33. Pilot J.G. Ingram injured and burned in escape via parachute.

C/n 201

Type Orion
Model 9D
Reg NC 230Y
Mfg 8/33
Eng P&W Wasp S1D1
ATC 514

Sold to American Airways, Inc. (later American Airlines, Inc.), Chicago (1933–34); their #149; ptd blue and orange. Converted by AA to Orion 9 under ATC 421 in 11/34. Blue Bird Air Service, Inc., Chicago (1934–36); Wyoming Air Service, Inc. (later Inland Air Lines, Inc.), Casper, Wyo. (1936–41). Harold S. Johnson, Oak Park, Ill. (1941); Aircraft Exporting Corp., N.Y.C. (1941–44). Alaska Star Airlines (later Alaska Airlines, Inc.), Anchorage (1944–?). Disposition unknown.

C/n 202

Type Orion
Model 9D
Reg NC 231Y, XA-BDZ (Mexico)
Mfg 8/33
Eng P&W Wasp S1D1
ATC 514

Sold to American Airways, Inc. (later American Airlines, Inc.), Chicago (1933–35); their #150; ptd blue and orange. Acc Dallas 11/25/33; repaired. Operated by AA as a cargo plane. Long & Harmon, Dallas (1935); Byrd-Frost Air Transport Co., Inc., Dallas (1935–36), pilot Joe Towle. Carlos Panini, México, D.F. (1936); cost $23,000. Exported for use of Spanish Republican Air Force (1937–?). Involved in Spanish Civil War. No record of disposition.

C/n 203

Type Vega
Model 5C
Reg NC 13705
Mfg 9/33
Eng P&W Wasp SC1
ATC 384

Sold to Shell Aviation Co., Ltd. (Shell Oil Co.), San Francisco (1933–44); ptd yellow-orange and red; named *Shell No. 7.* Wasp #5407 installed 1938. Charles H. Babb, Glendale, Calif. (1944); cost $6,000. Dwight W. Mercer, Mercer Air Service, Burbank, Calif. (1945–63). Disassembled and stored outdoors. G. E. Moxon, Los Angeles, 1963–88. John Desmond, Philadelphia, 1988, for restoration.

C/n 204

Type Orion
Model 9D-1
Reg NC 232Y, NR 232Y, XA-BDY (Mexico)
Mfg 10/33
Eng P&W Wasp S1D1 #2443
ATC Memo 2–464 of 12/1/33

Sold to John Mabee, Mabee Consolidated Corp., Tulsa (1933–34); special interior, couch and three chairs. F. C. Hall, Inc., Oklahoma City (1934–36), with Wasp #5441. Named *Sheridan of Oklahoma;* pilot Roy O. Hunt; flown in Bendix Race 1935 NAR. Fain Drilling Co., Oklahoma City (1936); General Development Co., Tulsa (1936). Carlos Panini, México, D.F. (1936); cost $23,000. Exported for use of Spanish Republican Air Force (1937–?). Involved in Spanish Civil War. No record of disposition.

C/n 205

Type Orion
Model 9D
Reg NC 13747, F-QAR (France)
Mfg 12/33
Eng P&W Wasp S1D1 #5450
ATC 514

Sold to Northwest Airways, Inc. (later Northwest Airlines, Inc.), St. Paul (1933–35); their #50; ptd white, black trim. Oil Field Airlines of Dallas, Inc., Dallas (1935–36); Charles H. Babb, N.Y.C. (1936). Rudolf Wolf Inc., N.Y.C. (1936–37). Exported via The Netherlands and France (reg F-AQAR applied?) to Spanish Republican Air Force (1937–?). Involved in Spanish Civil War. No record of disposition.

C/n 206

Type Orion
Model 9D
Reg NC 13748
Mfg 12/33
Eng P&W Wasp S1D1
ATC 514

Sold to Northwest Airways, Inc. (later Northwest Airlines, Inc.), St. Paul (1933–35); their #51; ptd white, black trim. Wyoming Air Service, Inc. (later Inland Air Lines, Inc.), Casper (1935–40); Harold S. Johnson, Joliet, Ill. (1940–41); Aircraft Exporting Corp., N.Y.C. (1941). On ferry flight to Alaska, burned after gear-up landing Pine Bluffs, Wyo., 9/30/41.

C/n 207

Type Orion
Model 9D
Reg NC 13749
Mfg 12/30/33
Eng P&W Wasp S1D1
ATC 514

Sold to Northwest Airways, Inc. (later Northwest Airlines, Inc.), St. Paul (1933–35); their #52; ptd white, black trim. Wyoming Air Service, Inc., Casper (1935–36). Washed out Buffalo, Wyo., 10/24/36.

C/n 208

Type Orion, UC–85 (USAAF)
Model 9D2
Reg X 799W, NC 799W, A.C. 42-62601
Mfg 6/34
Eng P&W Wasp S1D1 #5517
ATC Memo 2-488 of 9/11/34

Sold to Evening News Assn., Detroit (1934–41), used by *Detroit News* for newsgathering and broadcasting over Station WWJ. Special equipment, including pod wing camera; ptd red, white trim; named *Early Bird.* In active use 1934–38. Arthur D. Knapp, Mechanical Products, Inc., Jackson, Mich. (1941–42); Defense Supplies Corp., Washington, D.C. (1942). War Department, Washington, D.C. (1942–44). As UC-85 assigned to March Field, Calif.; used by Col. A. Paul Mantz; plane nicknamed "Scuttlebutt"; ptd olive drab, USAAF insignia. Danny A. Fowlie, Van Nuys, Calif. (1944); cost $6,511.48. Ohlsson & Rice Mfg. Co., Los Angeles (1944–45); F. H. Steward & Thelma M. Gibson, Chino, Calif. (1945–47). Installed engine and cowling from an AT-6. After acc Los Angeles, scrapped 11/47.

C/n 209

Type Orion
Model 9D
Reg F-AKHC (France)
Mfg 1934
Eng P&W Wasp S1D1
ATC none

Sold to racing pilot Michel Detroyat, Paris, France (1934) as an entry for the London-Melbourne MacRobertson Race of 10/34. Engine changed to Hispano-Suiza 9V Radial of 575 hp. Performance not up to expectations and Detroyat withdrew from the race. Ministere de L'Air, Paris (1934–36). Assigned to Centre d'Essais des Avions Nouveaux (CEPANA) and test-flown by various military pilots. By order of Pierre Cot, French Air Minister, flown in July 1936 to Spain by Eduoard Corniglion-Moulinier, with novelist André Malraux and wife, returning with new Spanish ambassador. Soon transferred to Spanish

Republican Government, Madrid (1936) and flown by French pilot Georges Cornez on liaison trips. Acc Muniesca, Spain 8/15/36. Wings sawed off after accident and no repairs made.

C/n 210

Type Vega, UC-101 (USAAF)
Model 5C
Reg NC 14236 A.C. 42-94148, NC 48610
Mfg 6/34
Eng P&W Wasp SC1 #5536
ATC 384

Last Vega built by LAC. Sold to W. P. Fuller, Sr. (later, W. P. (Frank) Fuller, Jr.), San Francisco (1934–36). Phillips Petroleum Co., Bartlesville, Okla. (1936–40); Wasp C #3104 installed 1938. Don Marshall, Dallas (1940–42). War Dept., U.S. Engineer's Office, Los Angeles (1942–44); completely rebuilt, with original Wasp SC1 #5536 reinstalled; cost $15,000. As UC-101 assigned to March Field, Calif. Back to Don Marshall, for Charles H. Babb, Burbank, Calif. (1944–45), cost $5,105. Ross B. Boardman, San Marino, Calif. (1945). Crashed El Paso 6/9/45. Pilot Raymond F. Darwin killed, three passengers injured.

C/n 211

Type Orion
Model 9D Special
Reg NR 14222
Mfg 11/34
Eng Wasp S1D1 #4838
ATC none

Special ship for Laura Ingalls, Newark (later Great Neck, N.Y.) (1934–36). No seating in cabin; 650-gal gas capacity. Ptd black, red trim; named *Auto-da-Fé*. Set nonstop transcontinental records with Miss Ingalls 7/11/35 and 9/12/35; second in Bendix Race 1936 NAR. Rudolf Wolf, Inc., N.Y.C. (1936–37). Exported via The Netherlands and France to Spanish Republican Air Force (1937–?). Involved in Spanish Civil War. Reported "crashed in Spain." No record.

C/n 212

Type Orion
Model 9F-1
Reg NC 14246, XA-BDO (Mexico)
Mfg 8/34
Eng WC SR-1820-F2
ATC 557

Sold to Phillips Petroleum Co., Bartlesville, Okla. (1934–36); flown by Phillips's aviation mgr. Will D. Parker. Fritz Bieler, México, D.F. (1936–37); Juan H. Garcia Echeveste ("citizen of unknown nationality") (1937). Exported to Spanish Republican Air Force (1937–?). Involved in Spanish Civil War. No record of disposition.

C/n 213

Type Altair
Model 8F
Reg X 14209, J-BAUC (Japan)
Mfg 1934
Eng P&W Wasp S1D1
ATC —

Tandem cockpits and cargo/passenger cabin. Exported and sold through Okura Trading Co. to Mainichi Shimbun (*Daily News*), Osaka, Japan (1934–44). Used for newsgathering throughout Japan. Destroyed in hangar at Haneda Airport, Tokyo, during bombing raid by USAAF in autumn 1944.

C/n 214 (Vega Co. c/n 1)

Type Altair
Model 8G
Reg NX 18149, NR 18149
Mfg 12/37
Eng Menasco Unitwin (2)
ATC none

A very special Altair, apparently built from spares three years after production of Lockheed single-engine series had ceased. Assembled to test the use and efficiency of a pair of 6-cylinder, in-line Menasco engines of 260-hp each, geared to a single propeller, called the Unitwin Installation. Built by Airover (name later changed to Vega Airplane Co., a special-purpose, wholly owned manufacturing subsidiary of Lockheed Aircraft Corp.), Burbank, Calif. (1937–40); originally listed as c/n 1 of Airover (or Vega). Named *Flying Test Stand*; most of testing done by pilot Bud Martin. Sold to Howard H. Batt, Santa Monica, Calif. (1940–42). Converted 9/40 under ATC

Last single-engine Lockheed, the Altair c/n 214 built in 1937.

Memo 2–423 of 10/8/32 to Altair 8D, with P&W Wasp C #3104; "Vega c/n 1" changed to LAC c/n 214 as of 6/19/42. CALIFORNIA AIRCRAFT CORP., Van Nuys (1942). BECHTEL-PRICE-CALAHAN CO., Edmonton, Alta. (1942–43?); Canadian reg (if any) unknown. B-P-C were contractors, building the Canol Project in northern Canada, and assembled a motley fleet of older aircraft to transport men and equipment from Edmonton to Norman Oil Wells. C/n 214 thought to have been among planes junked and burned when U.S. Army detachment took over B-P-C equipment *c.* 1943.

C/n EX-2

Type Air Express
Model 3
Reg 7955, NR 7955, NC 7955
Mfg 11/24/28
Eng P&W Wasp #984
ATC none

Originally c/n 5 (*q.v.*). Rebuilt after acc 6/6/28; used by LAC as demonstrator. First commercial airplane to be fitted with the newly developed NACA cowling. Given ATC 102 as of 1/11/29; ptd red and silver. Flown by Frank Hawks with Oscar Grubb to new nonstop transcontinental speed record 2/4/29. Sold to THE TEXAS CO., N.Y.C. (1929–30); ptd red, white trim; named *Texaco 5.* Flown by Hawks in record solo round-trip nonstop transcontinental flights 6/27–28/29, and on various intercity record hops. Fuselage only c/n 91 replaced original as of 1/9/30. Crashed West Palm Beach 1/17/30. Pilot Hawks unhurt, two passengers injured.

C/n 619

Type Vega
Model 5 Special
Reg NR 496M
Mfg 3/30 (Detroit)
Eng P&W Wasp C #1472
ATC —

Built at Detroit by William S. Brock and Edward F. Schlee, using parts in stock (except fuselage) of their Schlee-Brock Aircraft Corp., which was liquidating its assets. Fuselage supplied by LAC. Due to unexplained mixup, c/n 619 assigned to this fuselage and then the plane itself. Sold to WILLIAM S. BROCK, Detroit (1930). Radio equipped (Station KHILO); ptd red and cream. Flown by Brock and Schlee to new Florida-California round-trip speed record 6/17–18/30. CROSLEY RADIO CORP., Cincinnati (1930–32); named *The New Cincinnati;* flown by Brock in nonstop race 1930 NAR. Lent by Crosley to Ruth Nichols, Rye, N.Y., and prepared by Clarence Chamberlin, Jersey City, for Miss Nichols's record flights. Established women's transcontinental records 12/30, altitude record 3/6/31, speed record 4/13/31. Wire-braced l/g, Hamilton controllable-pitch propeller installed. Ptd white and gold; renamed *Crosley Radio Ship,* and then *Akita.* Beginning transatlantic flight attempt, cracked up St. John, N. B., 6/22/31; Miss Nichols hurt. Repaired 8/31 with new fuselage and stabilizer from LAC. Established distance record for women, Oakland–Louisville, Ky., 10/23/31. Caught fire and damaged Louisville 10/26/31; Miss Nichols escaped. Rebuilt by Chamberlin as a "sunken-wing Vega" (wing 14" down into fuselage), and bubble-type hatch over cockpit. Wooden belly skid attached, and conventional l/g made dropable. Cracked up Floyd Bennett Field, N.Y., 11/4/32. AVIAMENT CORP., Jersey City (1932–?). Wrecked aircraft stored, offered for sale. Eventually became unfit and scrapped.

C/n (none)

Type XP-900, YIP-24, YP-24 (USAAC)
Model (Pursuit plane by DAC)
Reg A.C. 32-320
Mfg 1931 (Detroit)
Eng Curtiss Conqueror V-1570C #587, A.C. #30-970
ATC —

Experimental 2P low-wing fighter. First Army Air Corps low-wing fighter and first with fully retractable l/g. Designed by DAC engineer Robert J. Woods. Metal fuselage built at Detroit attached to wooden wing shipped from LAC. Equipped with 602-hp, in-line engine; 3-bladed propeller; one .30-cal, one .50-cal machine gun firing through propeller, plus one flexible .30-cal gun aft. Tested at Detroit; delivered to U.S. ARMY AIR CORPS, Dayton, for evaluation 10/31. Crashed Wright Field, Ohio, 10/19/31 (test pilot ordered to abandon plane and leave via parachute when control lever for lowering l/g broke in flight). Total flying hours: 20.

KNOWN REGISTRATIONS
Single-Engine Lockheeds Since 1927

KEY

C/n = Constructor's number (*i.e.*, manufacturer's serial number; *cf.* the Individual Histories, *Supplement A*)

U.S. prefixes:

None = very early usage, or temporary

NC or C = Commercial

NX or X = Experimental

NR or R = Restricted

N = since 1948

U.S.A.

Prefix	Registration	Aircraft
NR	211	Sirius, c/n 140
NC	606	Vega, c/n 56
NX	913	Vega, c/n 1
	2779	Vega, c/n 1
	2788	Vega, c/n 1
	2804	Vega, c/n 1
NC	2845	Vega, c/n 61
NC	2846	Vega, c/n 62
NC	2874	Vega, c/n 59
NC	2875	Vega, c/n 60
NR	3057	Air Express, c/n 75; later NC
	3625	Vega, c/n 3; later X
X	3903	Vega, c/n 4
NC	4097	Vega, c/n 6
X	4769	Vega, c/n 7
	4897	Air Express, c/n 5
	5885	Vega, c/n 8
NC	6526	Vega, c/n 9
NC	6911	Vega, c/n 10
NC	7044	Vega, c/n 11
	7162	Vega, c/n 12; later C, NC
NC	7425	Vega, c/n 12B
NC	7426	Vega, c/n 14; later NR
NC	7427	Vega, c/n 15
NC	7428	Vega, c/n 16
X	7429	Vega, c/n 18; later NC, NR
X	7430	Vega, c/n 19
X	7439	Vega, c/n 17
X	7440	Vega, c/n 20; later NC
X	7441	Vega, c/n 21
NC	7805	Vega, c/n 28; later X, NR
NC	7894	Vega, c/n 29
	7895	Vega, c/n 30
NC	7896	Vega, c/n 31
NC	7952	Vega, c/n 22
NC	7953	Vega, c/n 23
NC	7954	Vega, c/n 24; later NR
	7955	Air Express, c/n EX–2; later NR, NC
NC	7973	Vega, c/n 32; later NR
X	8494	Sirius (& Altair), c/n 165; later NR
NC	8495	Vega, c/n 156
NC	8496	Vega, c/n 157
NC	8497	Vega, c/n 154
NC	9424	Vega, c/n 78
NR	12220	Orion, c/n 177; later NC
NC	12221	Orion, c/n 178
X	12222	Altair (& Orion), c/n 180; later NR, NC
NC	12223	Orion, c/n 181
NC	12224	Orion, c/n 182
NC	12225	Orion, c/n 183
NC	12226	Orion, c/n 184
NC	12227	Orion, c/n 185
NC	12228	Orion, c/n 186
X	12229	Orion, c/n 187; later NC
X	12230	Altair, c/n 188
X	12231	Orion, c/n 189
X	12232	Orion, c/n 190
NC	12277	Orion, c/n 192
NC	12278	Orion, c/n 193
NC	12282	Vega, c/n 194; later NR
NC	12283	Orion, c/n 195; later NR
NC	12284	Orion, c/n 196
NC	12285	Orion, c/n 197
NC	12286	Orion, c/n 198
NC	12287	Orion, c/n 199
NC	12288	Vega, c/n 161
NC	13705	Vega, c/n 203
NC	13747	Orion, c/n 205
NC	13748	Orion, c/n 206
NC	13749	Orion, c/n 207
NC	13976	Orion, c/n 174
NC	13977	Orion, c/n 169
X	14209	Altair, c/n 213
NR	14222	Orion, c/n 211
NC	14236	Vega, c/n 210
NC	14246	Orion, c/n 212
NX	18149	Altair, c/n 214; later NR
NC	19958	Vega, c/n 102
NC	48610	Vega, c/n 210
N	105D	Vega, c/n 72
N	174D	Vega, c/n 72
NC	31E	Vega, c/n 36
NC	32E	Vega, c/n 33
NR	33E	Vega, c/n 34
NC	34E	Vega, c/n 35; later X
NC	35E	Vega, c/n 37
NC	194E	Vega, c/n 25
NC	195E	Vega, c/n 26
	196E	Vega, c/n 27
NC	197E	Vega, c/n 38
	198E	Vega, c/n 39
NC	199E	Vega, c/n 40; later NR
NC	200E	Vega, c/n 41
NC	432E	Vega, c/n 48
NC	433E	Vega, c/n 49
NC	434E	Vega, c/n 50
NC	435E	Vega, c/n 51
NC	513E	Vega, c/n 52
NC	514E	Air Express, c/n 65
NC	574E	Vega, c/n 57
NC	623E	Vega, c/n 58
NC	624E	Vega, c/n 53
NC	625E	Vega, c/n 63; later NR
NC	657E	Vega, c/n 54
NC	658E	Vega, c/n 55
NC	857E	Vega, c/n 64
NC	858E	Vega, c/n 66
C	859E	Vega, c/n 67
NC	868E	Vega, c/n 68

NC	869E	Vega, c/n 69, 118; later NR
NC	870E	Vega, c/n 70
NC	871E	Vega, c/n 71
NC	891E	Vega, c/n 73
NC	892E	Vega, c/n 74
NC	898E	Vega, c/n 72
NC	306H	Air Express (& Vega), c/n 76
NC	307H	Air Express, c/n 77
NC	308H	Vega, c/n 79; later NR, X
NC	309H	Vega, c/n 80
NC	336H	Vega, c/n 81
NC	392H	Vega, c/n 84
R	393H	Vega, c/n 85
NC	394H	Vega, c/n 87
NC	395H	Vega, c/n 88
NC	396H	Vega, c/n 89
NC	397H	Vega, c/n 82
NC	497H	Vega, c/n 135
NR	856H	Explorer, c/n 2, 116
NC	974H	Vega, c/n 94
NC	975H	Vega, c/n 96
NC	504K	Vega, c/n 90
NC	505K	Vega, c/n 83
NC	522K	Air Express, c/n 92
NC	31M	Vega, c/n 98
NC	32M	Vega, c/n 102
NC	46M	Vega, c/n 97
NC	47M	Vega, c/n 99; later N
NC	48M	Vega, c/n 100
NC	49M	Vega, c/n 101
NC	239M	Vega, c/n 156
NC	483M	Vega, c/n 136
NC	496M	Vega, c/n 619
NC	534M	Vega, c/n 103
NC	536M	Vega, c/n 105
NC	537M	Vega, c/n 106
NC	538M	Vega, c/n 107
NC	539M	Vega, c/n 108; later NR
NC	540M	Vega, c/n 109
NC	102N	Vega, c/n 113
NC	105N	Vega, c/n 117; later NR
NC	106N	Vega, c/n 118
N	161N	Vega, c/n 41
NC	997N	Vega, c/n 139
NC	349V	Sirius, c/n 141
NR	500V	Vega, c/n 112
NR	12W	Sirius, c/n 142
NC	13W	Sirius (& Altair), c/n 143; later NR
NC	14W	Sirius, c/n 144
NC	15W	Sirius (& Altair), c/n 145; later NR
NC	16W	Sirius, c/n 146
NR	100W	Explorer, c/n 147
NR	101W	Explorer, c/n 148
NC	102W	Vega, c/n 119
NC	103W	Vega, c/n 120
NC	104W	Vega, c/n 121
NC	105W	Vega, c/n 122; later NR
NC	106W	Vega, c/n 123
NC	107W	Vega, c/n 124
NR	115W	Sirius, c/n 166
NR	116W	Sirius, c/n 150; later NC
NC	117W	Sirius, c/n 151
NR	118W	Sirius (& Altair), c/n 152; later NC, X
X	119W	Sirius (& Altair), c/n 153; later NR
NC	152W	Vega, c/n 125
NC	160W	Vega, c/n 126
NC	161W	Vega, c/n 127
NC	162W	Vega, c/n 128
NC	167W	Sirius, c/n 167
NC	176W	Vega, c/n 129
NC	288W	Vega, c/n 137
X	799W	Orion, c/n 208; later NC
NC	229Y	Orion, c/n 200
NC	230Y	Orion, c/n 201
NC	231Y	Orion, c/n 202
NC	232Y	Orion, c/n 204; later NR
NC	904Y	Vega, c/n 132
NC	905Y	Vega, c/n 133
NC	926Y	Vega, c/n 134; later NR
NC	934Y	Vega, c/n 138
NC	959Y	Vega, c/n 170
X	960Y	Orion, c/n 168; later NC
NC	964Y	Orion, c/n 169
NR	965Y	Vega, c/n 171; later X, NC
N	965Y	Vega, c/n 40
NC	972Y	Vega, c/n 160
NR	974Y	Air Express, c/n 130; later NC
NC	975Y	Orion, c/n 172
NC	980Y	Vega, c/n 191
NC	984Y	Orion, c/n 173
NC	988Y	Orion, c/n 174; later NR
NC	991Y	Orion, c/n 175
NR	998Y	Altair, c/n 176

U.S. Navy

9054	Altair, c/n 179

U.S. Army

A.C. 31–405	Vega, c/n 158
A.C. 31–408	Vega, c/n 159
A.C. 32–232	Altair, c/n 165
A.C. 32–320	XP–900, none
A.C. 32–393	Altair, c/n 153
A.C. 42–62601	Orion, c/n 208
A.C. 42–94148	Vega, c/n 210

Argentina

R–48	Vega, c/n 4

Australia

VH–USB	Altair, c/n 152
VH–UVK	Vega, c/n 155

Brazil

P–BDAH	Air Express, c/n 65

Canada

CF–AAL	Vega, c/n 30

Costa Rica

TI–62	Vega, c/n 96

France

F–AKHC	Orion, c/n 209
F–AQAR	Orion, c/n 205
F–AQAS	Orion, c/n 183
F–AQAV	Orion, c/n 185

Great Britain

G–ABGK	Vega, c/n 155
G–ADUS	Altair, c/n 152

Japan

J–BAMC	Altair, c/n 188
J–BAUC	Altair, c/n 213

Mexico

XA–BAM	Vega, c/n 80
XA–BAW	Vega, c/n 59
XA–BAY	Orion, c/n 169
XA–BDH	Orion, c/n 174
XA–BDO	Orion, c/n 212
XA–BDY	Orion, c/n 204
XA–BDZ	Orion, c/n 202
XA–BEI	Orion, c/n 169
XA–BEJ	Orion, c/n 173
XA–BEL	Orion, c/n 174
XA–BEU	Orion, c/n 181
XA–BFP	Vega, c/n 108
XA–BFR	Vega, c/n 124
XA–BFT	Vega, c/n 50
XA–BFU	Vega, c/n 23
XA–BHA	Vega, c/n 62
XA–BHA	Orion, c/n 181
XA–BHB	Vega, c/n 59
XA–BHB	Orion, c/n 182
XA–BHC	Vega, c/n 90
XA–BHC	Orion, c/n 183
XA–BHD	Orion, c/n 185
XA–BHE	Orion, c/n 186
XA–BHG	Vega, c/n 9
XA–BHI	Vega, c/n 103
XA–BHJ	Vega, c/n 61
XA–BHK	Vega, c/n 100
XA–BHL	Vega, c/n 71
XA–BHM	Vega, c/n 88 (reg reported applied for)
XA–BIT	Vega, c/n 139

XA–BKF	Vega, c/n 121
XA–BKG	Vega, c/n 58
XA–BLZ	Vega, c/n 109
XA–DAH	Vega, c/n 125
XA–DAI	Vega, c/n 102
XA–DAM	Vega, c/n 127
XA–DAY	Vega, c/n 157
XA–DEB	Vega, c/n 133
XA–DEC	Vega, c/n 60
XA–DOK	Vega, c/n 72
XA–FAF	Vega, c/n 121
XA–FAL	Vega, c/n 96
XB–AAD	Vega, c/n 103
XB–ADA	Sirius, c/n 149
XB–AHQ	Orion, c/n 172
XB–KAQ	Vega, c/n 96
XB–MAA	Vega, c/n 72

Nicaragua

AN–ABL	Vega, c/n 66
AN–ABP	Vega, c/n 30

Norway

N–41	Vega, c/n 34
LN–ABD	Vega, c/n 34

Panama

RX–14	Vega, c/n 81

Switzerland

CH–167	Orion, c/n 189
CH–168	Orion, c/n 190
HB–LAH	Orion, c/n 189
HB–LAJ	Orion, c/n 190

John Henry Mears's second City of New York, *with 20-year-old Elinor Smith, to whom it was given. Flown by her as Mrs. ? (below, with Bernt Balchen), and then acquired by Amelia Earhart.*

SUPPLEMENT C

MODEL SPECIFICATIONS AND QUANTITIES

(**ATC** = Approved Type Certificate; **P** = seating; **C** = closed cabin; **O** = open cockpit; **L** = landplane; **S** = seaplane; **WC** = Wright Cyclone; **DL** = metal fuselage; **C/n** = constructor's [serial] number; **L/g** = landing gear)

Model	ATC	— Date	Description	Engine	HP	Wing Position	Wing Span
Vega 1	49	7/9/28	5PCLM	WW J5	220–225	High	41′
Vega 5	93	12/1/28	5PCLM	P&W Wasp B	420–450	High	41′
—Seaplane	"	"	5PCSM	"	"	"	"
Vega Executive 5A	"	"	5PCLM	"	"	"	"
Air Express 3	102	1/11/29	5–7PCLM	P&W Wasp	420–450	Parasol	42′ 6″
Vega 2	140	4/29/29	5PCLM	WW J6	300	High	41′
Vega 5	169	6/28/29	6PCLM	P&W Wasp C	450	High	41′
Vega 5B	227	9/9/29	7PCLM	P&W Wasp C	450	High	41′
—Seaplane	"	"	7PCSM	"	"	"	"
Vega 2A	252	10/7/29	7PCLM	WW J6	300	High	41′
Sirius 8	300	3/14/30	2POLM	P&W Wasp C	450	Low	42′ 9¼″
Sirius 8A	"	"	"	"	"	"	"
Vega DL-1	308	4/2/30	7PCLM	P&W Wasp C1	450	High	41′
Vega DL-B	"	"	"	"	"	"	"
Sirius DL-2	378	10/27/30	1–2POLM	P&W Wasp C	450	Low	42′ 10″
Vega 5C	384	12/19/30	7PCLM	P&W Wasp C1	450	High	41′
—Seaplane	"	"	7PCSM	"	"	"	"
Orion 9	421	5/6/31	7PCLM	P&W Wasp SC	450	Low	42′ 9½″
Orion 9B	462	2/25/32	7PCLM	WC R–1820–E	575	Low	42′ 9¼″
Orion 9E	508	5/22/33	1–7PCLM	P&W Wasp SC1	450	Low	42′ 9¼″
Orion 9F	512	7/19/33	5–7PCLM	WC R–1820–F2	645	Low	42′ 9¼″
Orion 9D	514	8/31/33	1–7PCLM	P&W Wasp S1D1	550	Low	42′ 9¼″
Orion 9F-1	557	10/8/34	5–7PCLM	WC SR–1820–F2	650	Low	42′ 9¼″
Explorer 4	none	(1929)	1POLM	P&W Wasp	450	Low	48′ 6″
Explorer 7 (*special*)	none	(1930)	1POLM	P&W Wasp C	450	Low	48′ 6″
XP–900	none	(1931)	2P pursuit	Curtiss Conqueror V–1570C	602	Low	42′ 9¼″
Altair 8E	none	(1932)	1–4PCLM	P&W Wasp S1D1	550	Low	42′ 9¼″
Altair 8F	none	(1934)	1–4PCLM	P&W Wasp S1D1	550	Low	42′ 9¼″
Altair 8G	none	(1937)	2POLM	Menasco Unitwin	2 @ 260	Low	42′ 9¼″

SINGLE-ENGINE LOCKHEEDS COMPLETED/FLOWN 1927–37

M = monoplane; **WW** = Wright Whirlwind; **P&W** = Pratt & Whitney;

Wing (sq ft)	Length	Height	Empty Weight (lbs)	Gross Weight (lbs)	Top Speed (mph)	Orig-inals	Con-verted	Remarks
275	27′ 6″	8′ 4½″	1650–1875	2900–3470	135	28	—	C/ns 4, 17, 29, 30, 34, 40, 41 as seaplanes
275	27′ 6″	8′ 4½″	2492	4033	165	36	2	C/ns 38, 56, 58 converted; w/cowl 180–185 mph
"	"	"	2977	4698	157	—	5	W/cowl 172 mph
"	"	"	2492	4670	165	9	—	W/cowl 175 mph
288	27′ 6″	8′ 4½″	2533	4375	167	7	1	Open pilot's cockpit; w/cowl 176 mph; c/n 130 converted
275	27′ 6″	8′ 6″	2140	3853	160	5	1	C/n 57 as seaplane; c/n 30 converted
275	27′ 6″	8′ 6″	2465	4033	180	—	2	P increased; c/ns 78, 82
275	27′ 6″	8′ 6″	2490	4265	165	29	3	P increased; w/cowl 180 mph
"	"	"	2925	4750	157	—	2	C/ns 119, 120 w/Edo K floats; w/cowl 172 mph
275	27′ 6″	8′ 6″	2305	4220	160	1	—	P increased; c/n 83
294.1	27′ 6″	9′ 3″	2974	4600	173	5	—	2° dihedral; c/ns 140, 141, 142, 144, 149
"	27′ 10″	"	3056	"	"	8	—	Larger fin & rudder; c/n 153 first fully retractable l/g
275	27′ 6″	8′ 2″	2563	4270	178	4	—	By Detroit, Duralumin fuselage
"	"	"	"	"	"	3	1	Wire-braced l/g; c/n 135 converted
294.1	28′ 6″	9′ 2″	2958	5200	175	1	—	C/n 165, by Detroit
279	28′ 6″	9′ 2″	2565	4500	185	6	24	Larger tail
"	"	"	3153	4880	175	—	3	C/ns 55, 99, 101
294.1	27′ 6″	9′ 8″	3420	5400	227	14	1	2° & 3° dihedral; c/n 201 converted
294.1	28′ 11″	9′ 8″	3570	5400	195	2	—	3° dihedral; c/ns 189, 190
294.1	27′ 6″	9′ 8″	3860	5600	228	2	1	C/ns 193, 195; c/n 192 converted
294.1	27′ 11″	9′ 8″	3708	5400	242	1	—	C/n 196
294.1	28′ 4″	9′ 8″	3640	5800	226	10	—	Wing flaps; longer nose
294.1	28′ 1½″	9′ 5″	4100	5800	235	1	—	C/n 212
313	27′ 6″	8′ 2″	3075	9008	165	2	—	C/ns 2, 116
313	27′ 6″	8′ 2″	3075	9008	165	2	—	2° dihedral; c/ns 147, 148
292	28′ 9″	8′ 6″	3010	4360	214	1	—	USAAC YP–24 (no c/n)
294.1	28′ 11″	9′ 3″	3550	5800	220	1	—	C/n 188; tandem cockpits & cargo-or-P cabin
294.1	28′ 11″	9′ 3″	3650	5800	221	1	—	C/n 213; tandem cockpits & cargo-or-P cabin
294.1	28′ 11″	9′ 3″	—	—	—	1	—	C/n 214 *Flying Test Stand*

SUPPLEMENT C *(Continued)*

SPECIAL MODEL SPECIFICATIONS AND QUANTITIES

ATC = Approved Type Certificate; **P** = seating; **C** = closed cabin; **O** = open cockpit; **L** = landplane; **S** = seaplane; **WC** = Wright Cyclone; **DL** = metal fuselage; **C/n** = constructor's [serial] number; **L/g** = landing gear)

Model	ATC —	Date	Description	Engine	HP	Wing Position	Wing Span
Vega *(unassigned)*	none	(1928)	2PCLM	P&W Hornet	515	High	41′
Vega 5 Special	none	(1930)	1–2PCLM	P&W Wasp C	450	High	41′
Vega Special	2–256	8/13/30	3–5PCLM	P&W Wasp C	420	High	41′
—Seaplane	"	"	3–5PCSM	"	"	"	"
Vega 5B *(modified)*	2–274	9/29/30	7PCLM	P&W Wasp	420	High	41′
Vega 5A Special	2–284	10/10/30	5PCLM	P&W Wasp	450	High	41′
Vega DL-1 Special	2–316	1/3/31	5PCLM	P&W Wasp C1	420	High	41′
Vega DL-1B Special	none	(1930)	1PCLM	P&W Wasp C R–1340–17	600	High	41′
Orion 9	2–367	1/17/31	3–5PCLM	P&W Wasp C	450	Low	42′ 9¼″
Vega 5C Special	none	(1931)	1–2PCLM	P&W Wasp	450	High	41′
Sirius 8 Special	none	(1931)	2POSM	WC SR–1820–F2	650	Low	42′ 9¼″
Air Express Special	none	(1931)	1POLM	P&W Wasp	450	Parasol	42′ 6″
Sirius 8C	2–374	8/10/31	4PCLM	P&W Wasp C	450	Low	42′ 9¼″
Altair *(unassigned)*	none	(1931)	2POLM	P&W Wasp	450	Low	42′ 9¼″
Altair Special	none	(1931)	2POLM	WC R–1820–F2	645	Low	42′ 9¼″
Vega 2D	2–377	8/21/31	5PCL/SM	P&W Wasp Jr	300	High	41′
Vega 5C	2–385	9/22/31	3PCL/SM	P&W Wasp	420	High	41′
Altair DL–2A	2–386	10/17/31	2POLM	P&W Wasp E	450	Low	42′ 9¼″
Altair DL–2A	none	(1931)	2POLM	WC	645	Low	42′ 9¼″
Orion 9A Special	2–397	1/16/32	5PCLM	P&W Wasp C	450	Low	42′ 9¼″
Sirius 8 Special	2–400	2/4/32	2POLM	P&W Wasp	450	Low	42′ 9¼″
Orion 9C Special	2–416	7/11/32	3PCLM	WC SR–1820–F2	650	Low	42′ 9¼″
Altair 8D	2–423	10/8/32	2POLM	P&W Wasp SC1	450	Low	42′ 9¼″
Vega 1 Special	2–427	11/9/32	7PCLM	Packard Diesel R–980	225	High	41′
Orion 9 Special	none	(1932)	1PCLM	P&W Wasp	450	Low	42′ 9¼″
Vega 5C Special	none	(1933)	7PCLM	P&W Wasp SC1	450	High	41′
Vega DL–1B Special	2–448	5/29/33	7PCLM	P&W Wasp SC1	450	High	41′
Orion 9D–1	2–464	12/1/33	5–7PCLM	P&W Wasp S1D1	550	Low	42′ 9¼″
Orion 9D–2	2–488	9/11/34	5PCLM	P&W Wasp S1D1	550	Low	42′ 9¼″
Orion 9D Special	none	(1934)	1PCLM	P&W Wasp S1D1	550	Low	42′ 9¼″
Orion-Explorer *(special)*	none	(1935)	2PCL/SM	P&W Wasp S3H1	550	Low	48′ 6″

SINGLE-ENGINE LOCKHEEDS COMPLETED/FLOWN 1927–37

M = monoplane; **WW** = Wright Whirlwind; **P&W** = Pratt & Whitney;

Wing (sq ft)	Length	Height	Empty Weight (lbs)	Gross Weight (lbs)	Top Speed (mph)	Orig-inals	Con-verted	Remarks
275	27′ 6″	8′ 4½″	—	—	—	1	—	C/n 19, Thaw racer
275	27′ 6″	8′ 6″	—	—	—	1	—	C/n 619, built by Schlee-Brock
275	27′ 6″	8′ 2″	2842	4750	185	1	—	C/n 102 *Detroit News*
"	"	"	3245	4750	157	—	1	C/n 102 w/APCB 9500 floats
275	27′ 6″	8′ 6″	—	—	—	—	1	C/n 101; baggage compt sealed off
275	27′ 6″	8′ 6″	2492	4217	—	—	1	C/n 80 Executive; added equipment
275	27′ 6″	8′ 2″	2563	—	—	1	—	C/n 155, Kidston
275	27′ 6″	8′ 2″	—	—	221	1	—	C/n 159, Army Y1C–17; extra sreamlined
294.1	27′ 1″	9′ 8″	3420	—	—	—	2	Passenger P restored; c/ns 173, 174
275	27′ 6″	8′ 2″	—	—	—	1	—	C/n 171; Hi-Speed l/g
294.1	27′ 1″	9′ 3″	4289	7099	185	—	1	C/n 140, Lindbergh; Edo floats
288	27′ 6″	8′ 6″	—	—	—	1	—	C/n 130, Ingalls; wire & regular l/g
294.1	27′ 6″	9′ 3″	3354	4600	175	1	1	C/n 150; c/n 167 converted; Sport Cabin
294.1	27′ 10″	9′ 3″	3000	4600	224	—	2	C/ns 145, 153 from Sirius 8A
294.1	28′ 11″	9′ 3″	—	—	—	1	—	C/n 176, Macfadden
275	27′ 6″	8′ 2″	2405	3600	162	—	3	Engine change; c/ns 38, 40, 58
275	27′ 6″	8′ 2″	—	—	—	—	1	P change; c/n 55
294.1	27′ 6″	9′ 6″	3310	5200	204	1	1	C/n 180; c/n 165 converted
294.1	27′ 6″	9′ 6″	—	—	—	1	—	C/n 179, Navy XRO–1
294.1	28′	9′ 8″	3445	5410	227	1	—	3° dihedral, longer nose; c/n 187
294.1	27′ 6″	9′ 3″	—	5200	—	—	1	C/n 152, Fleming
294.1	27′ 6″	9′ 8″	3440	5824	200	—	1	C/n 180 *Shellightning*
294.1	27′ 1″	9′ 3″	3000	4600	227	—	3	2° dihedral; c/ns 143, 152 (Kingsford-Smith), 214
275	27′ 6″	8′ 2″	—	—	—	—	1	C/n 14, Chamberlin
294.1	27′ 6″	9′ 8″	—	—	—	1	—	C/n 192, TWA cargo carrier
275	28′ 6″	9′ 2″	—	—	—	1	—	C/n 194, Continental Oil
275	27′ 6″	8′ 2″	—	—	—	1	—	C/n 161, assembled by Von Hake
294.1	28′ 4″	9′ 8″	3640	5400	226	1	—	C/n 204; wing flaps
294.1	28′ 11″	9′ 8″	4182	5800	226	1	—	C/n 208; photo/radio ship; later USAAF UC–85
294.1	28′ 4″	9′ 8″	—	—	—	1	—	C/n 211, Ingalls racer *Auto-da-Fé*
313	27′ 6″	9′ 8″	—	—	—	—	1	C/n 195, Post; fixed l/g, also on floats

SUPPLEMENT D

CONDENSED PRODUCTION LIST OF SINGLE-ENGINE LOCKHEEDS 1927–37

(Compiled from Federal Aviation Agency and Lockheed records)

Of the 217 accountable constructor's numbers in the series (*cf. Supplement A* for dossiers of c/ns 1–214, plus special c/ns EX–2 and 619, and the XP–900 with no c/n), 198 individuals were completed and flown.

Built	Type	Model (General)	Individuals
110	Vega	—	Many variations of landing gear (*see* [a] [b] [c] *below*), tails, seating, doors, etc.
9	Vega	Executive	C/ns 72, 79, 80, 88, 89, 96, 107, 108, 132
10	Vega	DL (metal fuselage)	C/ns 135[c], 136[c], 137[c], 154[c], 155, 156, 157, 158, 159[c], 161[b]
8	Air Express	—	C/ns 5, EX–2, 65, 75, 76, 77, 92, 130[c] (c/n 76 converted to Vega)
4	Explorer	—	C/ns 2, 116, 147, 148
14	Sirius	—	C/ns 140[a], 141, 142, 143, 144, 145, 146, 149, 150, 151, 152, 153, 166, 167 (c/ns 143, 145, 152, 153 converted to Altair)
1	Sirius	DL (metal fuselage)	C/n 165 (converted to Altair)
4	Altair	—	C/ns 176, 188, 213, 214 (c/n 214 originally with Menasco Unitwin installation)
2	Altair	DL (metal fuselage)	C/ns 179, 180 (c/n 180 converted to Orion)
1	XP–900	Army pursuit plane (metal fuselage)	No c/n; USAACs YP-24
35	Orion	—	Many variations of cabin, tails, fairings, etc. (c/n 195 converted to Orion-Explorer[a])
198	= **Total Built**		

Not Built	Remarks	Individuals
6	Never fully assembled, or used as replacements; registrations canceled	C/ns 104, 110, 111, 114, 115, 131
10	Used as Fuselage Only replacements; registrations either never assigned or canceled	C/ns 42, 43, 44, 45, 46, 47, 86, 91, 93, 95
3	C/ns never assigned	C/ns 162, 163, 164
19	= **Total Not Built**	

NOTES

[a] Known to have flown as seaplanes: c/ns 4, 17, 25, 29, 30, 34, 40, 41, 48, 54, 55, 57, 81, 94, 99, 101, 102, 119, 120, 140, 195.

[b] Known to have flown on skis: c/ns 4, 17, 30, 34, 60, 64, 102, 161.

[c] Known to have flown with wire-braced landing gear: c/ns 9, 73, 99, 130, 135, 136, 137, 154, 159, 171, 619.

SUPPLEMENT E

AVERAGE PERFORMANCES OF SINGLE-ENGINE LOCKHEEDS 1927–37

(Cf. speeds, etc., in Supplement C)

Normal range varied from 700 to 1,000 miles in Vegas. With added fuel capacity, range could be extended to as much as 5,500 miles in an Explorer.

Landing speed varied from 50 mph for a Vega with the low-powered Wright Whirlwind engine to 60–65 mph for a cowled and panted Vega equipped with a Pratt & Whitney Wasp. The Orion and Altair landed faster: 65–70 mph—but this was cut to about 58 mph with the introduction of wing flaps.

Rate of climb varied from 1,300 feet per minute for a regular cowled and panted 7-place Vega to 1,480 fpm for the last Orion produced (1934). The Sirius and Explorer were slower climbers; 1,200 fpm. Tops was the XP-900 (the Army pursuit plane), which could make 1,820 fpm.

Service ceiling averaged out at about 22,000 feet for the entire single-engine series. Normal ceilings ranged from 15,000 feet for the early Vegas to 25,900 for the Altair. Colonel Lindbergh's Sirius had a ceiling of 26,100.

Seaplanes. Vegas on floats with a normal load of around 1,500 pounds took off in 15 seconds, with a light load were airborne in 12 seconds. Landing speed varied between 50–60 mph. Normal cruising range was 650 miles; cruising speed was about 130 mph.

SUPPLEMENT F

STANDARD EQUIPMENT AND TYPICAL PRICES Single-Engine Lockheeds Since 1928–34

In 1929 standard equipment on all models was: electric self-starter; Standard steel propeller; cabin heaters; Bendix brakes; magnetic compass; tachometer; altimeter; air speed indicator; bank and turn indicator; oil pressure gauge; 8-day clock; automatic fire extinguisher; navigation, dash, and cabin lights; First Aid kit.

Vega Executive standard extra equipment included: a folding desk; a new Corona typewriter; seats convertible to a lounge; lavatory, chemical toilet; extra baggage compartment.

In 1931 standard equipment for the Orion was: NACA cowling, and cylinder baffles; Lockheed retractable landing gear with oleo shock units; Goodrich semiballoon tires and brakes; Hamilton-Standard propeller; landing lights; two parachute flares; automatic pressure fire extinguisher; cabin heater; navigation, dome, and cabin lights; combination hand-electric inertia starter; magnetic compass; bank and turn, air speed, and rate of climb indicators; tachometer; altimeter; clock; oil pressure and temperature gauges; indirect instrument lighting. Tail wheel or skid optional. Bonded for radio.

Gasoline capacity could be varied from 100 gallons in standard tanks to 900 gallons for a long-range Explorer.

Oil capacity was ordinarily 10 gallons, but again could be arranged as high as 44 gallons for the Explorer.

Color. In 1930 was optional if 8 weeks allowed for delivery. Special upholstery $200 extra; special lettering and/or designs extra.

(Prices flyaway Burbank, Calif.)

Type	1928	1929	1930	1931	1934	Remarks
Vega (Wright Whirlwind)	$13,500	$14,750	$14,985	—	—	—
Vega (P&W Wasp)	$20,000	$18,900	$18,985	$19,000	$20,000	1930–31 with cowl & pants; 1934 Model 5C with cowl
Vega Executive (Wasp)	—	$19,250	$19,985	$20,000	—	1930–31 with cowl & pants
DL Vega (metal) (Wasp)	—	—	$21,985	$22,000	—	With NACA cowl
Air Express (Wasp)	$21,000	$21,250	$19,885	$20,000	—	With NACA cowl
Sirius (Wasp)	—	$18,500	$18,985	$19,000	—	With cowl & pants
Orion (Wasp)	—	—	—	$25,000	$20,000	1934 Model 9D
Altair (Wasp)	—	—	—	—	$25,000	1934 Model 8E

SUPPLEMENT G

TYPES PRODUCED BY YEARS Single-Engine Lockheeds 1927–37

Type	1927	1928	1929	1930	1931	1932	1933	1934	1937	Originals	Conversions	Final
Vega	2	29	60	29	4	1	3	1	—	129	1 from Air Express	130
Air Express	—	2	5	—	1	—	—	—	—	8	1 to Vega	7
Explorer	—	—	2	2	—	—	—	—	—	4	—	4
Sirius	—	—	1	14	—	—	—	—	—	15	5 to Altair	10
Altair	—	—	—	—	3	1	—	1	1	6	1 to Orion 5 from Sirius	10
Orion	—	—	—	—	17	1	13	4	—	35	1 from Altair	36
XP-900	—	—	—	—	1	—	—	—	—	1	—	1
Total	2	31	68	45[a]	26[b]	3[c]	16[d]	6	1	198	7	198

Notes:

By Lockheed Aircraft Corp. (LAC)	183
By Detroit Aircraft Corp. (DAC)	11
Assembled by others	4
	198

[a] Includes 9 DL (metal) Vegas & 1 DL Sirius by DAC; 1 Vega assembled by Schlee-Brock, Detroit.

[b] Includes 1 Vega assembled by Wedell-Williams, Patterson, La.; 2 DL Altairs completed by LAC; XP-900 built by DAC.

[c] Includes 1 Vega assembled under direction of Firman Gray, Burbank, Calif.

[d] Includes 1 DL Vega assembled under direction of Richard A. Von Hake, Burbank.

SUPPLEMENT H

SOME ADVANCES RECORDED BY/IN SINGLE-ENGINE LOCKHEEDS 1928–36

Event	Year	Plane	Notes
First trans-Arctic flight (Alaska-Spitzbergen)	1928	Vega	c/n 4
First nonstop flight Los Angeles–New York	1928	Vega	c/n 7, *Yankee Doodle*
First to fly coast to coast in under 24 hours	1928	Vega	" " "
First to fly nonstop coast to coast each way	1928	Vega	" " "
First to carry a passenger nonstop coast to coast each way	1928	Vega	" " "
First to fly from and over Antarctica	1928	Vega	c/n 4
First airplane from which new land was discovered	1928	Vega	c/n 4, over Antarctica
First commercial airplane to be fitted with NACA cowling	1929	Air Express	c/n EX–2
First nonstop flight Stateside to Alaska (Seattle-Juneau)	1929	Vega	c/n 48, *Juneau*
First solo nonstop transcontinental east-west flight (New York–Los Angeles)	1929	Air Express	c/n EX–2, *Texaco 5*
First solo nonstop transcontinental west-east flight (Los Angeles–New York)	1929	Air Express	" " "
First solo one-stop round-trip transcontinental flight (New York–Los Angeles–New York)	1929	Air Express	" " "
First nonstop flight New York–Mexico City	1930	Sirius	c/n 149, *Anahuac*
First nonstop flight New York–Canal Zone	1930	Explorer	c/n 148, *Blue Flash*
First commercial transport equipped with fully retractable landing gear	1931	Orion	c/n 168
First commercial airplane to make a record flight around the world	1931	Vega	c/n 122, *Winnie Mae*

Wilkins and Eielson prepare for their historic first flight over Antarctica.

Event	Year	Plane	Notes
First flight U.S.A.-Hungary	1931	Sirius	c/n 166, *Justice for Hungary*
First American commercial transport sold to foreign airline	1931	Orion	c/n 189, to Swissair
First to fly over three oceans	1931–33	Sirius	c/n 140, Lindberghs' N. Pacific, N. & S. Atlantic surveys
First U.S. military low-wing aircraft with fully retractable landing gear	1931	Altairs	c/n 153, USAAC; c/n 179, USN
First U.S. Army low-wing pursuit plane	1931	XP-900	c/n none, USAAC YP–24
First nonstop flight Montreal-Havana	1931	Altair	c/n 176, *The Gold Eagle*
First woman's solo flight across the Atlantic	1932	Vega	c/n 22
First woman's solo nonstop transcontinental west-east flight	1932	Vega	"
First nonstop flight New York–Norway	1933	Vega	c/n 118, *Century of Progress*
First nonstop flight New York–Berlin	1933	Vega	c/n 122, *Winnie Mae*
First solo flight around the world	1933	Vega	" "
First flight Australia-Oakland	1934	Altair	c/n 152, *Lady Southern Cross*
First woman's solo flight Honolulu-Oakland	1935	Vega	c/n 171
First nonstop flight Mexico City-New York	1935	Vega	"
First woman's solo nonstop transcontinental east-west flight	1935	Orion	c/n 211, *Auto-da-Fé*
First flight Tokyo-Manila and return	1935	Altair	c/n 188
First flight Cuba-Spain via South Atlantic	1936	Sirius	c/n 146, *4 de Septiembre*

Anahuac, *the first plane to fly nonstop from New York to Mexico City.*

SUPPLEMENT I

HOW LOCKHEED OWNERS NAMED THEIR PLANES

The Atmosphere and Heavenly Bodies

Aksarben Comet	c/n 76
Aquarius	c/n 49
Arcturus	c/n 26
Libra	c/n 50
Sirius	c/n 24
West Wind	c/n 181
South Wind	c/n 182
North Wind	c/n 183
East Wind	c/n 184
Winter Wind	c/n 185
Coast Wind	c/n 186

Beasts, Birds, and Bugs

Early Bird	c/n 208
Golden Eagle	c/n 1
Gold Eagle	c/n 176
Black Hornet	c/n 75
Gilmore Lion	c/n 75

Honoring Countries and Cities

Anahuac	c/n 149
City of New York	c/n 112
City of Tacoma	c/n 2
Crystal City	c/n 117
Fort Worth	c/n 18
Juneau	c/n 48
Justice for Hungary	c/n 166
Lituanica II	c/n 134
Richmond, Virginia, U.S.A.	c/n 152
The New Cincinnati	c/n 619

People

Doctor Brinkley III	c/n 196
Elizabeth Lind	c/n 40
Raymond Robins	c/n 92
Sheridan of Oklahoma	c/n 204
Winnie Mae of Oklahoma	c/ns 24, 122, 133

Products

Morell's Pride II (Ham)	c/n 161
Prest-O-Lite II (Batteries)	c/n 170
Shellightning (Petroleum)	c/n 180
Texaco 5 (Petroleum)	c/n EX–2
The General Tire (Rubber)	c/n 75
True Story (Magazine)	c/n 19

Roscoe Turner named his plane for his mascot and occasional passenger.

Other Languages

Akita (American Indian)	c/n 619
Auto-da-Fé (Portuguese)	c/n 211
4 de Septiembre (Cuban)	c/n 146
Tingmissartoq (Eskimo)	c/n 140
Qarrtsiluni (Eskimo)	c/n 34
Maraca (Portuguese)	c/n 65
Marajo (Portuguese)	c/n 77

Fanciful Names

Ariel	c/n 138
Blue Flash	c/n 148
Century of Progress	c/n 118
Nugget	c/n 99
Puck	c/n 155
The Blue Streak	c/n 80
The Cherokee	c/n 123
The Crusader	c/n 145
The Spirit of Fun	c/n 187
The Tester	c/n 18
The Viking	c/n 40
Yankee Doodle	c/ns 7, 148

And, of Course—The Ladies!

Lady Southern Cross	c/n 152
Miss Liberty	c/n 176
Miss McAleer	c/n 132
Miss Patsy	c/n 11
Miss Silvertown	c/n 79
Miss Stratosphere	c/n 143
Miss Streamline	c/ns 108, 156
Miss Teaneck	c/n 14
Mrs. ?	c/n 171

North Wind *in a publicity photo with its own collection of heavenly bodies.*

INDEX

Numbers in *italics* indicate illustrations. C/n references are to dossiers of individuals in Single-Engine Lockheed series, Supplement A.

ABOUT THE AUTHOR

A lifelong resident of New York State, Richard Sanders Allen grew up during the golden age of aviation. He has held numerous jobs, ranging from Wall Street office boy to Executive Director of the New York State American Revolution Bicentennial Commission. A veteran of the Air Transport Command of World War II, he was awarded a Guggenheim Fellowship in engineering history in 1962. Over the past forty years he has gained a distinguished reputation as a researcher, compiler, and writer in such diverse fields as nineteenth-century bridge-building and iron-making, the Spanish Civil War, and aviation history. *Revolution in the Sky* is an outgrowth of Rick Allen's early and consuming love of airplanes, flying, and flyers. He lives in Albany.

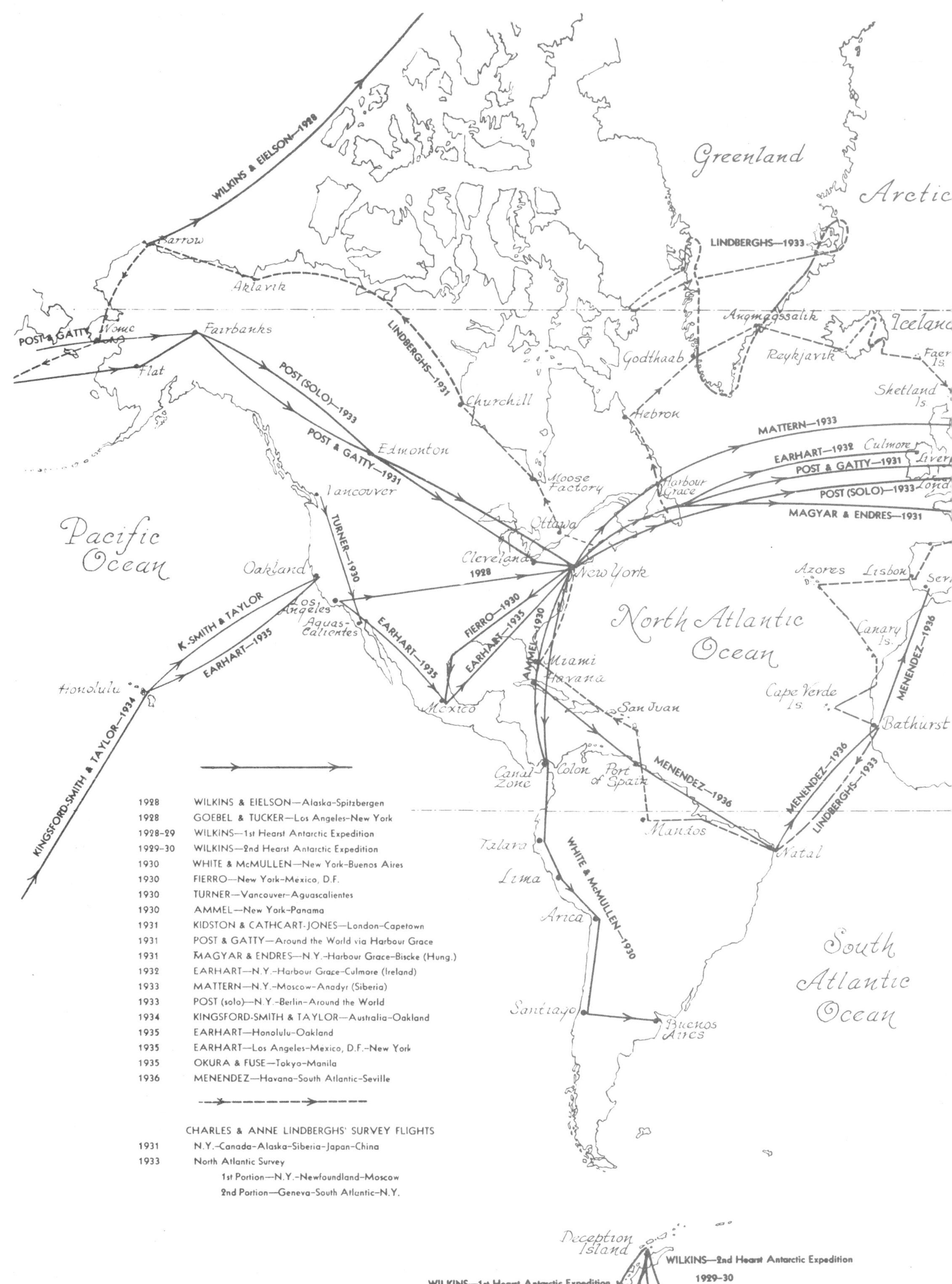

WILKINS & EIELSON—1928
Barrow
Aklavik
POST & GATTY
Nome
Fairbanks
Flat
LINDBERGHS—1931
POST (SOLO)—1933
POST & GATTY—1931
Edmonton
Churchill
Moose Factory
Ottawa
Greenland
Arctic
LINDBERGHS—1933
Angmagssalik
Iceland
Godthaab
Reykjavik
Faer Is.
Shetland Is.
Hebron
Harbour Grace
MATTERN—1933
EARHART—1932
Culmore
POST & GATTY—1931
POST (SOLO)—1933
MAGYAR & ENDRES—1931
Vancouver
TURNER—1930
Pacific Ocean
Cleveland
1928
New York
Oakland
K-SMITH & TAYLOR
EARHART—1935
Los Angeles
Aguascalientes
EARHART—1935
FIERRO—1930
EARHART—1935
AMMEL—1930
Miami
Havana
Mexico
Honolulu
KINGSFORD-SMITH & TAYLOR—1934
North Atlantic Ocean
Azores
Lisbon
Canary Is.
MENENDEZ—1936
Cape Verde Is.
Bathurst
San Juan
Canal Zone
Colon
Port of Spain
MENENDEZ—1936
MENENDEZ—1936
LINDBERGHS—1933
Manaos
Natal
Talara
Lima
WHITE & McMULLEN—1930
Arica
South Atlantic Ocean
Santiago
Buenos Aires
1928 WILKINS & EIELSON—Alaska-Spitzbergen
1928 GOEBEL & TUCKER—Los Angeles-New York
1928–29 WILKINS—1st Hearst Antarctic Expedition
1929–30 WILKINS—2nd Hearst Antarctic Expedition
1930 WHITE & McMULLEN—New York-Buenos Aires
1930 FIERRO—New York-México, D.F.
1930 TURNER—Vancouver-Aguascalientes
1930 AMMEL—New York-Panama
1931 KIDSTON & CATHCART-JONES—London-Capetown
1931 POST & GATTY—Around the World via Harbour Grace
1931 MAGYAR & ENDRES—N.Y.-Harbour Grace-Biscke (Hung.)
1932 EARHART—N.Y.-Harbour Grace-Culmore (Ireland)
1933 MATTERN—N.Y.-Moscow-Anadyr (Siberia)
1933 POST (solo)—N.Y.-Berlin-Around the World
1934 KINGSFORD-SMITH & TAYLOR—Australia-Oakland
1935 EARHART—Honolulu-Oakland
1935 EARHART—Los Angeles-Mexico, D.F.-New York
1935 OKURA & FUSE—Tokyo-Manila
1936 MENENDEZ—Havana-South Atlantic-Seville
CHARLES & ANNE LINDBERGHS' SURVEY FLIGHTS
1931 N.Y.-Canada-Alaska-Siberia-Japan-China
1933 North Atlantic Survey
1st Portion—N.Y.-Newfoundland-Moscow
2nd Portion—Geneva-South Atlantic-N.Y.
Deception Island
WILKINS—2nd Hearst Antarctic Expedition 1929–30
WILKINS—1st Hearst Antarctic Expedition 1928–29
Antarctica